CALIFORNIA'S

BEST FISHING WATERS™

182 Detailed Maps of 31 of the Best Rivers and Streams

Wilderness Adventures Press, Inc.™
Belgrade, Montana

Wilderness Adventures Press is dedicated to making these angling maps as accurate as possible. Please contact us at books@wildadvpress.com to let us know about any information in this book that you feel needs to be corrected. We appreciate your help.

Special thanks to Doug Brutocao at Doug's Bugs, Sandy Watts, and Woody Woodland at The Fly Shop for their help verifying information for certain waters.

This book was manufactured with an easy-open, lay-flat binding.

Published by Wilderness Adventures Press, Inc.™
45 Buckskin Road
Belgrade, MT 59714
866-400-2012
Website: www.wildadvpress.com
Email: books@wildadvpress.com

First Edition

Printed in Singapore

ISBN 1-932098-23-2

Table of Contents

Rivers

Rivers and Streams

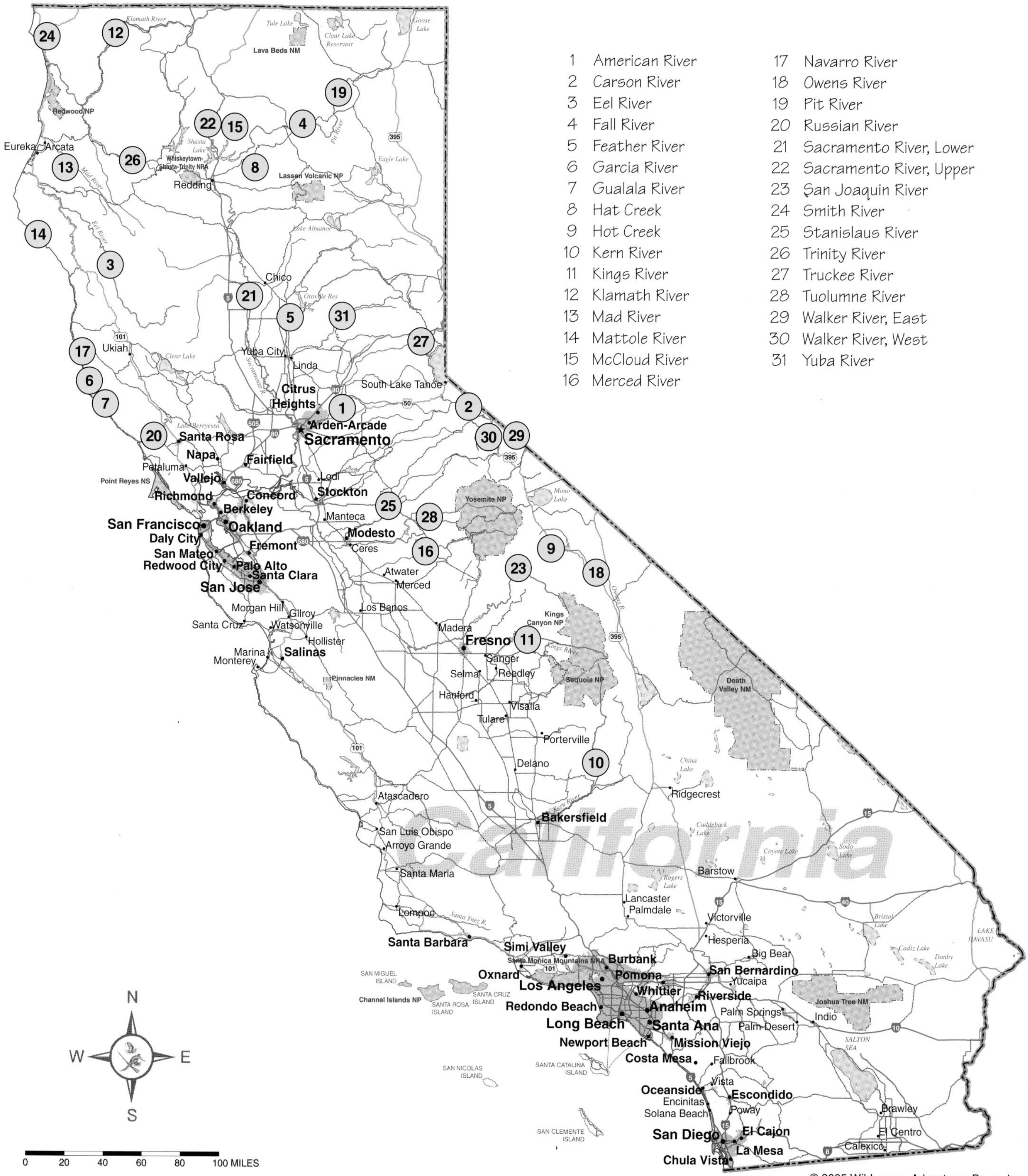

Introduction

The state of California has the most diverse array of angling opportunities in the country. From the thousands of high-country lakes and streams in the Sierra Nevada backcountry to massive reservoirs and famous trout streams to north-coast steelhead and salmon streams and warmwater action in Southern California, every type of freshwater angler can find a lifetime of fishing here. Add in the amazing saltwater fishing, and the possibilities are nearly endless. Just the Wild Trout Waters and catch-and-release waters cover 1,100 miles so far. Trout typically garner a lot of attention—and you'll find everything from wild and stocked brown, rainbow, and brook trout to goldens and cutthroats—but anadromous species like steelhead, king salmon, shad and stripers, and warmwater species like large and smallmouth bass also offer great fishing.

Countless books and articles have been written about California's fishing, but few seem to focus on the most important aspect for most anglers—access. How do you find the best areas to fish and the best access to those areas quickly and easily? The answers lie between these covers. Here we've chosen to concentrate on the best rivers and streams in the state because these are the waters where it's most difficult to pinpoint legal fishing access. All of these streams are located in central and northern California, although that is not to imply that Southern California doesn't also have excellent fishing. It's just that the premier larger rivers typically run to the coast or drain off the Sierra slopes farther north.

These maps are based on the U.S. Geological Survey maps, and a wealth of useful angling information is included on each one, along with an overview of the fishing. Official access points are clearly indicated, along with the boat ramps, campgrounds, and roads and trails that allow much wider possibilities. Some of the state's best rivers include miles of public access in the national forests, but most are a mix of public and private land, making knowledge about access critical to a good angling experience.

The waters presented here are listed in alphabetical order for easy reference without the need to consult an index for specific page numbers. For the best information on up-to-the-minute water conditions, contact angling stores and fly shops near the water you're planning to fish. And it's always a good idea to acquire a copy of the latest fishing regulations, as California has a long list of restrictions in place to protect its riverine resources, particularly along the coast. These are available online at the Department of Fish & Game website (www.dfg.ca.gov), where you'll also find license information and other useful tips. You can also help protect California's precious fishing waters by joining conservation organizations like Cal Trout (www.caltrout.org) or Trout Unlimited (www.tu.org).

California Resources

Department of Fish & Game
License and Revenue Branch

3211 S Street
Sacramento, CA 95816
(916) 227-2245
www.dfg.ca.gov

Department of Fish and Game
Fisheries Programs Branch

Ed Pert, Branch Chief
1416 Ninth Street
Sacramento, CA 95814
(916) 445-3417
www.dfg.ca.gov

California Fish and Game Commission

1416 Ninth Street
Sacramento, CA 95814
(916) 653-4899

Department of Parks and Recreation

1416 9th Street
Sacramento, CA 95814

P.O. Box 942896
Sacramento, CA 94296

Public Information Inquiries:
800-777-0369
(916) 653-6995
FAX (916) 654-6374
info@parks.ca.gov

BLM California State Office

2800 Cottage Way Suite W1834
Sacramento, CA 95825
Phone: (916) 978-4401
www.ca.blm.gov

Legend

- Interstate
- Primary Highway
- Road or Street
- Trails
- 5 Interstate Route
- 120 State Route
- 395 U.S. Route
- BLM - Public Land
- State - Public Land
- Indian Reservation
- National Forest
- Military Base
- Boat Launch
- Campsite
- Ferry
- Pump House
- Picnic Area
- Airport
- Rapids
- Dam
- Railroad

American River

The American River forks rise west and south of Lake Tahoe and flow generally west to Folsom Lake, where they join for the relatively short run to the lower Sacramento River at the city of Sacramento. Despite the high population center nearby, the lower river has good fishing for king salmon in the fall, steelhead in winter and spring, shad in May, and striped bass through midsummer. Above Folsom Lake, the three forks host some of the best whitewater rafting in the state, along with miles and miles of fine fishing for trout.

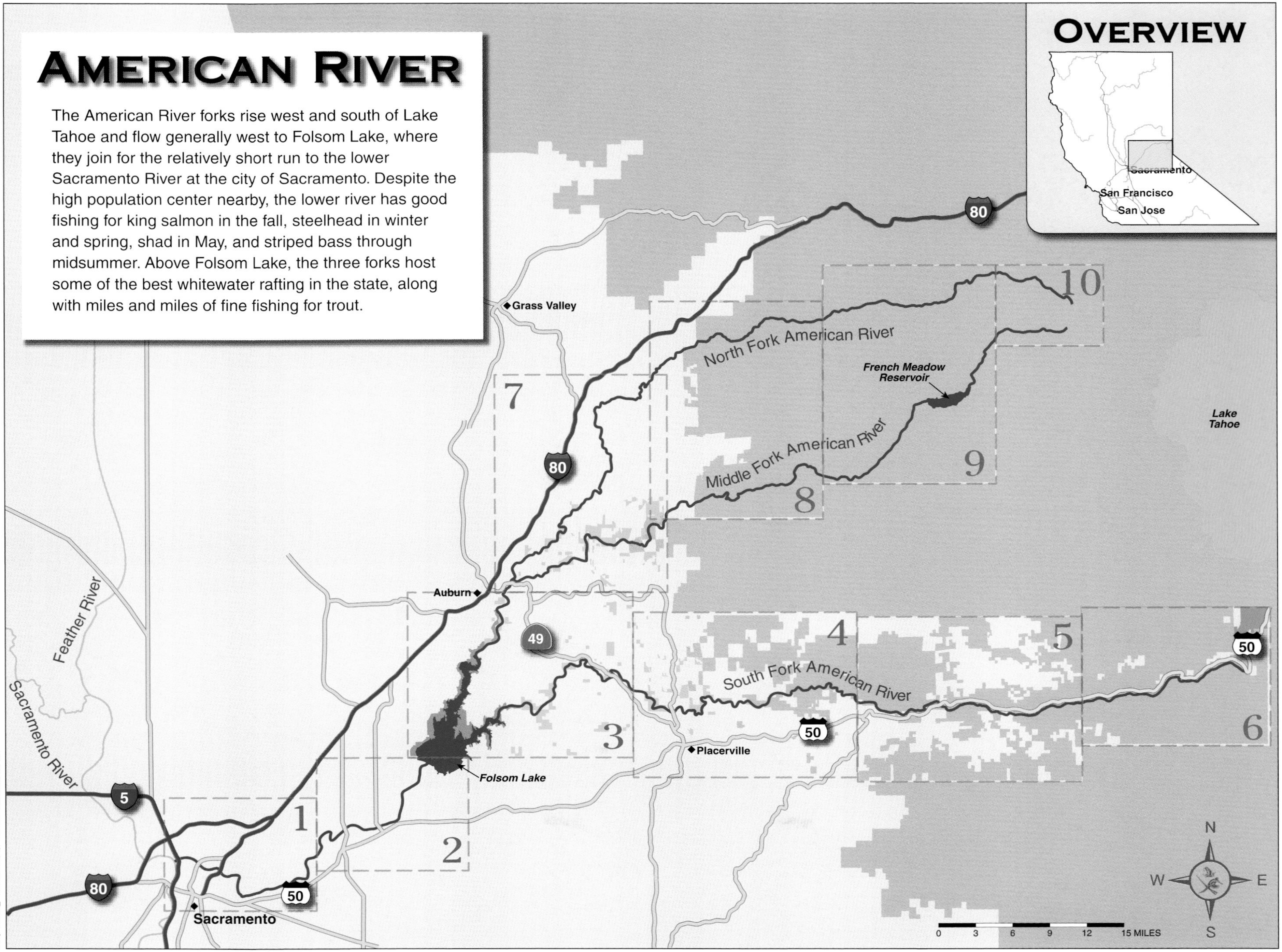

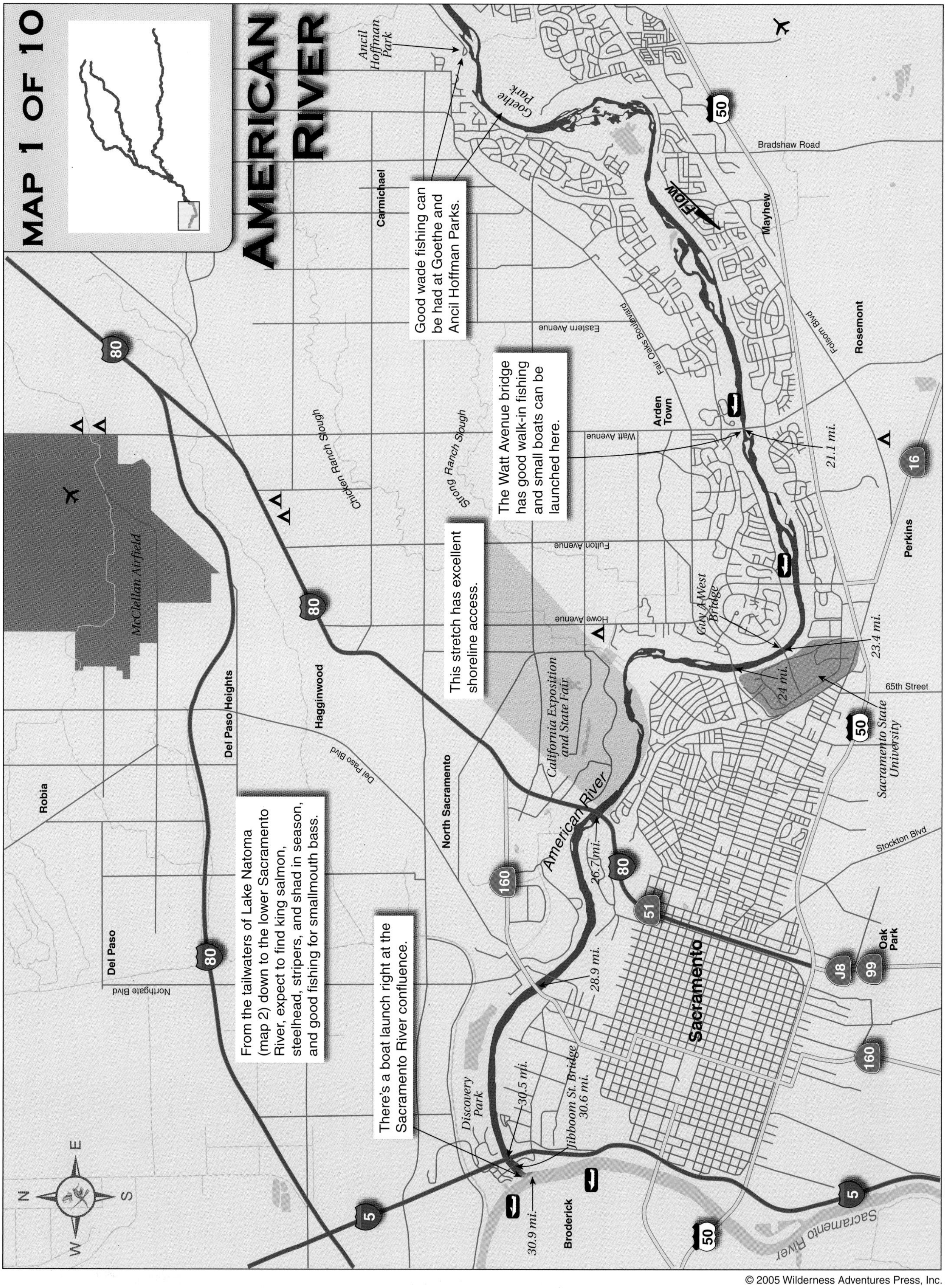

MAP 1 OF 10
AMERICAN RIVER
Good wade fishing can be had at Goethe and Ancil Hoffman Parks.
The Watt Avenue bridge has good walk-in fishing and small boats can be launched here.
This stretch has excellent shoreline access.
From the tailwaters of Lake Natoma (map 2) down to the lower Sacramento River, expect to find king salmon, steelhead, stripers, and shad in season, and good fishing for smallmouth bass.
There's a boat launch right at the Sacramento River confluence.
Ancil Hoffman Park
Goethe Park
Carmichael
Flow
Bradshaw Road
Mayhew
Rosemont
Folsom Blvd
Eastern Avenue
Fair Oaks Boulevard
Arden Town
Watt Avenue
21.1 mi.
Chicken Ranch Slough
Strong Ranch Slough
McClellan Airfield
Fulton Avenue
Perkins
Howe Avenue
Guy A West Bridge
23.4 mi.
24 mi.
65th Street
California Exposition and State Fair
Sacramento State University
Hagginwood
Del Paso Heights
Del Paso Blvd
North Sacramento
Robia
American River
26.7 mi.
Stockton Blvd
Oak Park
Del Paso
Northgate Blvd
28.9 mi.
Sacramento
Discovery Park
30.5 mi.
Jibboom St. Bridge 30.6 mi.
30.9 mi.
Broderick
Sacramento River
N
E
S
W
80
50
16
160
51
99
J8
5

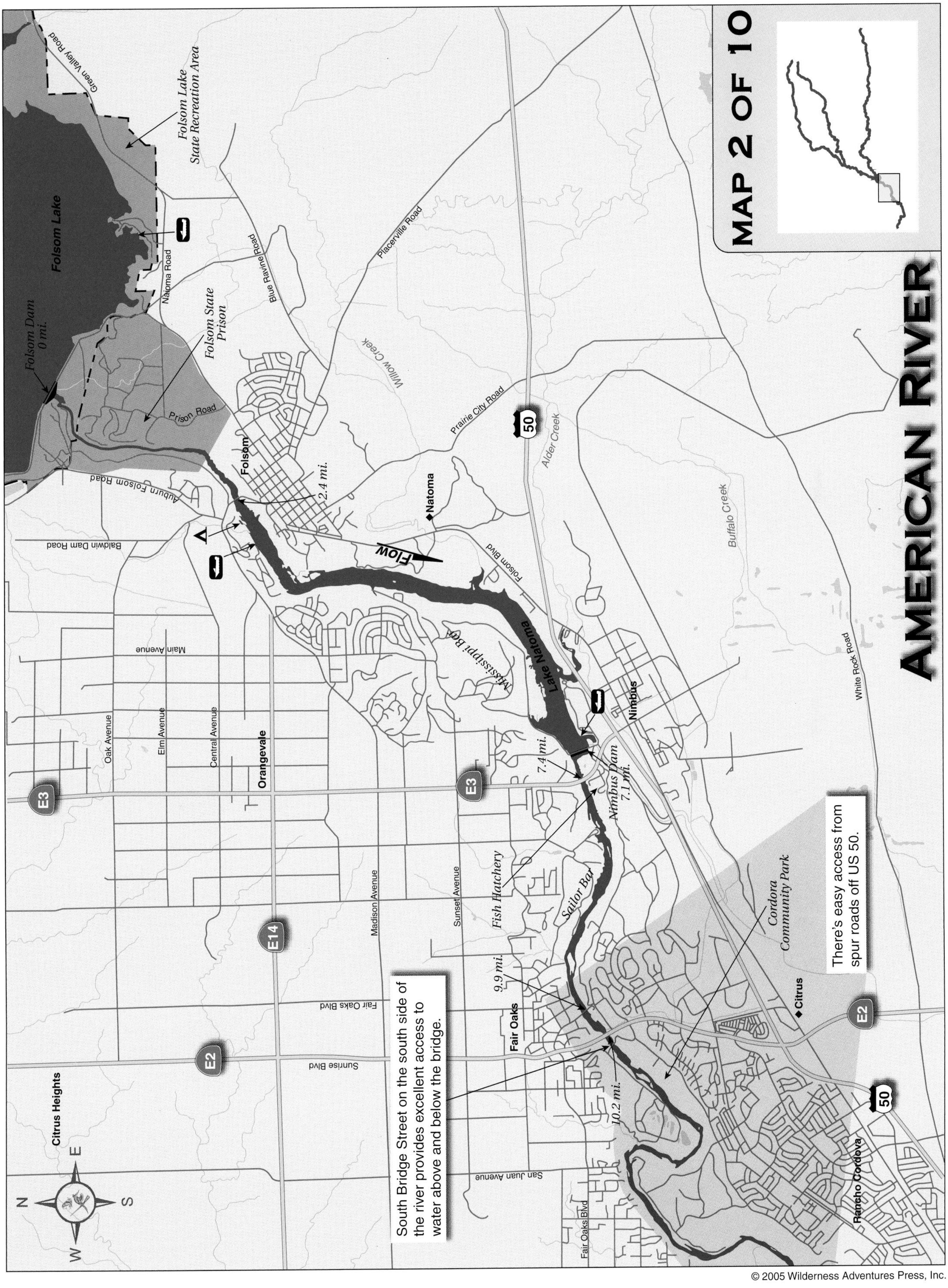
MAP 2 OF 10
AMERICAN RIVER
Folsom Lake
Folsom Dam
0 mi.
Folsom Lake
State Recreation Area
Folsom State
Prison
Green Valley Road
Natoma Road
Blue Ravine Road
Placerville Road
Prison Road
Willow Creek
Prairie City Road
Auburn Folsom Road
Folsom
2.4 mi.
Natoma
Alder Creek
Baldwin Dam Road
Flow
Folsom Blvd
Buffalo Creek
Main Avenue
Mississippi Bar
Lake Natoma
Nimbus
Oak Avenue
Elm Avenue
Central Avenue
Orangevale
E3
7.4 mi.
Nimbus Dam
7.1 mi.
White Rock Road
Madison Avenue
Sunset Avenue
Fish Hatchery
Sailor Bar
E14
Cordora
Community Park
There's easy access from
spur roads off US 50.
9.9 mi.
Fair Oaks
Fair Oaks Blvd
Citrus
E2
Sunrise Blvd
South Bridge Street on the south side of
the river provides excellent access to
water above and below the bridge.
10.2 mi.
Citrus Heights
50
San Juan Avenue
Rancho Cordova
Fair Oaks Blvd
N
E
S
W

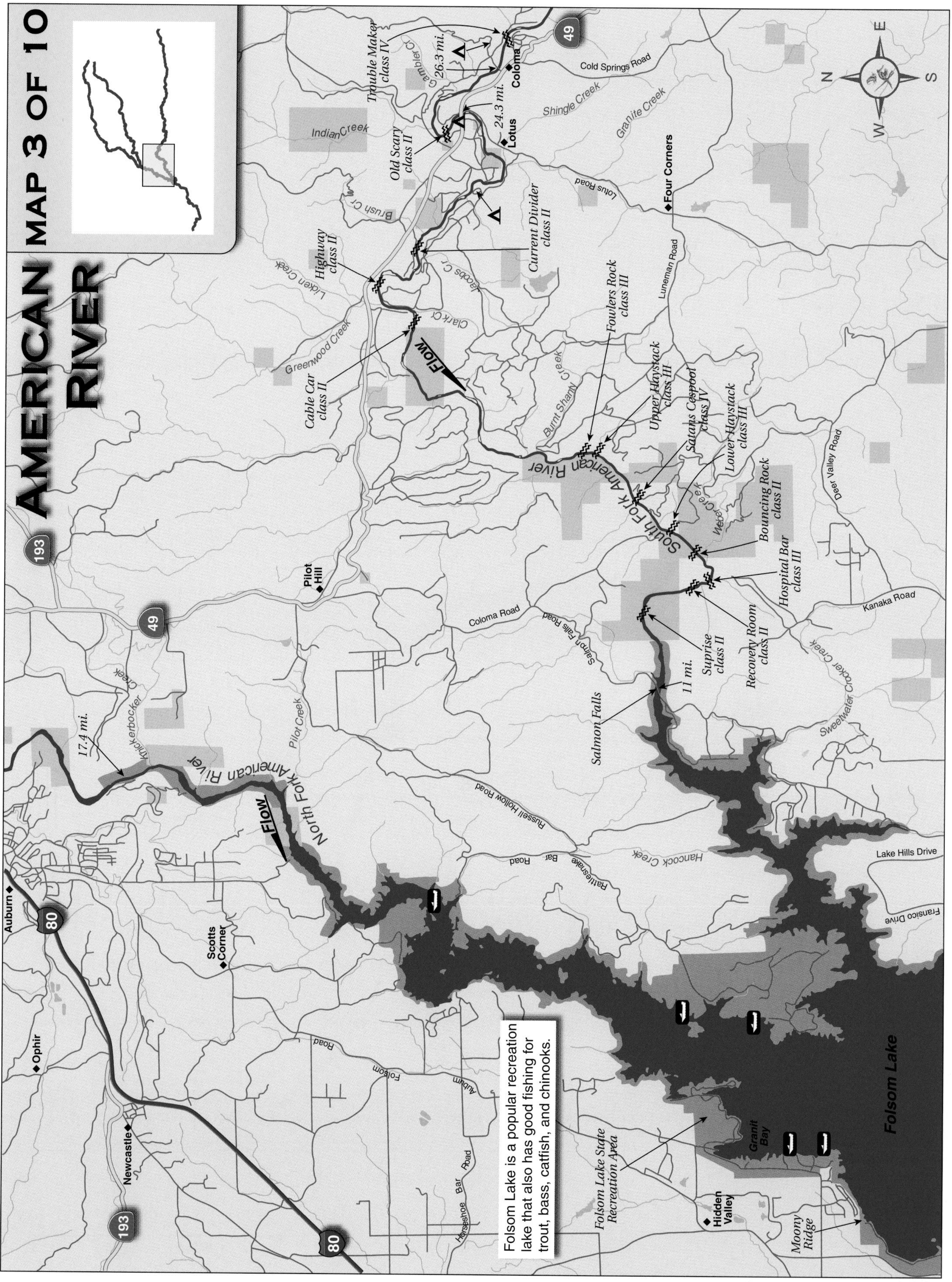
AMERICAN RIVER
MAP 3 OF 10
Folsom Lake is a popular recreation lake that also has good fishing for trout, bass, catfish, and chinooks.
Folsom Lake
Folsom Lake State Recreation Area
Granit Bay
Moony Ridge
Hidden Valley
Newcastle
Ophir
Auburn
Scotts Corner
Pilot Hill
Coloma
Lotus
Four Corners
North Fork American River
South Fork American River
Flow
17.4 mi.
11 mi.
24.3 mi.
26.3 mi.
Salmon Falls
Suprise class II
Recovery Room class II
Hospital Bar class III
Bouncing Rock class II
Lower Haystack class III
Satans Cesspool class IV
Upper Haystack class III
Fowlers Rock class III
Cable Car class II
Highway class II
Current Divider class II
Old Scary class II
Trouble Maker class IV
Knickerbocker Creek
Pilot Creek
Greenwood Creek
Clark Cr
Jacobs Cr
Brush Cr
Indian Creek
Gambler Cr
Shingle Creek
Granite Creek
Burnt Shanty Creek
Weber Creek
Sweetwater Creek
Hancock Creek
Coloma Road
Salmon Falls Road
Russell Hollow Road
Rattlesnake Bar Road
Folsom Auburn Road
Horseshoe Bar Road
Lotus Road
Luneman Road
Cold Springs Road
Deer Valley Road
Kanaka Road
Lake Hills Drive
Francisco Drive
80
193
49
N
E
S
W

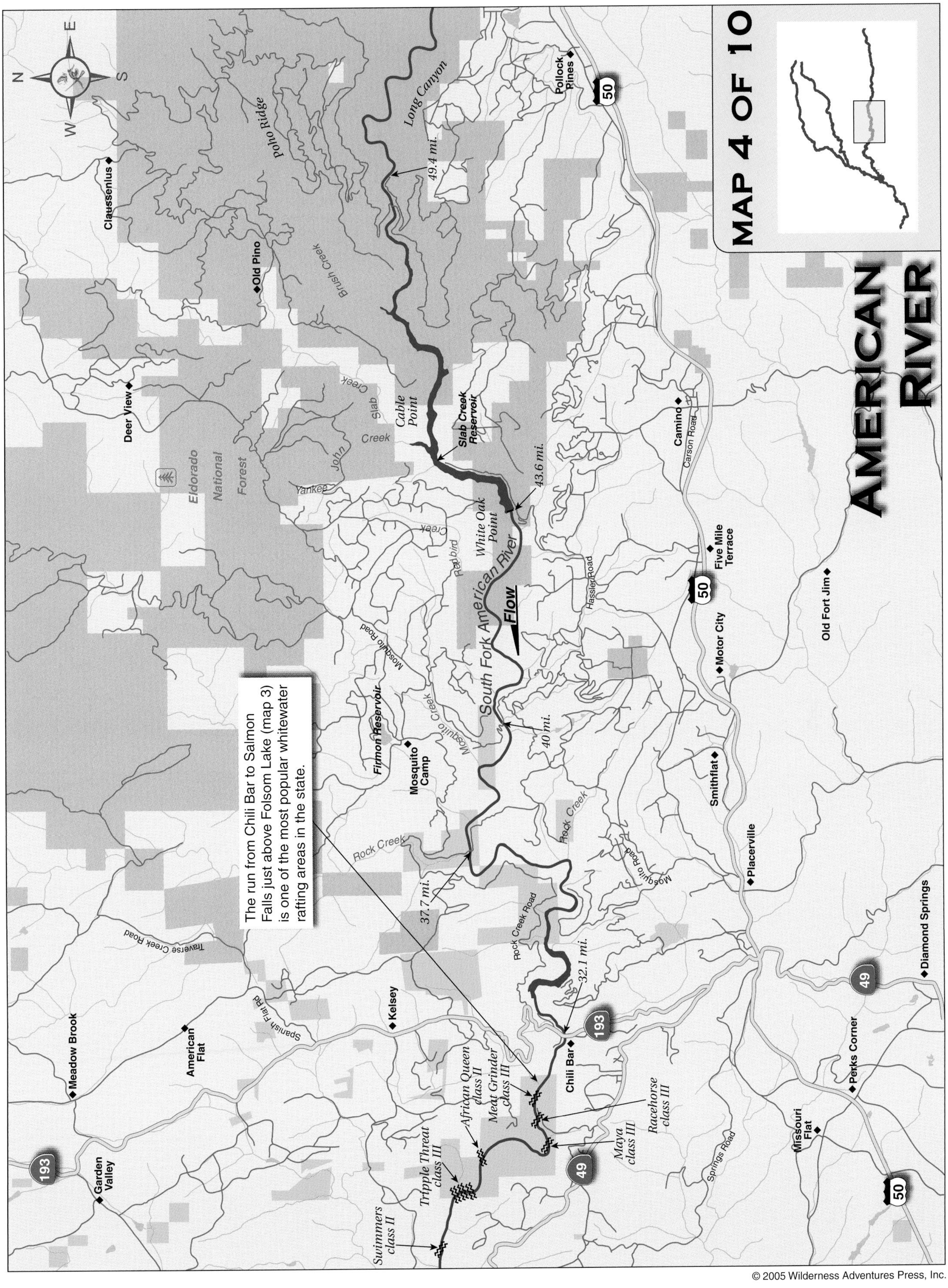
MAP 4 OF 10
AMERICAN RIVER
The run from Chili Bar to Salmon Falls just above Folsom Lake (map 3) is one of the most popular whitewater rafting areas in the state.
South Fork American River
Flow
Long Canyon
Poho Ridge
Brush Creek
49.4 mi.
43.6 mi.
40 mi.
37.7 mi.
32.1 mi.
Slab Creek Reservoir
Cable Point
White Oak Point
Slab Creek
John Creek
Yankee Creek
Redbird Creek
Eldorado National Forest
Mosquito Road
Mosquito Creek
Finnon Reservoir
Mosquito Camp
Rock Creek
Rock Creek Road
Hassler Road
Carson Road
Traverse Creek Road
Spanish Flat Rd
Springs Road
Swimmers class II
Tripple Threat class III
African Queen class II
Meat Grinder class III
Racehorse class III
Maya class III
Claussenius
Old Pino
Deer View
Pollock Pines
Camino
Five Mile Terrace
Old Fort Jim
Motor City
Smithflat
Placerville
Diamond Springs
Perks Corner
Missouri Flat
Chili Bar
Kelsey
American Flat
Meadow Brook
Garden Valley
193
50
49
N
E
S
W

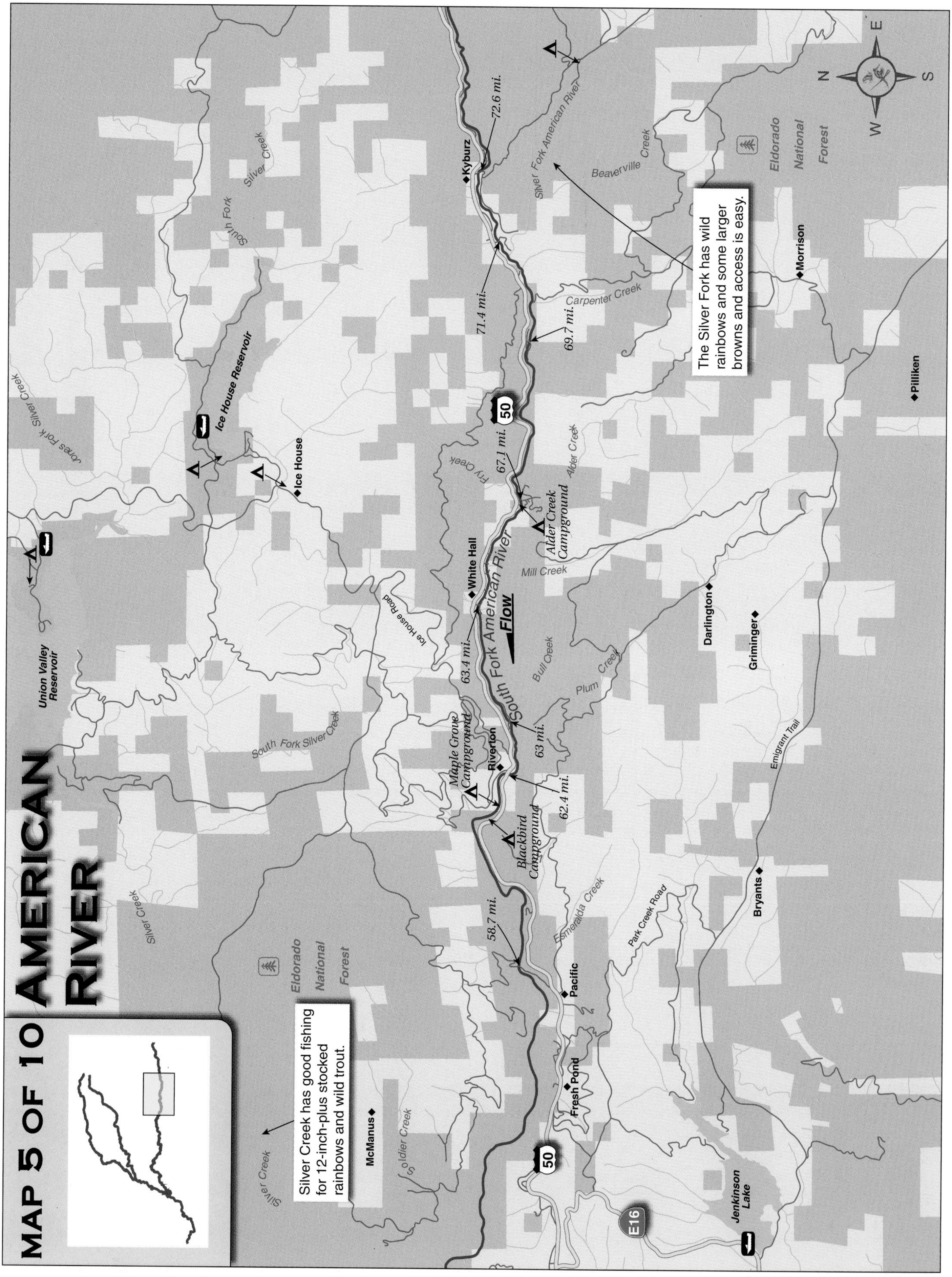
MAP 5 OF 10
AMERICAN RIVER
Silver Creek has good fishing for 12-inch-plus stocked rainbows and wild trout.
The Silver Fork has wild rainbows and some larger browns and access is easy.
South Fork American River
Flow
Silver Fork American River
Eldorado National Forest
Eldorado National Forest
Union Valley Reservoir
Ice House Reservoir
Ice House
Ice House Road
Jones Fork Silver Creek
South Fork Silver Creek
South Fork Silver Creek
Silver Creek
Silver Creek
Soldier Creek
McManus
Fresh Pond
Pacific
Esmeralda Creek
Park Creek Road
Bryants
Blackbird Campground
Maple Grove Campground
Riverton
Plum Creek
Bull Creek
Grimminger
Darlington
Emigrant Trail
White Hall
Mill Creek
Alder Creek Campground
Alder Creek
Fry Creek
Pilliken
Carpenter Creek
Morrison
Beaverville Creek
Kyburz
58.7 mi.
62.4 mi.
63 mi.
63.4 mi.
67.1 mi.
69.7 mi.
71.4 mi.
72.6 mi.
50
50
E16
Jenkinson Lake
N
S
E
W

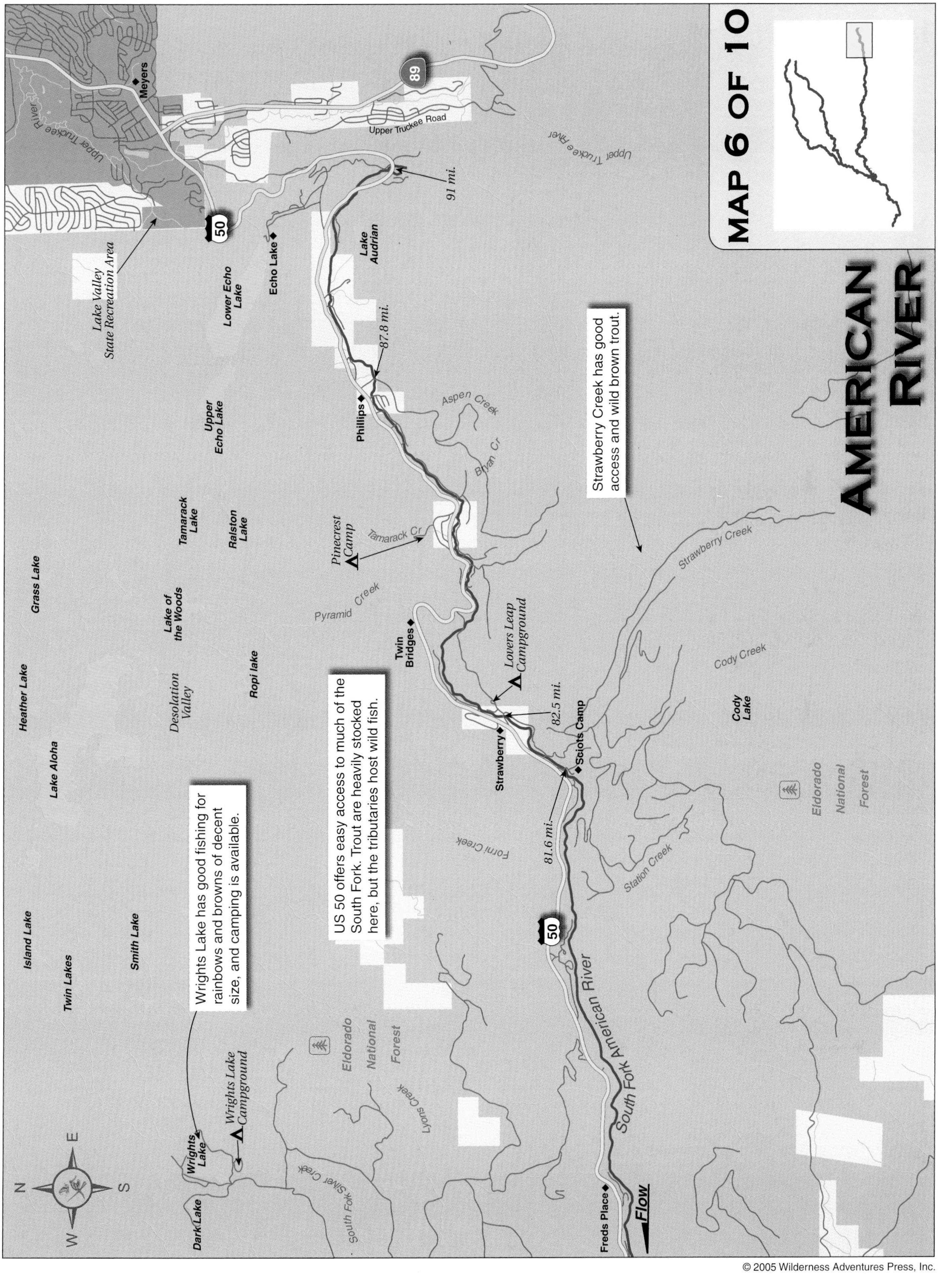
AMERICAN RIVER
MAP 6 OF 10
Strawberry Creek has good access and wild brown trout.
US 50 offers easy access to much of the South Fork. Trout are heavily stocked here, but the tributaries host wild fish.
Wrights Lake has good fishing for rainbows and browns of decent size, and camping is available.
Meyers
Upper Truckee River
Upper Truckee Road
89
50
Lake Valley State Recreation Area
Echo Lake
Lower Echo Lake
Upper Echo Lake
Lake Audrian
91 mi.
87.8 mi.
82.5 mi.
81.6 mi.
Phillips
Aspen Creek
Bryan Cr
Tamarack Lake
Ralston Lake
Pinecrest Camp
Tamarack Cr
Strawberry Creek
Grass Lake
Lake of the Woods
Pyramid Creek
Twin Bridges
Lovers Leap Campground
Heather Lake
Desolation Valley
Ropi lake
Cody Creek
Cody Lake
Sciots Camp
Strawberry
Lake Aloha
Eldorado National Forest
Forni Creek
Station Creek
Island Lake
Twin Lakes
Smith Lake
South Fork American River
Lyons Creek
Wrights Lake
Wrights Lake Campground
Dark Lake
South Fork Silver Creek
Freds Place
Flow
N
E
S
W

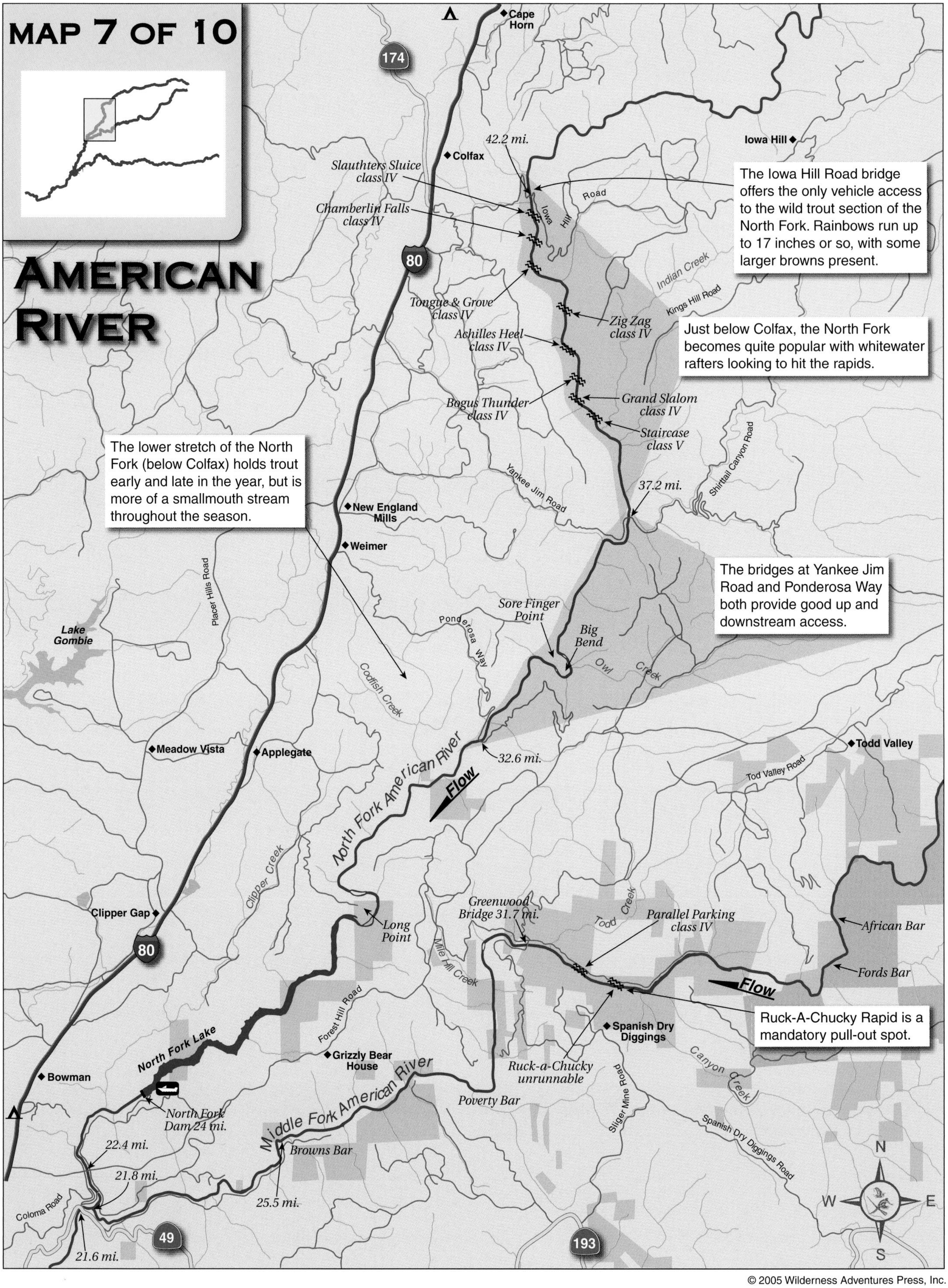
MAP 7 OF 10
AMERICAN RIVER
The Iowa Hill Road bridge offers the only vehicle access to the wild trout section of the North Fork. Rainbows run up to 17 inches or so, with some larger browns present.
Just below Colfax, the North Fork becomes quite popular with whitewater rafters looking to hit the rapids.
The lower stretch of the North Fork (below Colfax) holds trout early and late in the year, but is more of a smallmouth stream throughout the season.
The bridges at Yankee Jim Road and Ponderosa Way both provide good up and downstream access.
Ruck-A-Chucky Rapid is a mandatory pull-out spot.
Cape Horn
Colfax
Iowa Hill
42.2 mi.
Slauthters Sluice class IV
Chamberlin Falls class IV
Tongue & Grove class IV
Zig Zag class IV
Achilles Heel class IV
Bogus Thunder class IV
Grand Slalom class IV
Staircase class V
37.2 mi.
Iowa Hill Road
Indian Creek
Kings Hill Road
Shirttail Canyon Road
Yankee Jim Road
New England Mills
Weimer
Placer Hills Road
Lake Gombie
Sore Finger Point
Big Bend
Owl Creek
Ponderosa Way
Codfish Creek
32.6 mi.
Todd Valley
Tod Valley Road
Meadow Vista
Applegate
North Fork American River
Flow
Clipper Creek
Clipper Gap
Long Point
Greenwood Bridge 31.7 mi.
Todd Creek
Parallel Parking class IV
African Bar
Fords Bar
Mile Hill Creek
Forest Hill Road
Spanish Dry Diggings
Ruck-a-Chucky unrunnable
Canyon Creek
Grizzly Bear House
North Fork Lake
Bowman
North Fork Dam 24 mi.
Middle Fork American River
Poverty Bar
Sliger Mine Road
Spanish Dry Diggings Road
22.4 mi.
21.8 mi.
Browns Bar
25.5 mi.
Coloma Road
21.6 mi.
174
80
49
193
N
W
E
S

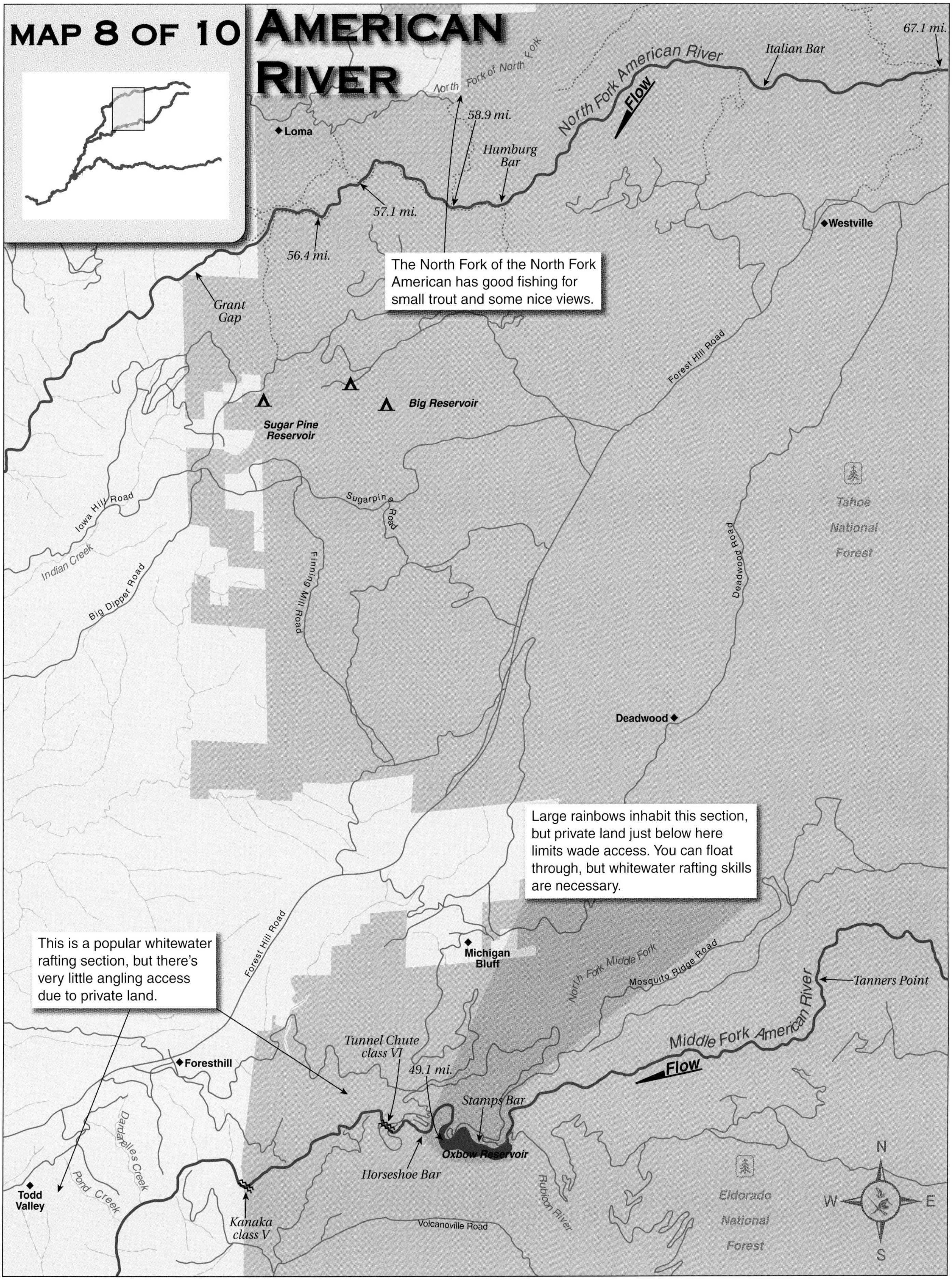

MAP 8 OF 10
AMERICAN RIVER
North Fork American River
North Fork of North Fork
Flow
67.1 mi.
Italian Bar
58.9 mi.
Humburg Bar
57.1 mi.
56.4 mi.
Loma
Grant Gap
Westville
The North Fork of the North Fork American has good fishing for small trout and some nice views.
Forest Hill Road
Big Reservoir
Sugar Pine Reservoir
Iowa Hill Road
Indian Creek
Sugarpine Road
Finning Mill Road
Big Dipper Road
Deadwood Road
Tahoe National Forest
Deadwood
Large rainbows inhabit this section, but private land just below here limits wade access. You can float through, but whitewater rafting skills are necessary.
This is a popular whitewater rafting section, but there's very little angling access due to private land.
Michigan Bluff
North Fork Middle Fork
Mosquito Ridge Road
Tanners Point
Middle Fork American River
Flow
Tunnel Chute class VI
49.1 mi.
Foresthill
Stamps Bar
Oxbow Reservoir
Horseshoe Bar
Dardanelles Creek
Pond Creek
Todd Valley
Kanaka class V
Volcanoville Road
Rubicon River
Eldorado National Forest
N
W
E
S

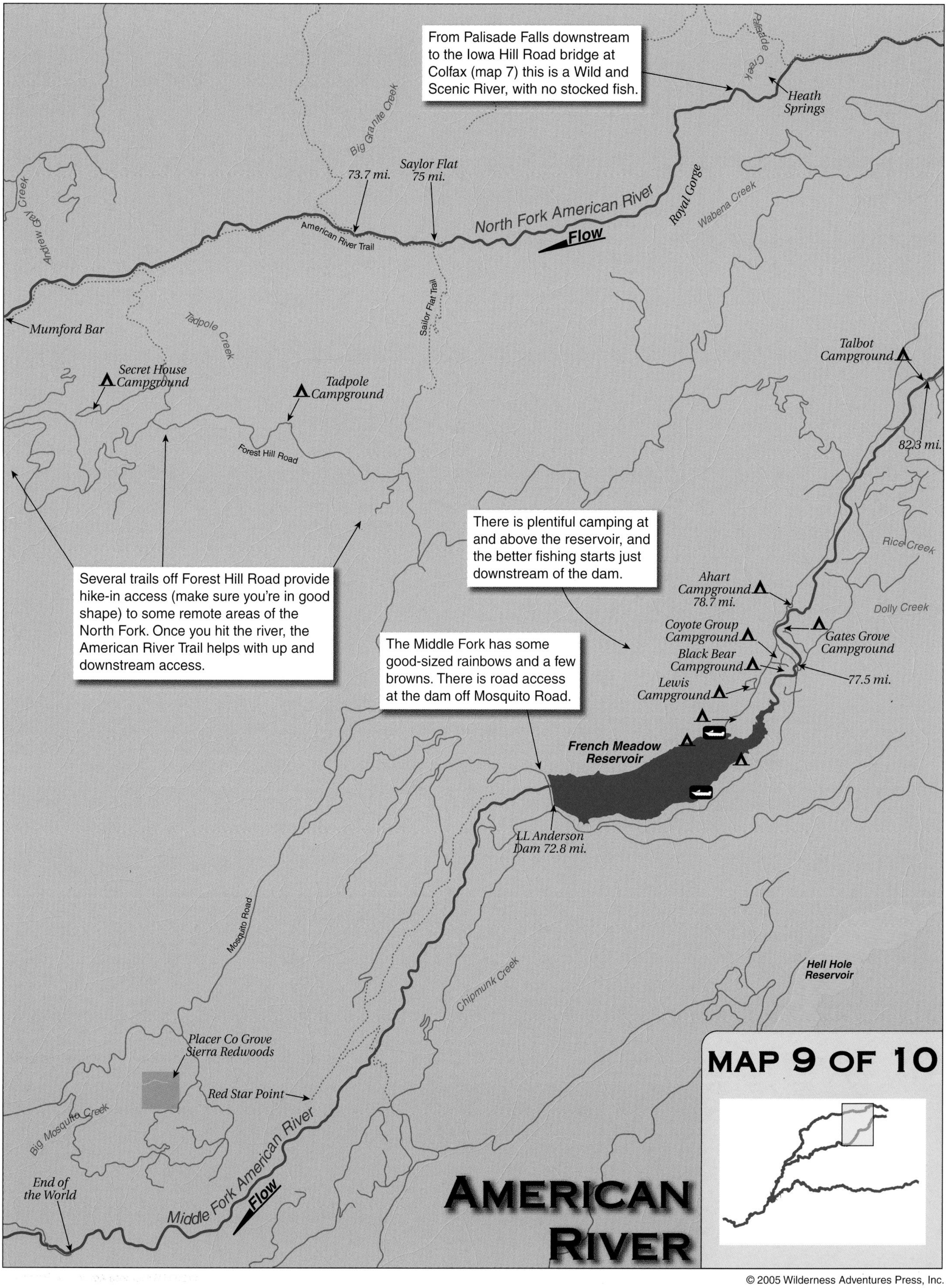
From Palisade Falls downstream to the Iowa Hill Road bridge at Colfax (map 7) this is a Wild and Scenic River, with no stocked fish.
Palisade Creek
Heath Springs
Big Granite Creek
73.7 mi.
Saylor Flat 75 mi.
Royal Gorge
Wabena Creek
North Fork American River
Flow
American River Trail
Andrew Gray Creek
Mumford Bar
Tadpole Creek
Sailor Flat Trail
Talbot Campground
Secret House Campground
Tadpole Campground
Forest Hill Road
82.3 mi.
There is plentiful camping at and above the reservoir, and the better fishing starts just downstream of the dam.
Rice Creek
Several trails off Forest Hill Road provide hike-in access (make sure you're in good shape) to some remote areas of the North Fork. Once you hit the river, the American River Trail helps with up and downstream access.
Ahart Campground 78.7 mi.
Dolly Creek
Coyote Group Campground
Gates Grove Campground
Black Bear Campground
The Middle Fork has some good-sized rainbows and a few browns. There is road access at the dam off Mosquito Road.
77.5 mi.
Lewis Campground
French Meadow Reservoir
LL Anderson Dam 72.8 mi.
Mosquito Road
Hell Hole Reservoir
Chipmunk Creek
MAP 9 OF 10
Placer Co Grove Sierra Redwoods
Red Star Point
Big Mosquito Creek
Middle Fork American River
Flow
End of the World
AMERICAN RIVER

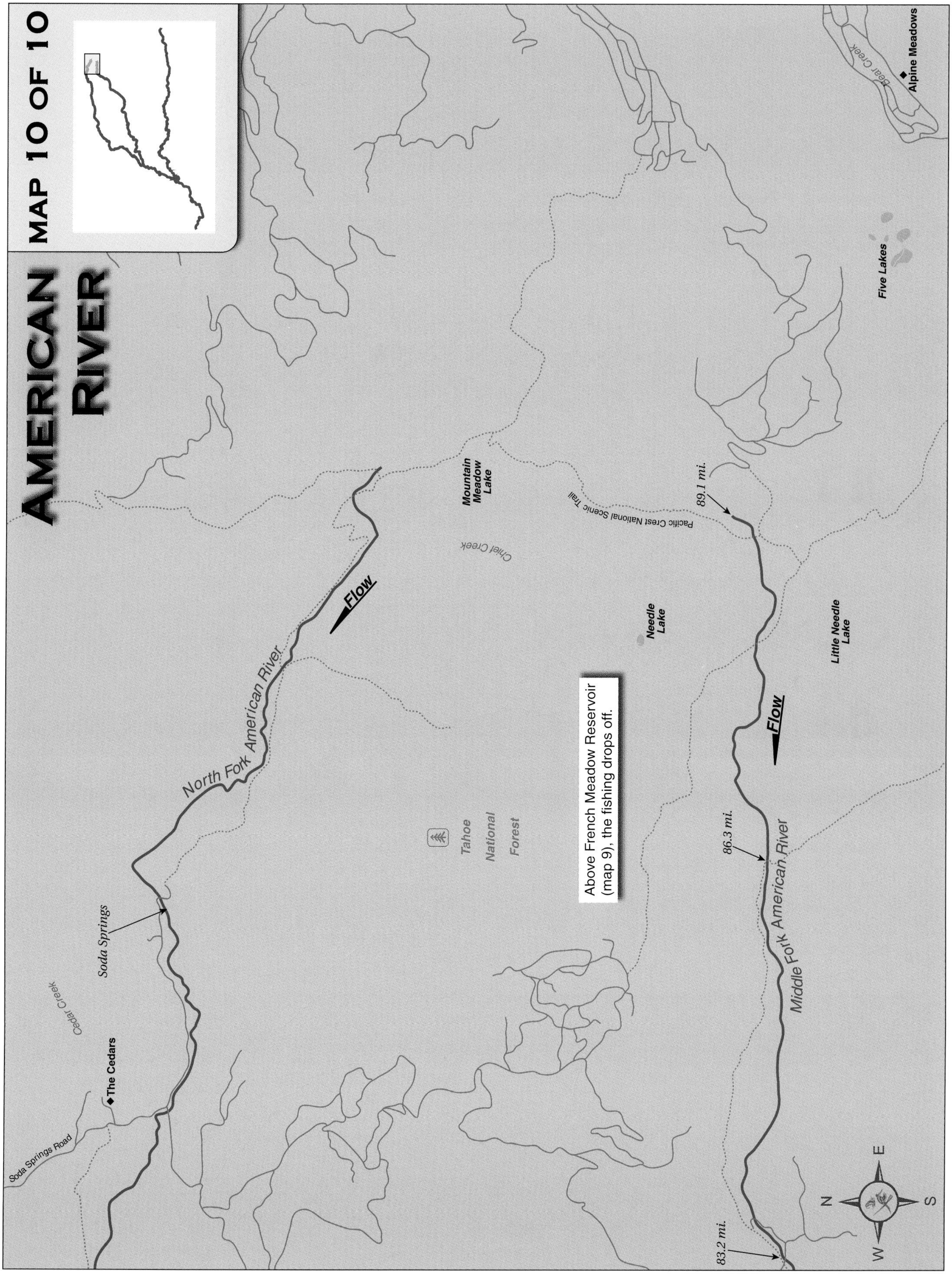
American River
Map 10 of 10
North Fork American River
Flow
Middle Fork American River
Flow
Soda Springs
Soda Springs Road
The Cedars
Cedar Creek
Tahoe National Forest
Above French Meadow Reservoir (map 9), the fishing drops off.
Mountain Meadow Lake
Chief Creek
Pacific Crest National Scenic Trail
Needle Lake
Little Needle Lake
Five Lakes
Alpine Meadows
Bear Creek
89.1 mi.
86.3 mi.
83.2 mi.
N
E
S
W

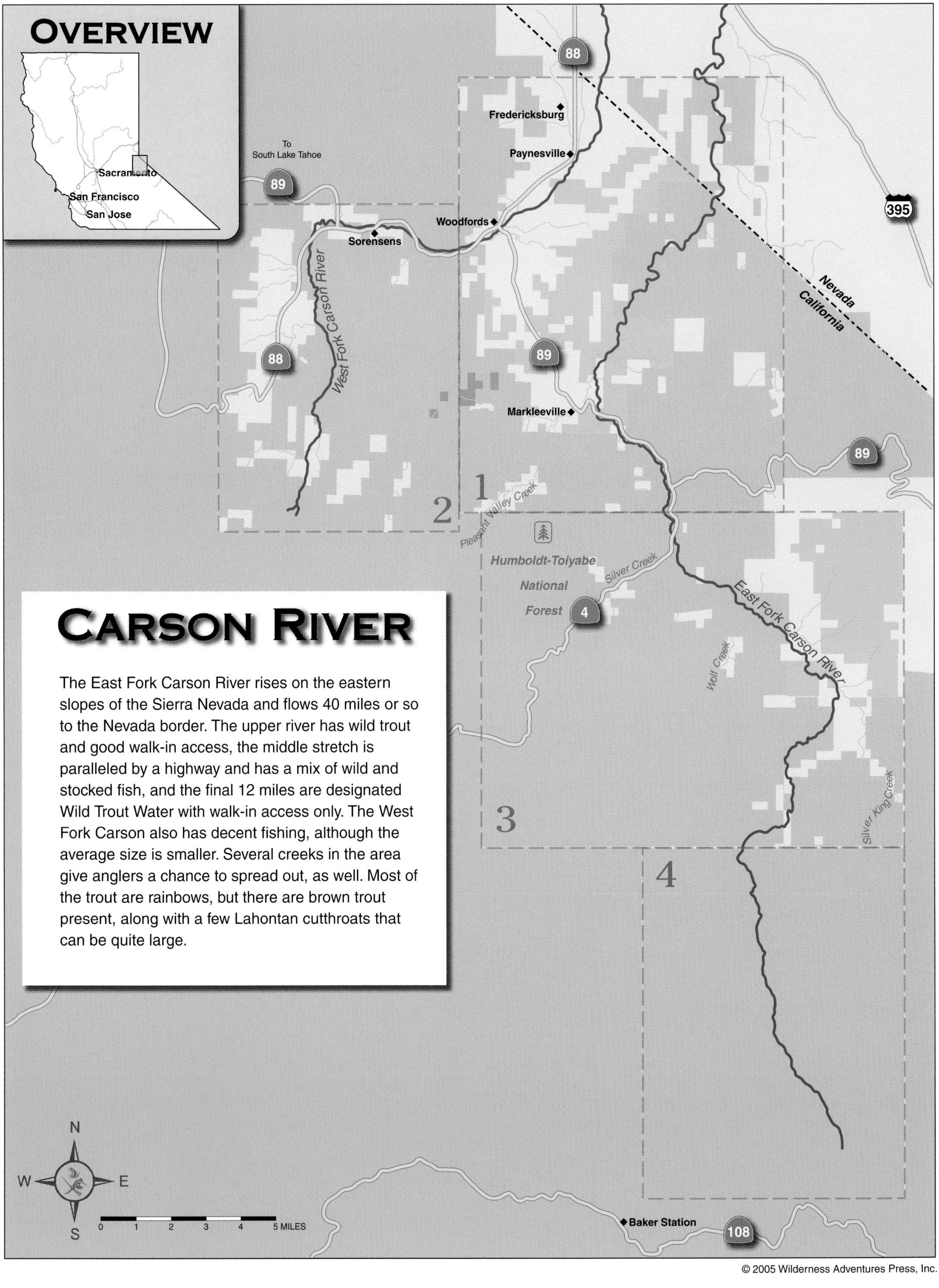

Carson River

The East Fork Carson River rises on the eastern slopes of the Sierra Nevada and flows 40 miles or so to the Nevada border. The upper river has wild trout and good walk-in access, the middle stretch is paralleled by a highway and has a mix of wild and stocked fish, and the final 12 miles are designated Wild Trout Water with walk-in access only. The West Fork Carson also has decent fishing, although the average size is smaller. Several creeks in the area give anglers a chance to spread out, as well. Most of the trout are rainbows, but there are brown trout present, along with a few Lahontan cutthroats that can be quite large.

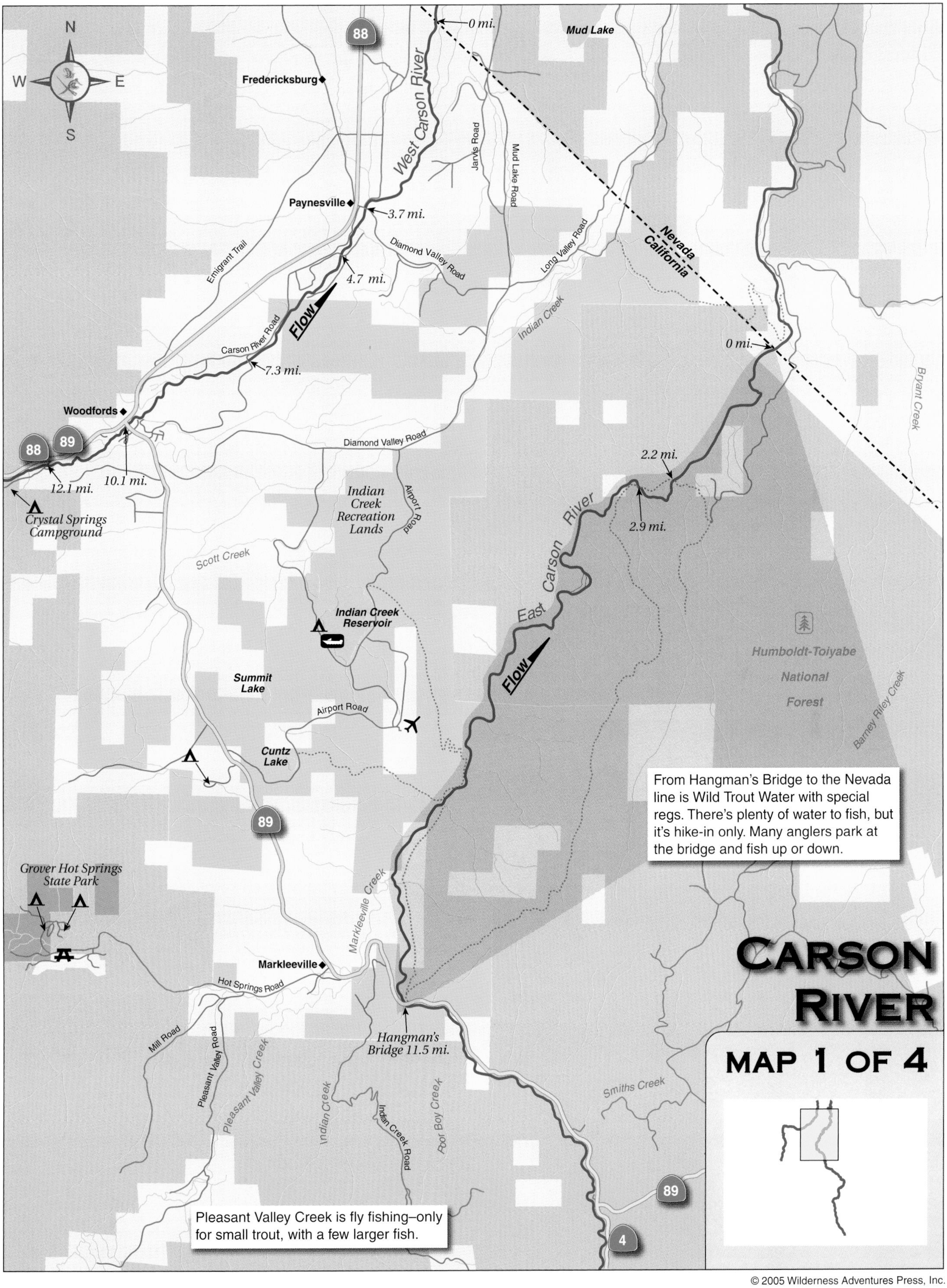

N
W
E
S
88
0 mi.
Mud Lake
Fredericksburg
West Carson River
Jarvis Road
Mud Lake Road
Paynesville
3.7 mi.
Diamond Valley Road
Long Valley Road
Nevada
California
Emigrant Trail
4.7 mi.
Flow
Indian Creek
Carson River Road
0 mi.
7.3 mi.
Bryant Creek
Woodfords
89
88
Diamond Valley Road
2.2 mi.
12.1 mi.
10.1 mi.
Crystal Springs Campground
Indian Creek Recreation Lands
Airport Road
East Carson River
2.9 mi.
Scott Creek
Indian Creek Reservoir
Flow
Humboldt-Toiyabe National Forest
Summit Lake
Airport Road
Barney Riley Creek
Cuntz Lake
From Hangman's Bridge to the Nevada line is Wild Trout Water with special regs. There's plenty of water to fish, but it's hike-in only. Many anglers park at the bridge and fish up or down.
89
Grover Hot Springs State Park
Markleeville Creek
Markleeville
CARSON RIVER
Hot Springs Road
Mill Road
Pleasant Valley Road
Pleasant Valley Creek
Hangman's Bridge 11.5 mi.
MAP 1 OF 4
Smiths Creek
Indian Creek
Indian Creek Road
Poor Boy Creek
89
Pleasant Valley Creek is fly fishing–only for small trout, with a few larger fish.
4

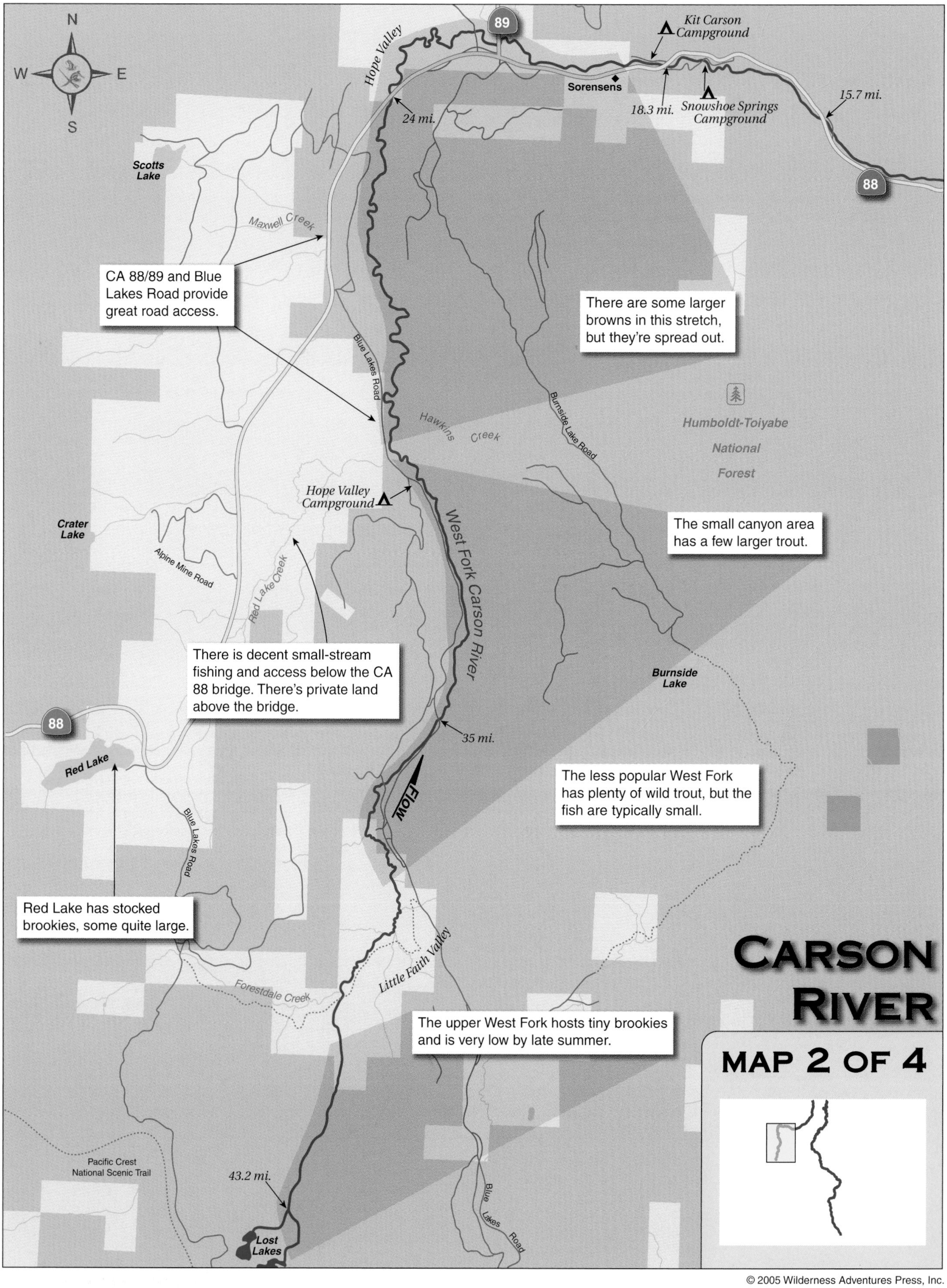
N
W
E
S
89
Kit Carson Campground
Hope Valley
Sorensens
18.3 mi.
Snowshoe Springs Campground
15.7 mi.
24 mi.
88
Scotts Lake
Maxwell Creek
CA 88/89 and Blue Lakes Road provide great road access.
There are some larger browns in this stretch, but they're spread out.
Blue Lakes Road
Hawkins Creek
Burnside Lake Road
Humboldt-Toiyabe National Forest
Hope Valley Campground
West Fork Carson River
The small canyon area has a few larger trout.
Crater Lake
Alpine Mine Road
Red Lake Creek
There is decent small-stream fishing and access below the CA 88 bridge. There's private land above the bridge.
Burnside Lake
88
35 mi.
Red Lake
Flow
The less popular West Fork has plenty of wild trout, but the fish are typically small.
Blue Lakes Road
Red Lake has stocked brookies, some quite large.
Little Faith Valley
Forestdale Creek
The upper West Fork hosts tiny brookies and is very low by late summer.
CARSON RIVER
MAP 2 OF 4
Pacific Crest National Scenic Trail
43.2 mi.
Blue Lakes Road
Lost Lakes

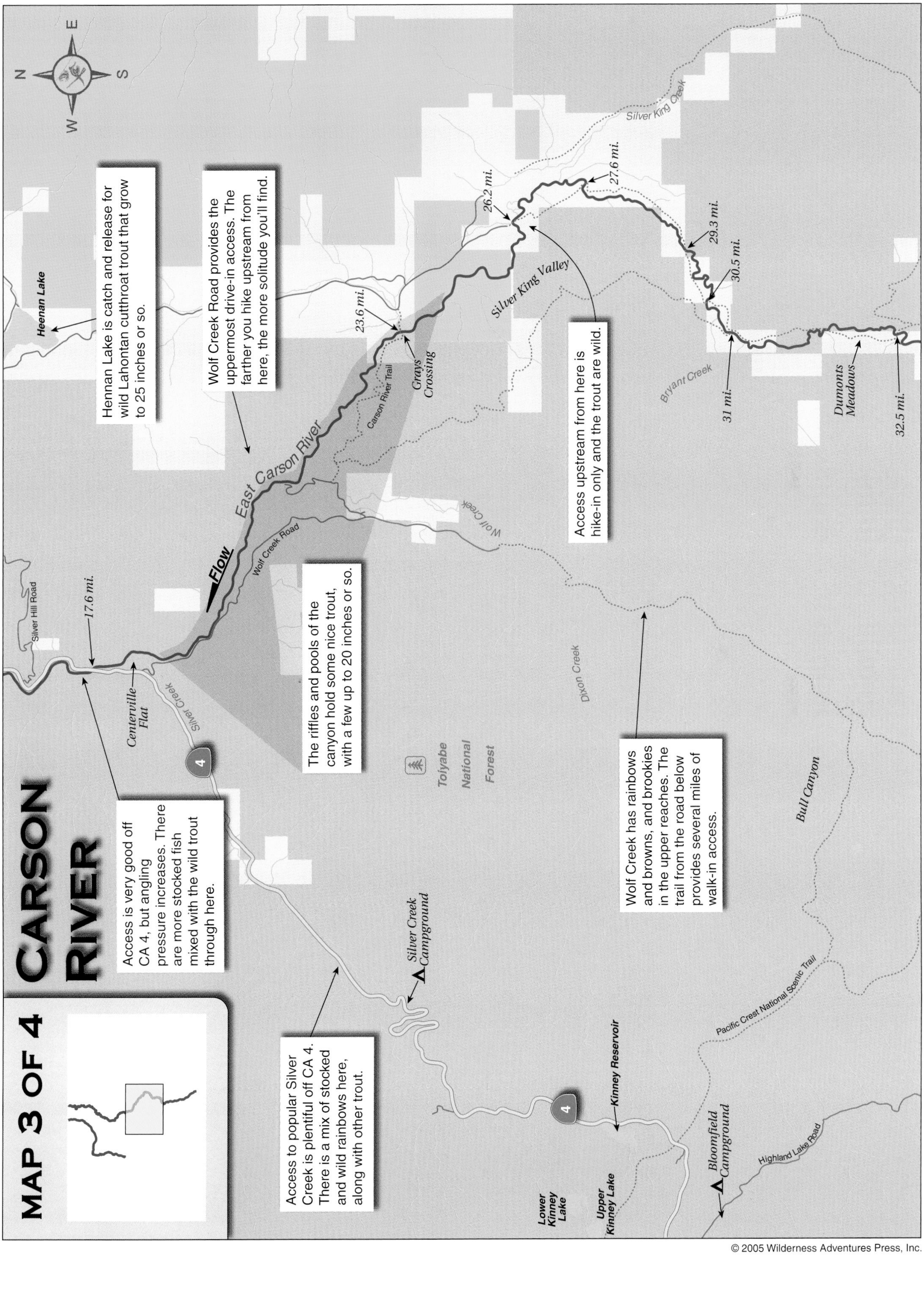
MAP 3 OF 4
CARSON RIVER
N
E
S
W
Hennan Lake is catch and release for wild Lahontan cutthroat trout that grow to 25 inches or so.
Wolf Creek Road provides the uppermost drive-in access. The farther you hike upstream from here, the more solitude you'll find.
Access upstream from here is hike-in only and the trout are wild.
The riffles and pools of the canyon hold some nice trout, with a few up to 20 inches or so.
Access is very good off CA 4, but angling pressure increases. There are more stocked fish mixed with the wild trout through here.
Wolf Creek has rainbows and browns, and brookies in the upper reaches. The trail from the road below provides several miles of walk-in access.
Access to popular Silver Creek is plentiful off CA 4. There is a mix of stocked and wild rainbows here, along with other trout.
Heenan Lake
Silver Hill Road
17.6 mi.
Flow
East Carson River
Wolf Creek Road
Carson River Trail
Grays Crossing
23.6 mi.
26.2 mi.
27.6 mi.
29.3 mi.
30.5 mi.
31 mi.
32.5 mi.
Silver King Valley
Silver King Creek
Bryant Creek
Dumonts Meadows
Wolf Creek
Dixon Creek
Centerville Flat
Silver Creek
4
Toiyabe National Forest
Bull Canyon
Silver Creek Campground
Pacific Crest National Scenic Trail
Kinney Reservoir
Lower Kinney Lake
Upper Kinney Lake
Bloomfield Campground
Highland Lake Road

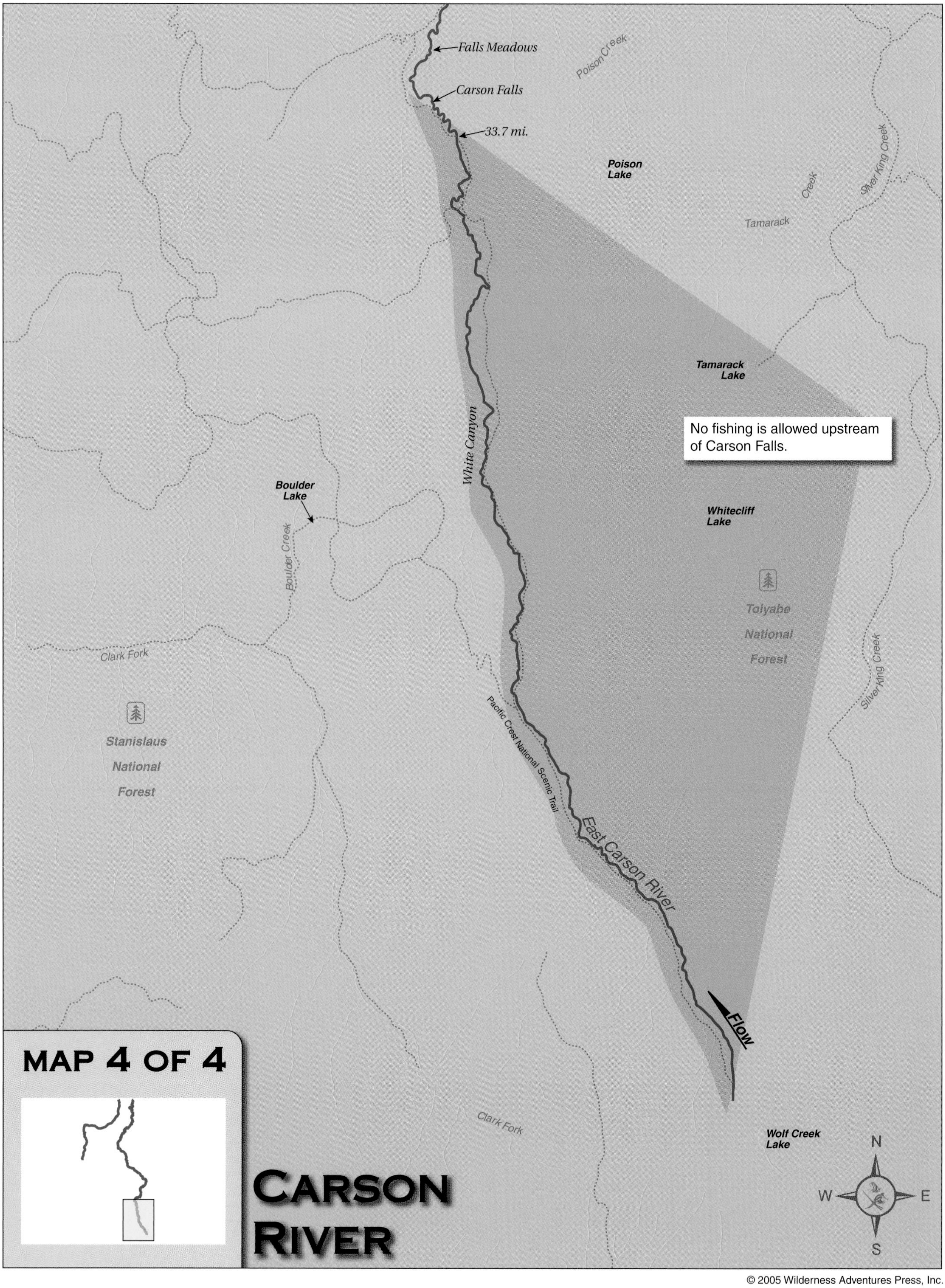
Falls Meadows
Carson Falls
33.7 mi.
Poison Creek
Poison Lake
Silver King Creek
Tamarack Creek
Tamarack Lake
No fishing is allowed upstream of Carson Falls.
White Canyon
Boulder Lake
Boulder Creek
Whitecliff Lake
Toiyabe National Forest
Clark Fork
Stanislaus National Forest
Pacific Crest National Scenic Trail
East Carson River
Flow
MAP 4 OF 4
Clark Fork
Wolf Creek Lake
CARSON RIVER
N
W
E
S

Eel River

The Eel River is located on the coast just south of Eureka in northern California. It has good runs of king salmon and steelhead, and the latter are sometimes quite large. Float-fishing is popular here, and this scenic river sees a lot of anglers from fall through spring. As with many coastal rivers, there are a host of complicated regulations governing the fishing and low-flow closures are always a possibility. Call 707-442-4502 or visit the Fish & Game website at www.dfg.ca.gov for the most current information. The nearby Van Duzen also offers anglers a shot at steelhead.

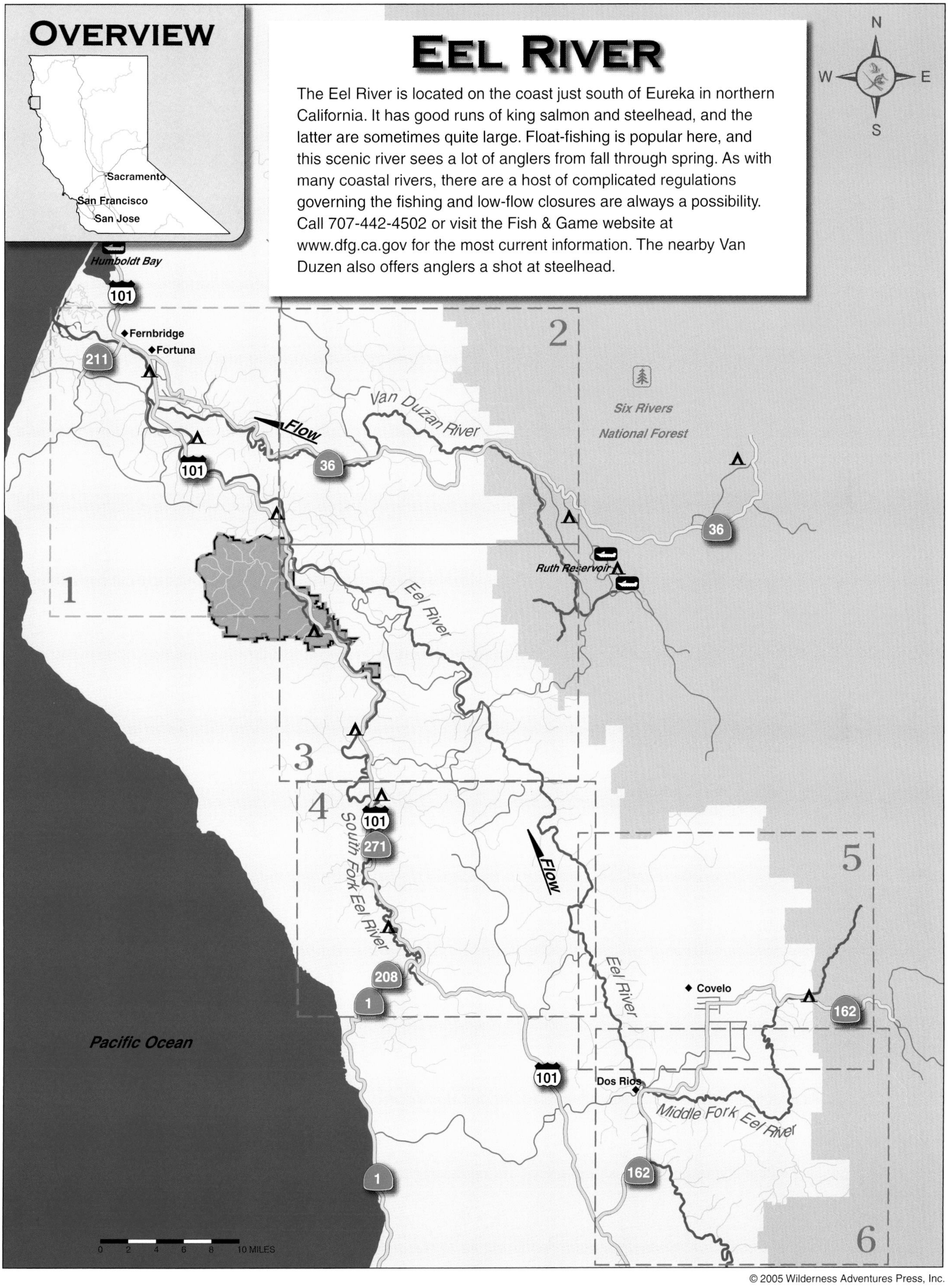

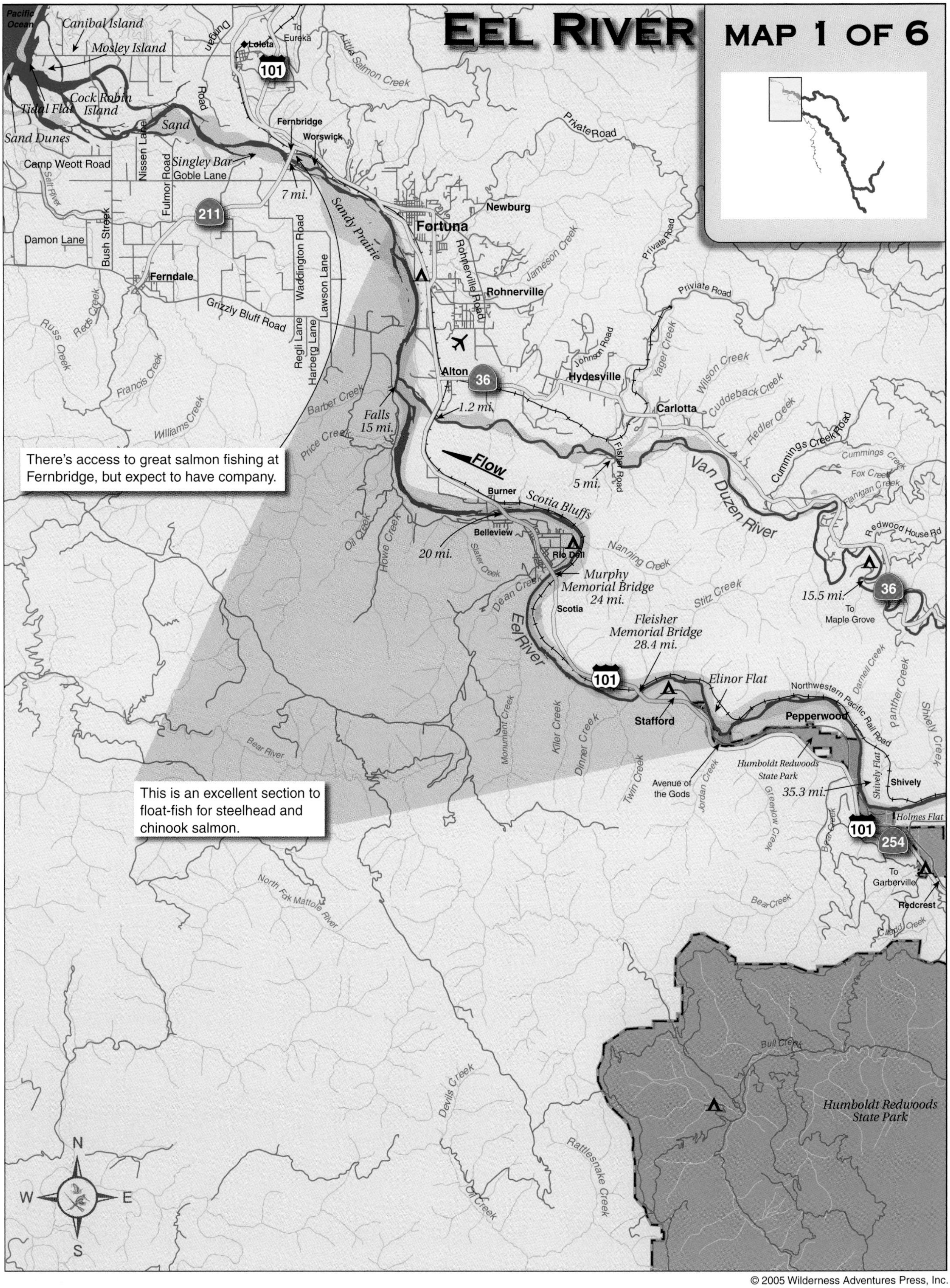
Eel River
Map 1 of 6
Pacific Ocean
Canibal Island
Mosley Island
Cock Robin Island
Tidal Flat
Sand Dunes
Sand
Singley Bar
Camp Weott Road
Goble Lane
Nissen Lane
Fulmor Road
Dungan Road
Loleta
To Eureka
101
Little Salmon Creek
Fernbridge
Worswick
Private Road
7 mi.
Salt River
211
Damon Lane
Bush Street
Ferndale
Waddington Road
Lawson Lane
Sandy Prairie
Fortuna
Newburg
Rohnerville Road
Rohnerville
Jameson Creek
Private Road
Priviate Road
Grizzly Bluff Road
Regli Lane
Harberg Lane
Russ Creek
Reas Creek
Francis Creek
Williams Creek
Barber Creek
Price Creek
Falls 15 mi.
Alton
36
1.2 mi.
Johnson Road
Hydesville
Yager Creek
Wilson Creek
Carlotta
Cuddeback Creek
Hedler Creek
Cummings Creek Road
Cummings Creek
Fox Creek
Flanigan Creek
There's access to great salmon fishing at Fernbridge, but expect to have company.
Flow
Fisher Road
5 mi.
Van Duzen River
Burner
Scotia Bluffs
Redwood House Rd
Oil Creek
Howe Creek
Belleview
20 mi.
Slater Creek
Rio Dell
Nanning Creek
Murphy Memorial Bridge 24 mi.
Dean Creek
Scotia
Stitz Creek
15.5 mi.
To Maple Grove
Eel River
Fleisher Memorial Bridge 28.4 mi.
Elinor Flat
Darnell Creek
Panther Creek
Shively Creek
Northwestern Pacific Rail Road
Stafford
Pepperwood
Monument Creek
Kiler Creek
Dinner Creek
Bear River
Twin Creek
Avenue of the Gods
Jordan Creek
Humboldt Redwoods State Park
Shively Flat
Shively
35.3 mi.
This is an excellent section to float-fish for steelhead and chinook salmon.
Greenlow Creek
Holmes Flat
Bear Creek
254
To Garberville
Redcrest
North Fork Mattole River
Bear Creek
Bull Creek
Humboldt Redwoods State Park
Devils Creek
Rattlesnake Creek
Oil Creek
N
W
E
S

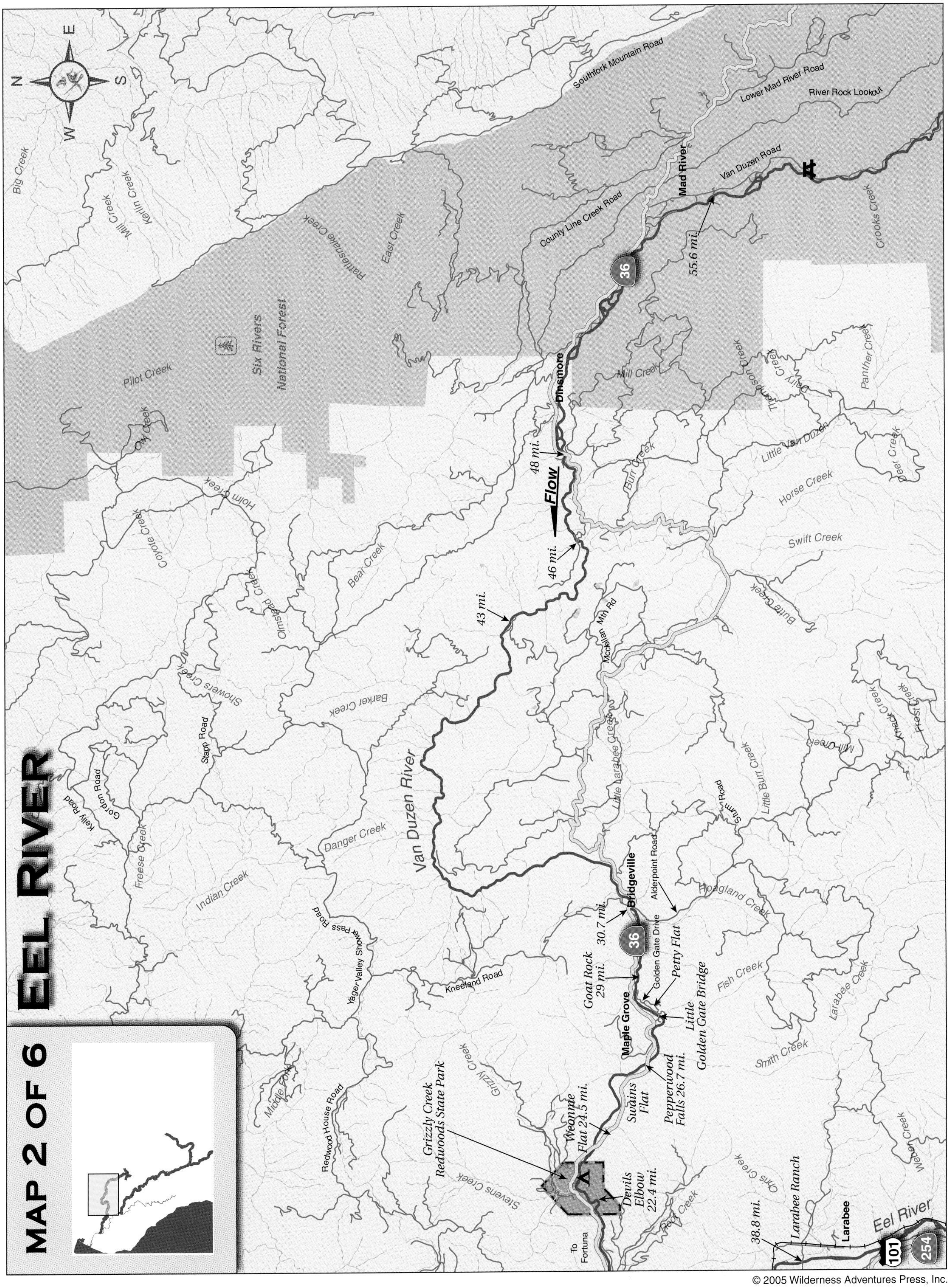
MAP 2 OF 6
EEL RIVER
Six Rivers National Forest
Van Duzen River
Flow
Mad River
Dinsmore
Bridgeville
Maple Grove
Larabee
Eel River
To Fortuna
Grizzly Creek Redwoods State Park
Devils Elbow 22.4 mi.
Weonnie Flat 24.5 mi.
Swains Flat
Pepperwood Falls 26.7 mi.
Little Golden Gate Bridge
Goat Rock 29 mi.
Golden Gate Drive
Petty Flat
30.7 mi.
43 mi.
46 mi.
48 mi.
55.6 mi.
38.8 mi.
Larabee Ranch
Alderpoint Road
Van Duzen Road
County Line Creek Road
Lower Mad River Road
Southfork Mountain Road
River Rock Lookout
Kneeland Road
Yager Valley Short Pass Road
Redwood House Road
Kelly Road
Gordon Road
Stapp Road
Mcclellan Mtn Rd
Pilot Creek
Big Creek
Mill Creek
Kerlin Creek
Rattlesnake Creek
East Creek
Holm Creek
Coyote Creek
Bear Creek
Olmstead Creek
Showers Creek
Barker Creek
Danger Creek
Freese Creek
Indian Creek
Grizzly Creek
Middle Fork
Stevens Creek
Red Creek
Burr Creek
Little Van Duzen
Horse Creek
Swift Creek
Butte Creek
Little Larabee Creek
Little Burr Creek
Hoagland Creek
Fish Creek
Smith Creek
Larabee Creek
Ohls Creek
Weber Creek
Crooks Creek
Thompson Creek
Panther Creek
Deer Creek
Frost Creek
36
101
254

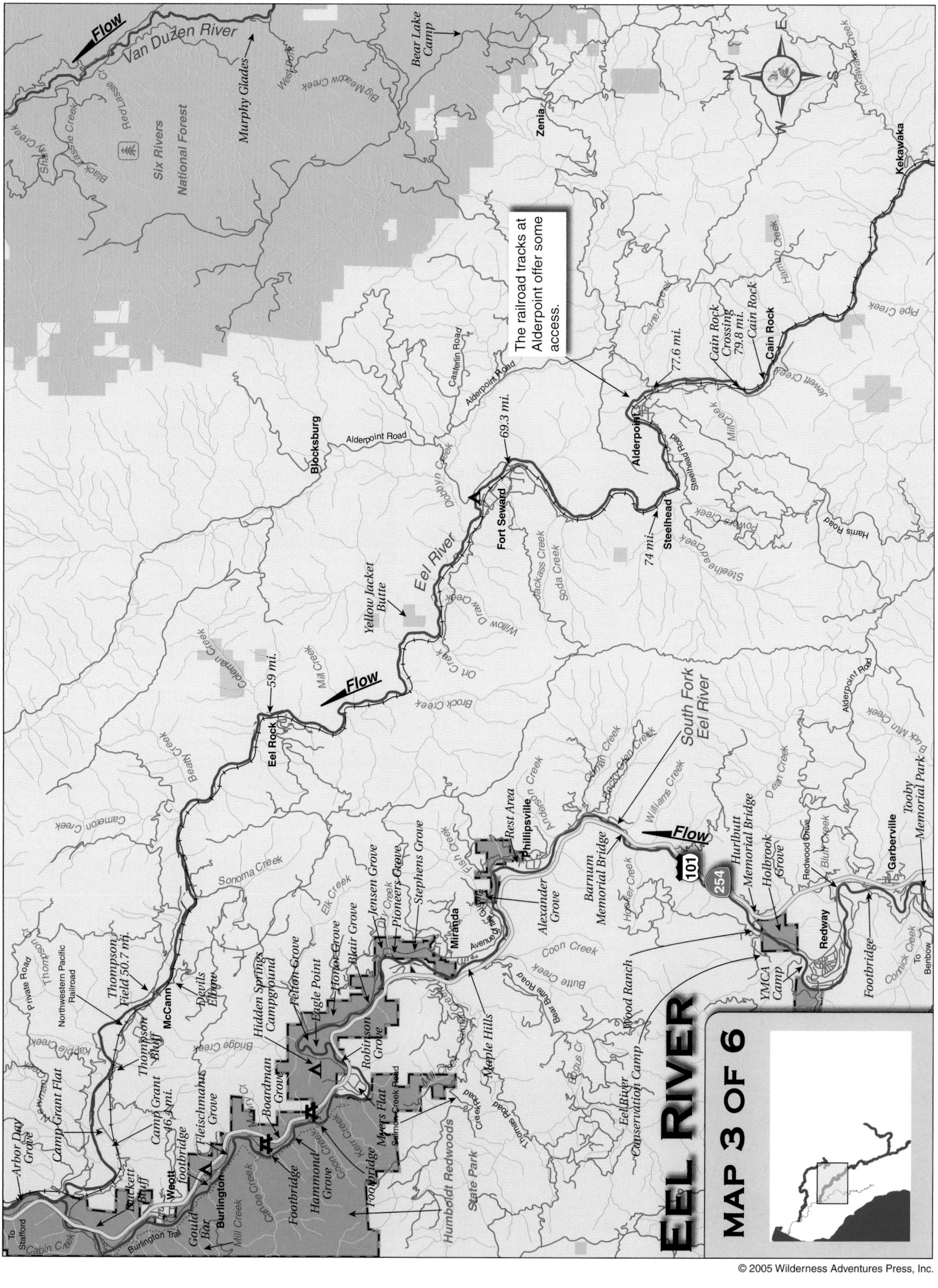
EEL RIVER
MAP 3 OF 6
The railroad tracks at Alderpoint offer some access.
Flow
Van Duzen River
Six Rivers National Forest
Murphy Glades
Bear Lake Camp
Zenia
Kekawaka
Cain Rock Crossing 79.8 mi.
Cain Rock
77.6 mi.
Alderpoint
Alderpoint Road
Casterlin Road
Blocksburg
69.3 mi.
Fort Seward
Steelhead
74 mi.
Eel River
Yellow Jacket Butte
59 mi.
Eel Rock
South Fork Eel River
Phillipsville
Rest Area
Barnum Memorial Bridge
Hurlbutt Memorial Bridge
Holbrook Grove
Garberville
Tooby Memorial Park
Redway
YMCA Camp
Footbridge
Miranda
Alexander Grove
Stephens Grove
Pioneers Grove
Jensen Grove
Blair Grove
Hocter Grove
Eagle Point
Felton Grove
Hidden Springs Campground
Robinson Grove
Maple Hills
Wood Ranch
Eel River Conservation Camp
Thompson Field 50.7 mi.
McCann
Devils Elbow
Thompson Bluff
Camp Grant Flat
Camp Grant 46.4 mi.
Fleischmann Grove
Boardman Grove
Myers Flat
Hammond Grove
Arbor Day Grove
Weott
Burlington
Gould Bar
Humboldt Redwoods State Park
Northwestern Pacific Railroad
Avenue of the Giants

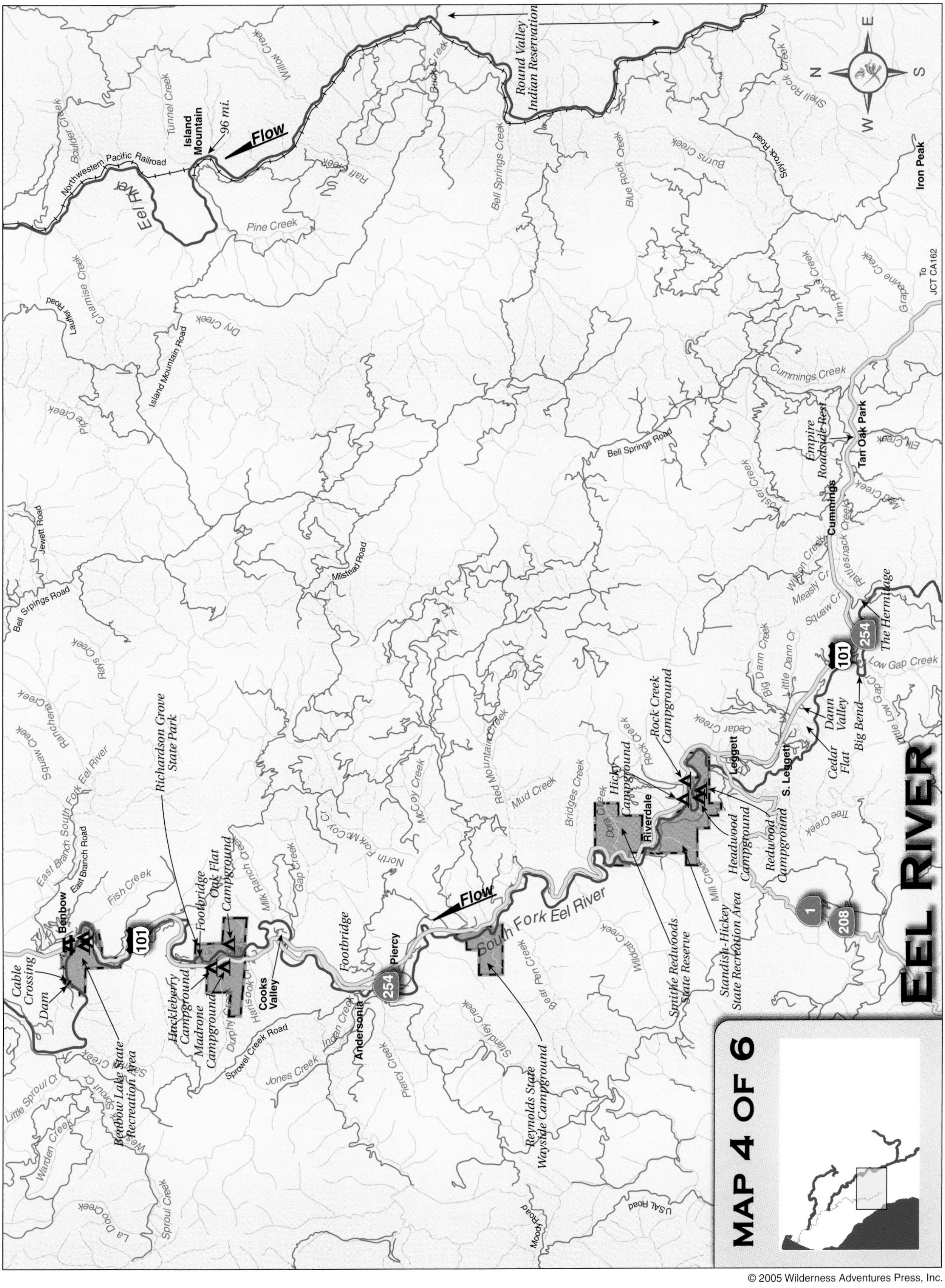
MAP 4 OF 6
EEL RIVER
Eel River
Flow
Island Mountain
96 mi.
Northwestern Pacific Railroad
Round Valley Indian Reservation
South Fork Eel River
Benbow
Cable Crossing
Dam
Benbow Lake State Recreation Area
Richardson Grove State Park
Footbridge
Oak Flat Campground
Huckleberry Campground
Madrone Campground
Cooks Valley
Piercy
Andersonia
Reynolds State Wayside Campground
Smithe Redwoods State Reserve
Standish-Hickey State Recreation Area
Riverdale
Hickey Campground
Rock Creek Campground
Headwood Campground
Redwood Campground
Leggett
S. Leggett
Cedar Flat
Dann Valley
Big Bend
The Hermitage
Cummings
Empire Roadside Rest
Tan Oak Park
Iron Peak
To JCT CA162
Bell Springs Road
Milstead Road
Island Mountain Road
Spyrock Road
Sprowel Creek Road
East Branch Road
Jewett Road
Laufler Road
Moody Road
USAL Road
Pine Creek
Bell Springs Creek
Blue Rock Creek
Burns Creek
Cummings Creek
Rattlesnack Creek
Low Gap Creek
Mill Creek
Dora Creek
Rock Creek
Mud Creek
Red Mountain Creek
McCoy Creek
North Fork McCoy Cr
Bear Pen Creek
Standley Creek
Piercy Creek
Jones Creek
Indian Creek
Harisook Creek
Durphy Creek
Milk Ranch Creek
Gap Creek
Fish Creek
East Branch South Fork Eel River
Squaw Creek
Rancheria Creek
Rays Creek
Dry Creek
Chamise Creek
Tunnel Creek
Boulder Creek
Willow Creek
Buck Creek
Raft Creek
Wildcat Creek
Cedar Creek
Big Dann Creek
Little Dann Cr
Squaw Cr
Measly Cr
Wilson Creek
Foster Creek
Twin Rocks Creek
Grapevine Creek
Elk Creek
Mad Creek
Tree Creek
Bridges Creek
Shell Rock Creek
Little Sproul Cr
Warden Creek
Sproul Creek
La Doo Creek
N
S
E
W
101
254
1
208

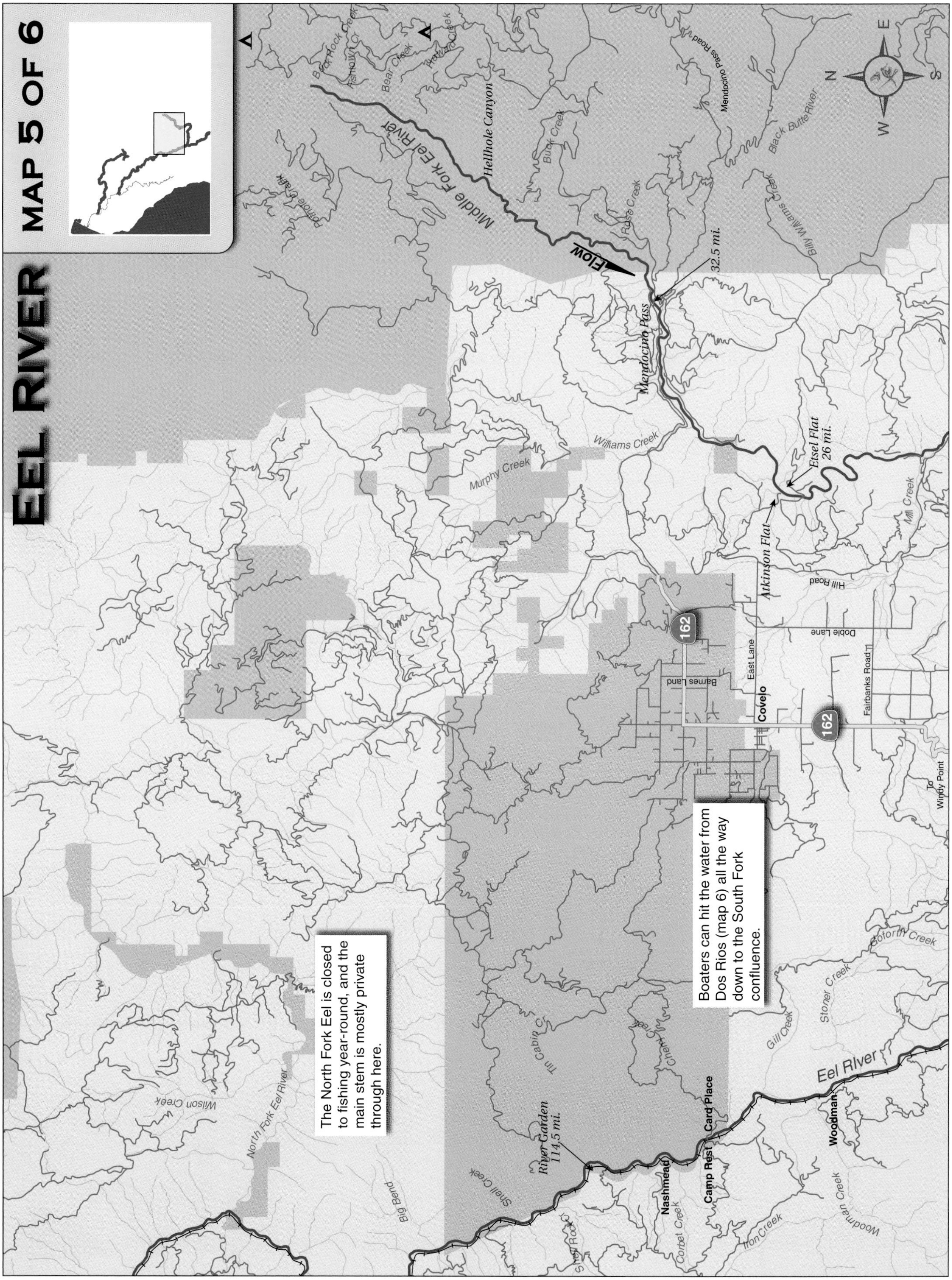
EEL RIVER
MAP 5 OF 6
Middle Fork Eel River
Hellhole Canyon
Flow
32.5 mi.
Mendocino Pass
Mendocino Pass Road
Bear Creek
Fishbowl Cr.
Buck Creek
Rose Creek
Black Butte River
Billy Williams Creek
Williams Creek
Murphy Creek
Etsel Flat
26 mi.
Atkinson Flat
Mill Creek
Hill Road
Dobie Lane
East Lane
Barnes Land
Covelo
162
Fairbanks Road
To Windy Point
Boaters can hit the water from Dos Rios (map 6) all the way down to the South Fork confluence.
The North Fork Eel is closed to fishing year-round, and the main stem is mostly private through here.
Wilson Creek
North Fork Eel River
Big Bend
Shell Creek
River Garden
114.5 mi.
Tin Cabin C.
Cherry Creek
Card Place
Camp Rest
Nashmead
Corbet Creek
Iron Creek
Woodman
Woodman Creek
Gill Creek
Stoner Creek
Eel River
N
E
S
W

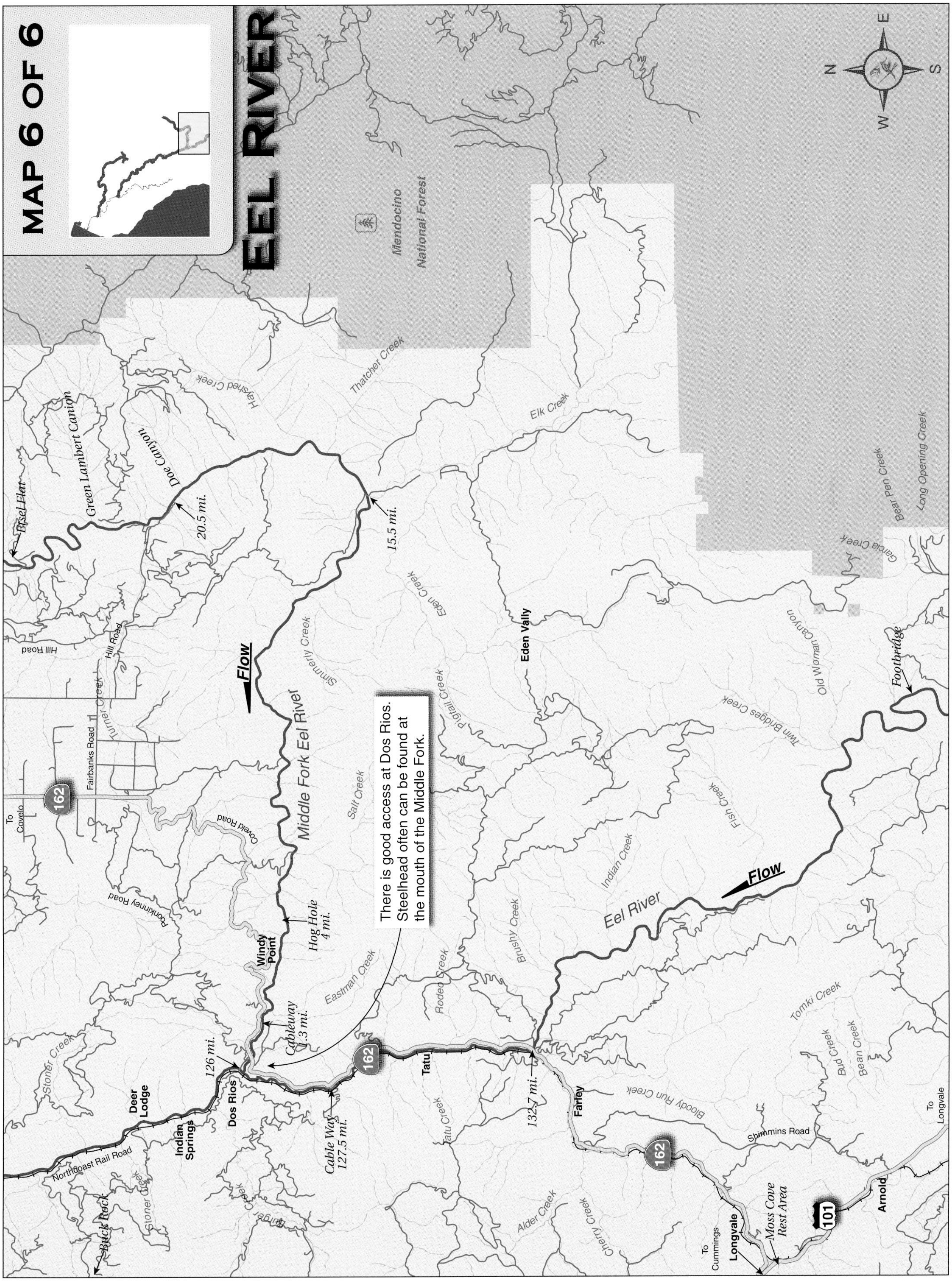
MAP 6 OF 6
EEL RIVER
Mendocino National Forest
Thatcher Creek
Haysfied Creek
Elk Creek
Long Opening Creek
Bear Pen Creek
Garcia Creek
Green Lambert Canion
Doe Canyon
Brsel Flat
20.5 mi.
15.5 mi.
Eden Creek
Hill Road
Hill Road
Eden Vally
Old Woman Canyon
Footbridge
Simmerly Creek
Flow
Turner Creek
Fairbanks Road
Middle Fork Eel River
Pigtail Creek
Twin Bridges Creek
To Covelo
162
Covelo Road
Salt Creek
Fish Creek
There is good access at Dos Rios. Steelhead often can be found at the mouth of the Middle Fork.
Indian Creek
Flow
Eel River
Poonkinney Road
Hog Hole 4 mi.
Windy Point
Eastman Creek
Brushy Creek
Rodeo Creek
Tomki Creek
Cableway 1.3 mi.
Stoner Creek
126 mi.
Deer Lodge
Dos Rios
162
Tatu
132.7 mi.
Farley
Bloody Run Creek
Bud Creek
Bean Creek
Indian Springs
Cable Way 127.5 mi.
Tatu Creek
Shimmins Road
162
To Longvale
Northoast Rail Road
Buck Rock
Stoner Creek
Alder Creek
Cherry Creek
To Cummings
Longvale
Moss Cove Rest Area
101
Arnold
N
E
S
W

Fall River

The Fall River begins near Thousand Springs northwest of McArthur and flows gently for 17 miles, eventually dumping into the Pit River, another excellent trout stream. The Fall is a spring creek with very clear water and very challenging fishing, but the payoff is wild trout that grow quite large. Prolific hatches throughout the year help anglers target rising fish, mostly rainbows and a few browns. There is a two-fish limit here, but due to the fishing pressure and the fact that these are wild fish, anglers typically release everything they catch. This is a special fishery that all anglers should work to protect. Because the river flows almost entirely through private land fishing is usually done from boats, which can be launched at just two sites. It's also possible to pay for access to the water through area ranches.

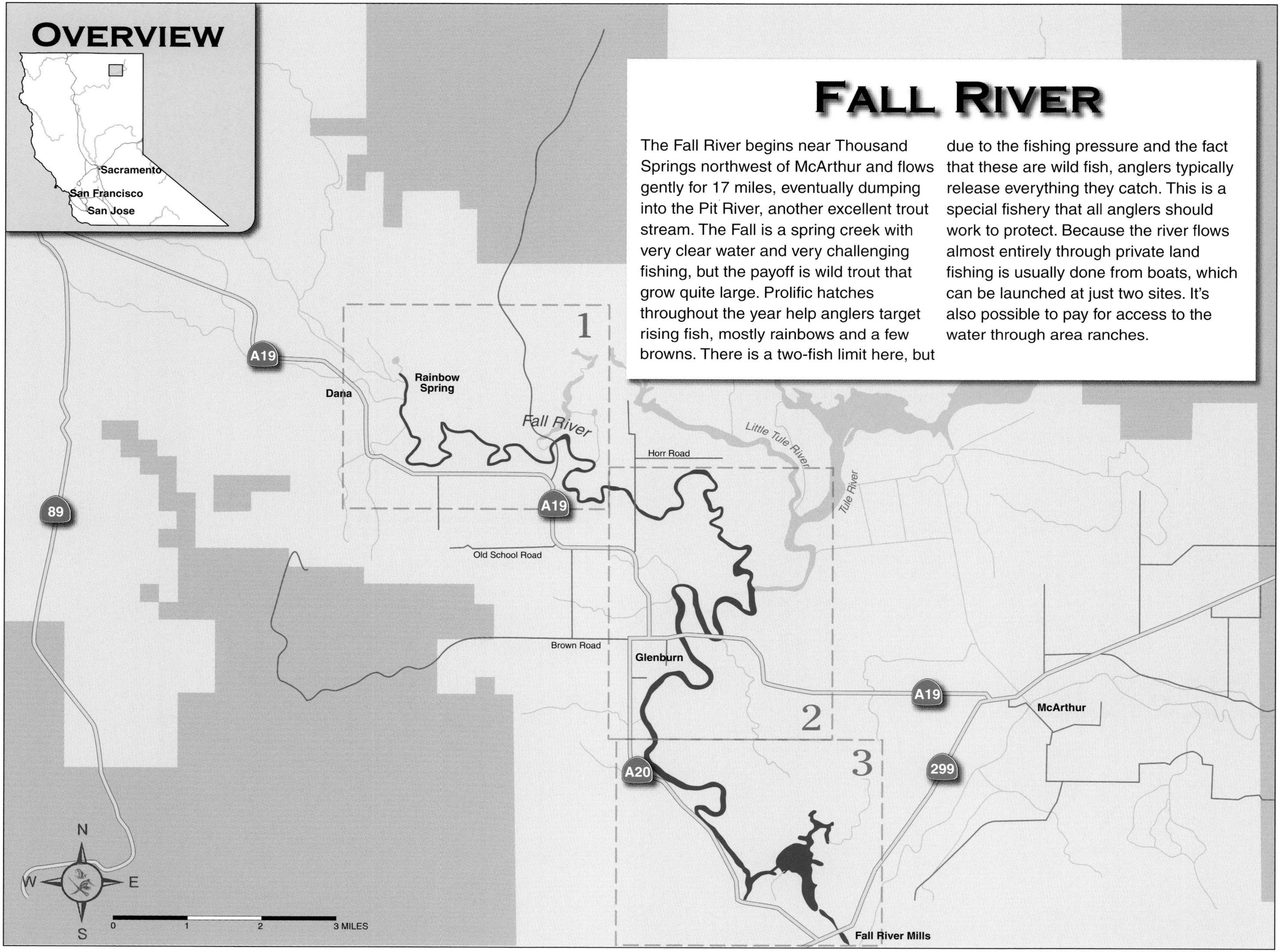

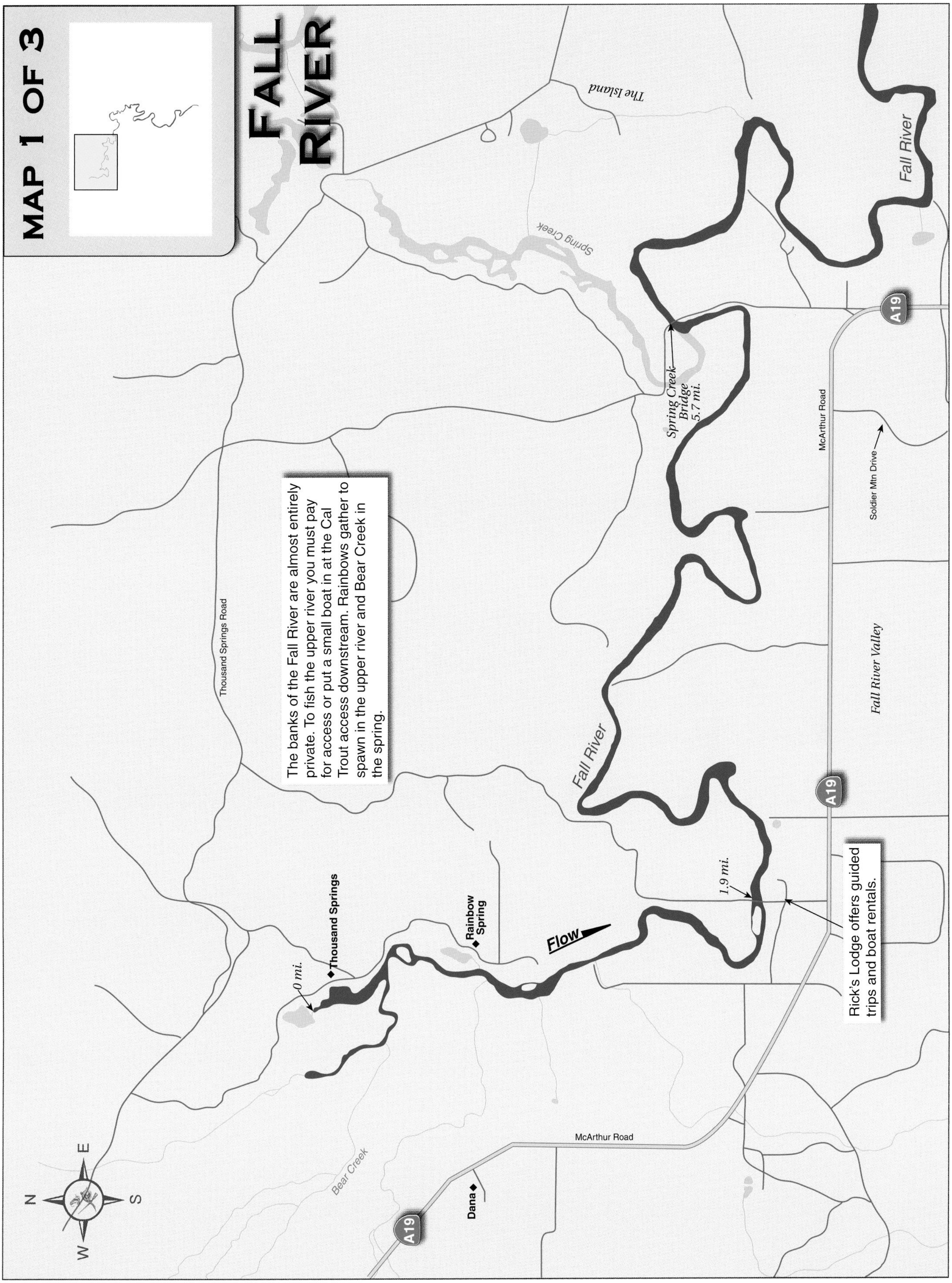
MAP 1 OF 3
FALL RIVER
The Island
Spring Creek
Fall River
Spring Creek Bridge 5.7 mi.
McArthur Road
Soldier Mtn Drive
Fall River Valley
A19
Thousand Springs Road
The banks of the Fall River are almost entirely private. To fish the upper river you must pay for access or put a small boat in at the Cal Trout access downstream. Rainbows gather to spawn in the upper river and Bear Creek in the spring.
Fall River
1.9 mi.
Rick's Lodge offers guided trips and boat rentals.
Thousand Springs
0 mi.
Rainbow Spring
Flow
McArthur Road
Bear Creek
Dana
A19
N
E
S
W

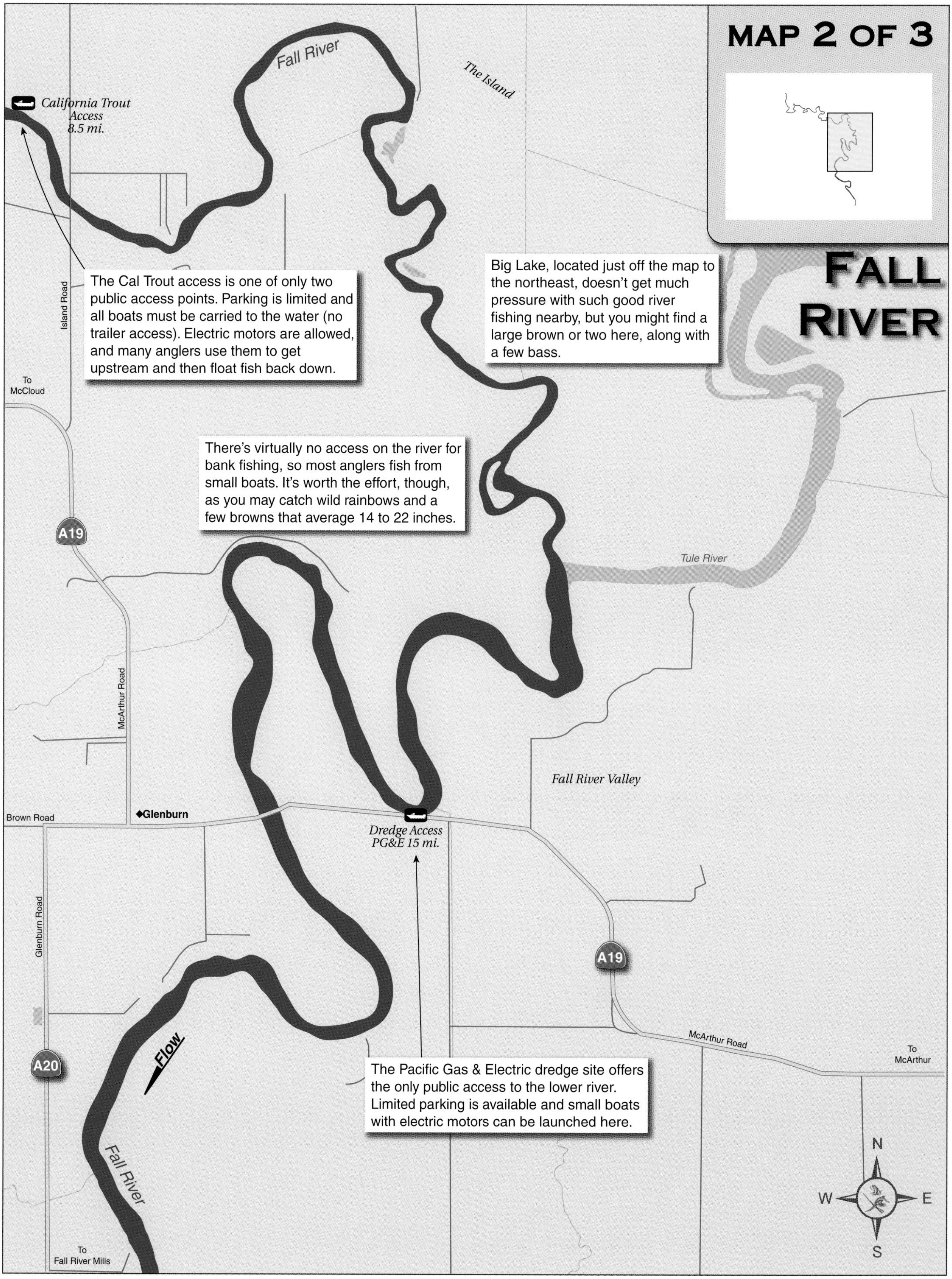
MAP 2 OF 3
FALL RIVER
California Trout Access 8.5 mi.
Fall River
The Island
The Cal Trout access is one of only two public access points. Parking is limited and all boats must be carried to the water (no trailer access). Electric motors are allowed, and many anglers use them to get upstream and then float fish back down.
Big Lake, located just off the map to the northeast, doesn't get much pressure with such good river fishing nearby, but you might find a large brown or two here, along with a few bass.
Island Road
To McCloud
There's virtually no access on the river for bank fishing, so most anglers fish from small boats. It's worth the effort, though, as you may catch wild rainbows and a few browns that average 14 to 22 inches.
A19
Tule River
McArthur Road
Fall River Valley
Brown Road
Glenburn
Dredge Access PG&E 15 mi.
Glenburn Road
A19
A20
Flow
McArthur Road
To McArthur
The Pacific Gas & Electric dredge site offers the only public access to the lower river. Limited parking is available and small boats with electric motors can be launched here.
N
W
E
S
Fall River
To Fall River Mills

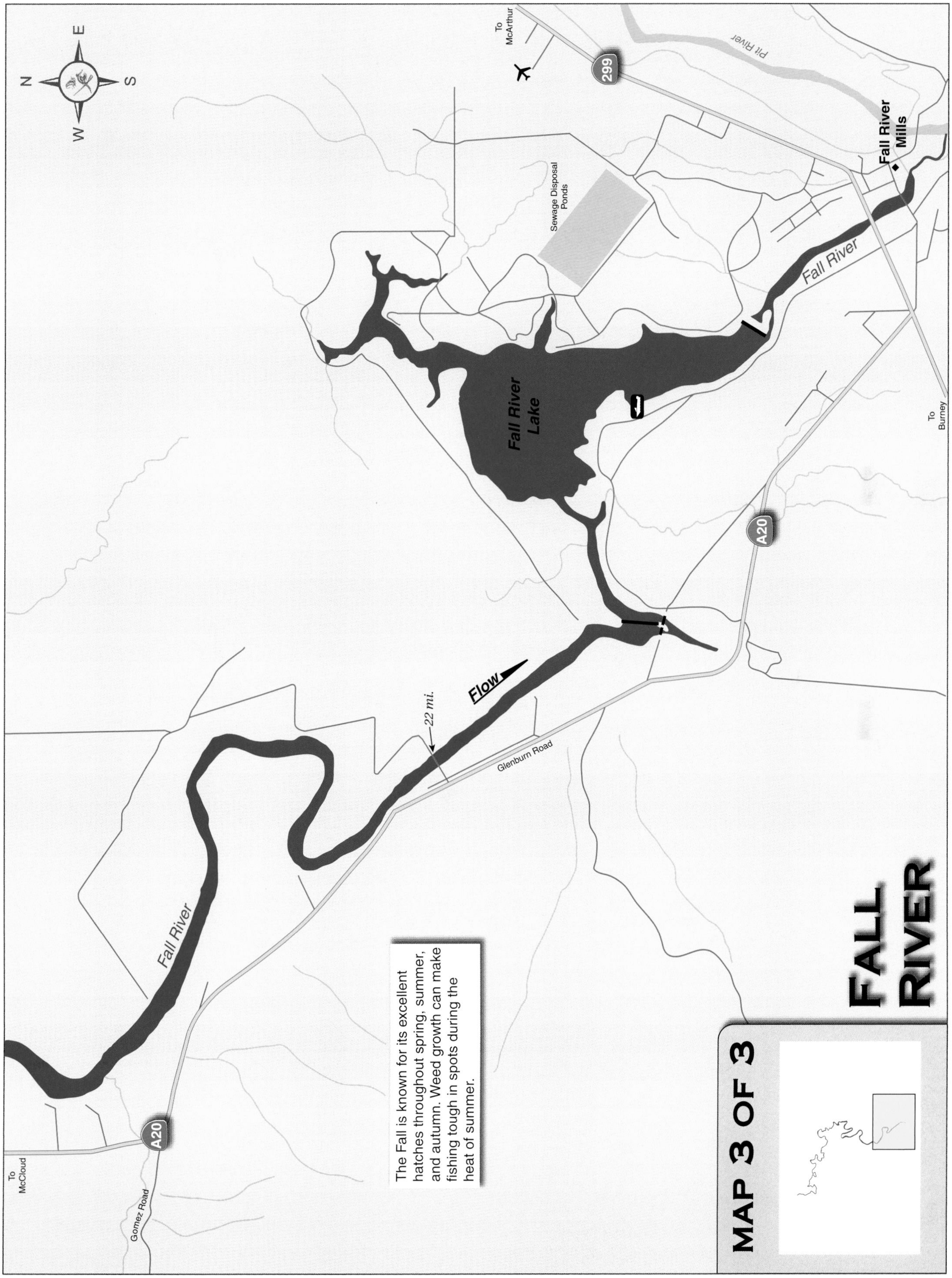
FALL RIVER
MAP 3 OF 3
N
E
S
W
To McArthur
Pit River
299
Fall River Mills
Sewage Disposal Ponds
Fall River
Fall River Lake
To Burney
A20
Flow
22 mi.
Glenburn Road
Fall River
The Fall is known for its excellent hatches throughout spring, summer, and autumn. Weed growth can make fishing tough in spots during the heat of summer.
To McCloud
Gomez Road
A20

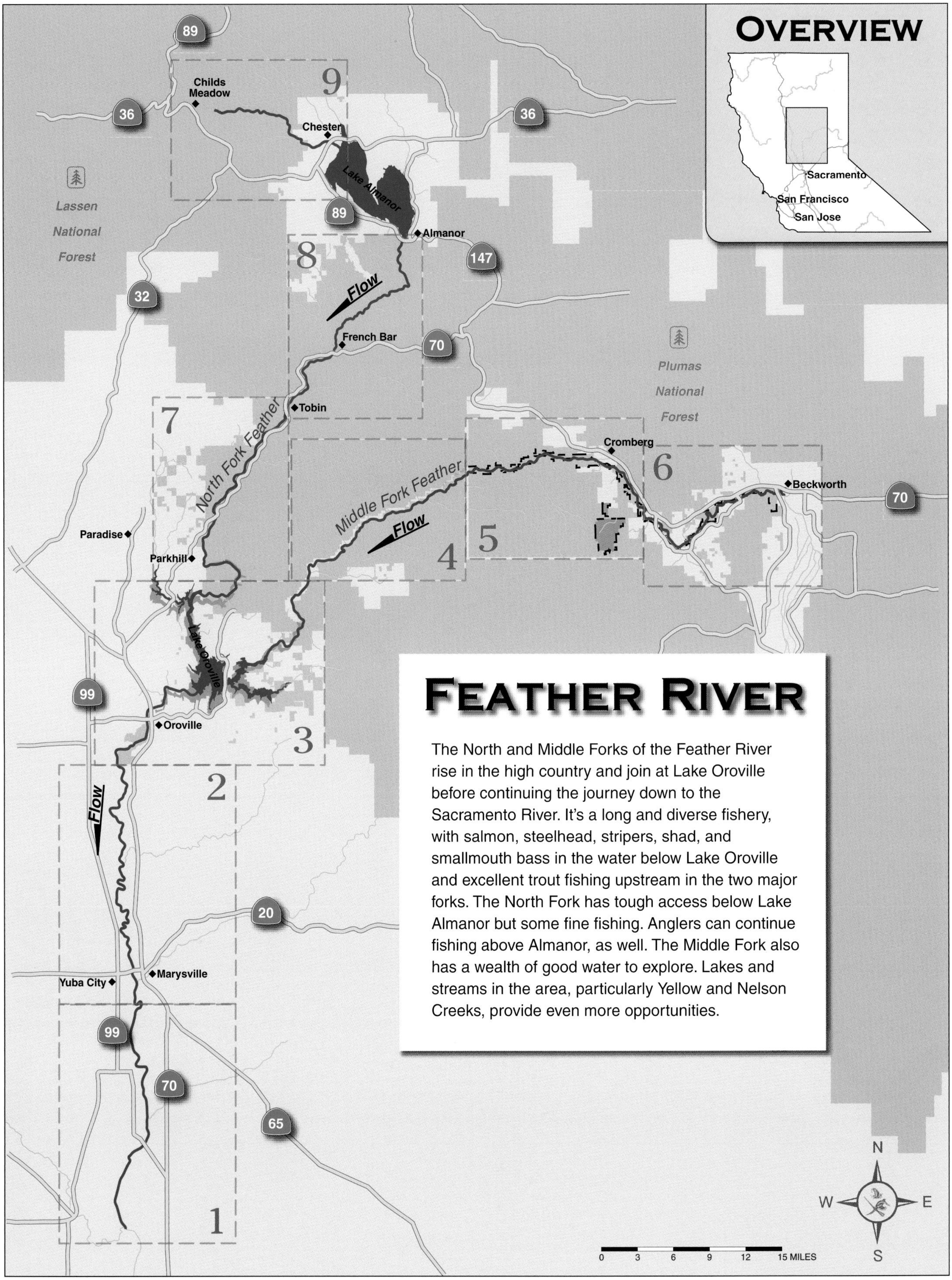

Feather River

The North and Middle Forks of the Feather River rise in the high country and join at Lake Oroville before continuing the journey down to the Sacramento River. It's a long and diverse fishery, with salmon, steelhead, stripers, shad, and smallmouth bass in the water below Lake Oroville and excellent trout fishing upstream in the two major forks. The North Fork has tough access below Lake Almanor but some fine fishing. Anglers can continue fishing above Almanor, as well. The Middle Fork also has a wealth of good water to explore. Lakes and streams in the area, particularly Yellow and Nelson Creeks, provide even more opportunities.

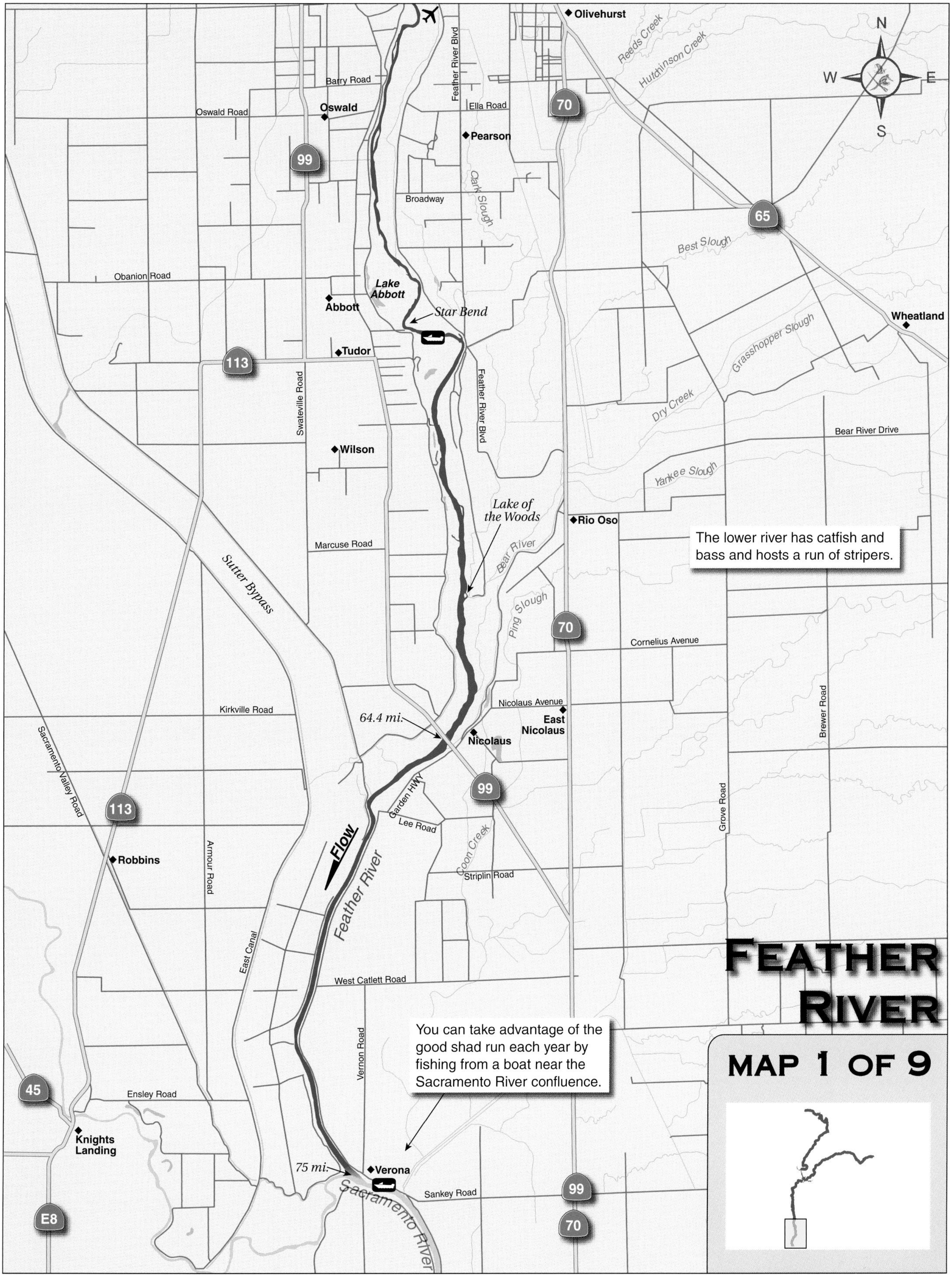
Olivehurst
Reeds Creek
Hutchinson Creek
N
W
E
S
Barry Road
Feather River Blvd
Ella Road
Oswald Road
Oswald
Pearson
70
99
Broadway
Clark Slough
65
Best Slough
Obanion Road
Lake Abbott
Abbott
Star Bend
Wheatland
Grasshopper Slough
Tudor
113
Swateville Road
Feather River Blvd
Dry Creek
Bear River Drive
Wilson
Yankee Slough
Lake of the Woods
Rio Oso
The lower river has catfish and bass and hosts a run of stripers.
Marcuse Road
Bear River
Sutter Bypass
Ping Slough
70
Cornelius Avenue
Nicolaus Avenue
East Nicolaus
Kirkville Road
64.4 mi.
Nicolaus
Brewer Road
Sacramento Valley Road
99
Garden HWY
113
Lee Road
Grove Road
Coon Creek
Robbins
Armour Road
Flow
Feather River
Striplin Road
FEATHER RIVER
East Canal
West Catlett Road
You can take advantage of the good shad run each year by fishing from a boat near the Sacramento River confluence.
Vernon Road
MAP 1 OF 9
45
Ensley Road
Knights Landing
75 mi.
Verona
Sankey Road
99
Sacramento River
E8
70

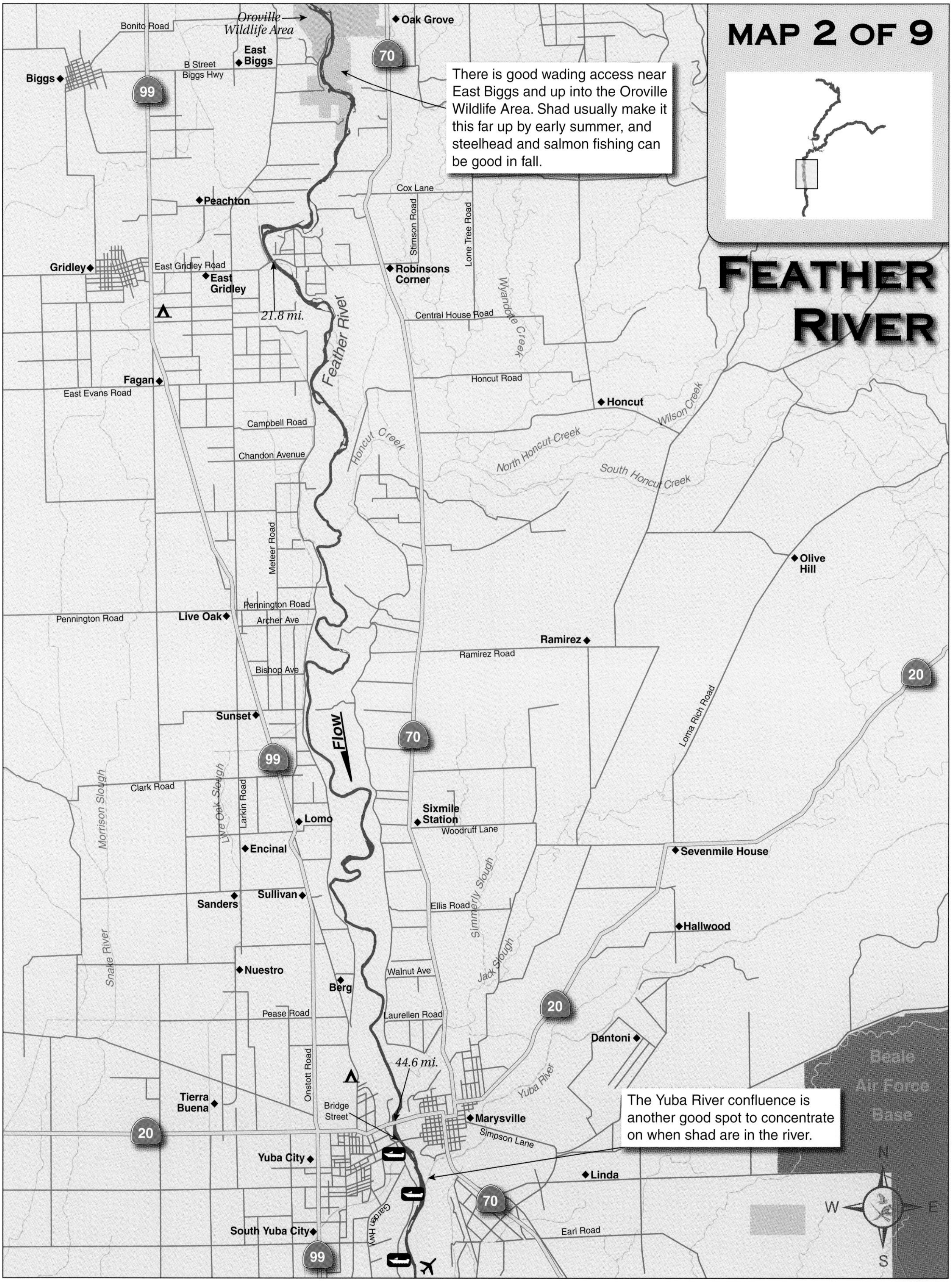

MAP 2 OF 9
FEATHER RIVER
There is good wading access near East Biggs and up into the Oroville Wildlife Area. Shad usually make it this far up by early summer, and steelhead and salmon fishing can be good in fall.
The Yuba River confluence is another good spot to concentrate on when shad are in the river.
Oroville Wildlife Area
Oak Grove
Bonito Road
East Biggs
B Street
Biggs Hwy
Biggs
Peachton
Cox Lane
Stimson Road
Lone Tree Road
Gridley
East Gridley Road
East Gridley
Robinsons Corner
21.8 mi.
Feather River
Central House Road
Wyandotte Creek
Fagan
East Evans Road
Honcut Road
Honcut
Wilson Creek
Campbell Road
Honcut Creek
North Honcut Creek
Chandon Avenue
South Honcut Creek
Meteer Road
Olive Hill
Pennington Road
Live Oak
Archer Ave
Ramirez
Ramirez Road
Bishop Ave
Loma Rich Road
Sunset
Flow
Morrison Slough
Clark Road
Live Oak Slough
Larkin Road
Lomo
Sixmile Station
Woodruff Lane
Encinal
Sevenmile House
Sanders
Sullivan
Ellis Road
Simmerly Slough
Hallwood
Snake River
Nuestro
Berg
Walnut Ave
Jack Slough
Pease Road
Laurellen Road
Dantoni
Beale Air Force Base
44.6 mi.
Onstott Road
Yuba River
Tierra Buena
Bridge Street
Marysville
Simpson Lane
Yuba City
Linda
Garden Hwy
South Yuba City
Earl Road
N
W
E
S

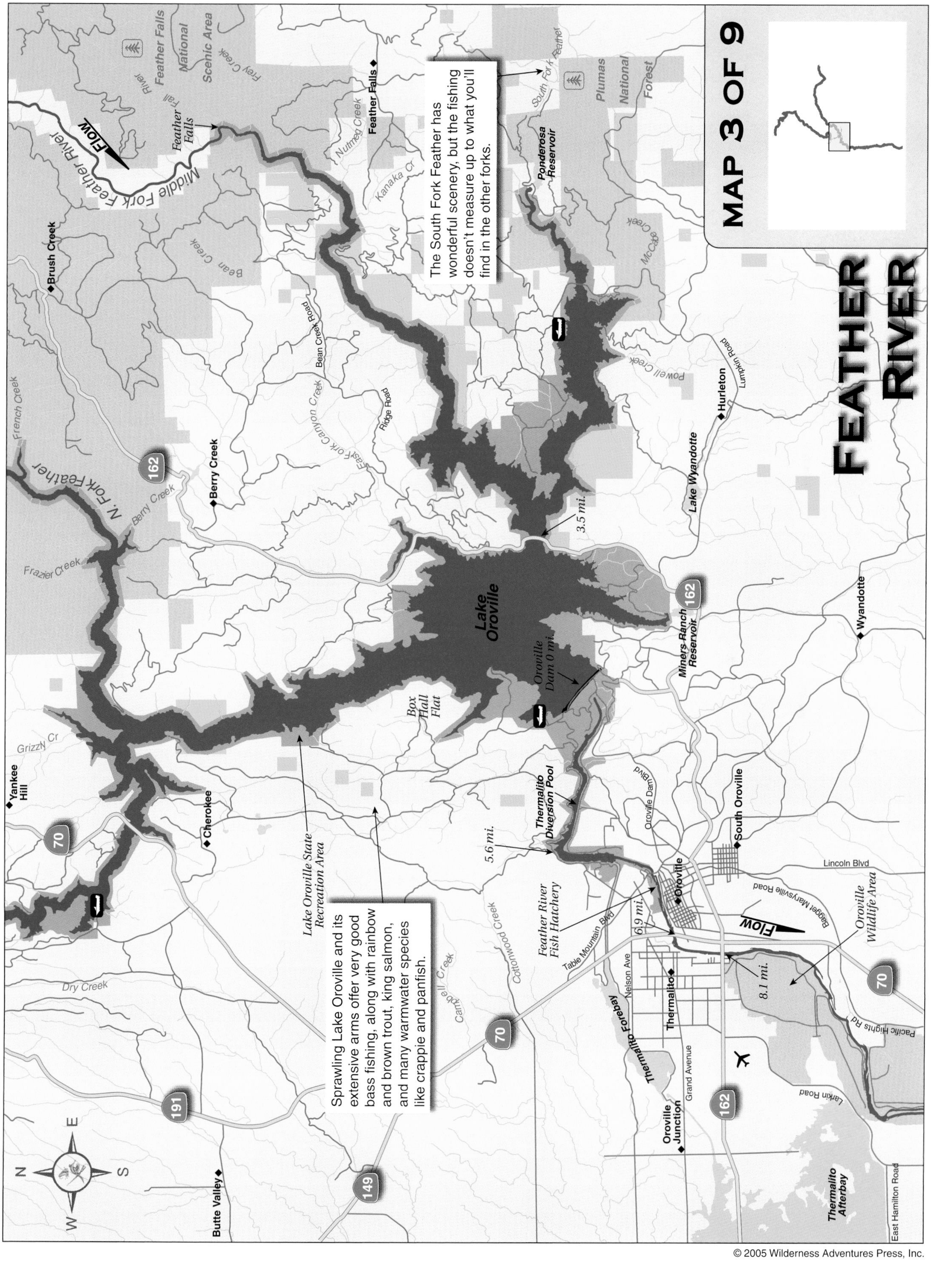
Feather River
Map 3 of 9
The South Fork Feather has wonderful scenery, but the fishing doesn't measure up to what you'll find in the other forks.
Sprawling Lake Oroville and its extensive arms offer very good bass fishing, along with rainbow and brown trout, king salmon, and many warmwater species like crappie and panfish.
Lake Oroville
Lake Oroville State Recreation Area
Box Flat
Oroville Dam 0 mi.
3.5 mi.
5.6 mi.
6.9 mi.
8.1 mi.
Thermalito Diversion Pool
Feather River Fish Hatchery
Thermalito Forebay
Thermalito Afterbay
Oroville Wildlife Area
Miners Ranch Reservoir
Ponderosa Reservoir
Feather Falls National Scenic Area
Plumas National Forest
Middle Fork Feather River
N. Fork Feather
South Fork Feather
Feather Falls
Fall River
Flow
Oroville
South Oroville
Thermalito
Oroville Junction
Cherokee
Yankee Hill
Berry Creek
Brush Creek
Hurleton
Lake Wyandotte
Wyandotte
Butte Valley
French Creek
Frazier Creek
Berry Creek
Grizzly Cr
Bean Creek
Nutmeg Creek
Kanaka Cr
Frey Creek
Powell Creek
McCabe Creek
East Fork Canyon Creek
Cottonwood Creek
Dry Creek
Bean Creek Road
Ridge Road
Lumpkin Road
Oroville Dam Blvd
Table Mountain Blvd
Nelson Ave
Grand Avenue
Lincoln Blvd
Baggett Marysville Road
Pacific Heights Rd
Larkin Road
East Hamilton Road
70
162
191
149
N
E
S
W

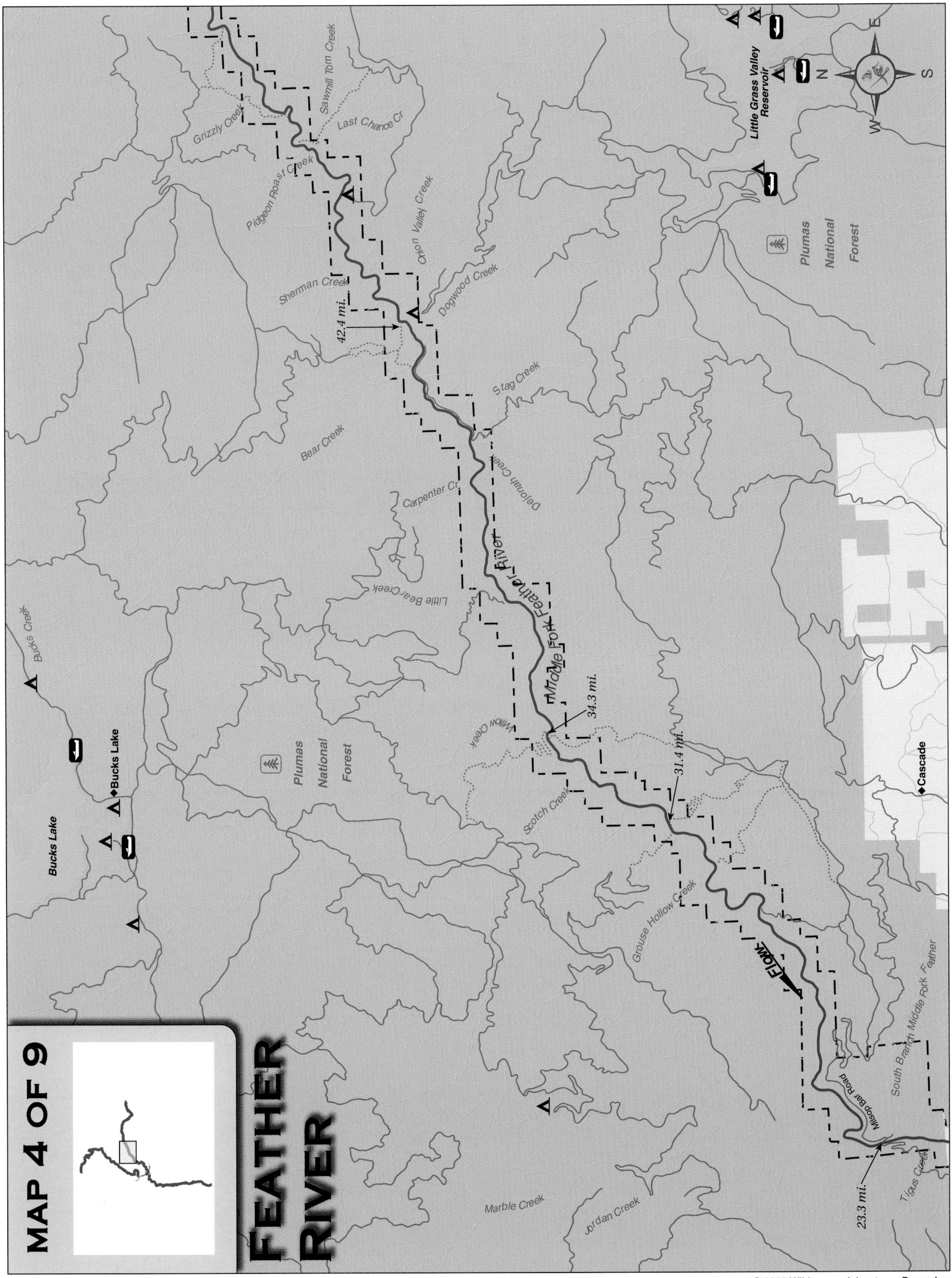
MAP 4 OF 9
FEATHER RIVER
Middle Fork Feather River
Flow
42.4 mi.
34.3 mi.
31.4 mi.
23.3 mi.
Plumas National Forest
Plumas National Forest
Bucks Lake
Bucks Lake
Bucks Creek
Little Grass Valley Reservoir
Cascade
Grizzly Creek
Sawmill Tom Creek
Last Chance Cr
Pidgeon Roast Creek
Onion Valley Creek
Sherman Creek
Dogwood Creek
Stag Creek
Bear Creek
Carpenter Cr
Dejonah Creek
Little Bear Creek
Willow Creek
Scotch Creek
Grouse Hollow Creek
South Branch Middle Fork Feather
Milsap Bar Road
Tigus Creek
Marble Creek
Jordan Creek
N
S
E
W

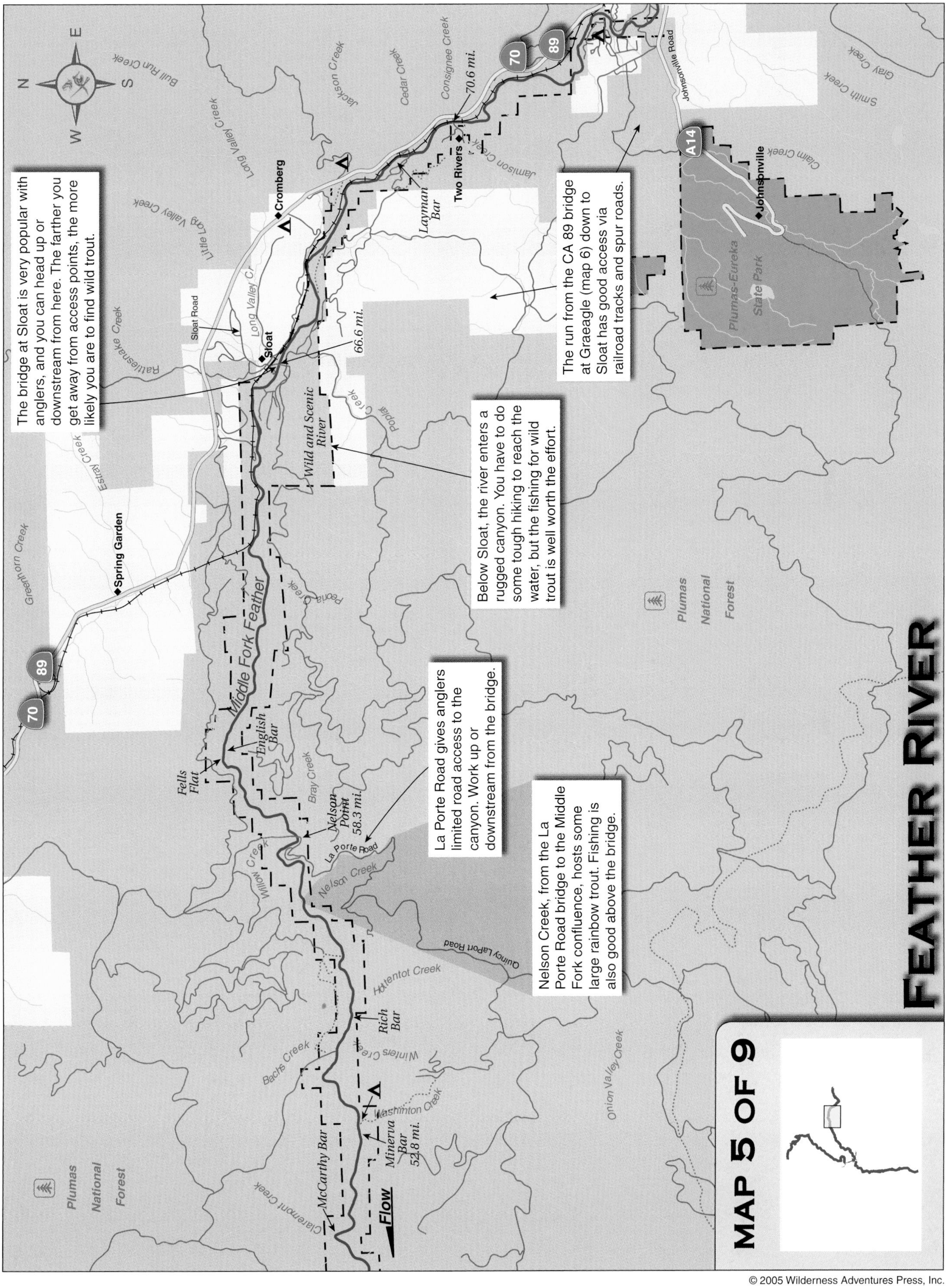
FEATHER RIVER
MAP 5 OF 9
The bridge at Sloat is very popular with anglers, and you can head up or downstream from here. The farther you get away from access points, the more likely you are to find wild trout.
The run from the CA 89 bridge at Graeagle (map 6) down to Sloat has good access via railroad tracks and spur roads.
Below Sloat, the river enters a rugged canyon. You have to do some tough hiking to reach the wild water, but the fishing for wild trout is well worth the effort.
La Porte Road gives anglers limited road access to the canyon. Work up or downstream from the bridge.
Nelson Creek, from the La Porte Road bridge to the Middle Fork confluence, hosts some large rainbow trout. Fishing is also good above the bridge.
Middle Fork Feather
Flow
Sloat
Sloat Road
Cromberg
Two Rivers
Spring Garden
Johnsonville
Johnsonville Road
Plumas-Eureka State Park
Plumas National Forest
Wild and Scenic River
70.6 mi.
66.6 mi.
58.3 mi.
52.8 mi.
Layman Bar
English Bar
Fells Flat
Nelson Point
Rich Bar
Minerva Bar
McCarthy Bar
La Porte Road
Quincy LaPort Road
Nelson Creek
Long Valley Cr
Little Long Valley Creek
Long Valley Creek
Bull Run Creek
Jackson Creek
Cedar Creek
Consignee Creek
Jamison Creek
Rattlesnake Creek
Estray Creek
Greenhorn Creek
Poplar Creek
Peona Creek
Bray Creek
Willow Creek
Hottentot Creek
Bachs Creek
Winters Creek
Washington Creek
Claremont Creek
Onion Valley Creek
Claim Creek
Smith Creek
Gray Creek
70
89
A14
N
E
S
W

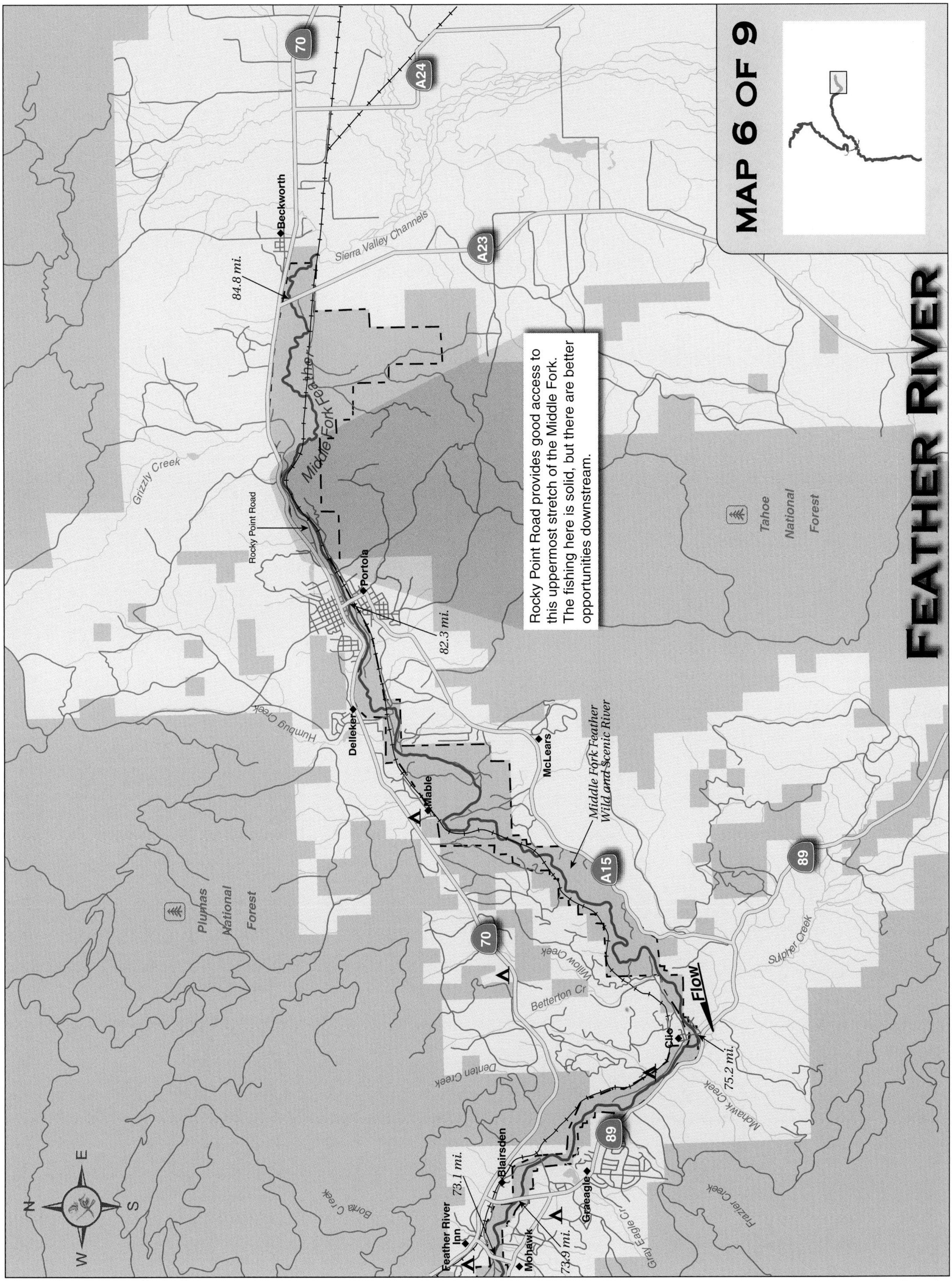
Feather River
Map 6 of 9
Rocky Point Road provides good access to this uppermost stretch of the Middle Fork. The fishing here is solid, but there are better opportunities downstream.
Middle Fork Feather
Middle Fork Feather Wild and Scenic River
Rocky Point Road
Flow
84.8 mi.
82.3 mi.
75.2 mi.
73.9 mi.
73.1 mi.
Beckworth
Portola
Delleker
Mabie
McLears
Clio
Blairsden
Graeagle
Mohawk
Feather River Inn
Sierra Valley Channels
Grizzly Creek
Humbug Creek
Willow Creek
Betterton Cr
Denten Creek
Bonta Creek
Gray Eagle Cr
Frazier Creek
Mohawk Creek
Sulpher Creek
Tahoe National Forest
Plumas National Forest
70
A24
A23
A15
89
N
E
S
W

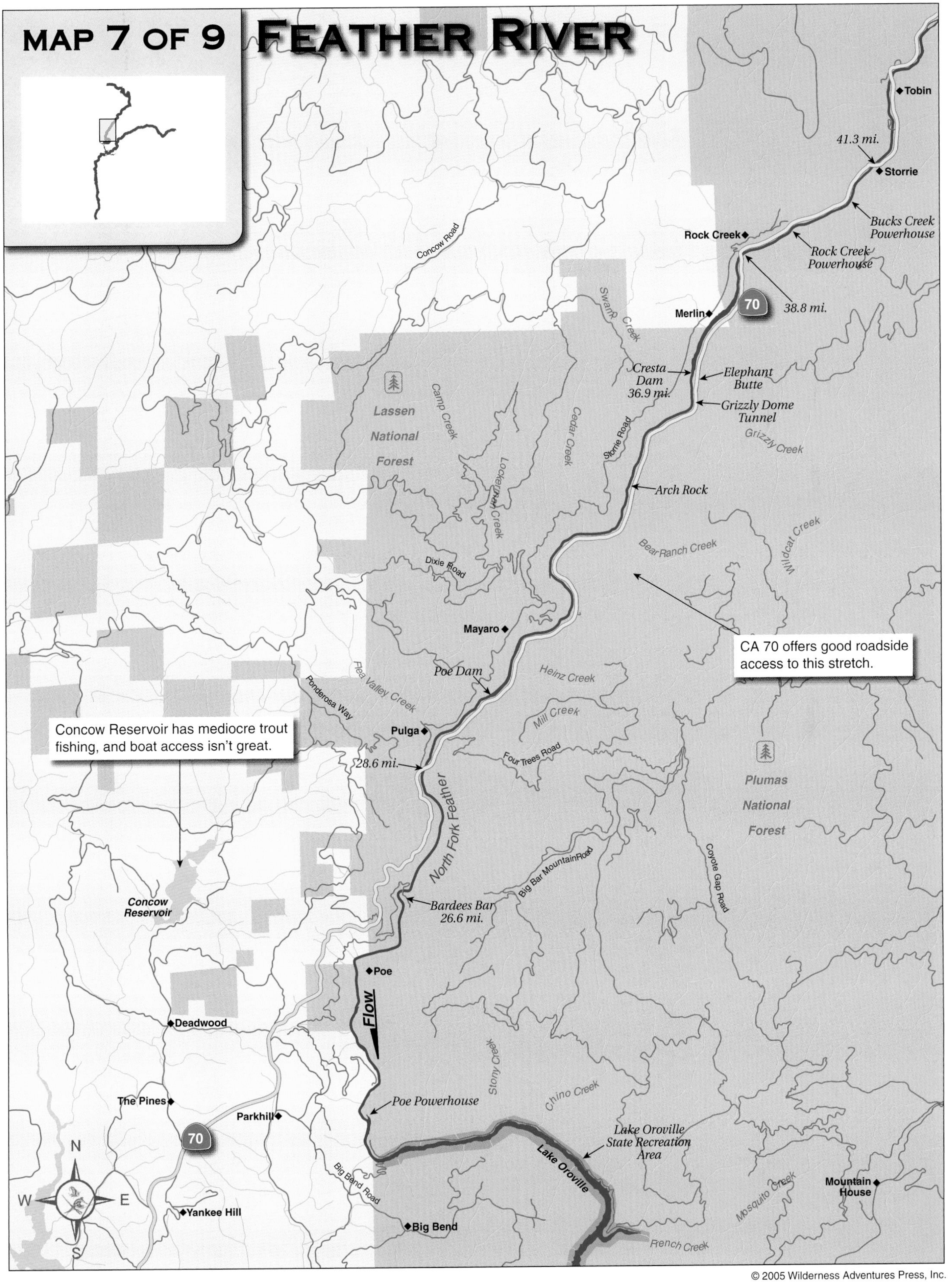
MAP 7 OF 9
FEATHER RIVER
Tobin
41.3 mi.
Storrie
Bucks Creek Powerhouse
Rock Creek
Rock Creek Powerhouse
38.8 mi.
70
Merlin
Concow Road
Swamp Creek
Cresta Dam 36.9 mi.
Elephant Butte
Grizzly Dome Tunnel
Grizzly Creek
Lassen National Forest
Camp Creek
Cedar Creek
Storrie Road
Arch Rock
Lockerman Creek
Bear Ranch Creek
Wildcat Creek
Dixie Road
Mayaro
CA 70 offers good roadside access to this stretch.
Poe Dam
Heinz Creek
Flea Valley Creek
Ponderosa Way
Mill Creek
Pulga
Concow Reservoir has mediocre trout fishing, and boat access isn't great.
28.6 mi.
Four Trees Road
Plumas National Forest
North Fork Feather
Big Bar Mountain Road
Coyote Gap Road
Concow Reservoir
Bardees Bar 26.6 mi.
Poe
Flow
Deadwood
Stony Creek
Chino Creek
The Pines
Poe Powerhouse
Parkhill
70
Lake Oroville State Recreation Area
Lake Oroville
N
W
E
S
Big Bend Road
Mosquito Creek
Mountain House
Yankee Hill
Big Bend
French Creek

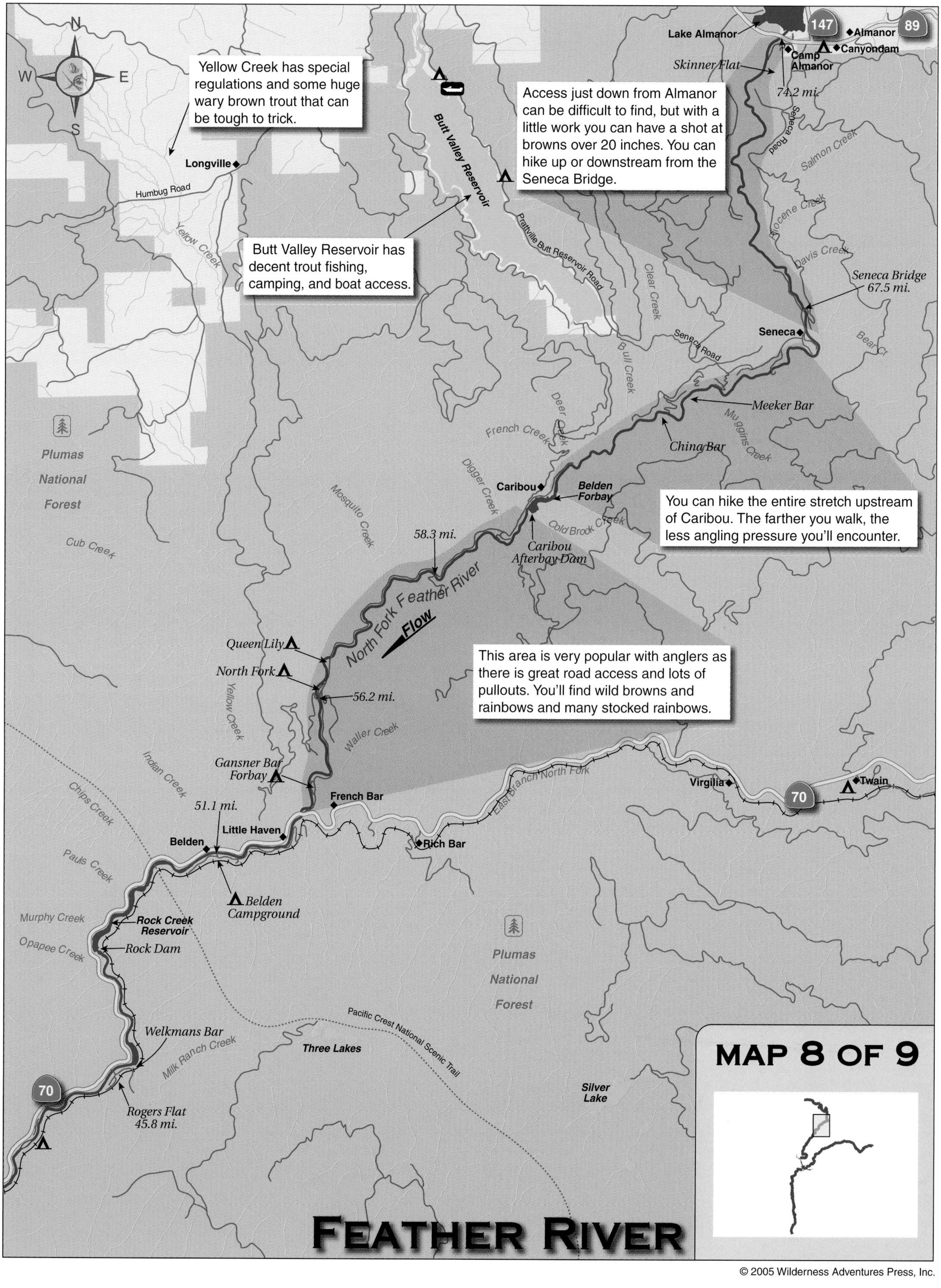
N
S
E
W
Yellow Creek has special regulations and some huge wary brown trout that can be tough to trick.
Butt Valley Reservoir
Access just down from Almanor can be difficult to find, but with a little work you can have a shot at browns over 20 inches. You can hike up or downstream from the Seneca Bridge.
Lake Almanor
147
Almanor
89
Camp Almanor
Canyondam
Skinner Flat
74.2 mi.
Seneca Road
Salmon Creek
Longville
Humbug Road
Yellow Creek
Butt Valley Reservoir has decent trout fishing, camping, and boat access.
Prattville Butt Reservoir Road
Clear Creek
Miocene Creek
Davis Creek
Seneca Bridge
67.5 mi.
Seneca
Seneca Road
Bear Cr
Bull Creek
Meeker Bar
Muggins Creek
China Bar
Deer Creek
French Creek
Digger Creek
Caribou
Belden Forbay
You can hike the entire stretch upstream of Caribou. The farther you walk, the less angling pressure you'll encounter.
Plumas National Forest
Mosquito Creek
Cold Brook Creek
Cub Creek
58.3 mi.
Caribou Afterbay Dam
North Fork Feather River
Flow
Queen Lily
North Fork
56.2 mi.
This area is very popular with anglers as there is great road access and lots of pullouts. You'll find wild browns and rainbows and many stocked rainbows.
Yellow Creek
Waller Creek
Indian Creek
Gansner Bar Forbay
East Branch North Fork
Virgilia
70
Twain
Chips Creek
51.1 mi.
French Bar
Belden
Little Haven
Rich Bar
Pauls Creek
Belden Campground
Murphy Creek
Rock Creek Reservoir
Rock Dam
Opapee Creek
Plumas National Forest
Pacific Crest National Scenic Trail
Welkmans Bar
Milk Ranch Creek
Three Lakes
70
Rogers Flat
45.8 mi.
Silver Lake
MAP 8 OF 9
FEATHER RIVER

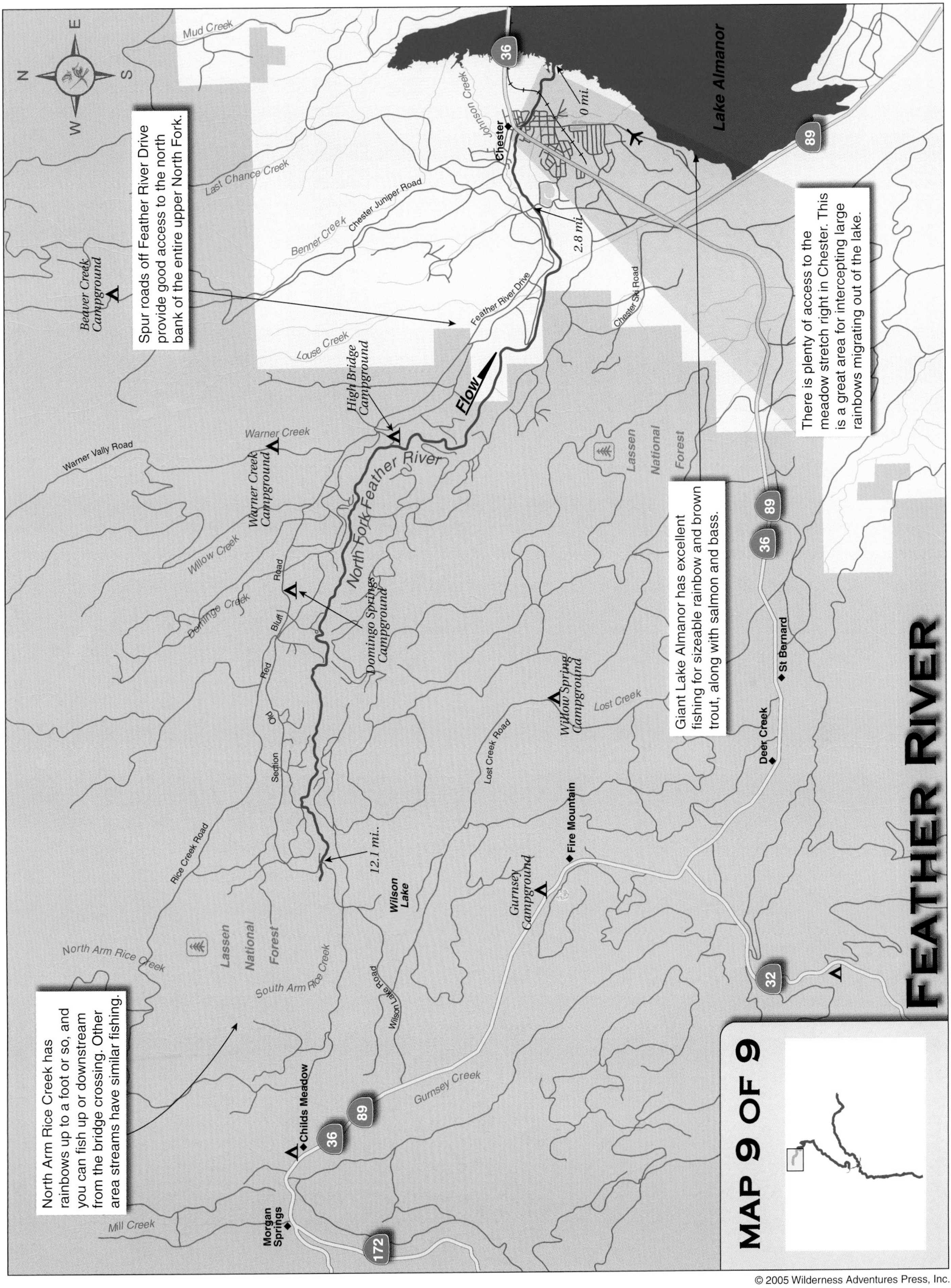
Feather River
Map 9 of 9
Spur roads off Feather River Drive provide good access to the north bank of the entire upper North Fork.
There is plenty of access to the meadow stretch right in Chester. This is a great area for intercepting large rainbows migrating out of the lake.
Giant Lake Almanor has excellent fishing for sizeable rainbow and brown trout, along with salmon and bass.
North Arm Rice Creek has rainbows up to a foot or so, and you can fish up or downstream from the bridge crossing. Other area streams have similar fishing.
Lake Almanor
Chester
0 mi.
2.8 mi.
12.1 mi..
Flow
North Fork Feather River
Mud Creek
Johnson Creek
Last Chance Creek
Chester Juniper Road
Benner Creek
Feather River Drive
Chester Ski Road
Louse Creek
Beaver Creek Campground
High Bridge Campground
Warner Creek
Warner Vally Road
Warner Creek Campground
Willow Creek
Domingo Creek
Domingo Springs Campground
Old Red Bluff Road
Section
Lassen National Forest
Willow Spring Campground
Lost Creek
Lost Creek Road
St Bernard
Deer Creek
Fire Mountain
Wilson Lake
Gurnsey Campground
Rice Creek Road
North Arm Rice Creek
South Arm Rice Creek
Wilson Lake Road
Gurnsey Creek
Childs Meadow
Morgan Springs
Mill Creek
36
89
32
172

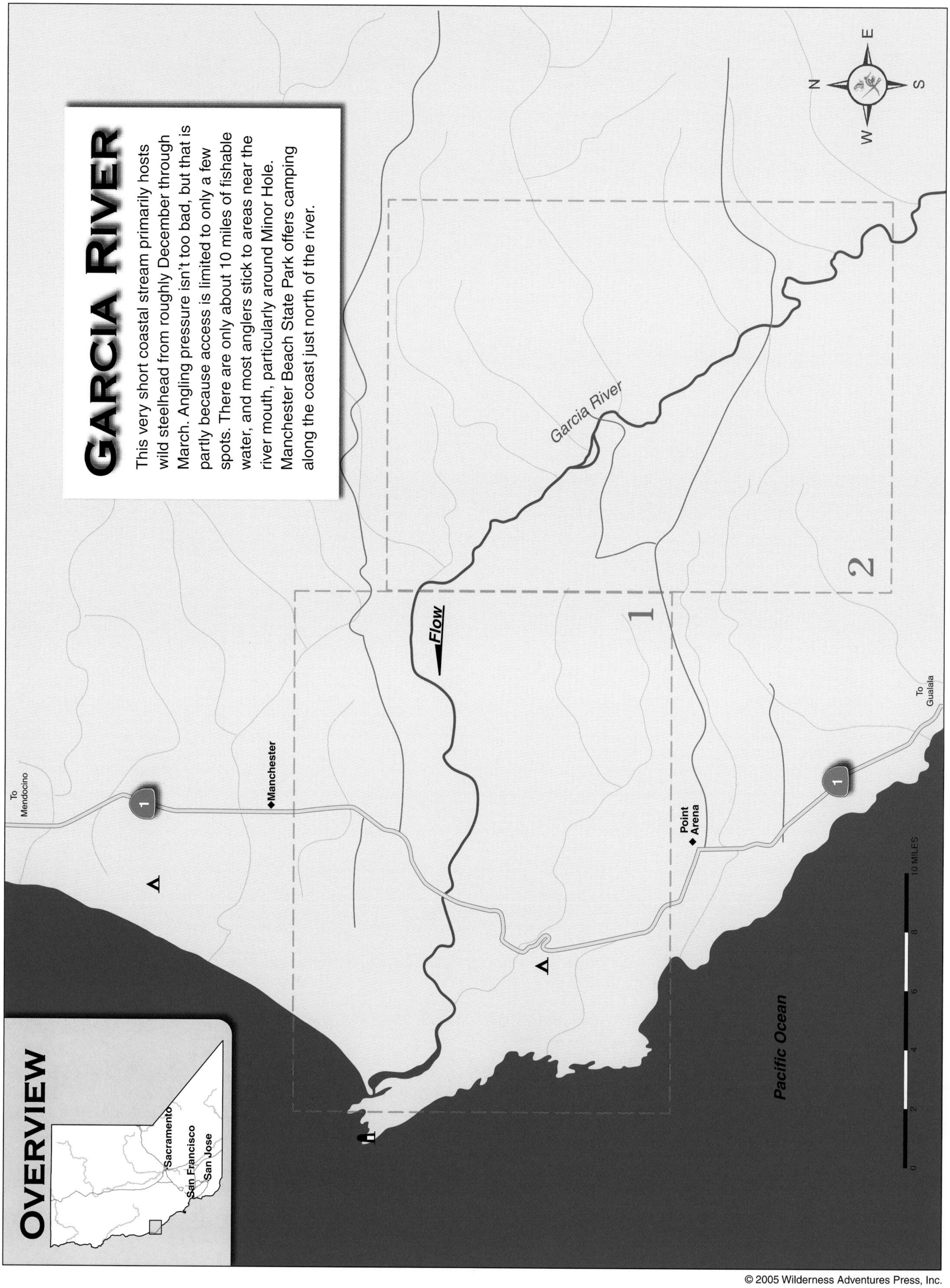
GARCIA RIVER
This very short coastal stream primarily hosts wild steelhead from roughly December through March. Angling pressure isn't too bad, but that is partly because access is limited to only a few spots. There are only about 10 miles of fishable water, and most anglers stick to areas near the river mouth, particularly around Minor Hole. Manchester Beach State Park offers camping along the coast just north of the river.
OVERVIEW
Sacramento
San Francisco
San Jose
To Mendocino
1
Manchester
Garcia River
Flow
1
2
Point Arena
To Gualala
Pacific Ocean
N
E
S
W
0
2
4
6
8
10 MILES

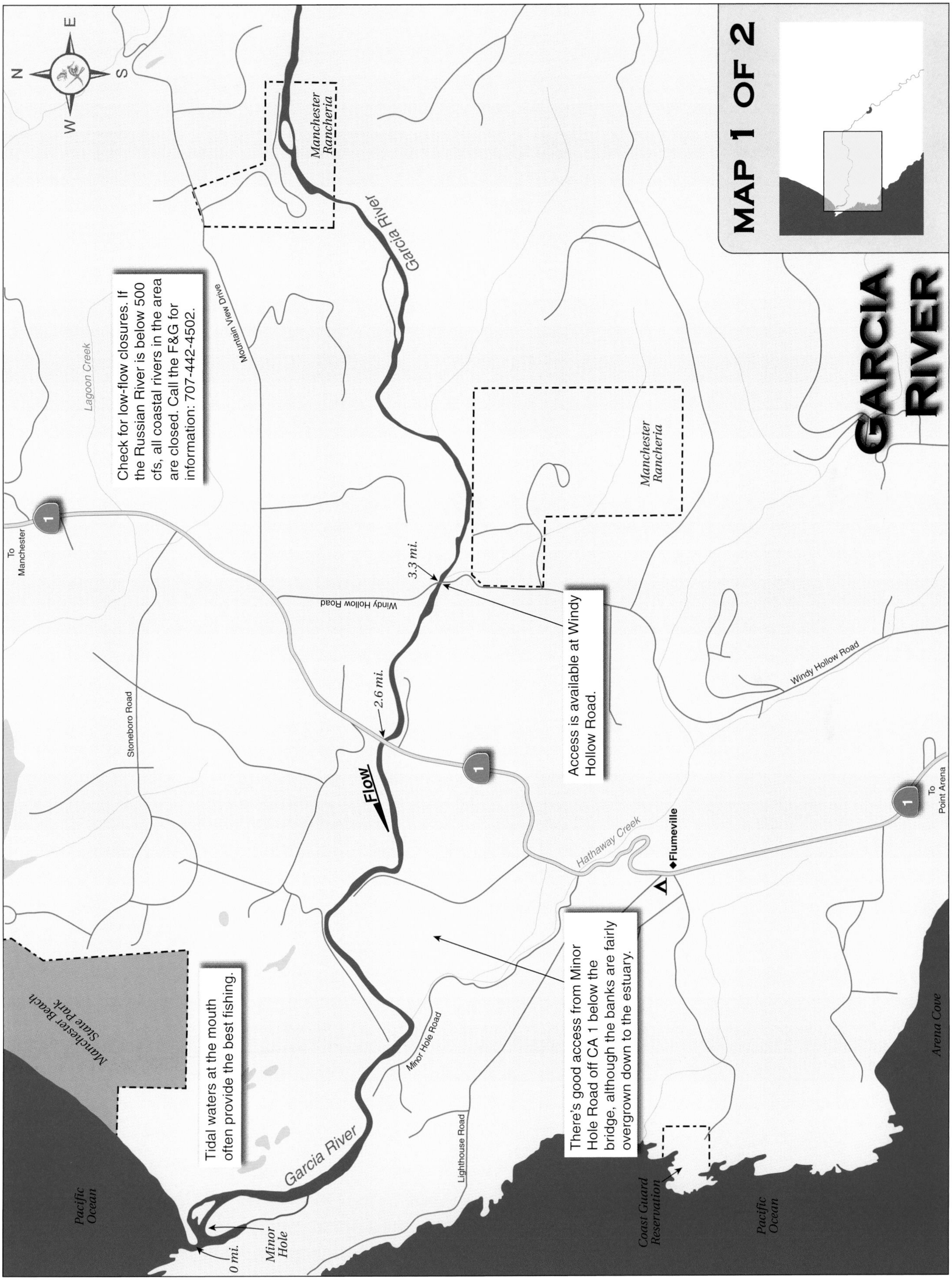
GARCIA RIVER
MAP 1 OF 2
N
E
S
W
Check for low-flow closures. If the Russian River is below 500 cfs, all coastal rivers in the area are closed. Call the F&G for information: 707-442-4502.
Access is available at Windy Hollow Road.
There's good access from Minor Hole Road off CA 1 below the bridge, although the banks are fairly overgrown down to the estuary.
Tidal waters at the mouth often provide the best fishing.
Manchester Rancheria
Manchester Rancheria
Garcia River
Garcia River
Mountain View Drive
Lagoon Creek
To Manchester
1
1
1
Windy Hollow Road
Windy Hollow Road
3.3 mi.
2.6 mi.
0 mi.
Stoneboro Road
Flow
Hathaway Creek
Flumeville
To Point Arena
Manchester Beach State Park
Minor Hole Road
Lighthouse Road
Minor Hole
Pacific Ocean
Pacific Ocean
Coast Guard Reservation
Arena Cove

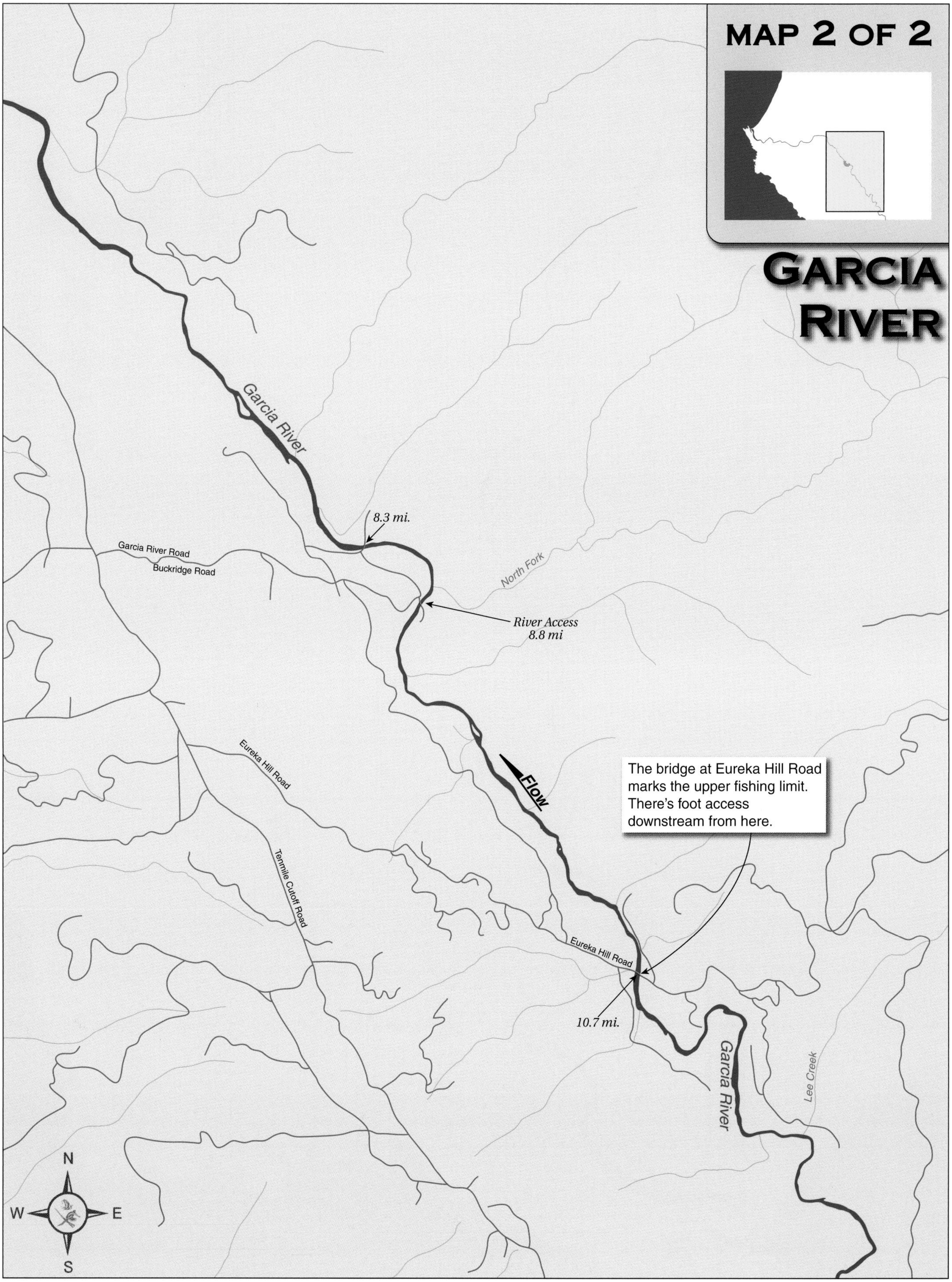
MAP 2 OF 2
GARCIA RIVER
Garcia River
8.3 mi.
Garcia River Road
Buckridge Road
North Fork
River Access
8.8 mi
Eureka Hill Road
Flow
The bridge at Eureka Hill Road marks the upper fishing limit. There's foot access downstream from here.
Tenmile Cutoff Road
Eureka Hill Road
10.7 mi.
Garcia River
Lee Creek
N
W
E
S

Gualala River

This short river has open gravel bars and large pools that host primarily wild steelhead from roughly December through March. Steelhead weighing well into the double-digits are possible, and they can be a real thrill in such small water. Angling pressure can be heavy at the peak of the run, but there is decent wading access to much of the fishable water. Most anglers hit the holding water from the mouth up to the North Fork Hole.

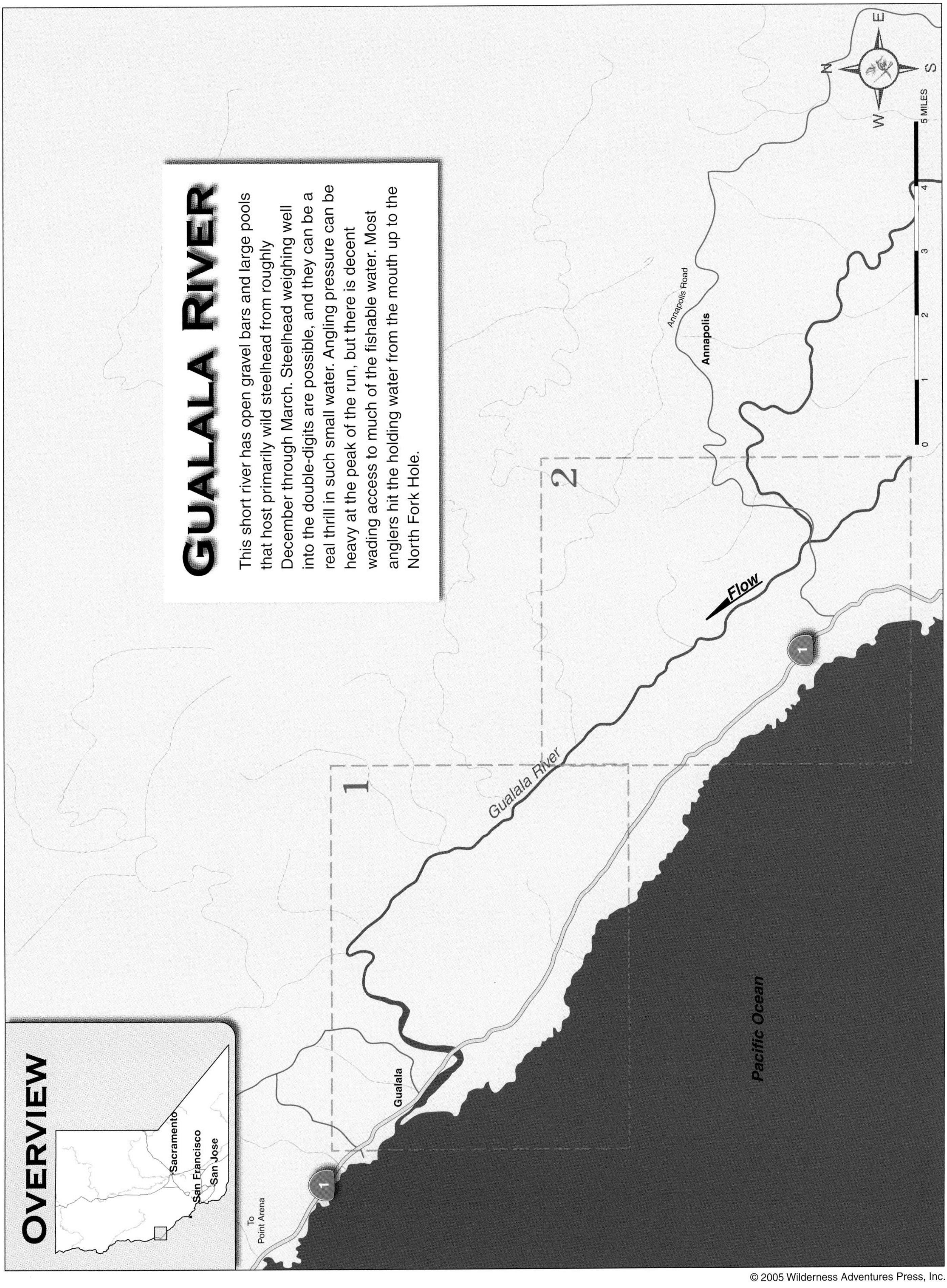

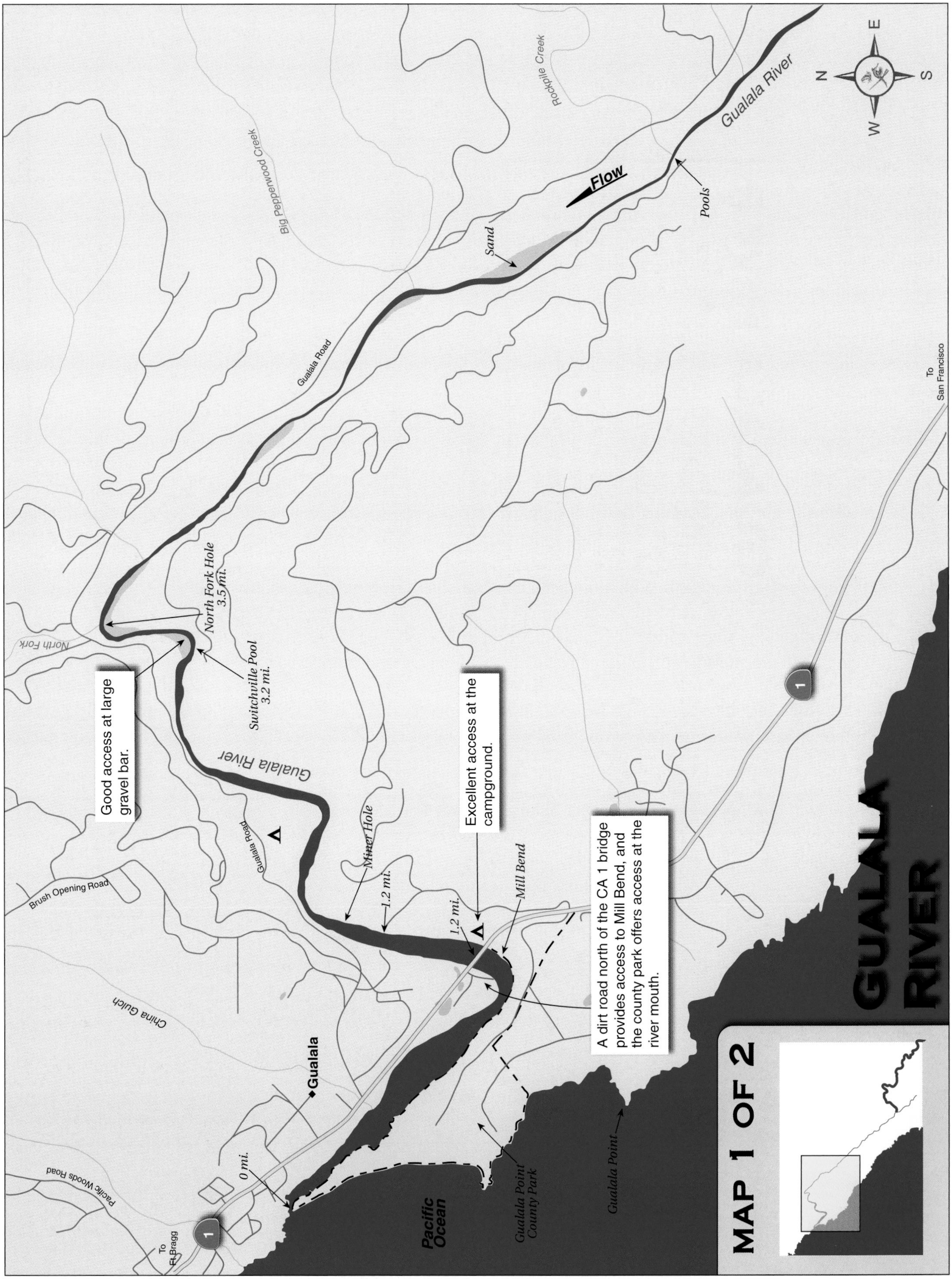
Gualala River
Flow
Pools
Sand
Rockpile Creek
Big Pepperwood Creek
Gualala Road
North Fork Hole
3.5 mi.
North Fork
Switchville Pool
3.2 mi.
Good access at large gravel bar.
Gualala River
Gualala Road
Excellent access at the campground.
Miner Hole
1.2 mi.
1.2 mi.
Mill Bend
A dirt road north of the CA 1 bridge provides access to Mill Bend, and the county park offers access at the river mouth.
Brush Opening Road
China Gulch
Gualala
0 mi.
Pacific Woods Road
To Ft. Bragg
1
Pacific Ocean
Gualala Point County Park
Gualala Point
To San Francisco
N
E
S
W
MAP 1 OF 2
GUALALA RIVER

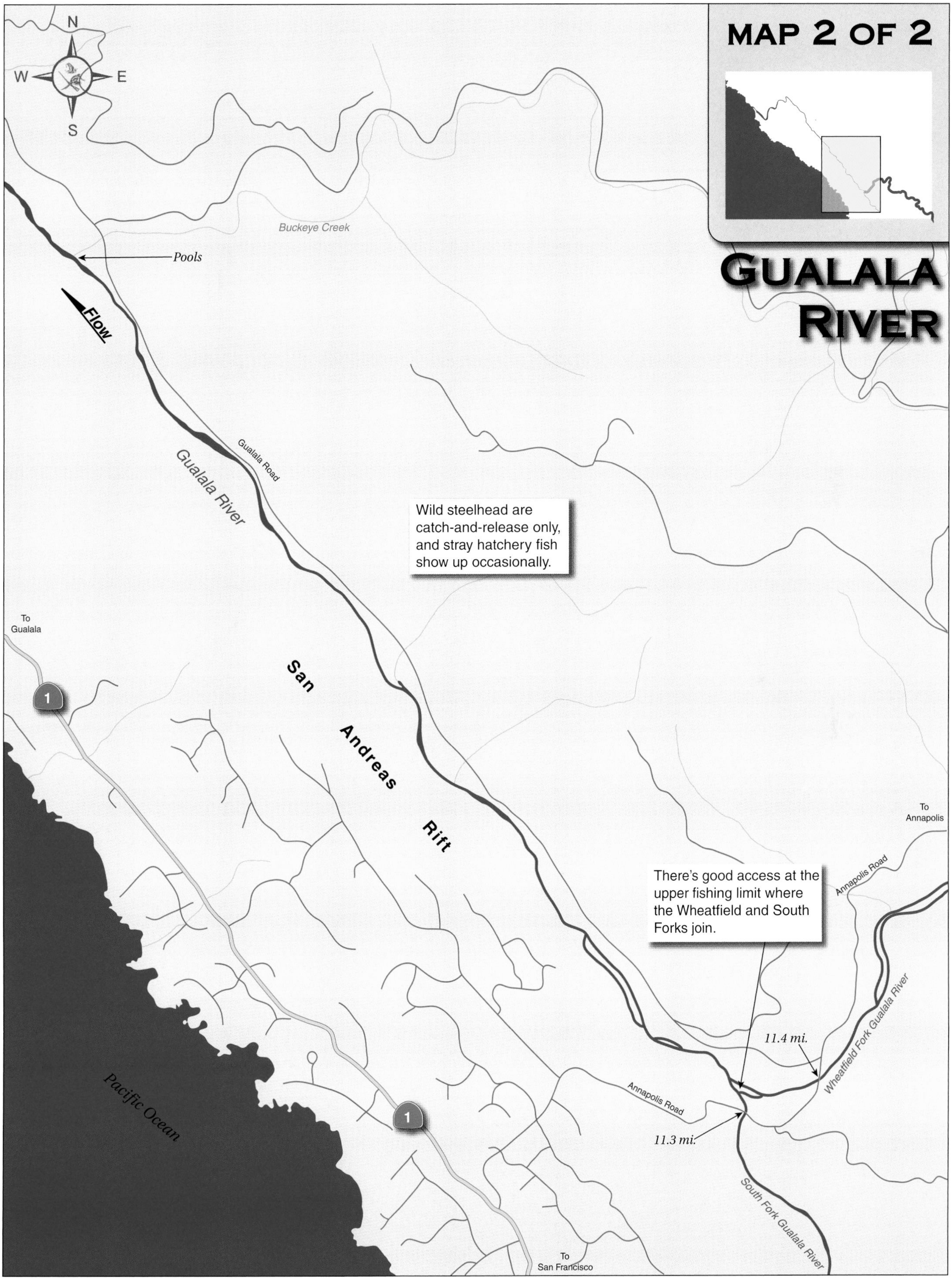
MAP 2 OF 2
GUALALA RIVER
N
W
E
S
Buckeye Creek
Pools
Flow
Gualala Road
Gualala River
Wild steelhead are catch-and-release only, and stray hatchery fish show up occasionally.
To Gualala
1
San Andreas Rift
To Annapolis
Annapolis Road
There's good access at the upper fishing limit where the Wheatfield and South Forks join.
Wheatfield Fork Gualala River
11.4 mi.
Annapolis Road
11.3 mi.
Pacific Ocean
1
South Fork Gualala River
To San Francisco

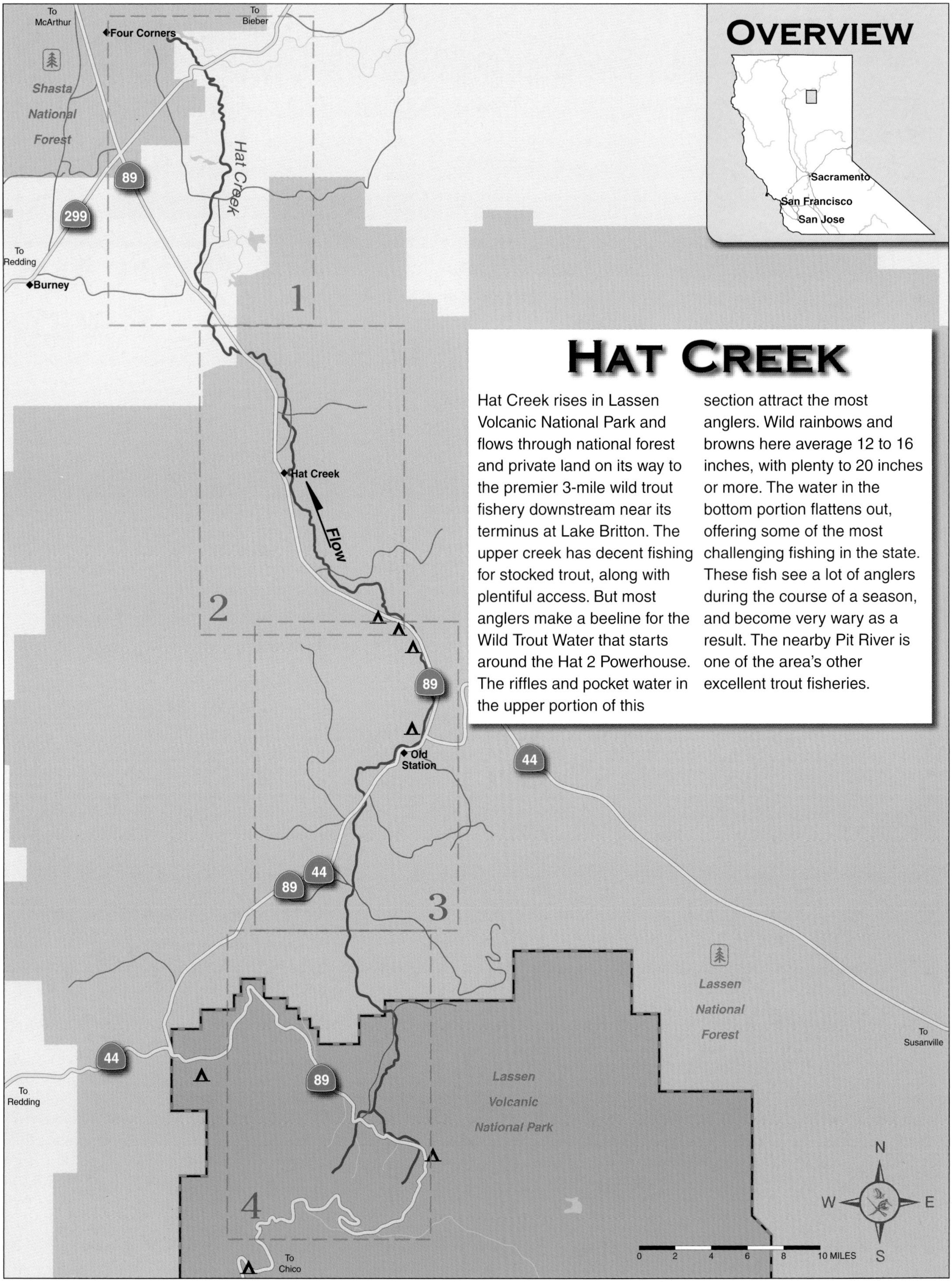

HAT CREEK

Hat Creek rises in Lassen Volcanic National Park and flows through national forest and private land on its way to the premier 3-mile wild trout fishery downstream near its terminus at Lake Britton. The upper creek has decent fishing for stocked trout, along with plentiful access. But most anglers make a beeline for the Wild Trout Water that starts around the Hat 2 Powerhouse. The riffles and pocket water in the upper portion of this section attract the most anglers. Wild rainbows and browns here average 12 to 16 inches, with plenty to 20 inches or more. The water in the bottom portion flattens out, offering some of the most challenging fishing in the state. These fish see a lot of anglers during the course of a season, and become very wary as a result. The nearby Pit River is one of the area's other excellent trout fisheries.

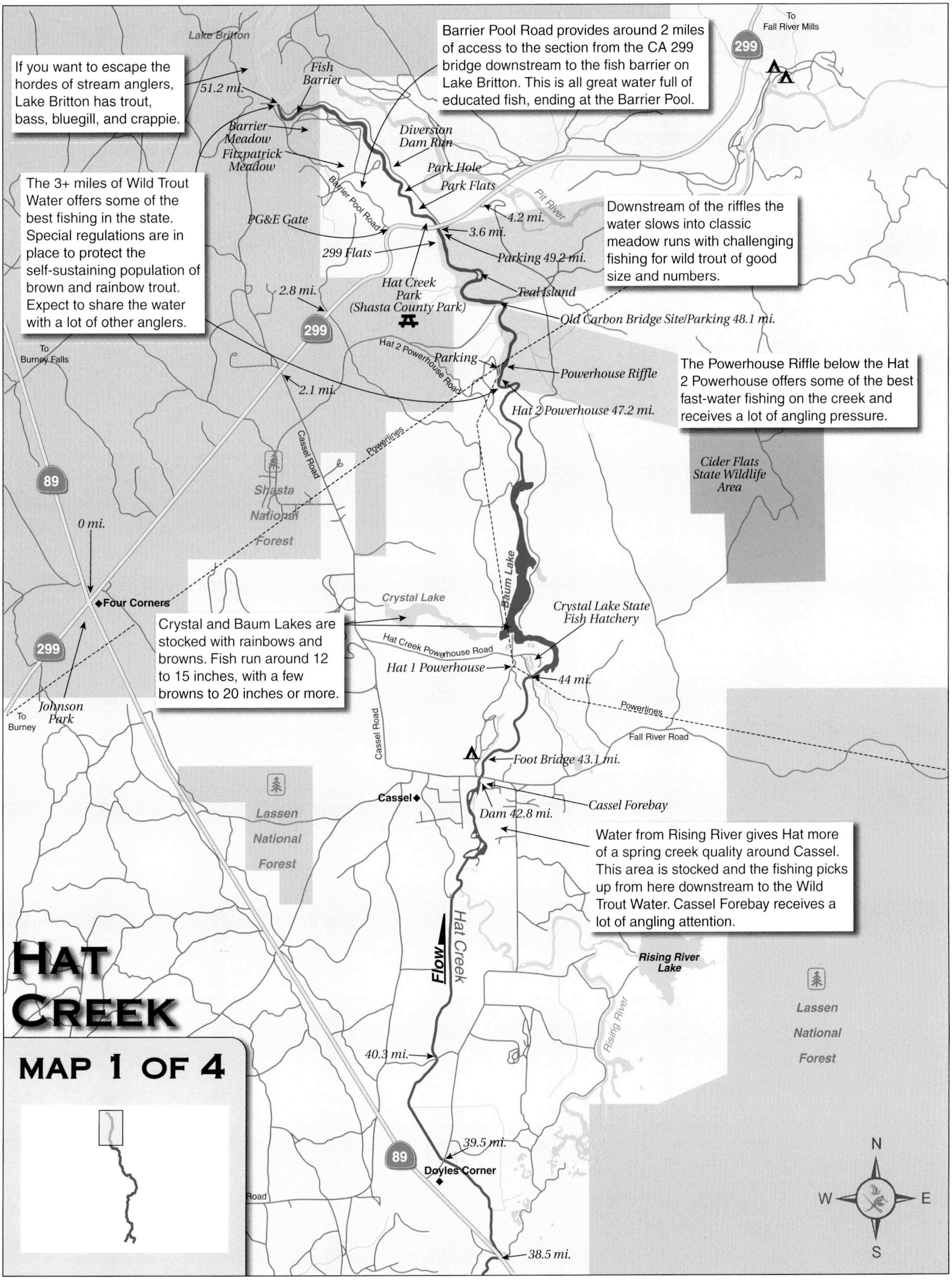
Hat Creek
Map 1 of 4
Lake Britton
If you want to escape the hordes of stream anglers, Lake Britton has trout, bass, bluegill, and crappie.
51.2 mi.
Fish Barrier
Barrier Pool Road provides around 2 miles of access to the section from the CA 299 bridge downstream to the fish barrier on Lake Britton. This is all great water full of educated fish, ending at the Barrier Pool.
To Fall River Mills
299
Barrier Meadow
Fitzpatrick Meadow
Diversion Dam Run
Park Hole
Park Flats
Pit River
Barrier Pool Road
The 3+ miles of Wild Trout Water offers some of the best fishing in the state. Special regulations are in place to protect the self-sustaining population of brown and rainbow trout. Expect to share the water with a lot of other anglers.
PG&E Gate
4.2 mi.
3.6 mi.
Parking 49.2 mi.
Downstream of the riffles the water slows into classic meadow runs with challenging fishing for wild trout of good size and numbers.
299 Flats
Hat Creek Park (Shasta County Park)
Teal Island
2.8 mi.
Old Carbon Bridge Site/Parking 48.1 mi.
To Burney Falls
Hat 2 Powerhouse Road
Parking
Powerhouse Riffle
The Powerhouse Riffle below the Hat 2 Powerhouse offers some of the best fast-water fishing on the creek and receives a lot of angling pressure.
2.1 mi.
Hat 2 Powerhouse 47.2 mi.
Powerlines
Cassel Road
Cider Flats State Wildlife Area
89
Shasta National Forest
0 mi.
Baum Lake
Four Corners
Crystal Lake
Crystal Lake State Fish Hatchery
Crystal and Baum Lakes are stocked with rainbows and browns. Fish run around 12 to 15 inches, with a few browns to 20 inches or more.
Hat Creek Powerhouse Road
Hat 1 Powerhouse
44 mi.
Johnson Park
To Burney
Powerlines
Fall River Road
Cassel Road
Foot Bridge 43.1 mi.
Cassel
Cassel Forebay
Dam 42.8 mi.
Lassen National Forest
Water from Rising River gives Hat more of a spring creek quality around Cassel. This area is stocked and the fishing picks up from here downstream to the Wild Trout Water. Cassel Forebay receives a lot of angling attention.
Flow
Hat Creek
Rising River Lake
Rising River
Lassen National Forest
40.3 mi.
39.5 mi.
Doyles Corner
Road
38.5 mi.
N
W
E
S

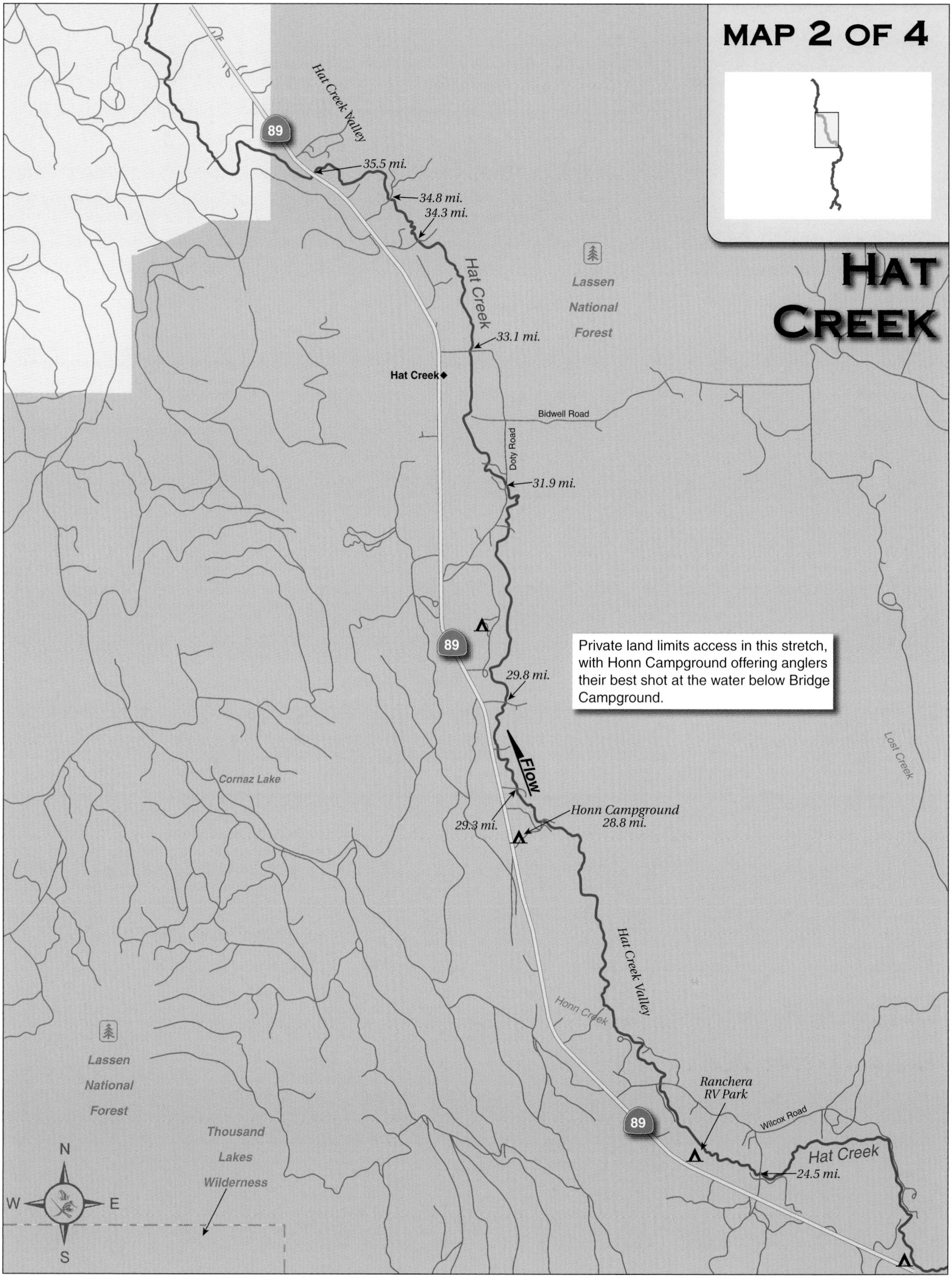
MAP 2 OF 4
HAT CREEK
Hat Creek Valley
89
35.5 mi.
34.8 mi.
34.3 mi.
Hat Creek
Lassen National Forest
33.1 mi.
Hat Creek
Bidwell Road
Doty Road
31.9 mi.
Private land limits access in this stretch, with Honn Campground offering anglers their best shot at the water below Bridge Campground.
29.8 mi.
Flow
Cornaz Lake
Lost Creek
Honn Campground 28.8 mi.
29.3 mi.
Hat Creek Valley
Honn Creek
Lassen National Forest
Thousand Lakes Wilderness
Rancheria RV Park
Wilcox Road
Hat Creek
24.5 mi.
N
W
E
S

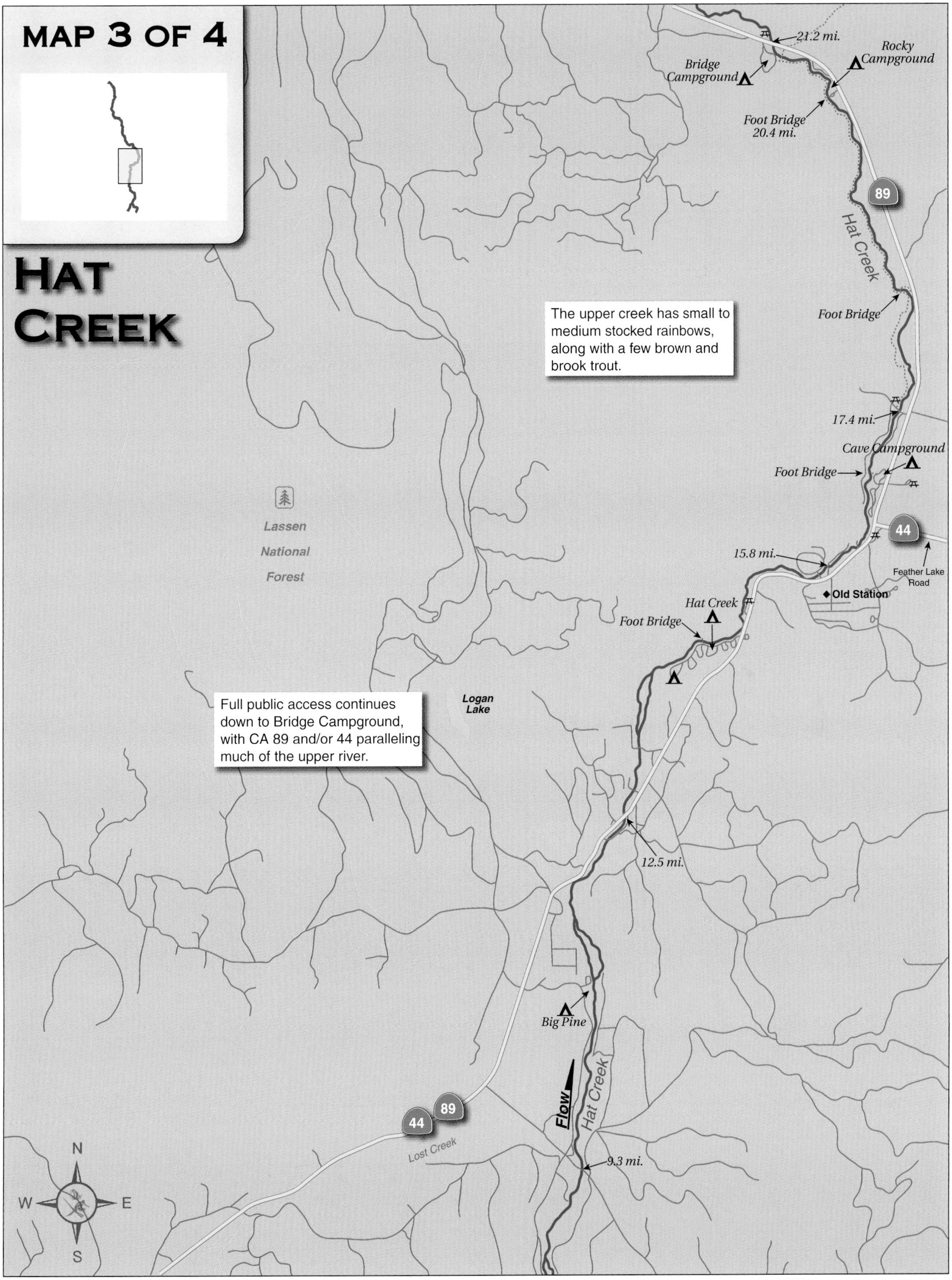
MAP 3 OF 4
HAT CREEK
21.2 mi.
Rocky Campground
Bridge Campground
Foot Bridge 20.4 mi.
89
Hat Creek
Foot Bridge
The upper creek has small to medium stocked rainbows, along with a few brown and brook trout.
17.4 mi.
Cave Campground
Foot Bridge
44
15.8 mi.
Feather Lake Road
Old Station
Hat Creek
Foot Bridge
Lassen National Forest
Logan Lake
Full public access continues down to Bridge Campground, with CA 89 and/or 44 paralleling much of the upper river.
12.5 mi.
Big Pine
Flow
Hat Creek
44
89
Lost Creek
9.3 mi.
N
W
E
S

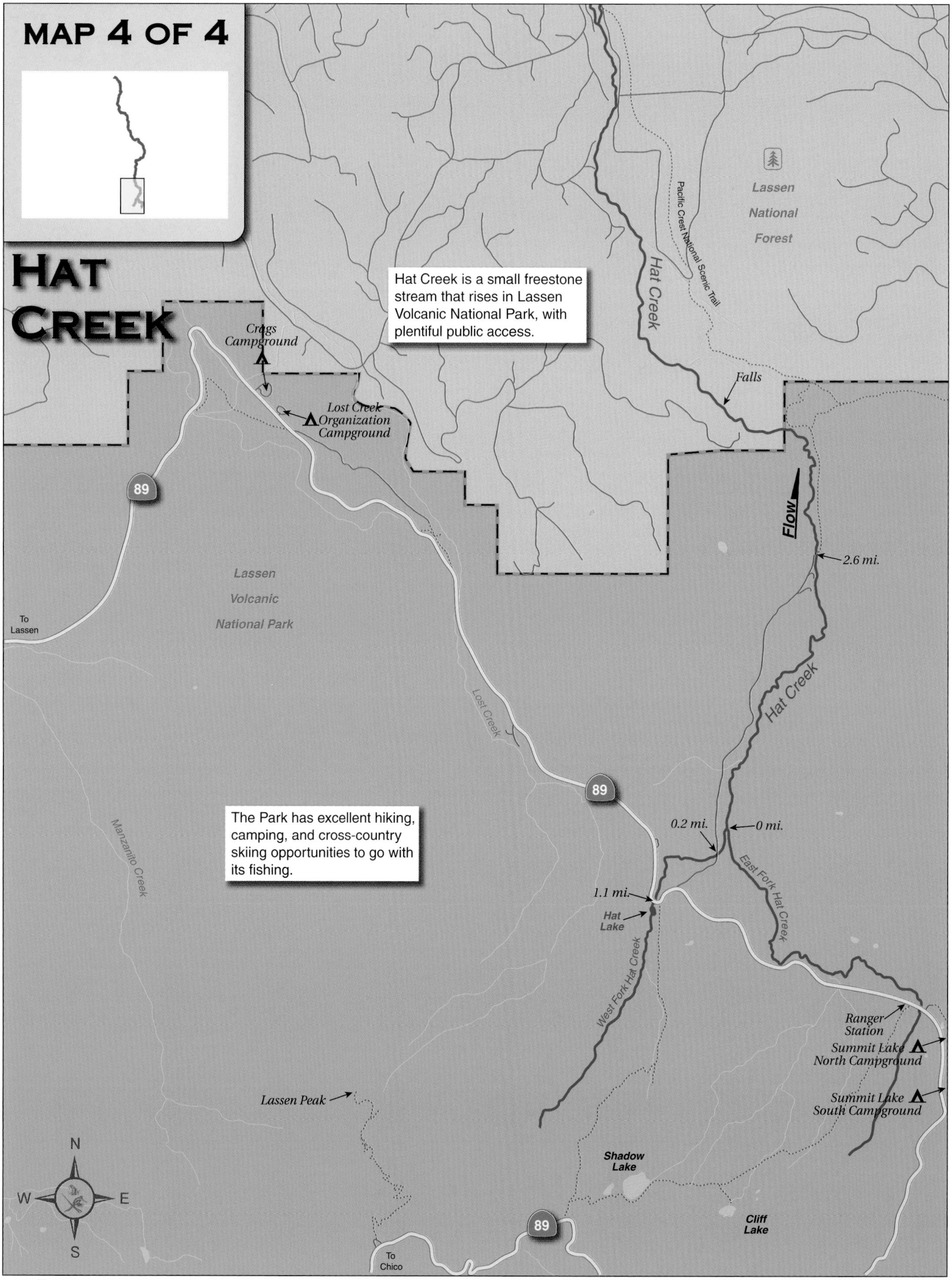
MAP 4 OF 4
HAT CREEK
Hat Creek is a small freestone stream that rises in Lassen Volcanic National Park, with plentiful public access.
The Park has excellent hiking, camping, and cross-country skiing opportunities to go with its fishing.
Lassen National Forest
Pacific Crest National Scenic Trail
Hat Creek
Falls
Crags Campground
Lost Creek Organization Campground
89
Flow
2.6 mi.
Lassen Volcanic National Park
To Lassen
Lost Creek
Hat Creek
0.2 mi.
0 mi.
East Fork Hat Creek
1.1 mi.
Hat Lake
Manzanito Creek
West Fork Hat Creek
Ranger Station
Summit Lake North Campground
Summit Lake South Campground
Lassen Peak
Shadow Lake
Cliff Lake
To Chico
N
W
E
S

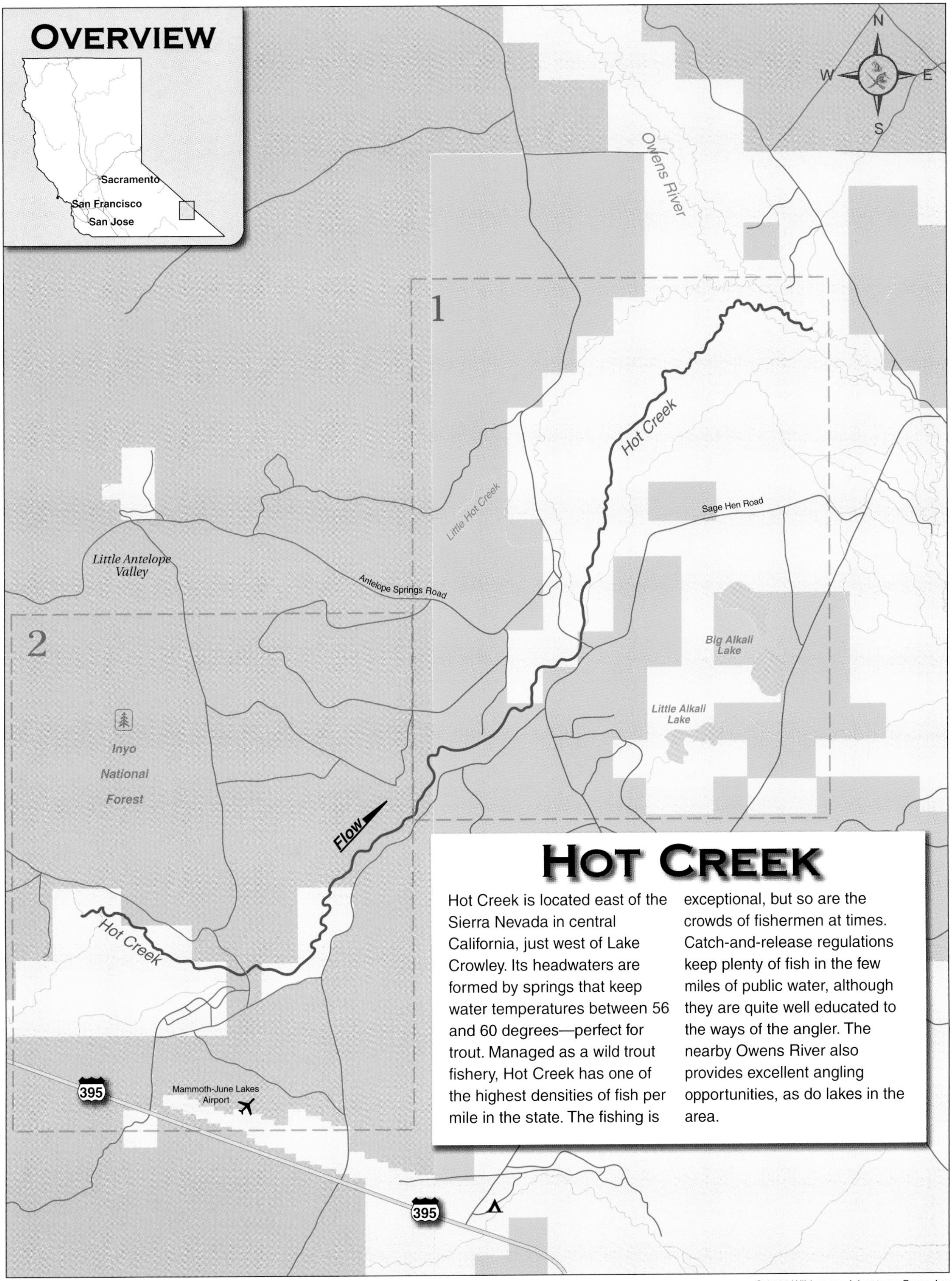

HOT CREEK

Hot Creek is located east of the Sierra Nevada in central California, just west of Lake Crowley. Its headwaters are formed by springs that keep water temperatures between 56 and 60 degrees—perfect for trout. Managed as a wild trout fishery, Hot Creek has one of the highest densities of fish per mile in the state. The fishing is exceptional, but so are the crowds of fishermen at times. Catch-and-release regulations keep plenty of fish in the few miles of public water, although they are quite well educated to the ways of the angler. The nearby Owens River also provides excellent angling opportunities, as do lakes in the area.

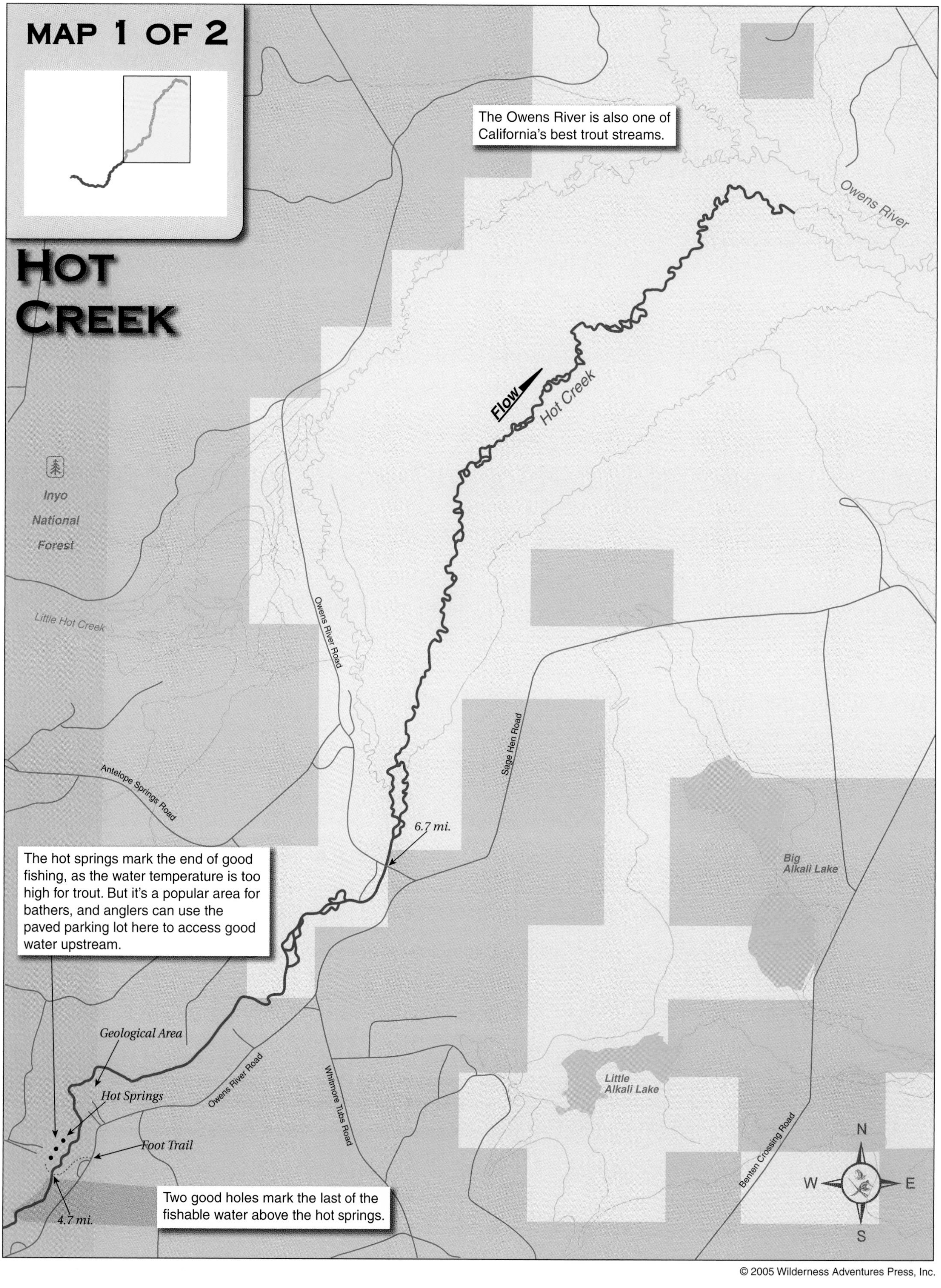
MAP 1 OF 2
HOT CREEK
The Owens River is also one of California's best trout streams.
Owens River
Flow
Hot Creek
Inyo National Forest
Little Hot Creek
Owens River Road
Sage Hen Road
Antelope Springs Road
6.7 mi.
The hot springs mark the end of good fishing, as the water temperature is too high for trout. But it's a popular area for bathers, and anglers can use the paved parking lot here to access good water upstream.
Big Alkali Lake
Geological Area
Hot Springs
Owens River Road
Whitmore Tubs Road
Little Alkali Lake
Foot Trail
Benten Crossing Road
N
W
E
S
4.7 mi.
Two good holes mark the last of the fishable water above the hot springs.

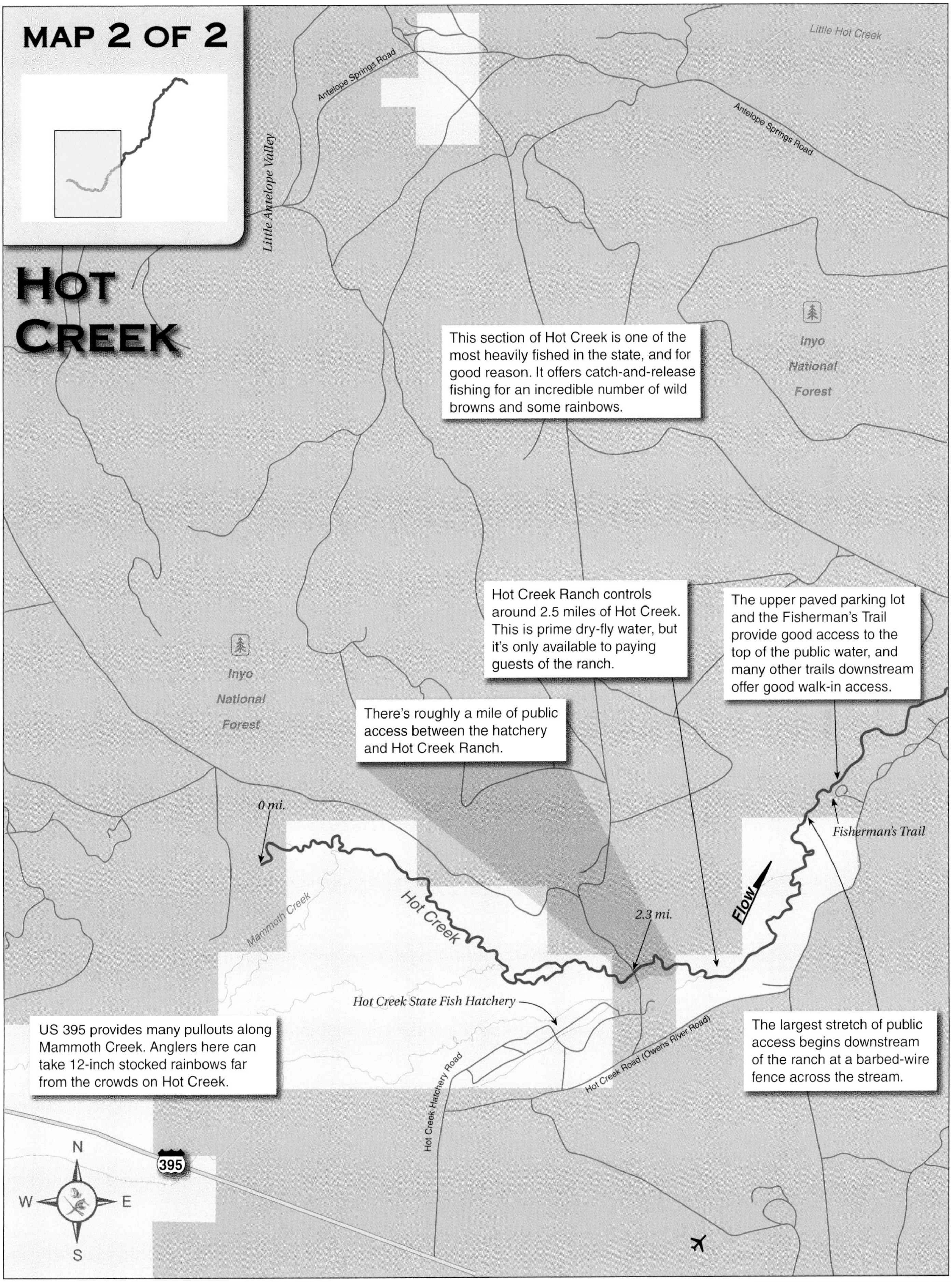
MAP 2 OF 2
HOT CREEK
Little Antelope Valley
Antelope Springs Road
Antelope Springs Road
Little Hot Creek
Inyo National Forest
This section of Hot Creek is one of the most heavily fished in the state, and for good reason. It offers catch-and-release fishing for an incredible number of wild browns and some rainbows.
Inyo National Forest
Hot Creek Ranch controls around 2.5 miles of Hot Creek. This is prime dry-fly water, but it's only available to paying guests of the ranch.
The upper paved parking lot and the Fisherman's Trail provide good access to the top of the public water, and many other trails downstream offer good walk-in access.
There's roughly a mile of public access between the hatchery and Hot Creek Ranch.
0 mi.
Fisherman's Trail
Mammoth Creek
Hot Creek
Flow
2.3 mi.
Hot Creek State Fish Hatchery
US 395 provides many pullouts along Mammoth Creek. Anglers here can take 12-inch stocked rainbows far from the crowds on Hot Creek.
Hot Creek Hatchery Road
Hot Creek Road (Owens River Road)
The largest stretch of public access begins downstream of the ranch at a barbed-wire fence across the stream.
395
N
W
E
S

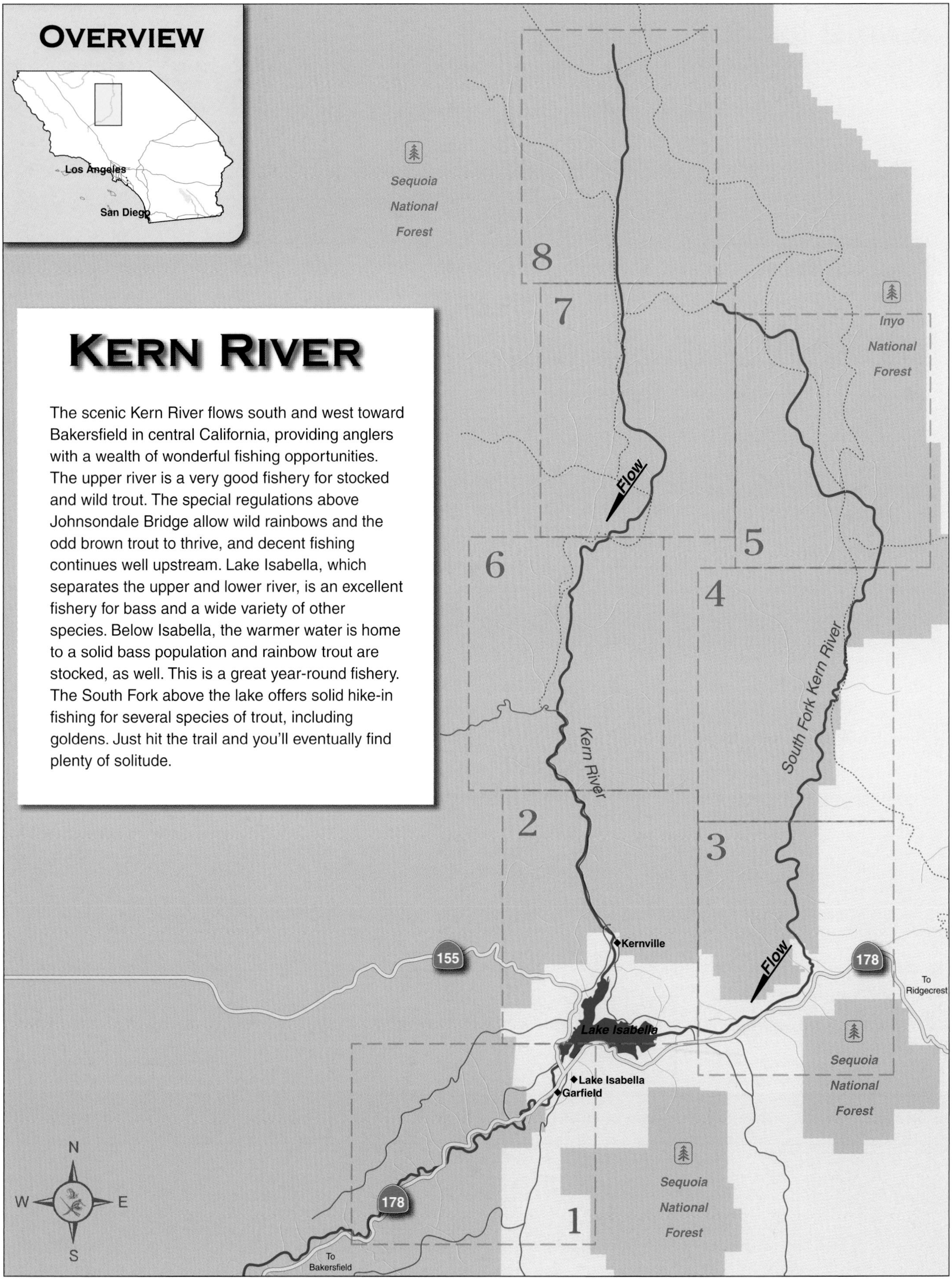

KERN RIVER

The scenic Kern River flows south and west toward Bakersfield in central California, providing anglers with a wealth of wonderful fishing opportunities. The upper river is a very good fishery for stocked and wild trout. The special regulations above Johnsondale Bridge allow wild rainbows and the odd brown trout to thrive, and decent fishing continues well upstream. Lake Isabella, which separates the upper and lower river, is an excellent fishery for bass and a wide variety of other species. Below Isabella, the warmer water is home to a solid bass population and rainbow trout are stocked, as well. This is a great year-round fishery. The South Fork above the lake offers solid hike-in fishing for several species of trout, including goldens. Just hit the trail and you'll eventually find plenty of solitude.

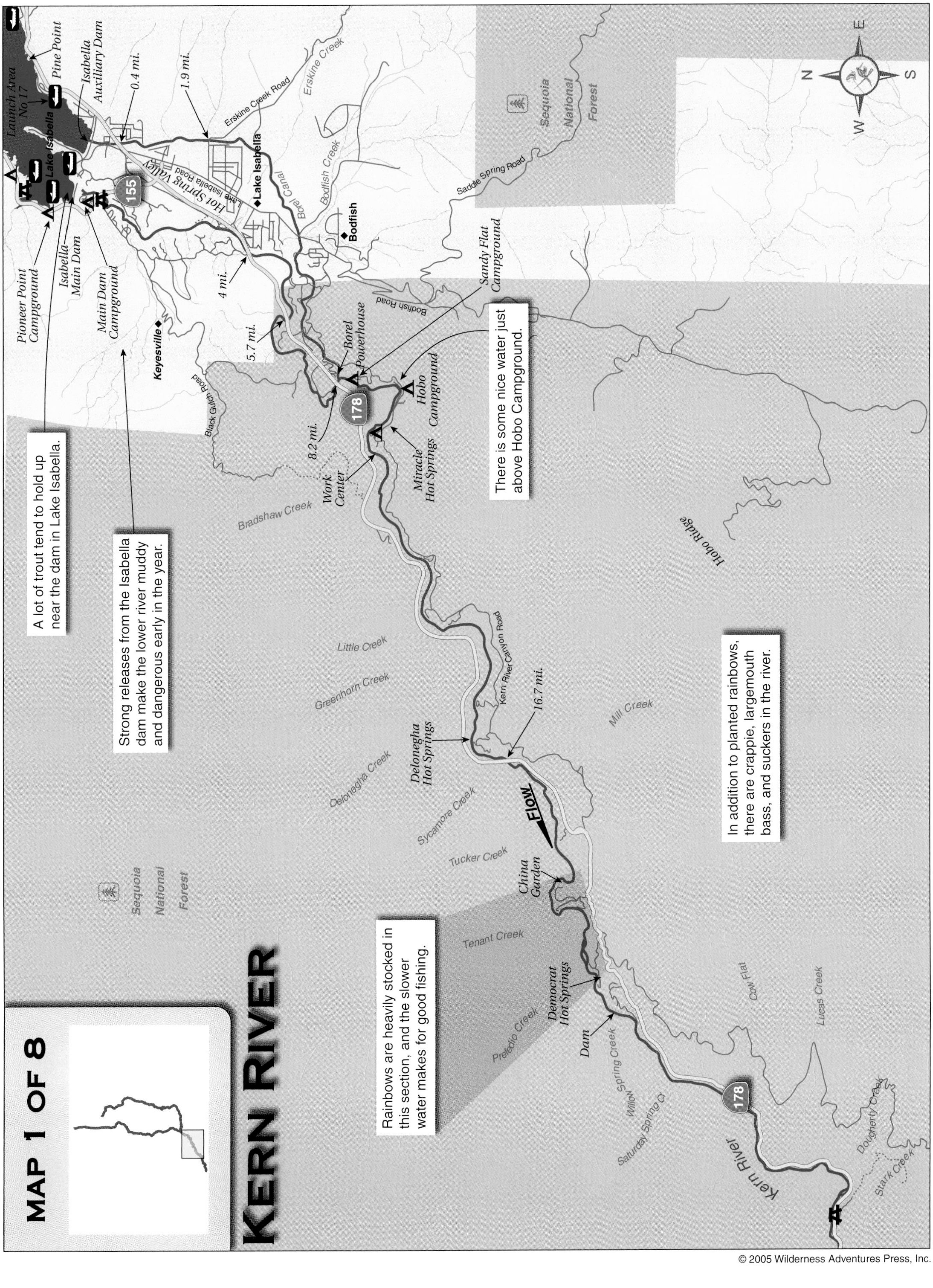
MAP 1 OF 8
KERN RIVER
A lot of trout tend to hold up near the dam in Lake Isabella.
Strong releases from the Isabella dam make the lower river muddy and dangerous early in the year.
There is some nice water just above Hobo Campground.
In addition to planted rainbows, there are crappie, largemouth bass, and suckers in the river.
Rainbows are heavily stocked in this section, and the slower water makes for good fishing.
Launch Area No 17
Pine Point
Isabella Auxiliary Dam
0.4 mi.
1.9 mi.
Lake Isabella
Pioneer Point Campground
Isabella Main Dam
Main Dam Campground
Hot Spring Valley
Lake Isabella Road
Erskine Creek Road
Erskine Creek
Bodfish Creek
Borel Canal
Bodfish
4 mi.
5.7 mi.
8.2 mi.
16.7 mi.
Keyesville
Black Gulch Road
Bodfish Road
Borel Powerhouse
Sandy Flat Campground
Hobo Campground
Miracle Hot Springs
Work Center
Saddle Spring Road
Sequoia National Forest
Bradshaw Creek
Hobo Ridge
Little Creek
Greenhorn Creek
Kern River Canyon Road
Delonegha Hot Springs
Delonegha Creek
Mill Creek
Sycamore Creek
Flow
Tucker Creek
China Garden
Tenant Creek
Democrat Hot Springs
Prelodio Creek
Dam
Willow Spring Creek
Saturday Spring Cr.
Cow Flat
Lucas Creek
Dougherty Creek
Stark Creek
Kern River
155
178
N
E
S
W

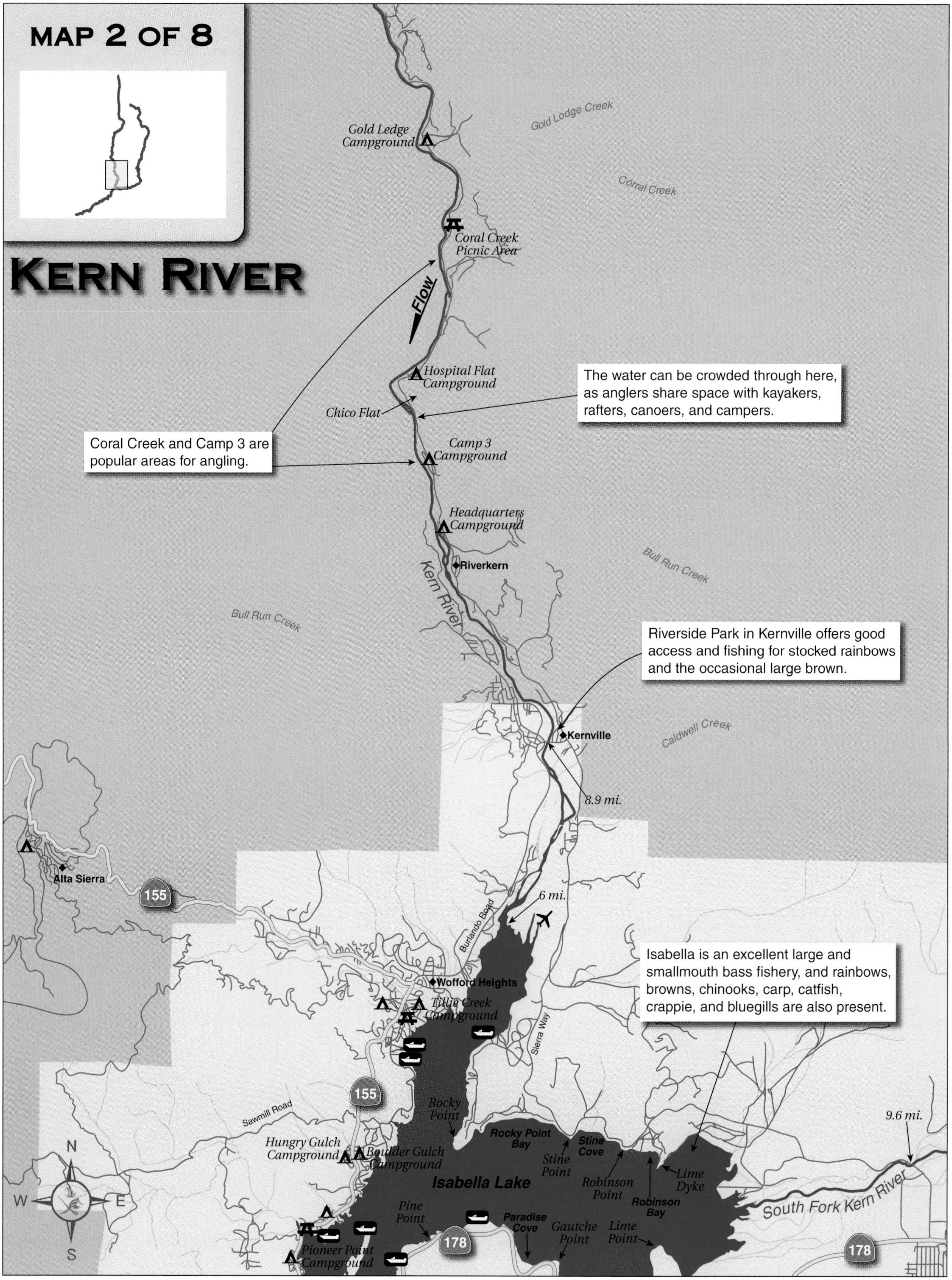
MAP 2 OF 8
KERN RIVER
Gold Ledge Campground
Gold Lodge Creek
Corral Creek
Coral Creek Picnic Area
Flow
Hospital Flat Campground
Chico Flat
The water can be crowded through here, as anglers share space with kayakers, rafters, canoers, and campers.
Coral Creek and Camp 3 are popular areas for angling.
Camp 3 Campground
Headquarters Campground
Riverkern
Kern River
Bull Run Creek
Bull Run Creek
Riverside Park in Kernville offers good access and fishing for stocked rainbows and the occasional large brown.
Kernville
Caldwell Creek
8.9 mi.
Alta Sierra
155
6 mi.
Burlando Road
Wofford Heights
Tillie Creek Campground
Sierra Way
Isabella is an excellent large and smallmouth bass fishery, and rainbows, browns, chinooks, carp, catfish, crappie, and bluegills are also present.
155
Sawmill Road
Rocky Point
Rocky Point Bay
Stine Cove
Stine Point
Robinson Point
Robinson Bay
Lime Dyke
9.6 mi.
Hungry Gulch Campground
Boulder Gulch Campground
Isabella Lake
South Fork Kern River
Pine Point
Paradise Cove
Gautche Point
Lime Point
178
178
Pioneer Point Campground
N
W
E
S

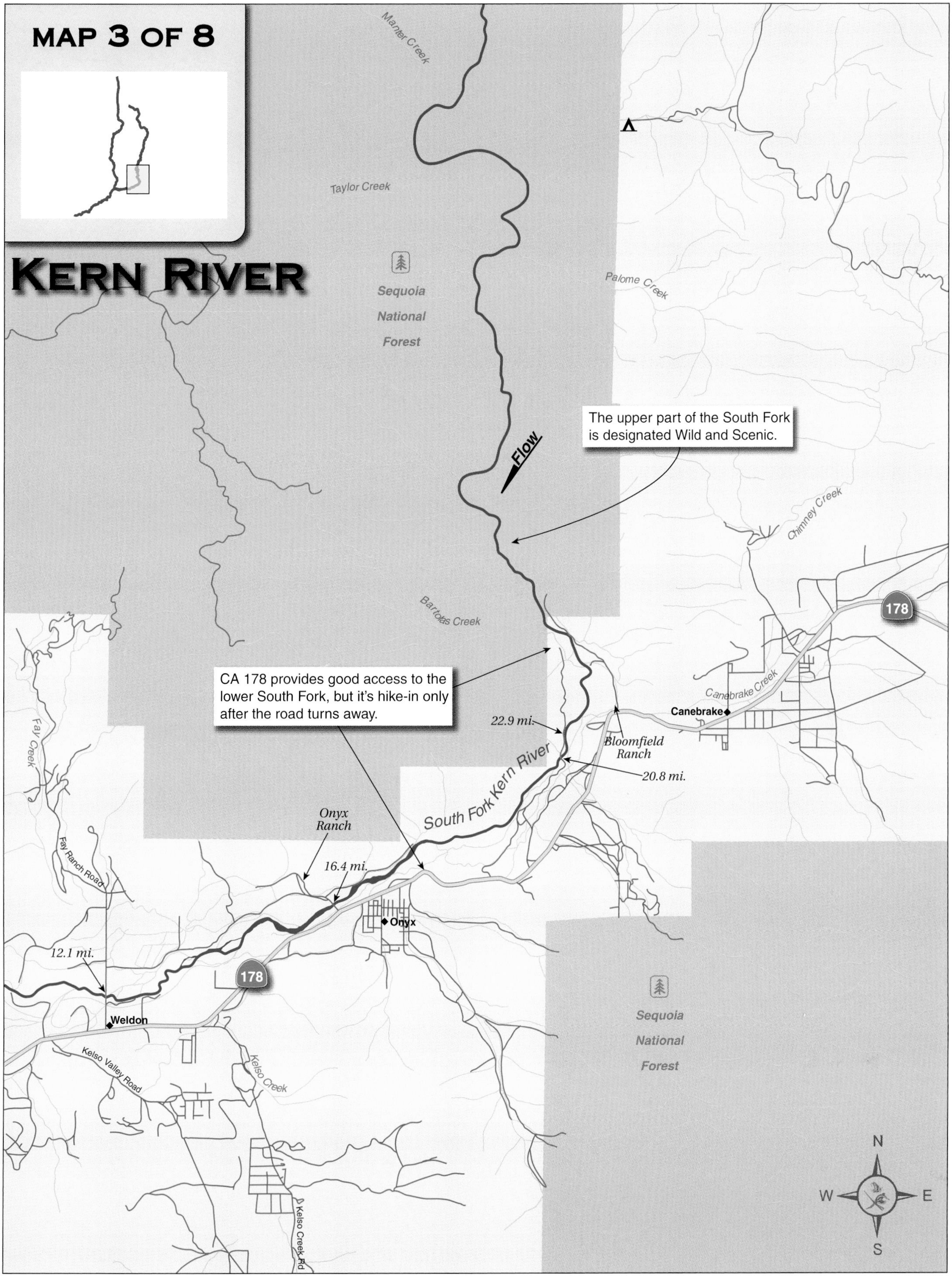
MAP 3 OF 8
KERN RIVER
Manter Creek
Taylor Creek
Sequoia National Forest
Palome Creek
Flow
The upper part of the South Fork is designated Wild and Scenic.
Chimney Creek
Bartolas Creek
178
CA 178 provides good access to the lower South Fork, but it's hike-in only after the road turns away.
Canebrake Creek
Canebrake
22.9 mi.
Bloomfield Ranch
20.8 mi.
South Fork Kern River
Fay Creek
Onyx Ranch
16.4 mi.
Fay Ranch Road
Onyx
12.1 mi.
178
Weldon
Kelso Valley Road
Kelso Creek
Sequoia National Forest
Kelso Creek Rd
N
W
E
S

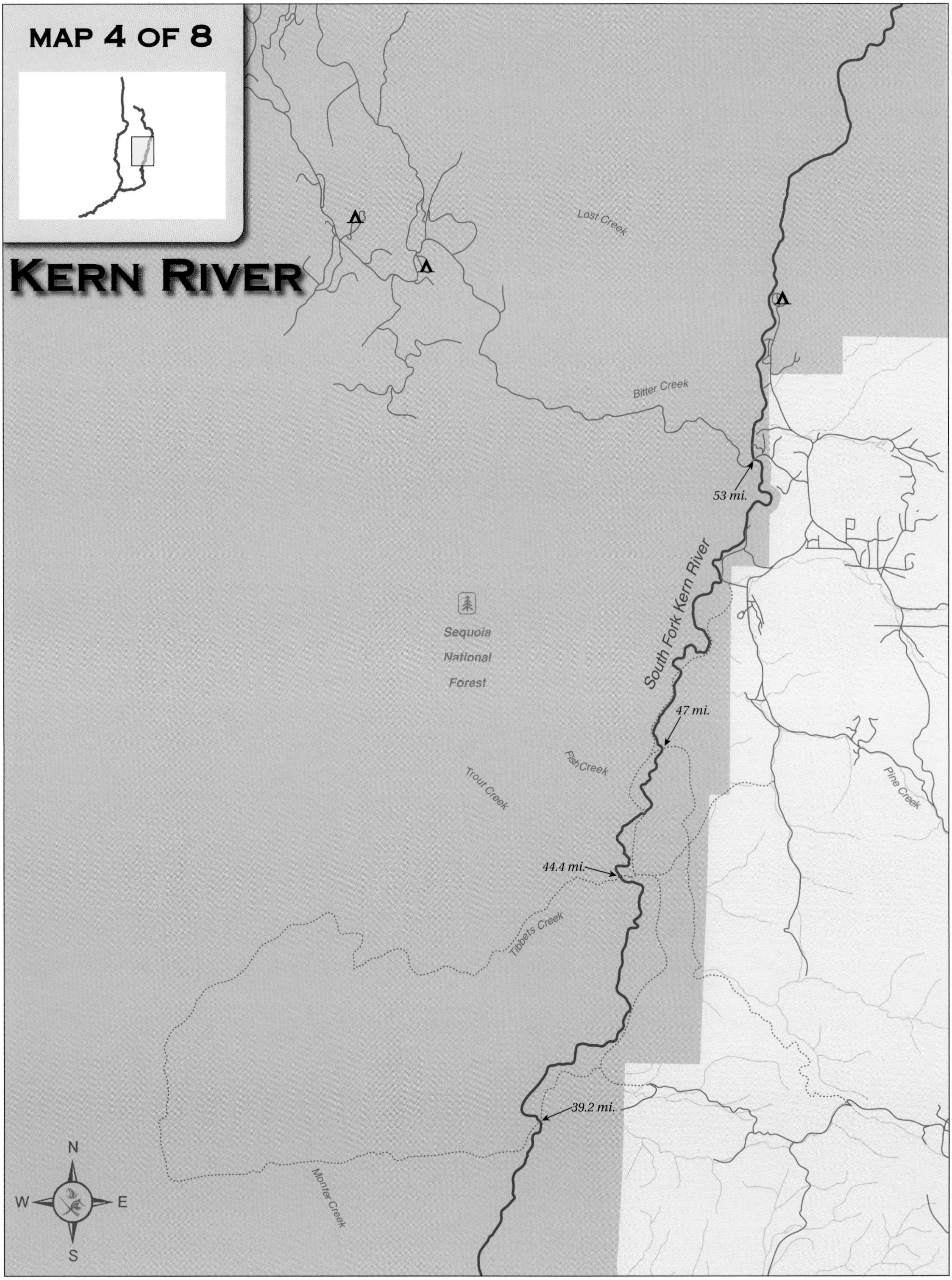
MAP 4 OF 8
KERN RIVER
Lost Creek
Bitter Creek
53 mi.
South Fork Kern River
Sequoia
National
Forest
47 mi.
Fish Creek
Trout Creek
Pine Creek
44.4 mi.
Tibbets Creek
39.2 mi.
Monter Creek
N
W
E
S

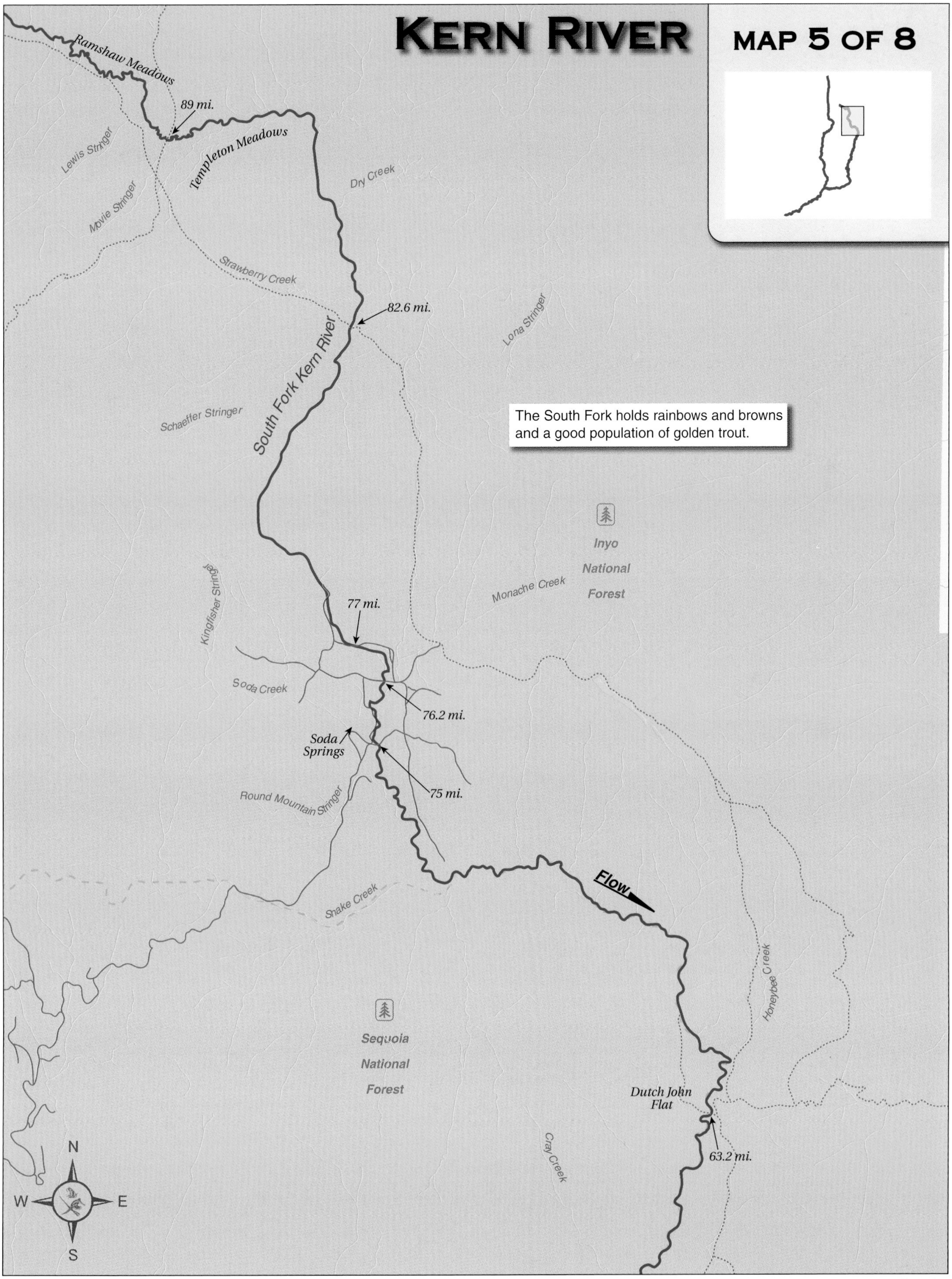
KERN RIVER
MAP 5 OF 8
Ramshaw Meadows
89 mi.
Templeton Meadows
Lewis Stringer
Movie Stringer
Dry Creek
Strawberry Creek
82.6 mi.
Lona Stringer
South Fork Kern River
Schaeffer Stringer
The South Fork holds rainbows and browns and a good population of golden trout.
Inyo National Forest
Monache Creek
Kingfisher Stringer
77 mi.
Soda Creek
76.2 mi.
Soda Springs
75 mi.
Round Mountain Stringer
Flow
Snake Creek
Honeybee Creek
Sequoia National Forest
Dutch John Flat
63.2 mi.
Cray Creek
N
W
E
S

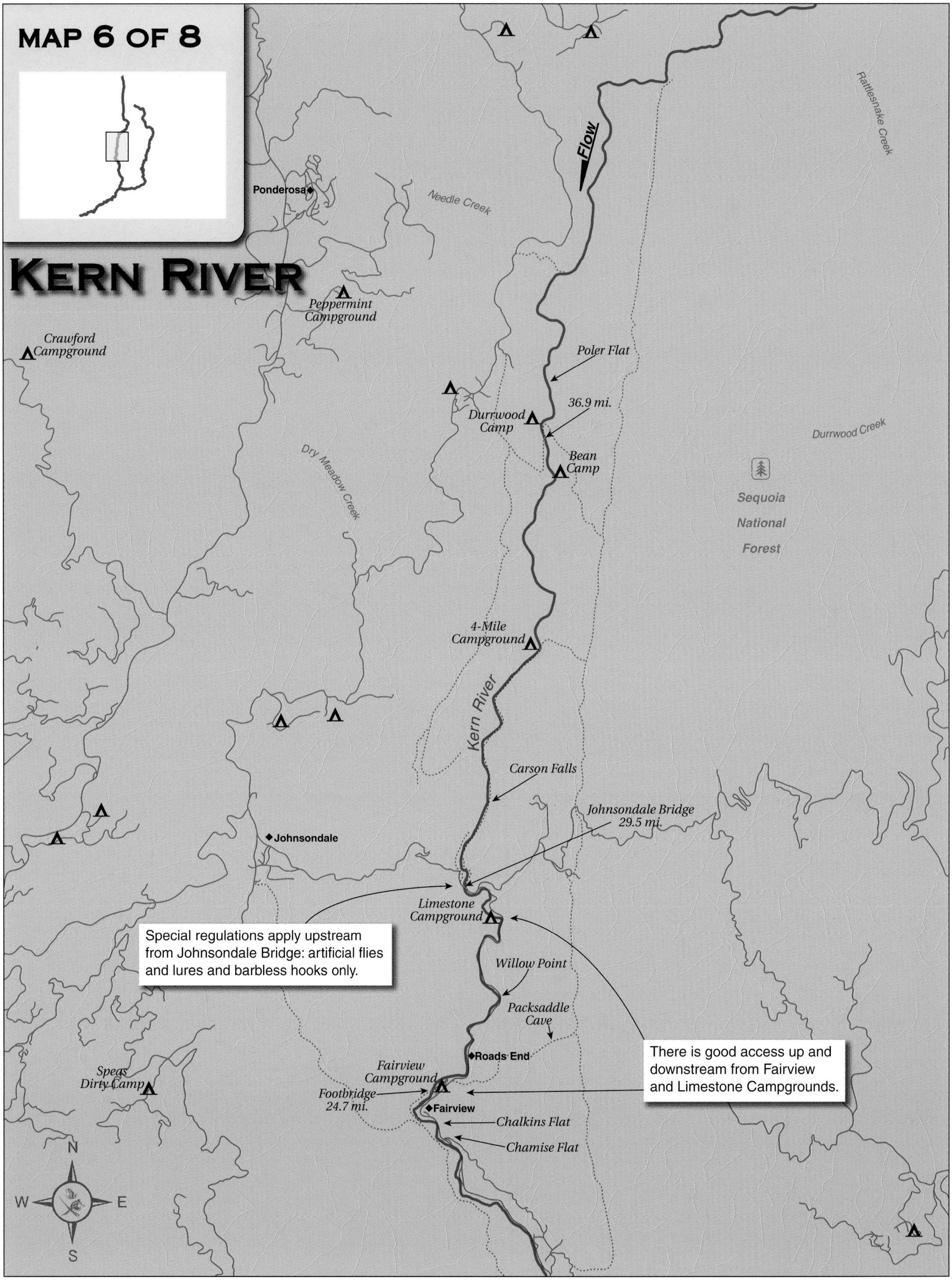

MAP 6 OF 8
KERN RIVER
Ponderosa
Needle Creek
Flow
Rattlesnake Creek
Peppermint Campground
Crawford Campground
Poler Flat
36.9 mi.
Durrwood Camp
Bean Camp
Durrwood Creek
Dry Meadow Creek
Sequoia National Forest
4-Mile Campground
Kern River
Carson Falls
Johnsondale Bridge 29.5 mi.
Johnsondale
Limestone Campground
Special regulations apply upstream from Johnsondale Bridge: artificial flies and lures and barbless hooks only.
Willow Point
Packsaddle Cave
Roads End
There is good access up and downstream from Fairview and Limestone Campgrounds.
Fairview Campground
Footbridge 24.7 mi.
Fairview
Chalkins Flat
Chamise Flat
Speas Dirty Camp
N
W
E
S

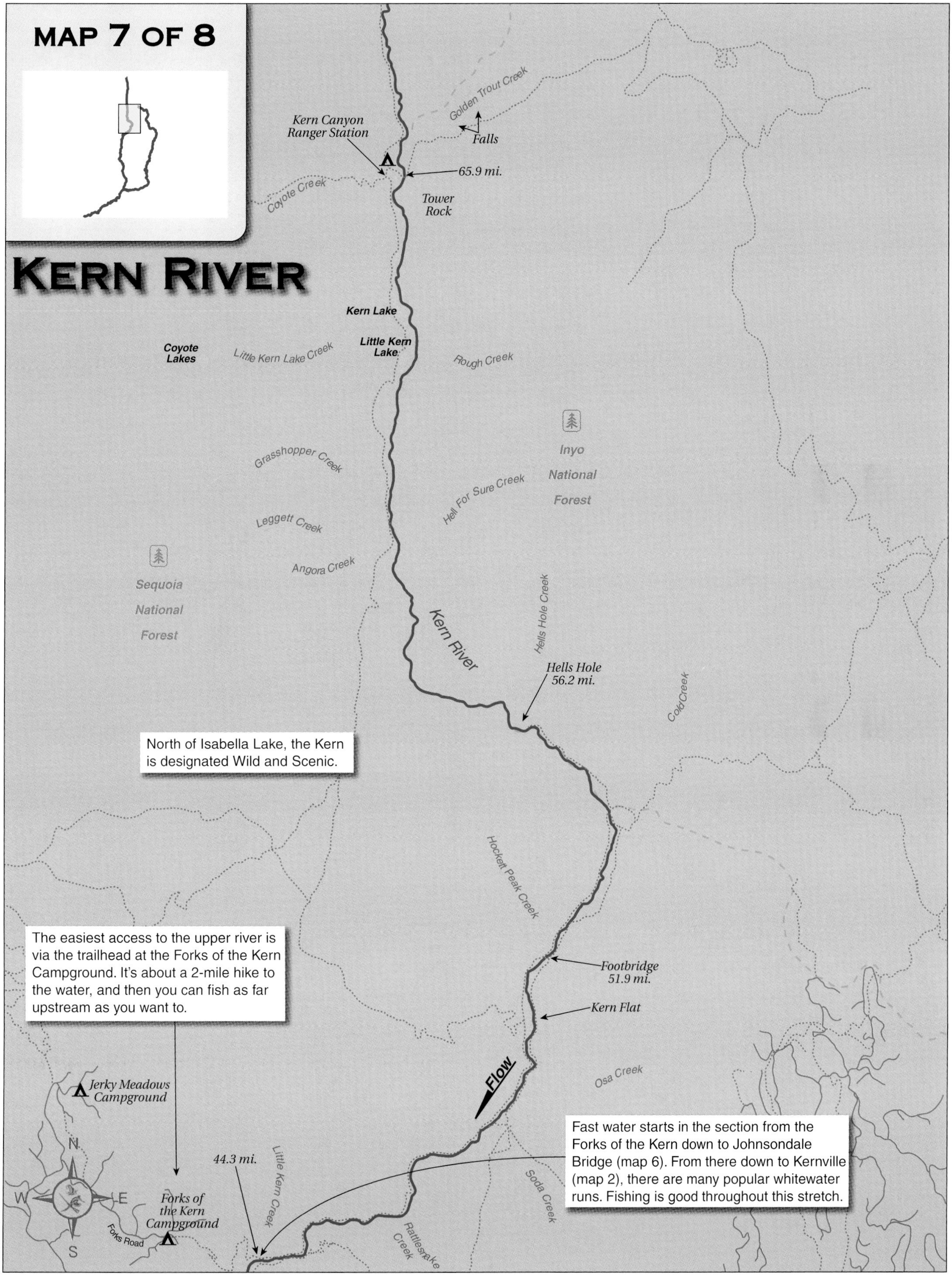
MAP 7 OF 8
KERN RIVER
Kern Canyon Ranger Station
Golden Trout Creek
Falls
65.9 mi.
Coyote Creek
Tower Rock
Kern Lake
Little Kern Lake
Coyote Lakes
Little Kern Lake Creek
Rough Creek
Inyo National Forest
Grasshopper Creek
Hell For Sure Creek
Leggett Creek
Angora Creek
Sequoia National Forest
Kern River
Hells Hole Creek
Hells Hole 56.2 mi.
Cold Creek
North of Isabella Lake, the Kern is designated Wild and Scenic.
Hockett Peak Creek
The easiest access to the upper river is via the trailhead at the Forks of the Kern Campground. It's about a 2-mile hike to the water, and then you can fish as far upstream as you want to.
Footbridge 51.9 mi.
Kern Flat
Flow
Osa Creek
Jerky Meadows Campground
N
W
E
S
44.3 mi.
Little Kern Creek
Forks of the Kern Campground
Forks Road
Rattlesnake Creek
Soda Creek
Fast water starts in the section from the Forks of the Kern down to Johnsondale Bridge (map 6). From there down to Kernville (map 2), there are many popular whitewater runs. Fishing is good throughout this stretch.

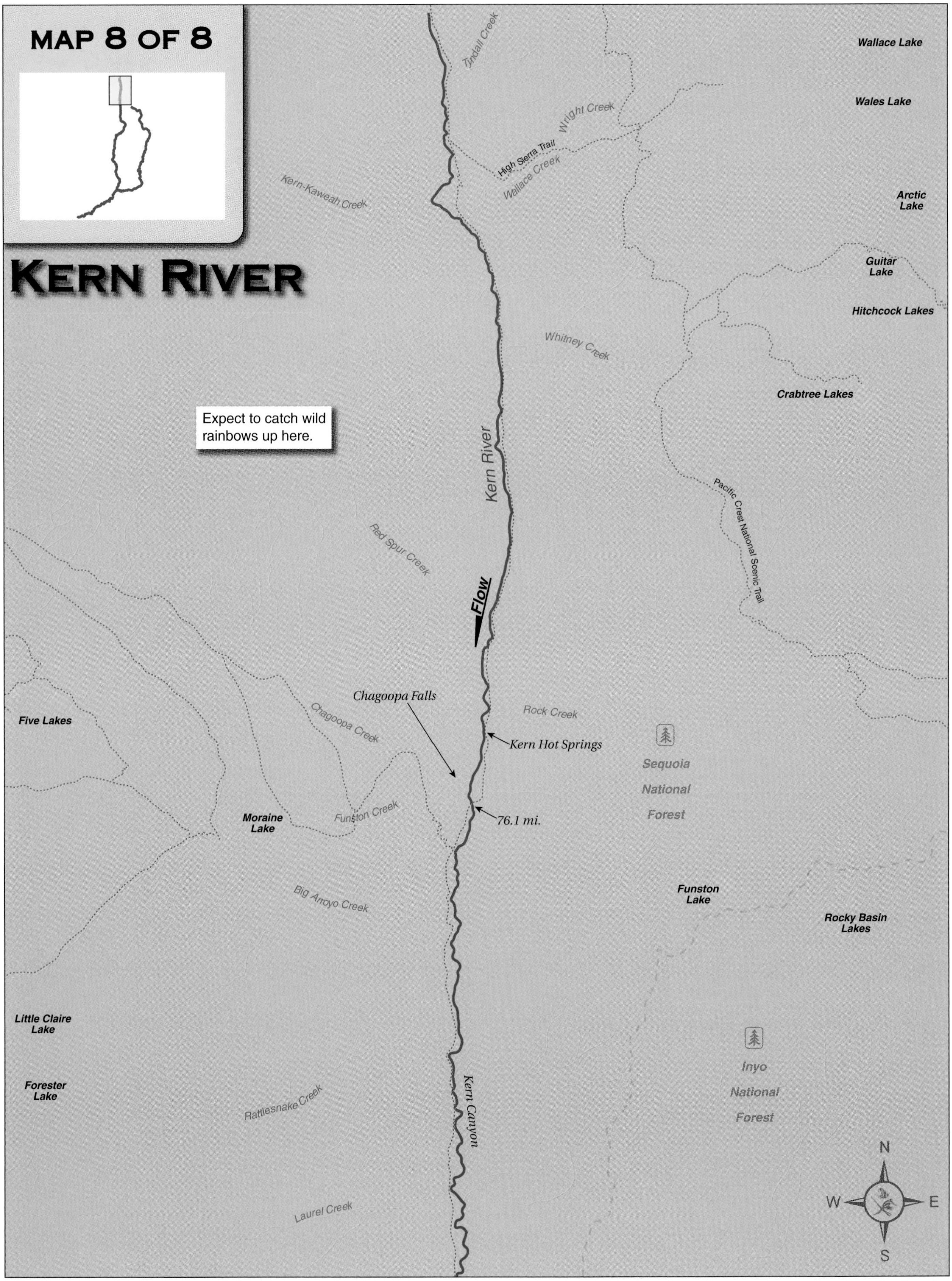
MAP 8 OF 8
KERN RIVER
Expect to catch wild rainbows up here.
Tyndall Creek
Wright Creek
High Sierra Trail
Wallace Creek
Kern-Kaweah Creek
Wallace Lake
Wales Lake
Arctic Lake
Guitar Lake
Hitchcock Lakes
Whitney Creek
Crabtree Lakes
Kern River
Pacific Crest National Scenic Trail
Red Spur Creek
Flow
Chagoopa Falls
Chagoopa Creek
Rock Creek
Kern Hot Springs
Sequoia National Forest
Five Lakes
Moraine Lake
Funston Creek
76.1 mi.
Big Arroyo Creek
Funston Lake
Rocky Basin Lakes
Little Claire Lake
Forester Lake
Rattlesnake Creek
Kern Canyon
Inyo National Forest
Laurel Creek
N
W
E
S

KINGS RIVER

The Kings River flows west off the Sierra Nevada in central California, with the upper river exiting Kings Canyon National Park below Cedar Grove. It's a pleasant little stream that is open year-round to angling. The upper river is often snowed in during winter, but above and below Pine Flat Reservoir you can fish in any season. The lower river mostly has stocked trout, but above the reservoir there are plenty of wild trout. Most of these fish aren't huge, but they're fun to catch and there are some surprises now and then. Spring and fall usually offer the best fishing.

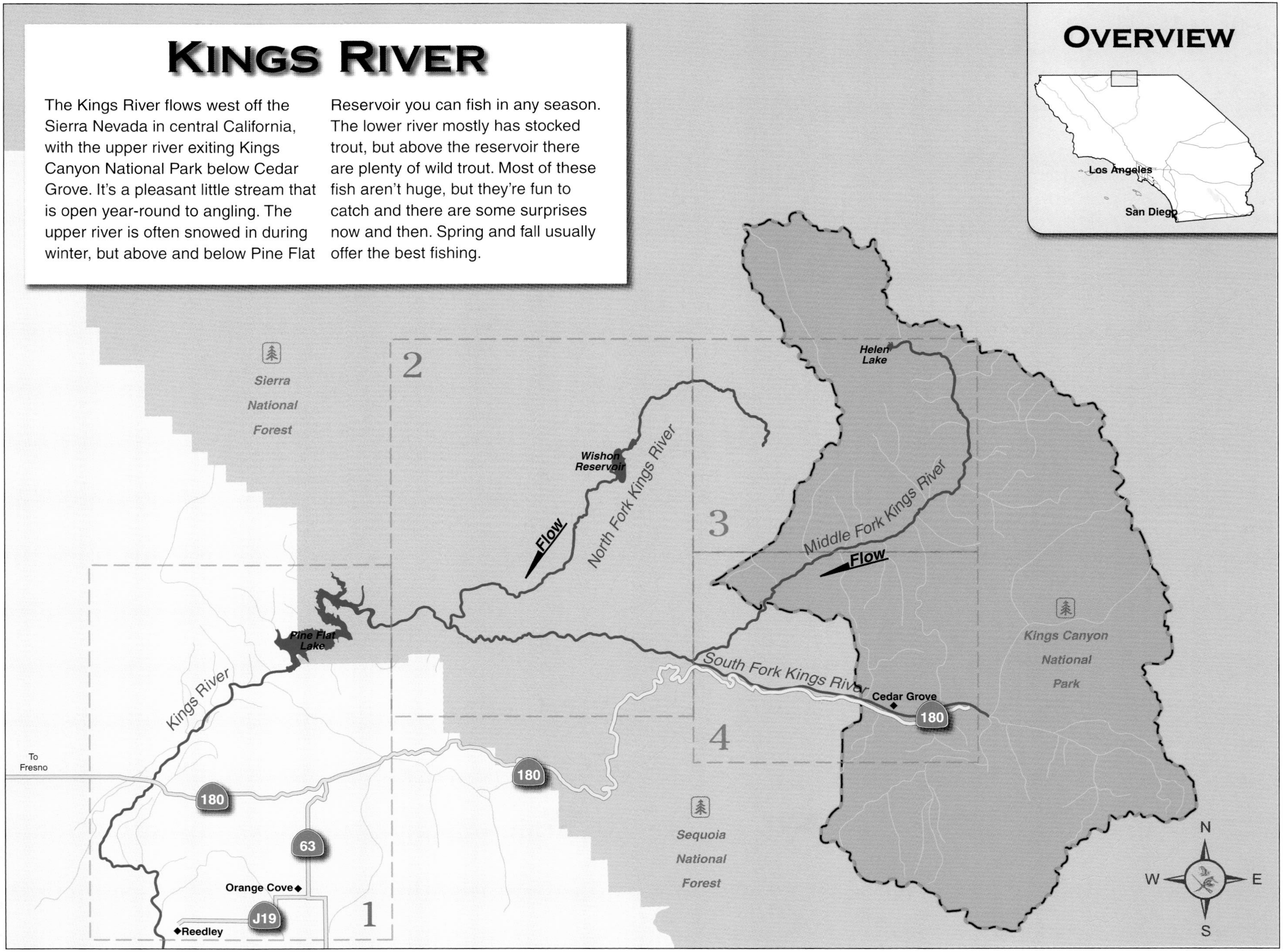

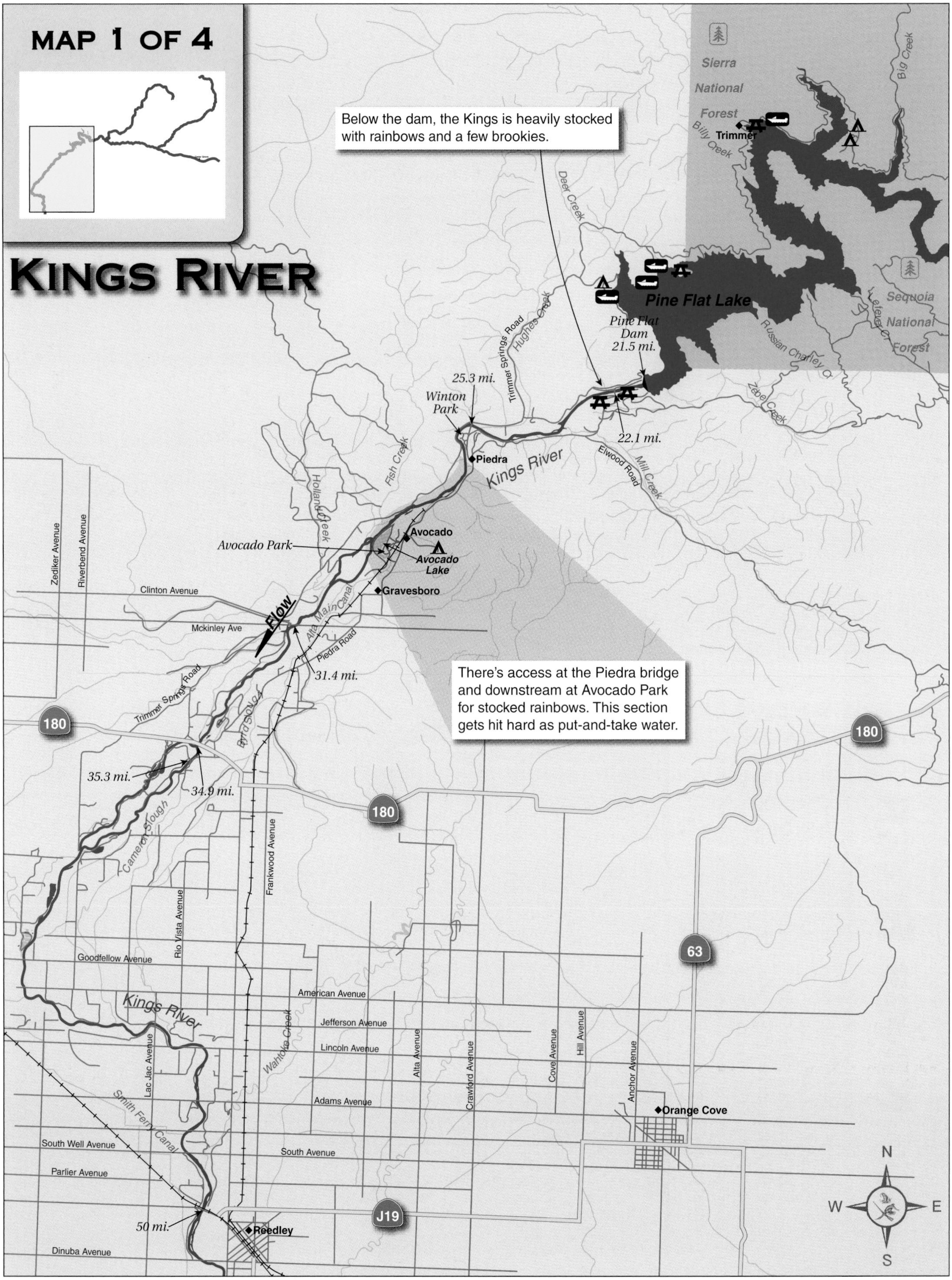
MAP 1 OF 4
KINGS RIVER
Below the dam, the Kings is heavily stocked with rainbows and a few brookies.
There's access at the Piedra bridge and downstream at Avocado Park for stocked rainbows. This section gets hit hard as put-and-take water.
Sierra National Forest
Sequoia National Forest
Trimmer
Billy Creek
Big Creek
Deer Creek
Pine Flat Lake
Pine Flat Dam 21.5 mi.
22.1 mi.
25.3 mi.
Winton Park
Piedra
Kings River
Trimmer Springs Road
Hughes Creek
Russian Charley Cr.
Zebe Creek
Elwood Road
Mill Creek
Fish Creek
Holland Creek
Avocado
Avocado Park
Avocado Lake
Gravesboro
Alta Main Canal
Piedra Road
31.4 mi.
Flow
Clinton Avenue
Mckinley Ave
Zediker Avenue
Riverbend Avenue
Trimmer Springs Road
Byrd Slough
180
35.3 mi.
34.9 mi.
Cameron Slough
Frankwood Avenue
Rio Vista Avenue
Goodfellow Avenue
63
American Avenue
Jefferson Avenue
Lincoln Avenue
Kings River
Wahtoke Creek
Lac Jac Avenue
Alta Avenue
Crawford Avenue
Cove Avenue
Hill Avenue
Anchor Avenue
Adams Avenue
Orange Cove
Smith Ferry Canal
South Well Avenue
South Avenue
Parlier Avenue
50 mi.
J19
Reedley
Dinuba Avenue
N
S
E
W

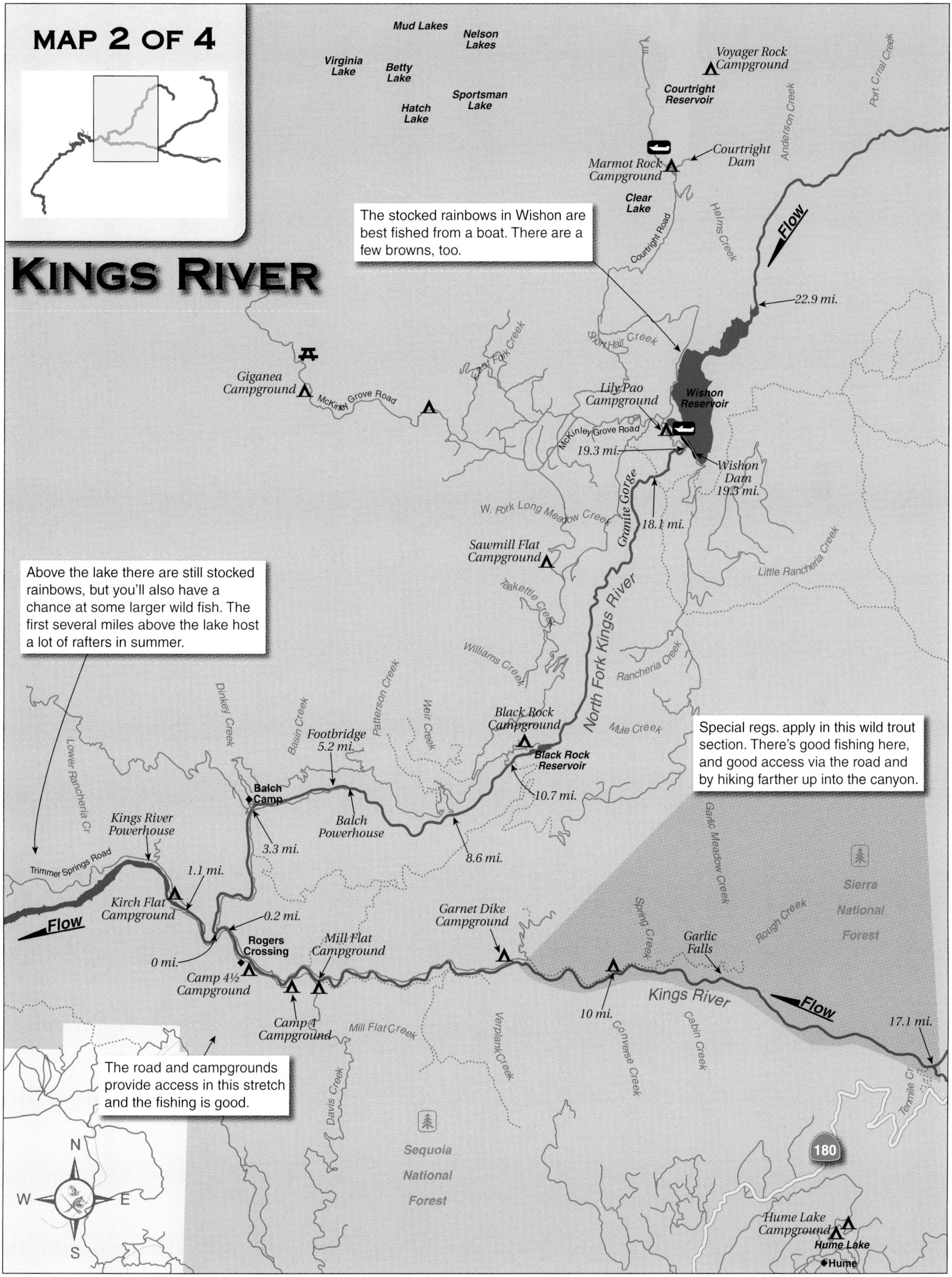
MAP 2 OF 4
KINGS RIVER
Mud Lakes
Nelson Lakes
Virginia Lake
Betty Lake
Sportsman Lake
Hatch Lake
Voyager Rock Campground
Courtright Reservoir
Courtright Dam
Marmot Rock Campground
Clear Lake
Anderson Creek
Port Cral Creek
Helms Creek
Courtright Road
Flow
The stocked rainbows in Wishon are best fished from a boat. There are a few browns, too.
22.9 mi.
Short Hair Creek
Giganea Campground
McKinley Grove Road
Lily Pao Campground
Wishon Reservoir
19.3 mi.
Wishon Dam 19.3 mi.
Granite Gorge
18.1 mi.
W. Fork Long Meadow Creek
Sawmill Flat Campground
Little Rancheria Creek
Above the lake there are still stocked rainbows, but you'll also have a chance at some larger wild fish. The first several miles above the lake host a lot of rafters in summer.
Teakettle Creek
North Fork Kings River
Williams Creek
Rancheria Creek
Dinkey Creek
Basin Creek
Patterson Creek
Weir Creek
Footbridge 5.2 mi.
Black Rock Campground
Black Rock Reservoir
Mule Creek
Special regs. apply in this wild trout section. There's good fishing here, and good access via the road and by hiking farther up into the canyon.
Lower Rancheria Cr
Balch Camp
Kings River Powerhouse
Balch Powerhouse
10.7 mi.
3.3 mi.
8.6 mi.
Trimmer Springs Road
1.1 mi.
Garlic Meadow Creek
Sierra National Forest
Kirch Flat Campground
Flow
0.2 mi.
Garnet Dike Campground
Spring Creek
Rough Creek
Rogers Crossing
Mill Flat Campground
Garlic Falls
0 mi.
Camp 4½ Campground
Kings River
Flow
Camp 4 Campground
Mill Flat Creek
Verplank Creek
10 mi.
Converse Creek
Cabin Creek
17.1 mi.
The road and campgrounds provide access in this stretch and the fishing is good.
Davis Creek
Tenmile Cr
Sequoia National Forest
180
N
W
E
S
Hume Lake Campground
Hume Lake
Hume

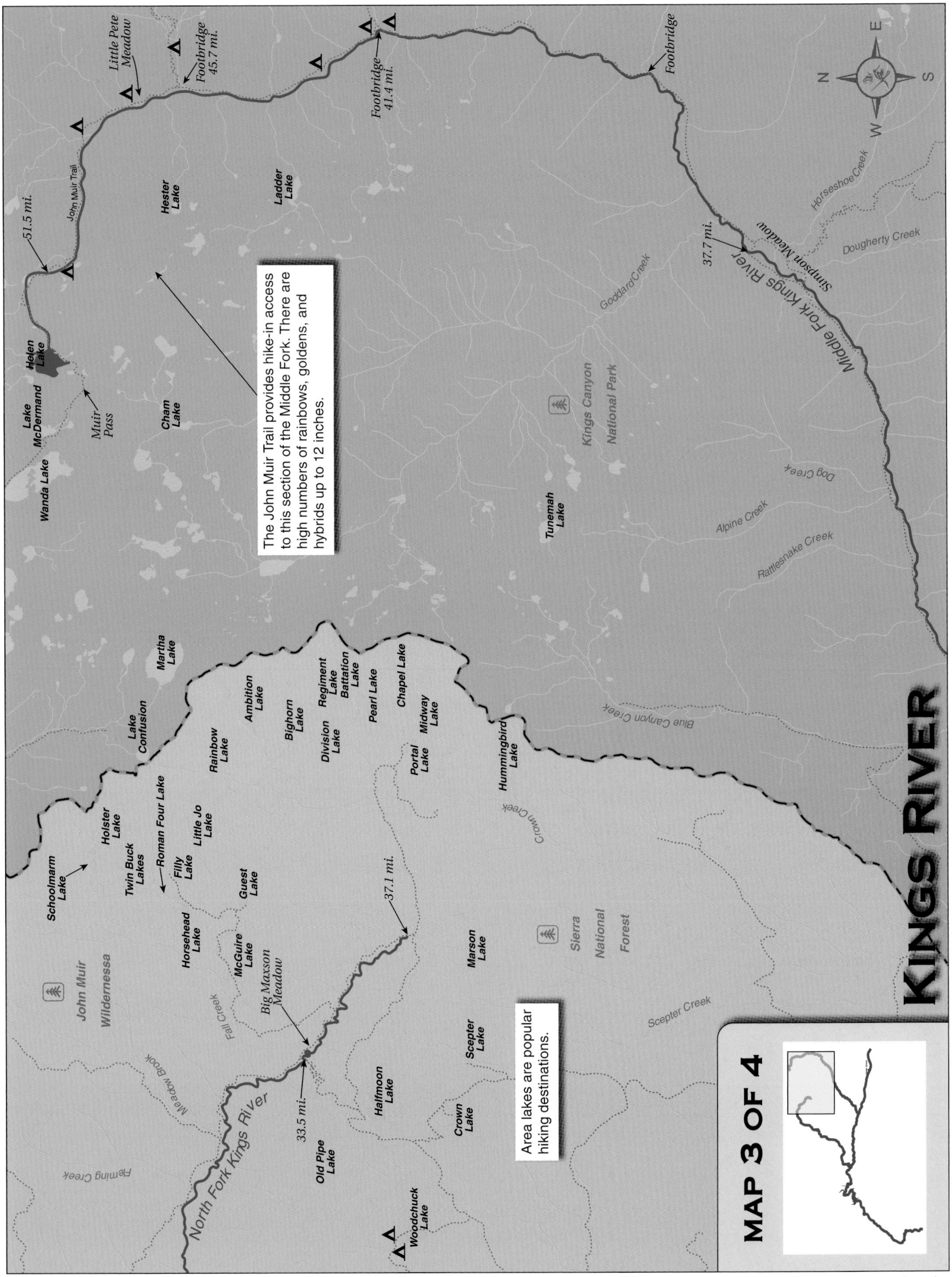
Kings River
Map 3 of 4
The John Muir Trail provides hike-in access to this section of the Middle Fork. There are high numbers of rainbows, goldens, and hybrids up to 12 inches.
Area lakes are popular hiking destinations.
Middle Fork Kings River
North Fork Kings River
John Muir Trail
Kings Canyon National Park
Sierra National Forest
John Muir Wilderness
Little Pete Meadow
Footbridge 45.7 mi.
Footbridge 41.4 mi.
Footbridge
51.5 mi.
37.7 mi.
37.1 mi.
33.5 mi.
Simpson Meadow
Big Maxson Meadow
Muir Pass
Helen Lake
Lake McDermand
Wanda Lake
Cham Lake
Hester Lake
Ladder Lake
Tunemah Lake
Martha Lake
Lake Confusion
Ambition Lake
Regiment Lake
Battation Lake
Chapel Lake
Pearl Lake
Bighorn Lake
Division Lake
Midway Lake
Rainbow Lake
Portal Lake
Hummingbird Lake
Holster Lake
Schoolmarm Lake
Twin Buck Lakes
Roman Four Lake
Little Jo Lake
Filly Lake
Guest Lake
Horsehead Lake
McGuire Lake
Marson Lake
Scepter Lake
Halfmoon Lake
Crown Lake
Old Pipe Lake
Woodchuck Lake
Goddard Creek
Horseshoe Creek
Dougherty Creek
Dog Creek
Alpine Creek
Rattlesnake Creek
Blue Canyon Creek
Crown Creek
Scepter Creek
Fall Creek
Meadow Brook
Fleming Creek
N
S
E
W

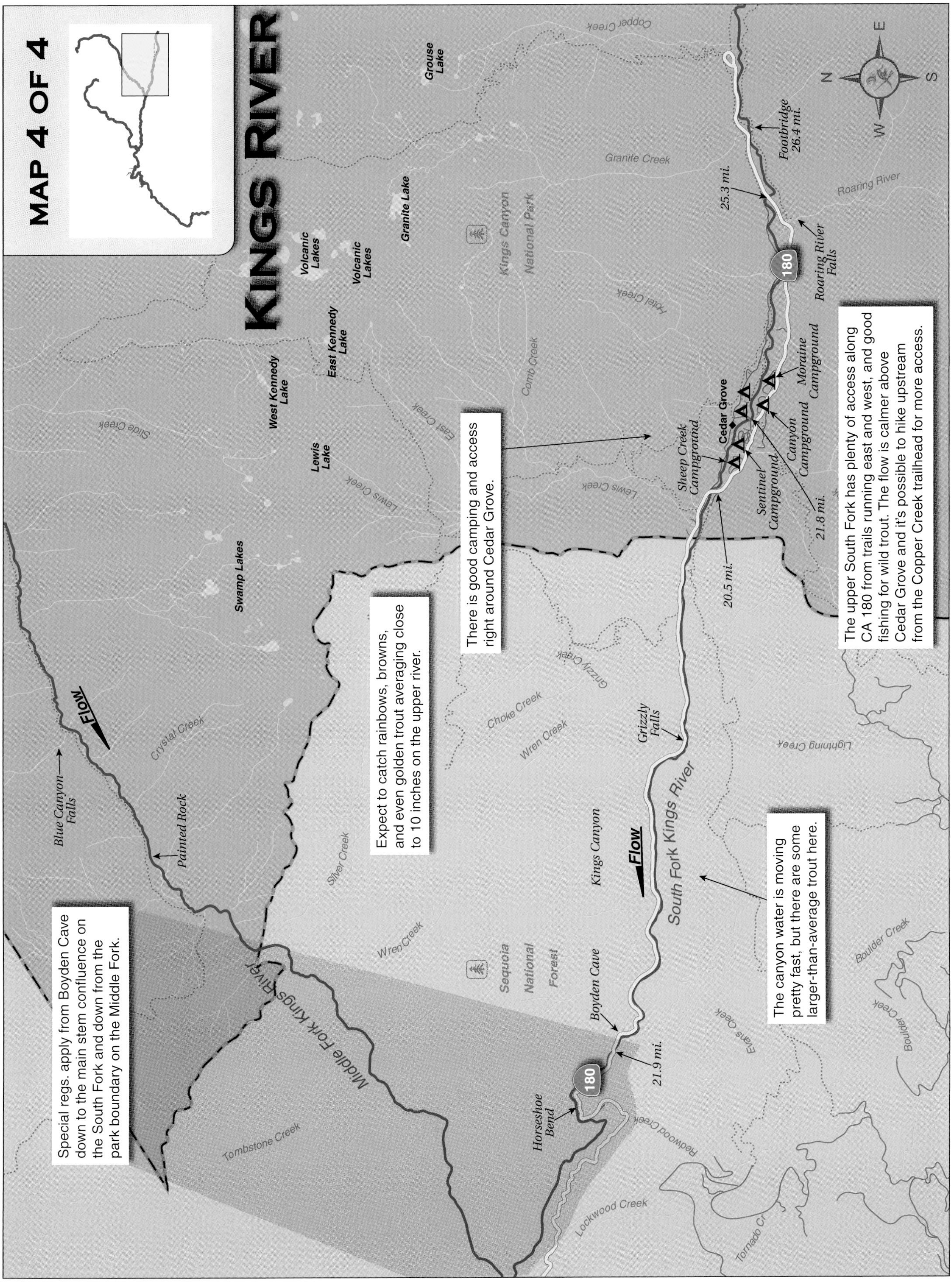
MAP 4 OF 4
KINGS RIVER
Special regs. apply from Boyden Cave down to the main stem confluence on the South Fork and down from the park boundary on the Middle Fork.
Expect to catch rainbows, browns, and even golden trout averaging close to 10 inches on the upper river.
There is good camping and access right around Cedar Grove.
The canyon water is moving pretty fast, but there are some larger-than-average trout here.
The upper South Fork has plenty of access along CA 180 from trails running east and west, and good fishing for wild trout. The flow is calmer above Cedar Grove and it's possible to hike upstream from the Copper Creek trailhead for more access.
Blue Canyon Falls
Painted Rock
Crystal Creek
FLOW
Swamp Lakes
West Kennedy Lake
East Kennedy Lake
Lewis Lake
Volcanic Lakes
Volcanic Lakes
Granite Lake
Grouse Lake
Slide Creek
Lewis Creek
East Creek
Comb Creek
Kings Canyon National Park
Hotel Creek
Granite Creek
Copper Creek
Roaring River
Roaring River Falls
Footbridge 26.4 mi.
25.3 mi.
180
Cedar Grove
Sheep Creek Campground
Sentinel Campground
Canyon Campground
Moraine Campground
21.8 mi.
20.5 mi.
Grizzly Creek
Choke Creek
Wren Creek
Grizzly Falls
Lightning Creek
Silver Creek
Kings Canyon
Flow
South Fork Kings River
Wren Creek
Sequoia National Forest
Boyden Cave
21.9 mi.
180
Horseshoe Bend
Middle Fork Kings River
Tombstone Creek
Evans Creek
Boulder Creek
Boulder Creek
Redwood Creek
Lockwood Creek
Tornado Cr
N
S
E
W

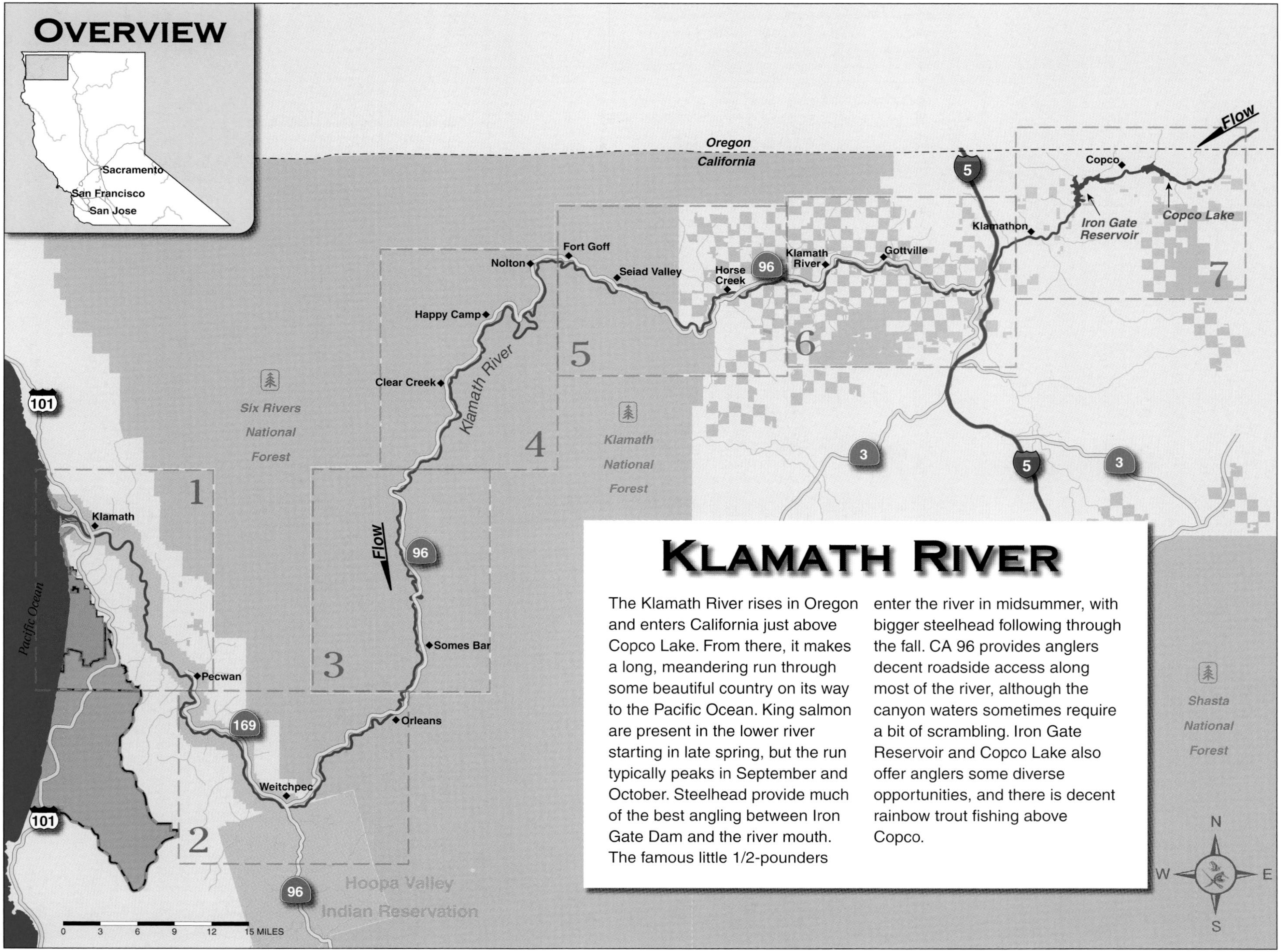

Klamath River

The Klamath River rises in Oregon and enters California just above Copco Lake. From there, it makes a long, meandering run through some beautiful country on its way to the Pacific Ocean. King salmon are present in the lower river starting in late spring, but the run typically peaks in September and October. Steelhead provide much of the best angling between Iron Gate Dam and the river mouth. The famous little 1/2-pounders enter the river in midsummer, with bigger steelhead following through the fall. CA 96 provides anglers decent roadside access along most of the river, although the canyon waters sometimes require a bit of scrambling. Iron Gate Reservoir and Copco Lake also offer anglers some diverse opportunities, and there is decent rainbow trout fishing above Copco.

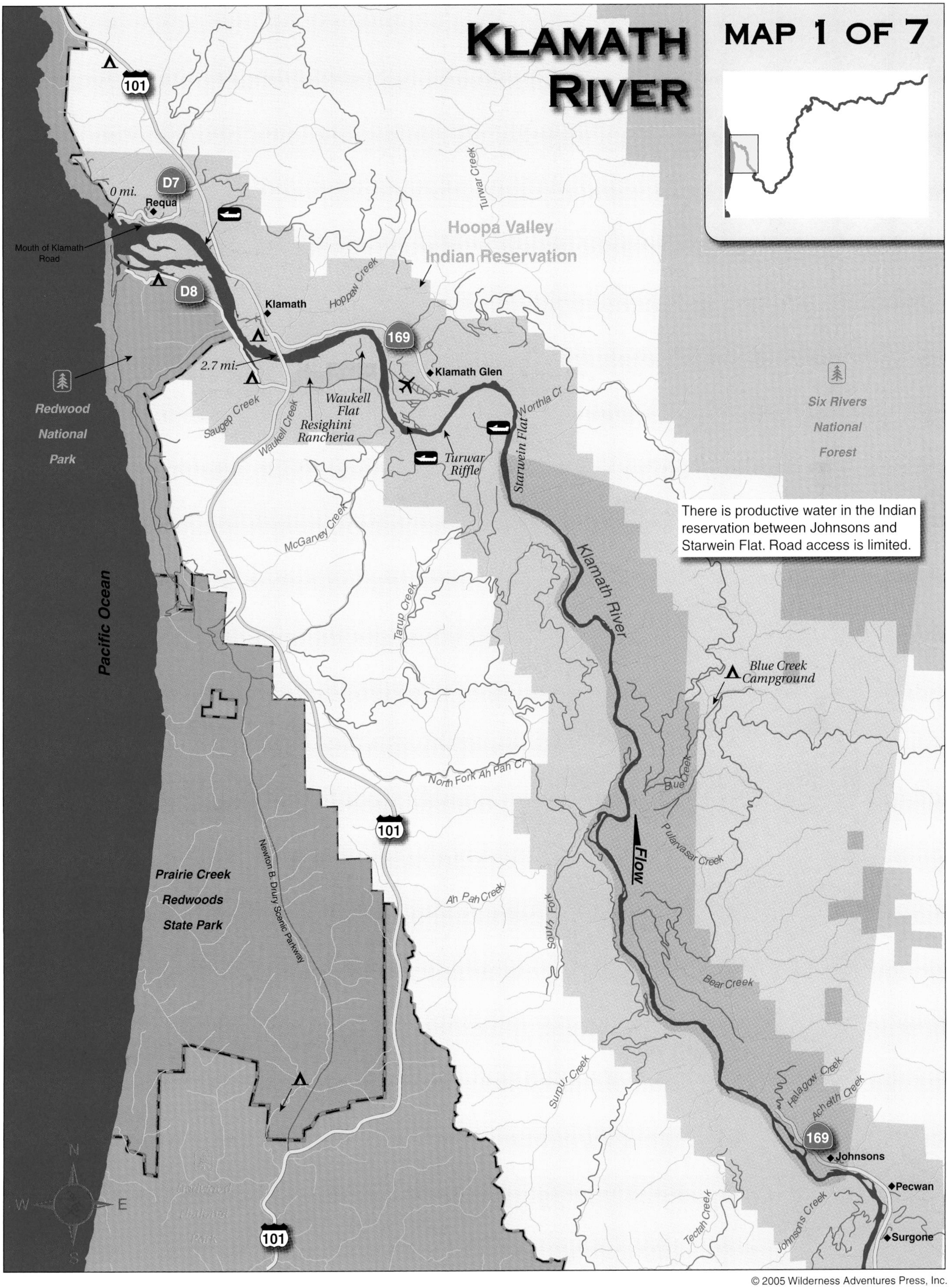
Klamath River
Map 1 of 7
Hoopa Valley
Indian Reservation
Six Rivers
National
Forest
Redwood
National
Park
Pacific Ocean
Prairie Creek
Redwoods
State Park
There is productive water in the Indian reservation between Johnsons and Starwein Flat. Road access is limited.
0 mi.
Requa
D7
D8
101
169
Mouth of Klamath Road
Klamath
Hoppaw Creek
2.7 mi.
Klamath Glen
Waukell Flat
Resighini Rancheria
Saugep Creek
Waukell Creek
Turwar Riffle
Turwar Creek
Starwein Flat
Northla Cr
McGarvey Creek
Tarup Creek
Klamath River
Blue Creek Campground
Blue Creek
North Fork Ah Pah Cr
Flow
Pularvasar Creek
Ah Pah Creek
South Fork
Newton B. Drury Scenic Parkway
Bear Creek
Surpur Creek
Halagow Creek
Acheth Creek
Johnsons
Pecwan
Surgone
Johnsons Creek
Tectah Creek
N
S
E
W

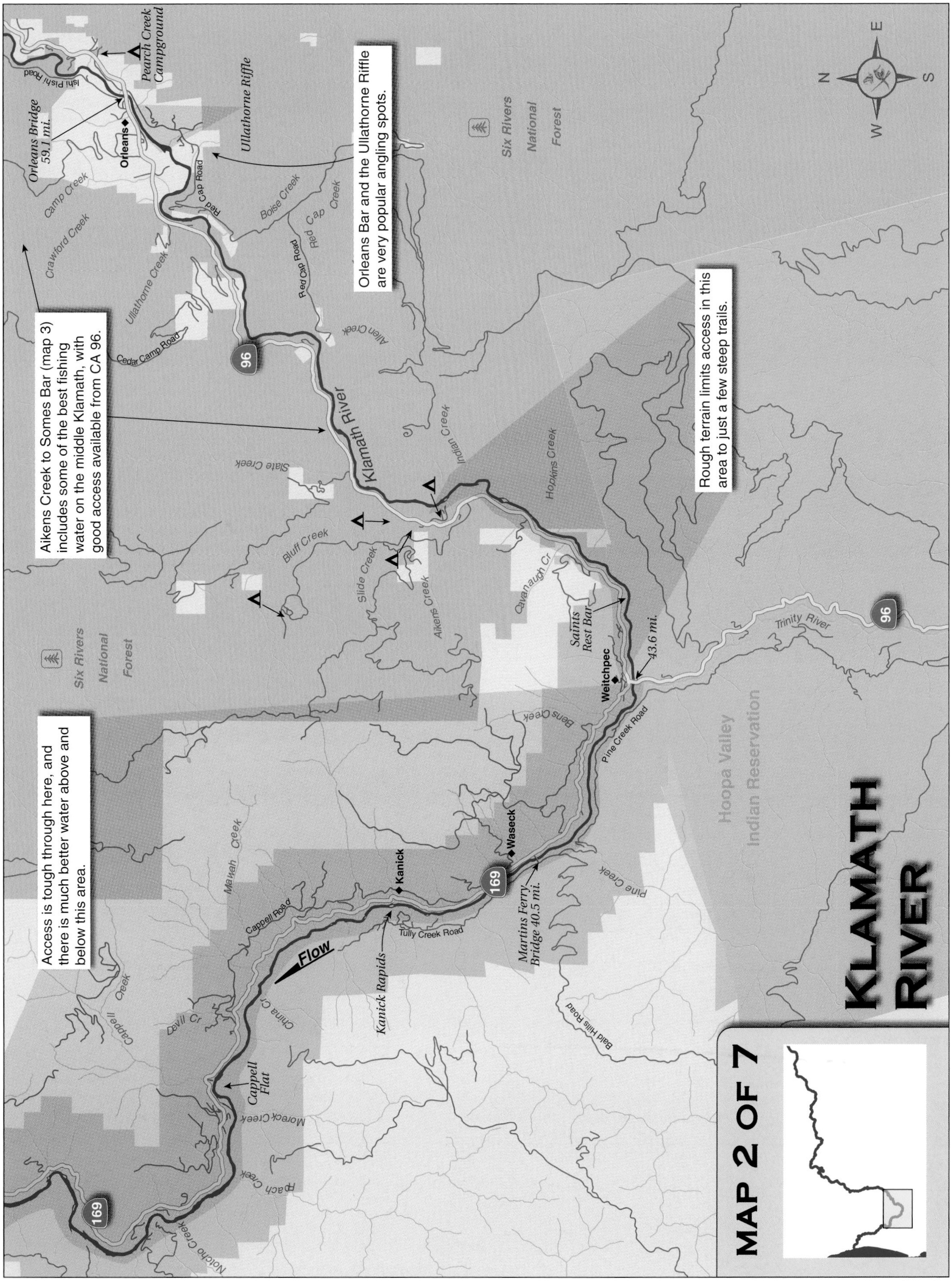
KLAMATH RIVER
MAP 2 OF 7
Access is tough through here, and there is much better water above and below this area.
Aikens Creek to Somes Bar (map 3) includes some of the best fishing water on the middle Klamath, with good access available from CA 96.
Orleans Bar and the Ullathorne Riffle are very popular angling spots.
Rough terrain limits access in this area to just a few steep trails.
Orleans Bridge 59.1 mi.
Pearch Creek Campground
Ishi Pishi Road
Orleans
Ullathorne Riffle
Camp Creek
Crawford Creek
Red Cap Road
Boise Creek
Red Cap Creek
Ullathorne Creek
Cedar Camp Road
Allen Creek
Klamath River
Six Rivers National Forest
Slate Creek
Indian Creek
Hopkins Creek
Bluff Creek
Slide Creek
Aikens Creek
Cavanaugh Cr.
Saints Rest Bar
43.6 mi.
Weitchpec
Trinity River
96
Bens Creek
Pine Creek Road
Hoopa Valley Indian Reservation
Mawah Creek
Waseck
Kanick
169
Cappell Road
Tully Creek Road
Martins Ferry Bridge 40.5 mi.
Pine Creek
Flow
Kanick Rapids
Cappell Creek
Devil Cr
China Cr
Bald Hills Road
Cappell Flat
Moreck Creek
Roach Creek
Notcho Creek
N
E
S
W

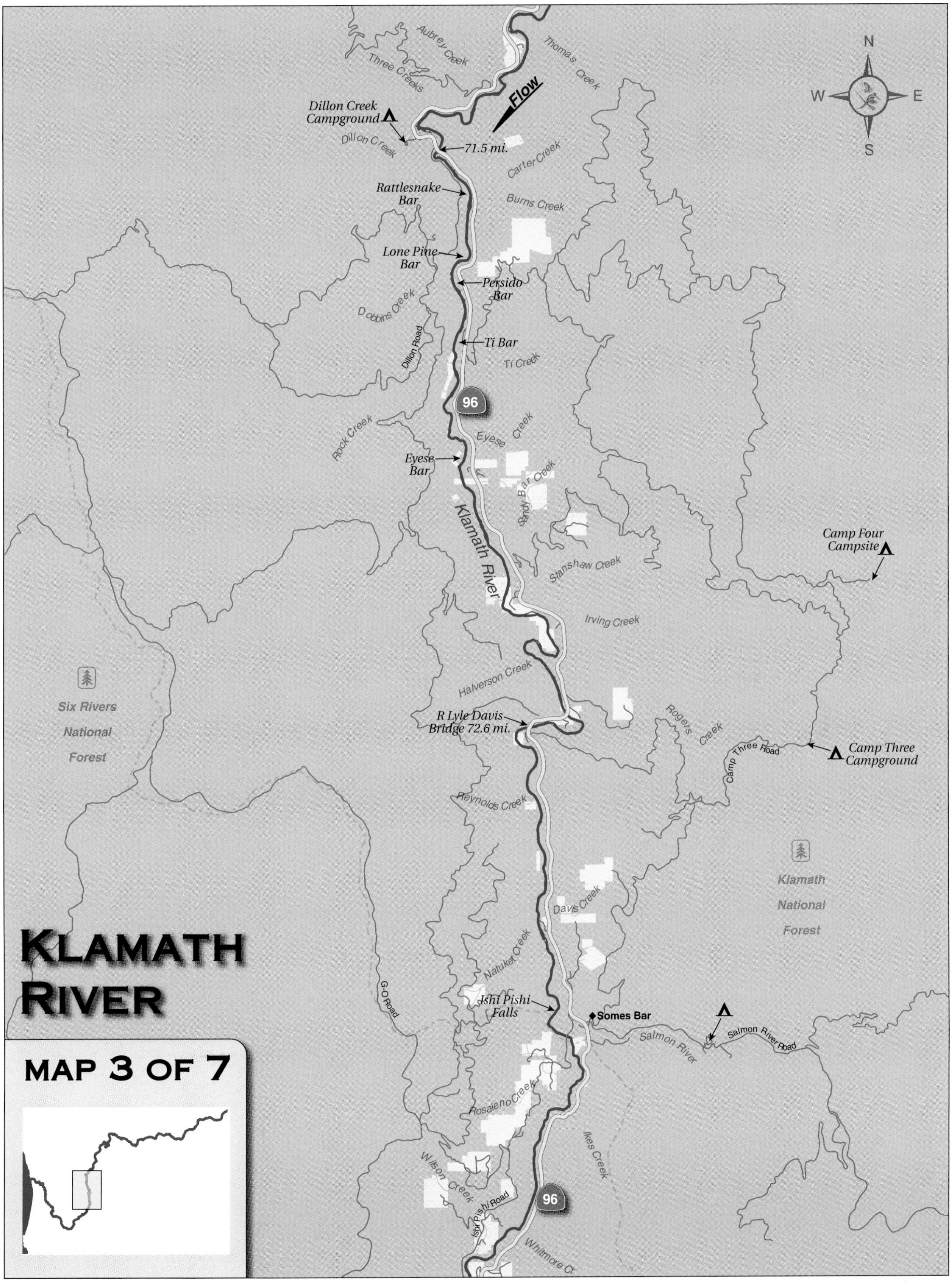

Aubrey Creek
Three Creeks
Thomas Creek
Flow
Dillon Creek Campground
Dillon Creek
71.5 mi.
Carter Creek
Rattlesnake Bar
Burns Creek
Lone Pine Bar
Persido Bar
Dobbins Creek
Dillon Road
Ti Bar
Ti Creek
96
Rock Creek
Eyese Creek
Eyese Bar
Sandy Bar Creek
Klamath River
Camp Four Campsite
Stanshaw Creek
Irving Creek
Six Rivers National Forest
Halverson Creek
R Lyle Davis Bridge 72.6 mi.
Rogers Creek
Camp Three Road
Camp Three Campground
Reynolds Creek
Klamath National Forest
Davis Creek
KLAMATH RIVER
Natuket Creek
G-O Road
Ishi Pishi Falls
Somes Bar
Salmon River
Salmon River Road
MAP 3 OF 7
Rosaleno Creek
Ikes Creek
Wilson Creek
Ishi Pishi Road
Whitmore Cr
N
W
E
S

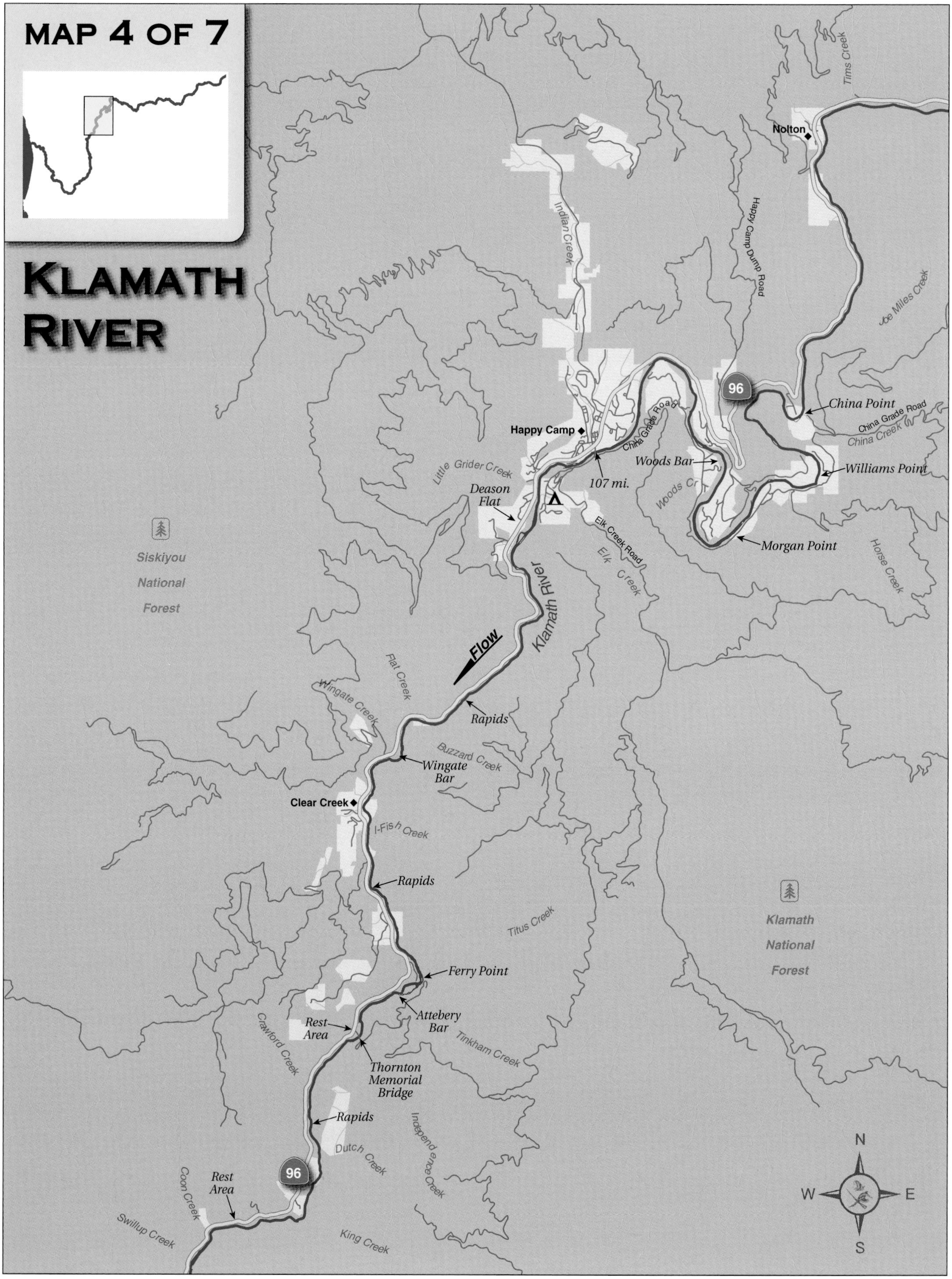
MAP 4 OF 7
KLAMATH RIVER
Nolton
Tims Creek
Happy Camp Dump Road
Indian Creek
Joe Miles Creek
96
China Point
China Grade Road
China Creek
Happy Camp
China Grade Road
Woods Bar
Williams Point
Little Grider Creek
107 mi.
Woods Cr
Deason Flat
Morgan Point
Elk Creek Road
Elk Creek
Horse Creek
Siskiyou National Forest
Klamath River
Flow
Flat Creek
Wingate Creek
Rapids
Buzzard Creek
Wingate Bar
Clear Creek
I-Fish Creek
Rapids
Titus Creek
Klamath National Forest
Ferry Point
Attebery Bar
Rest Area
Crawford Creek
Tinkham Creek
Thornton Memorial Bridge
Rapids
Independence Creek
Dutch Creek
96
Rest Area
Coon Creek
Swillup Creek
King Creek
N
W
E
S

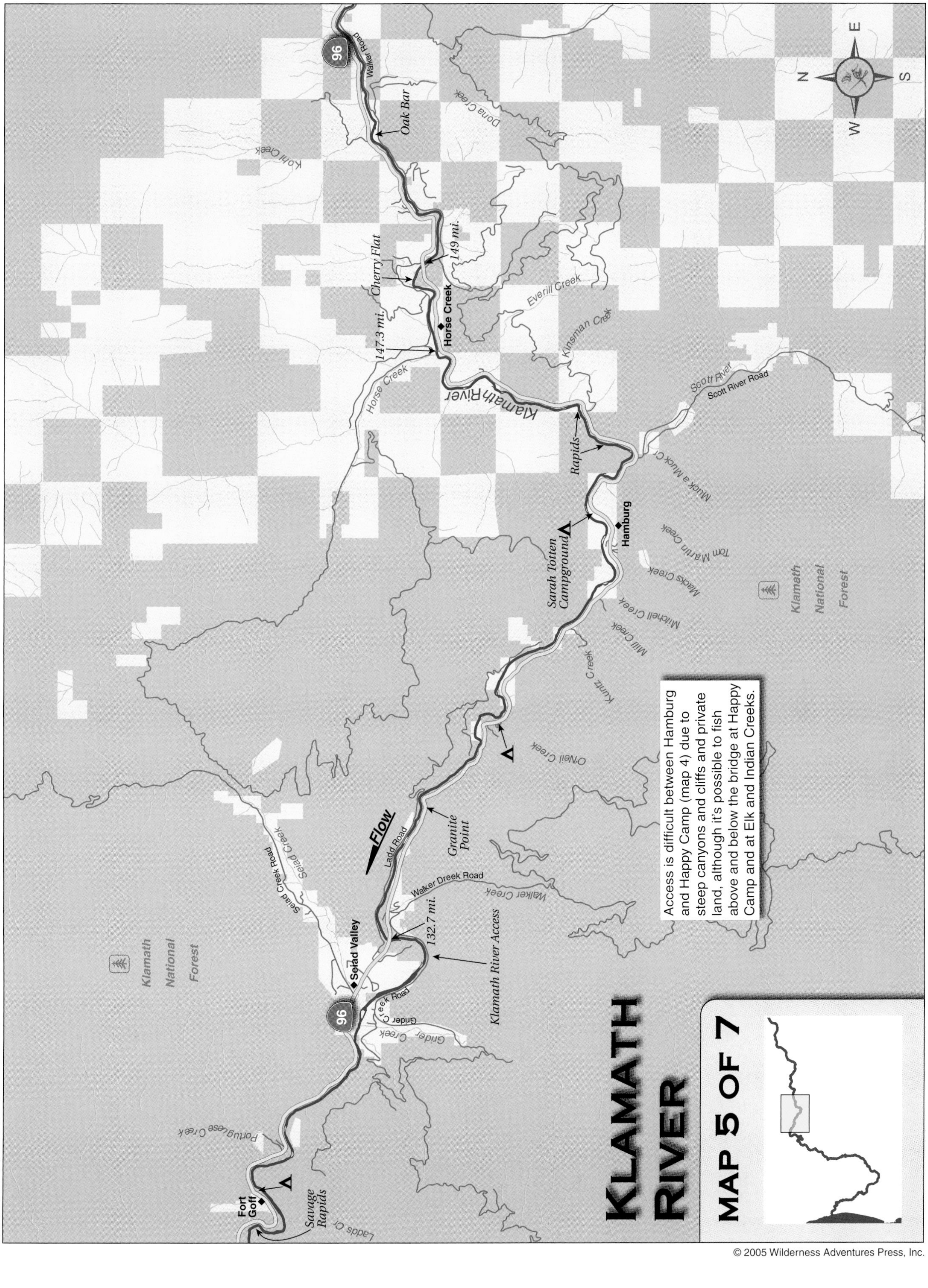
KLAMATH RIVER
MAP 5 OF 7
Access is difficult between Hamburg and Happy Camp (map 4) due to steep canyons and cliffs and private land, although it's possible to fish above and below the bridge at Happy Camp and at Elk and Indian Creeks.
Klamath National Forest
Klamath National Forest
Fort Goff
Savage Rapids
Ladds Cr
Portuguese Creek
96
Grider
Grider Creek
Creek Road
Seiad Valley
Seiad Creek Road
Seiad Creek
Klamath River Access
132.7 mi.
Walker Dreek Road
Walker Creek
Ladd Road
Flow
Granite Point
O'Neil Creek
Kuntz Creek
Mill Creek
Mitchell Creek
Macks Creek
Tom Martin Creek
Sarah Totten Campground
Hamburg
Muck a Muck Cr
Rapids
Scott River
Scott River Road
Klamath River
Horse Creek
Kinsman Creek
Everill Creek
147.3 mi.
Horse Creek
Cherry Flat
149 mi.
Oak Bar
Dona Creek
Kohl Creek
Walker Road
96
N
E
S
W

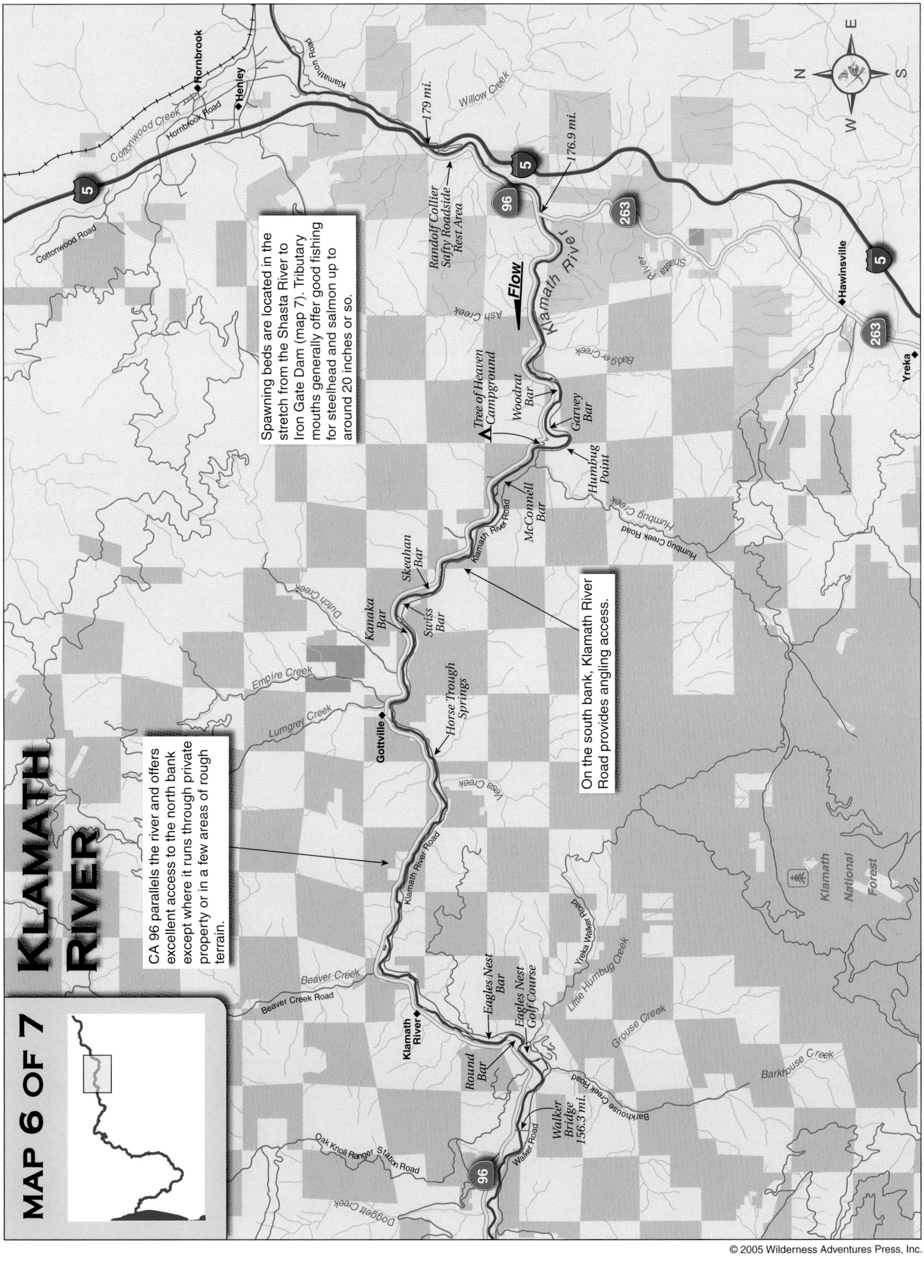
MAP 6 OF 7
KLAMATH RIVER
CA 96 parallels the river and offers excellent access to the north bank except where it runs through private property or in a few areas of rough terrain.
Spawning beds are located in the stretch from the Shasta River to Iron Gate Dam (map 7). Tributary mouths generally offer good fishing for steelhead and salmon up to around 20 inches or so.
On the south bank, Klamath River Road provides angling access.
Klamath River
Flow
Klamath River Road
Hornbrook
Henley
Hornbrook Road
Cottonwood Creek
Cottonwood Road
Klamathon Road
Willow Creek
179 mi.
176.9 mi.
Randolf Collier Safty Roadside Rest Area
Shasta River
Hawinsville
Yreka
Ash Creek
Badger Creek
Tree of Heaven Campground
Woodrat Bar
Garvey Bar
Humbug Point
Humbug Creek
Humbug Creek Road
McConnell Bar
Skeahan Bar
Swiss Bar
Kanaka Bar
Dutch Creek
Empire Creek
Lumgrey Creek
Gottville
Horse Trough Springs
Vesa Creek
Klamath National Forest
Yreka Walker Road
Little Humbug Creek
Beaver Creek
Beaver Creek Road
Eagles Nest Bar
Eagles Nest Golf Course
Klamath River
Round Bar
Grouse Creek
Barkhouse Creek
Barkhouse Creek Road
Walker Bridge 156.3 mi.
Walker Road
Oak Knoll Ranger Station Road
Doggett Creek
N
E
S
W

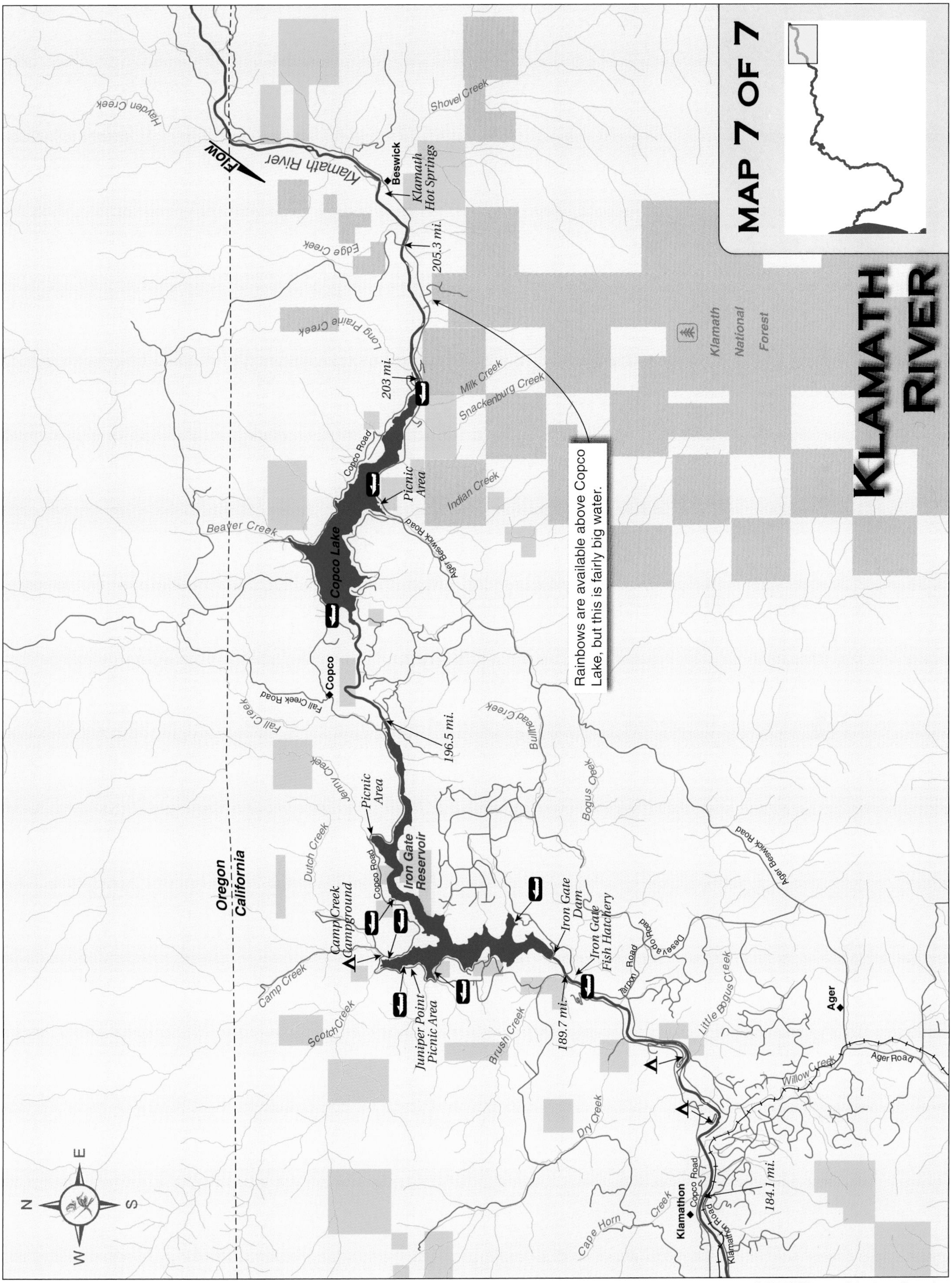
MAP 7 OF 7
KLAMATH RIVER
Klamath National Forest
Rainbows are available above Copco Lake, but this is fairly big water.
Flow
Klamath River
Beswick
Klamath Hot Springs
205.3 mi.
203 mi.
196.5 mi.
189.7 mi.
184.1 mi.
Copco Lake
Copco
Copco Road
Picnic Area
Iron Gate Reservoir
Iron Gate Dam
Iron Gate Fish Hatchery
Camp Creek Campground
Juniper Point Picnic Area
Oregon
California
Ager
Ager Road
Ager Beswick Road
Klamathon
Klamathon Road
Tarpon Road
Fall Creek Road
Hayden Creek
Shovel Creek
Edge Creek
Long Praire Creek
Milk Creek
Snackenburg Creek
Indian Creek
Beaver Creek
Fall Creek
Bullhead Creek
Jenny Creek
Dutch Creek
Bogus Creek
Camp Creek
Scotch Creek
Brush Creek
Little Bogus Creek
Willow Creek
Dry Creek
Cape Horn Creek
N
E
S
W

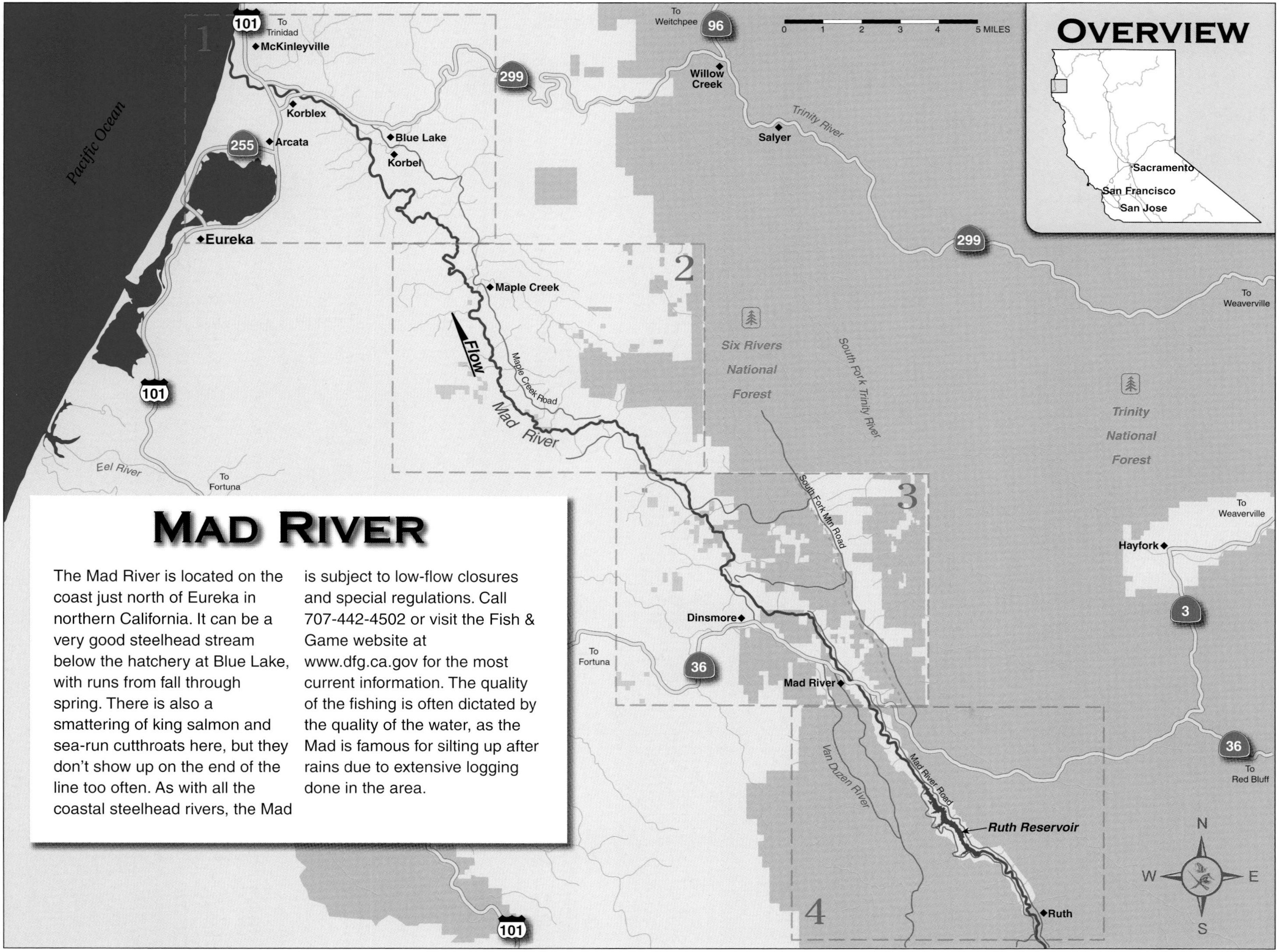

MAD RIVER

The Mad River is located on the coast just north of Eureka in northern California. It can be a very good steelhead stream below the hatchery at Blue Lake, with runs from fall through spring. There is also a smattering of king salmon and sea-run cutthroats here, but they don't show up on the end of the line too often. As with all the coastal steelhead rivers, the Mad is subject to low-flow closures and special regulations. Call 707-442-4502 or visit the Fish & Game website at www.dfg.ca.gov for the most current information. The quality of the fishing is often dictated by the quality of the water, as the Mad is famous for silting up after rains due to extensive logging done in the area.

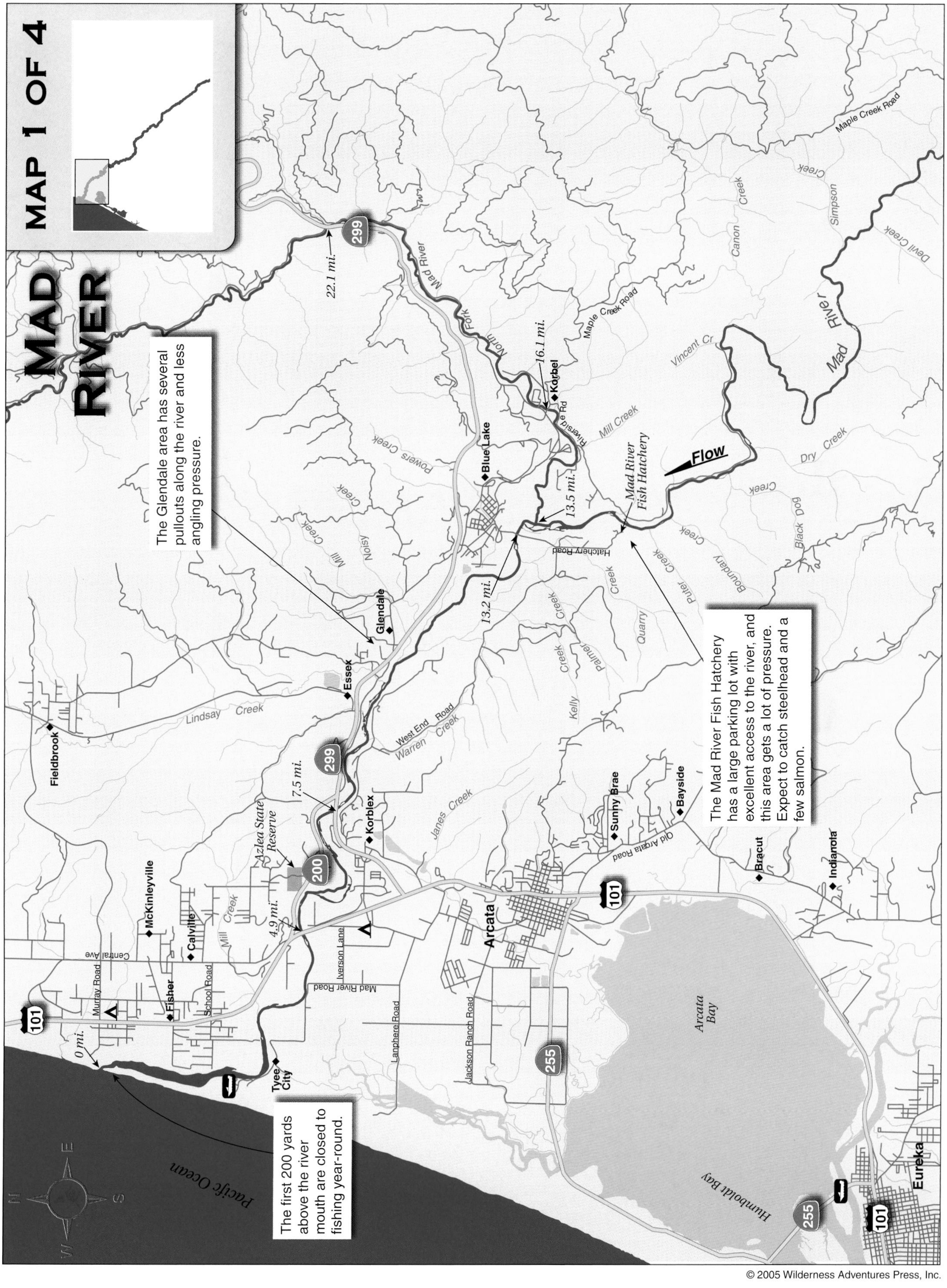
MAP 1 OF 4
MAD RIVER
The Glendale area has several pullouts along the river and less angling pressure.
The Mad River Fish Hatchery has a large parking lot with excellent access to the river, and this area gets a lot of pressure. Expect to catch steelhead and a few salmon.
The first 200 yards above the river mouth are closed to fishing year-round.
Flow
Mad River Fish Hatchery
0 mi.
4.9 mi.
7.5 mi.
13.2 mi.
13.5 mi.
16.1 mi.
22.1 mi.
Pacific Ocean
Arcata Bay
Humboldt Bay
Azlea State Reserve
Fieldbrook
McKinleyville
Calville
Fisher
Tyee City
Korblex
Essex
Glendale
Blue Lake
Korbel
Arcata
Sunny Brae
Bayside
Bracut
Indianola
Eureka
Central Ave
Murray Road
School Road
Iverson Lane
Mad River Road
Lanphere Road
Jackson Ranch Road
Old Arcata Road
West End Road
Hatchery Road
Riverside Rd
Maple Creek Road
Lindsay Creek
Mill Creek
Warren Creek
Janes Creek
Kelly Creek
Palmer Creek
Quarry Creek
Puter Creek
Boundary Creek
Black Dog Creek
Dry Creek
Mill Creek
Vincent Cr
Powers Creek
Noisy Creek
Canon Creek
Simpson Creek
Devil Creek
North Fork Mad River
Mad River
101
299
200
255

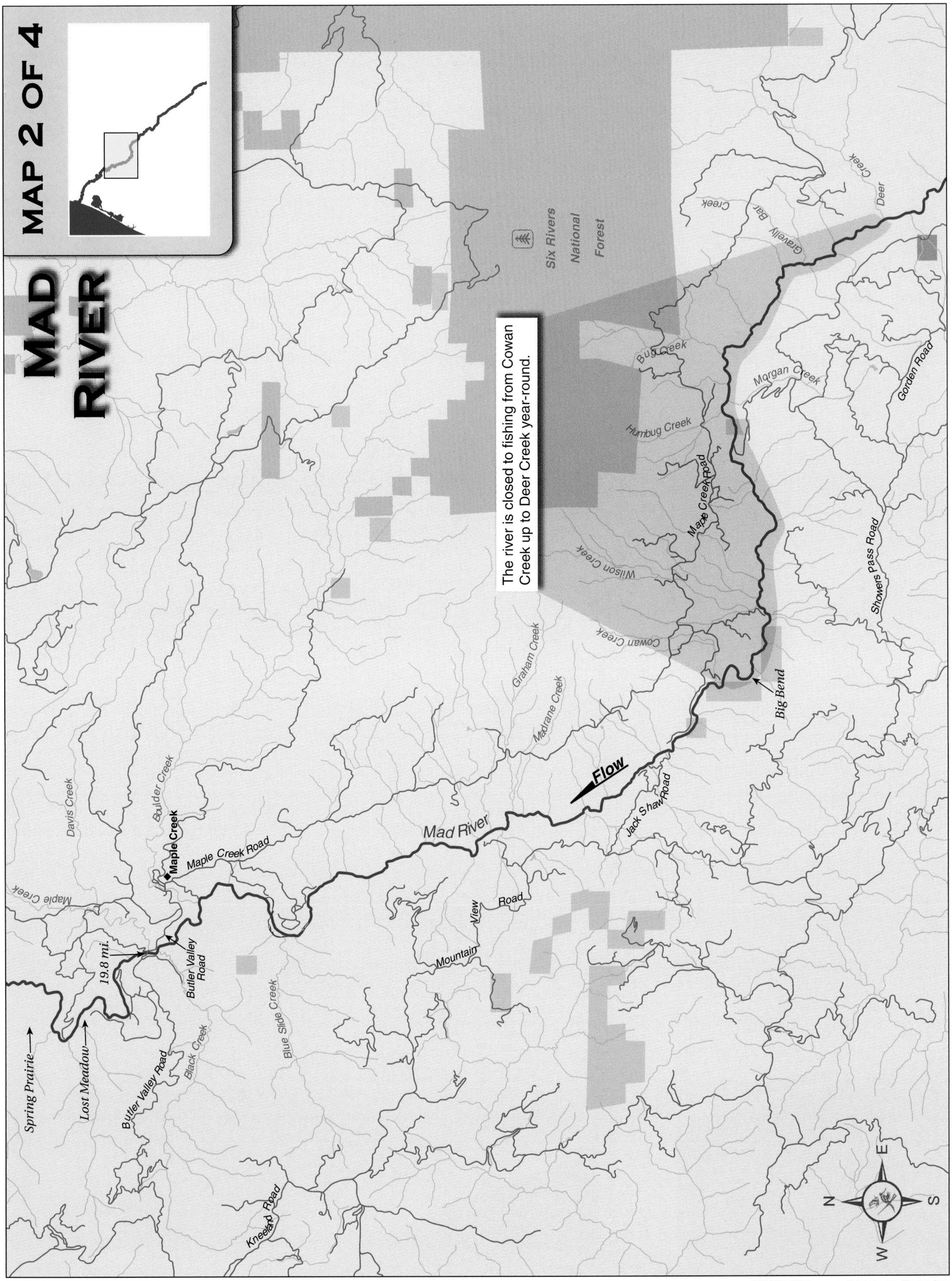
MAP 2 OF 4
MAD RIVER
Six Rivers National Forest
The river is closed to fishing from Cowan Creek up to Deer Creek year-round.
Deer Creek
Gravelly Bar Creek
Bug Creek
Morgan Creek
Gordon Road
Humbug Creek
Maple Creek Road
Wilson Creek
Showers Pass Road
Cowan Creek
Graham Creek
Madrane Creek
Big Bend
Flow
Jack Shaw Road
Mad River
Maple Creek Road
Maple Creek
Boulder Creek
Davis Creek
Maple Creek
Mountain View Road
19.8 mi.
Butler Valley Road
Blue Slide Creek
Black Creek
Spring Prairie
Lost Meadow
Butler Valley Road
Kneeland Road
N
E
S
W

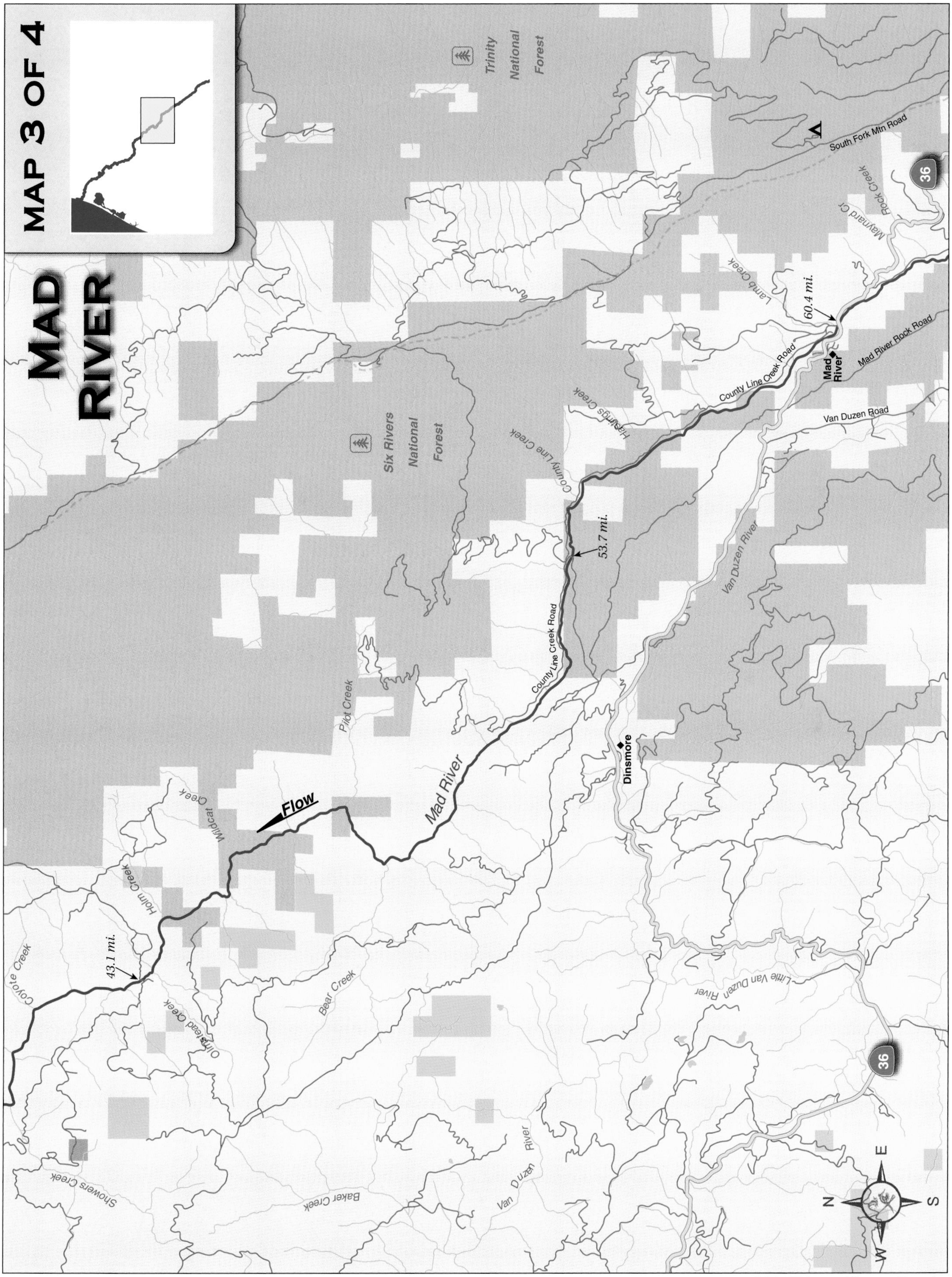
MAP 3 OF 4
MAD RIVER
Trinity National Forest
Six Rivers National Forest
South Fork Mtn Road
36
Rock Creek
Maynard Cr
Lamb Creek
60.4 mi.
Mad River Rock Road
Mad River
County Line Creek Road
Hastings Creek
Van Duzen Road
County Line Creek
53.7 mi.
Van Duzen River
County Line Creek Road
Pilot Creek
Dinsmore
Mad River
Flow
Wildcat Creek
Holm Creek
43.1 mi.
Coyote Creek
Olmstead Creek
Bear Creek
Little Van Duzen River
36
Van Duzen River
Baker Creek
Showers Creek
N
E
S
W

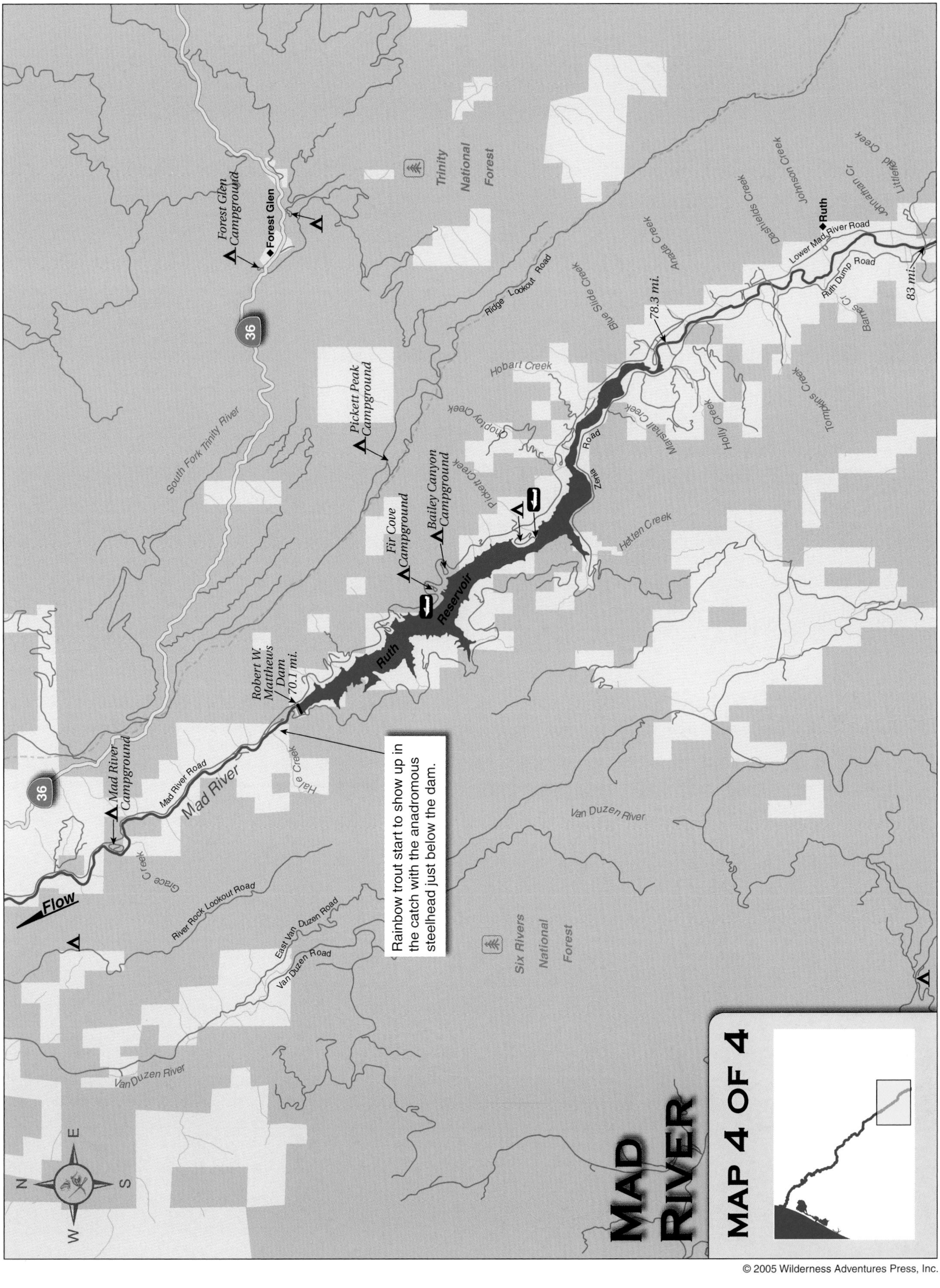
MAD RIVER
MAP 4 OF 4
Rainbow trout start to show up in the catch with the anadromous steelhead just below the dam.
Robert W. Matthews Dam 70.1 mi.
Ruth Reservoir
78.3 mi.
83 mi.
Mad River
Mad River Road
Mad River Campground
Forest Glen Campground
Forest Glen
Pickett Peak Campground
Fir Cove Campground
Bailey Canyon Campground
South Fork Trinity River
Trinity National Forest
Six Rivers National Forest
Ridge Lookout Road
Zenia Road
Lower Mad River Road
Ruth Dump Road
Ruth
River Rock Lookout Road
East Van Duzen Road
Van Duzen Road
Van Duzen River
Grace Creek
Hale Creek
Pickett Creek
Choptoy Creek
Hobart Creek
Hetten Creek
Marshall Creek
Holly Creek
Tompkins Creek
Barnes Cr.
Blue Slide Creek
Anada Creek
Dashields Creek
Johnson Creek
Johnathan Cr
Littlefield Creek
Flow
36
N
E
S
W

Mattole River

Pressure is generally light on the Mattole because it's a long drive from any major towns. The steelhead are relatively large though, and they're usually in the river from around December or January through March, depending on water levels. Access is fairly good from the mouth upstream to the upper limit at Honeydew Creek. It's possible to launch boats at several points and wade access is available from spur roads.

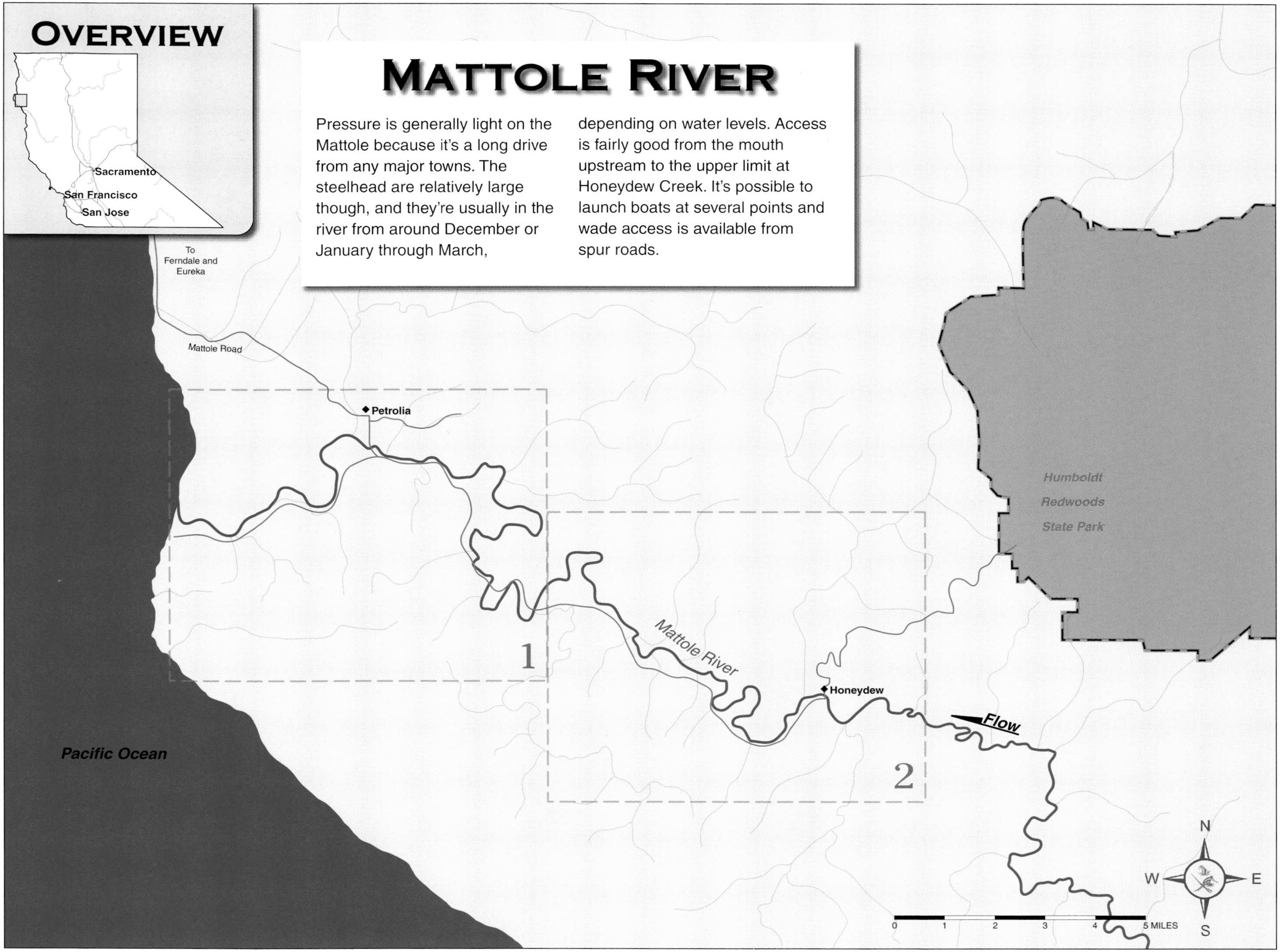

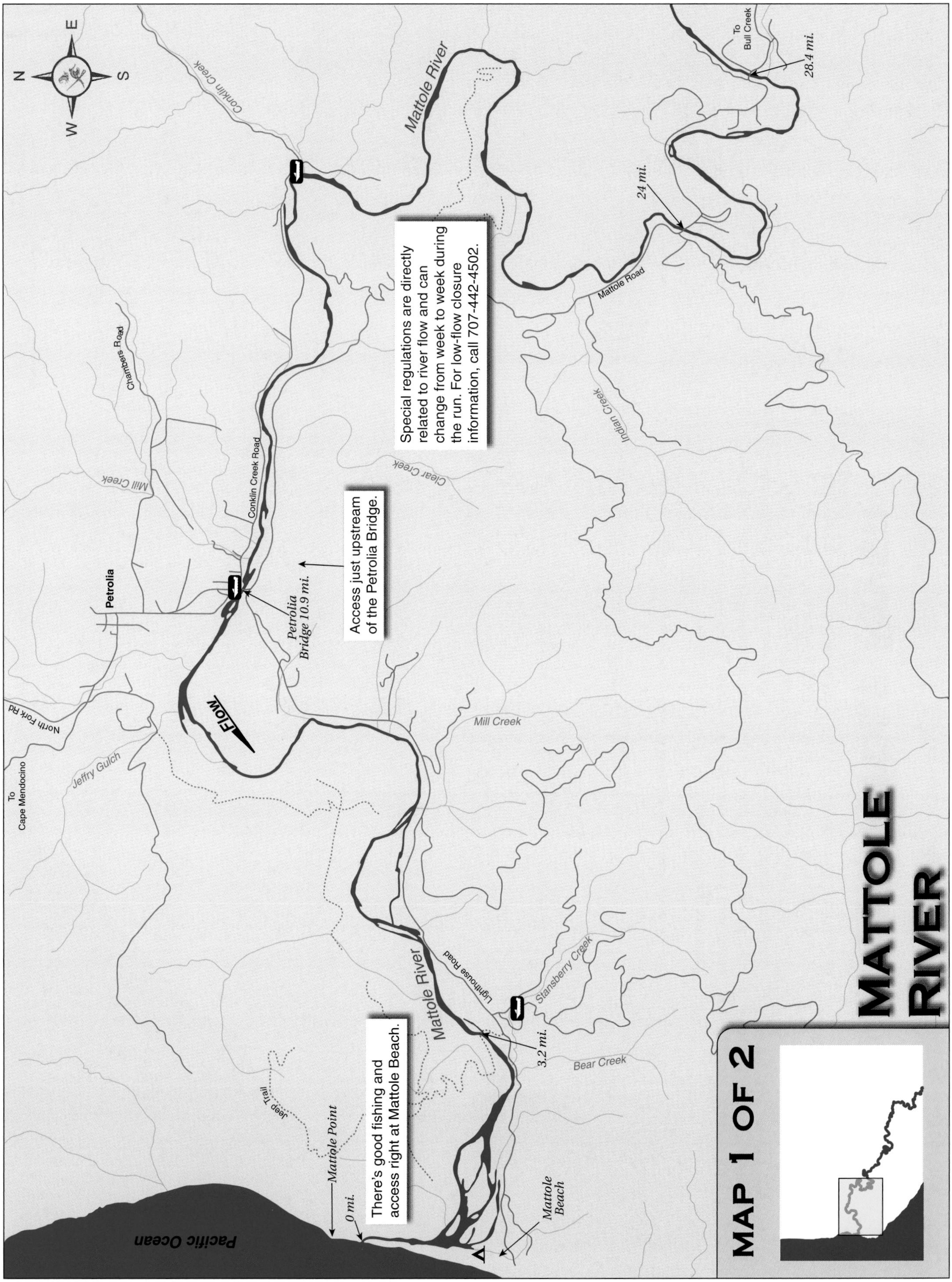
MATTOLE RIVER
MAP 1 OF 2
N
E
S
W
Pacific Ocean
Mattole Point
0 mi.
There's good fishing and access right at Mattole Beach.
Mattole Beach
Jeep Trail
Mattole River
Lighthouse Road
Stansberry Creek
Bear Creek
3.2 mi.
Jeffry Gulch
To Cape Mendocino
North Fork Rd
Flow
Mill Creek
Petrolia
Petrolia Bridge 10.9 mi.
Access just upstream of the Petrolia Bridge.
Conklin Creek Road
Mill Creek
Clear Creek
Chambers Road
Special regulations are directly related to river flow and can change from week to week during the run. For low-flow closure information, call 707-442-4502.
Indian Creek
Mattole Road
Conklin Creek
Mattole River
24 mi.
To Bull Creek
28.4 mi.

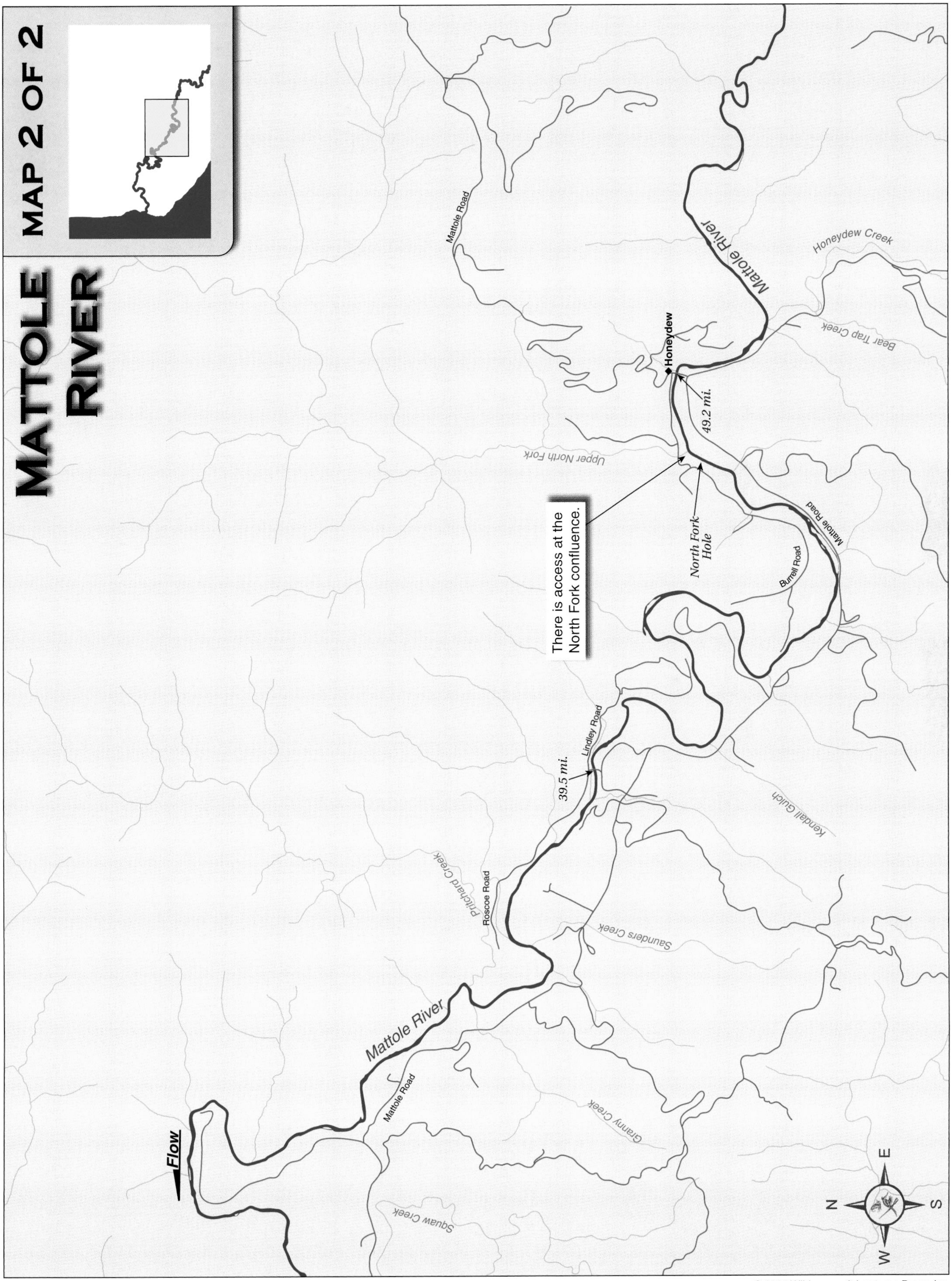
Mattole River
Map 2 of 2
Mattole Road
Mattole River
Honeydew Creek
Bear Trap Creek
Honeydew
49.2 mi.
Upper North Fork
There is access at the North Fork confluence.
North Fork Hole
Mattole Road
Burrell Road
Lindley Road
39.5 mi.
Kendall Gulch
Pritchard Creek
Roscoe Road
Saunders Creek
Mattole River
Mattole Road
Granny Creek
Flow
Squaw Creek
N
E
S
W

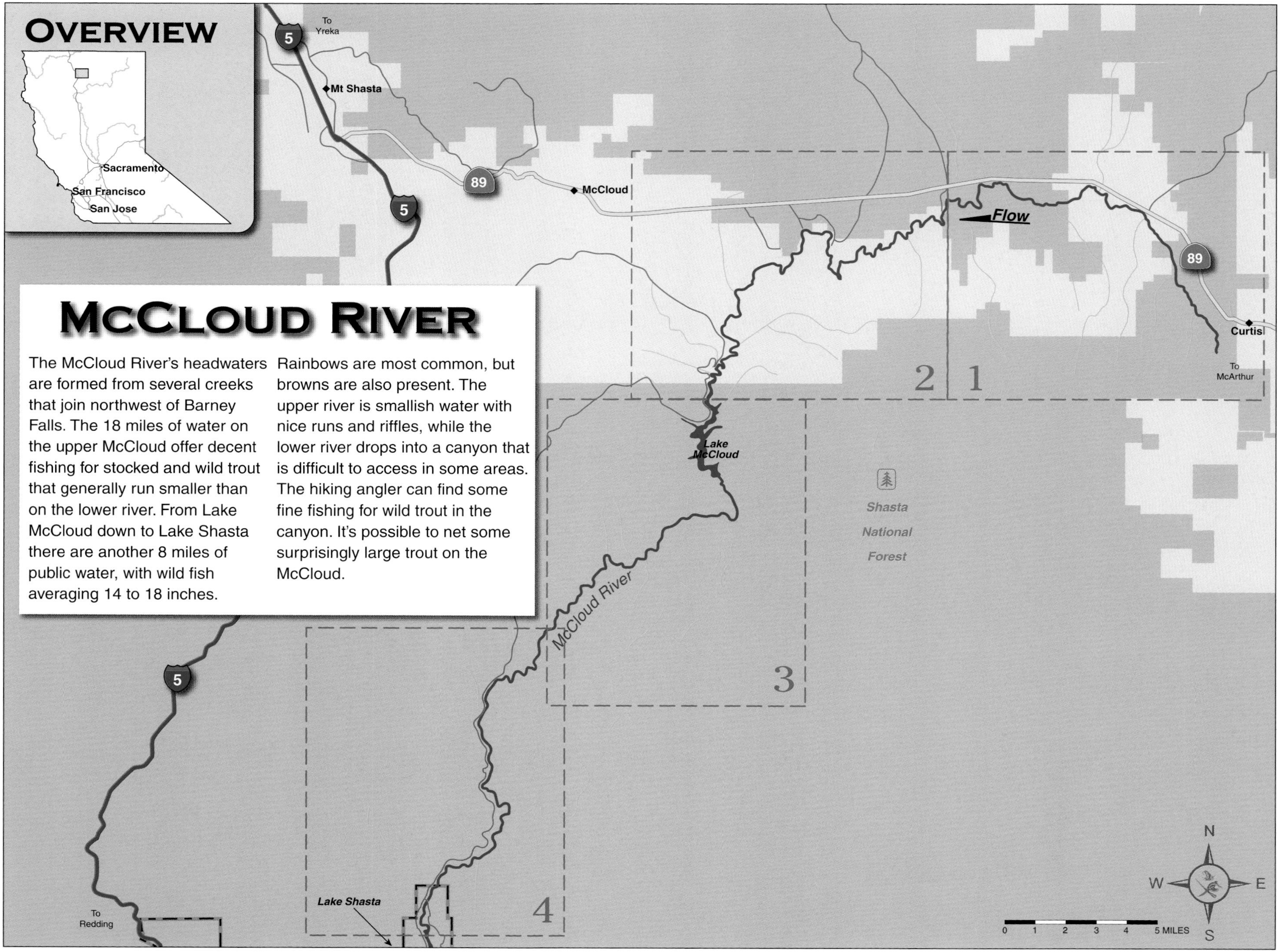

McCloud River

The McCloud River's headwaters are formed from several creeks that join northwest of Barney Falls. The 18 miles of water on the upper McCloud offer decent fishing for stocked and wild trout that generally run smaller than on the lower river. From Lake McCloud down to Lake Shasta there are another 8 miles of public water, with wild fish averaging 14 to 18 inches.

Rainbows are most common, but browns are also present. The upper river is smallish water with nice runs and riffles, while the lower river drops into a canyon that is difficult to access in some areas. The hiking angler can find some fine fishing for wild trout in the canyon. It's possible to net some surprisingly large trout on the McCloud.

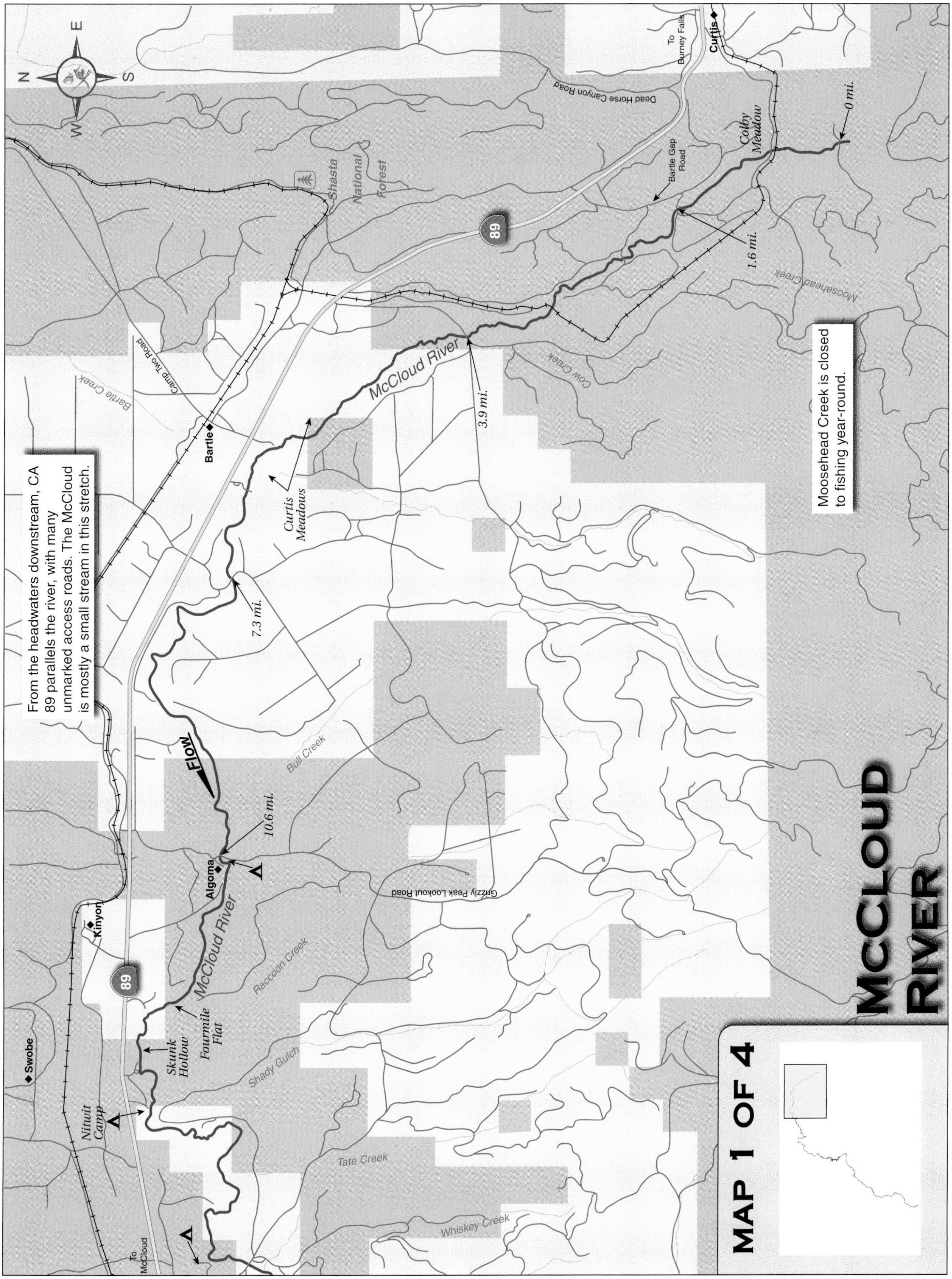
McCLOUD RIVER
MAP 1 OF 4
From the headwaters downstream, CA 89 parallels the river, with many unmarked access roads. The McCloud is mostly a small stream in this stretch.
Moosehead Creek is closed to fishing year-round.
N
E
S
W
Shasta National Forest
89
To Burney Falls
Curtis
Dead Horse Canyon Road
Bartle Gap Road
Colby Meadow
0 mi.
1.6 mi.
Moosehead Creek
Cow Creek
3.9 mi.
McCloud River
Camp Two Road
Bartle Creek
Bartle
Curtis Meadows
7.3 mi.
Flow
Bull Creek
10.6 mi.
Algoma
Grizzly Peak Lookout Road
Kinyon
Raccoon Creek
Fourmile Flat
Skunk Hollow
Swobe
Shady Gulch
Nitwit Camp
Tate Creek
Whiskey Creek
To McCloud

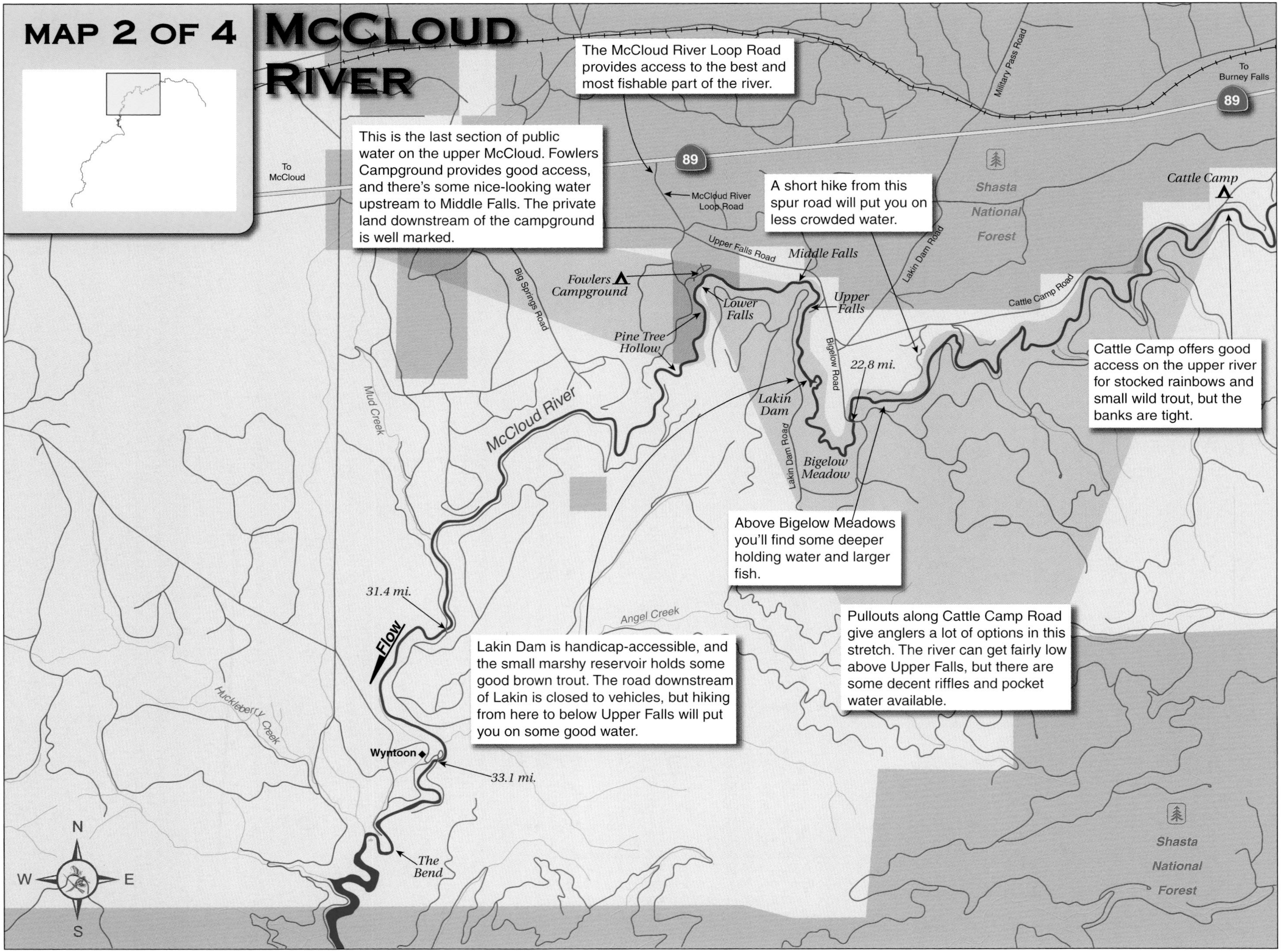
MAP 2 OF 4
McCLOUD RIVER
The McCloud River Loop Road provides access to the best and most fishable part of the river.
This is the last section of public water on the upper McCloud. Fowlers Campground provides good access, and there's some nice-looking water upstream to Middle Falls. The private land downstream of the campground is well marked.
A short hike from this spur road will put you on less crowded water.
Cattle Camp offers good access on the upper river for stocked rainbows and small wild trout, but the banks are tight.
Above Bigelow Meadows you'll find some deeper holding water and larger fish.
Pullouts along Cattle Camp Road give anglers a lot of options in this stretch. The river can get fairly low above Upper Falls, but there are some decent riffles and pocket water available.
Lakin Dam is handicap-accessible, and the small marshy reservoir holds some good brown trout. The road downstream of Lakin is closed to vehicles, but hiking from here to below Upper Falls will put you on some good water.
To McCloud
To Burney Falls
89
Military Pass Road
McCloud River Loop Road
Upper Falls Road
Big Springs Road
Lakin Dam Road
Cattle Camp Road
Bigelow Road
Shasta National Forest
Cattle Camp
Fowlers Campground
Middle Falls
Upper Falls
Lower Falls
Pine Tree Hollow
Lakin Dam
Bigelow Meadow
22.8 mi.
31.4 mi.
33.1 mi.
McCloud River
Mud Creek
Angel Creek
Huckleberry Creek
Flow
Wyntoon
The Bend
N
S
E
W

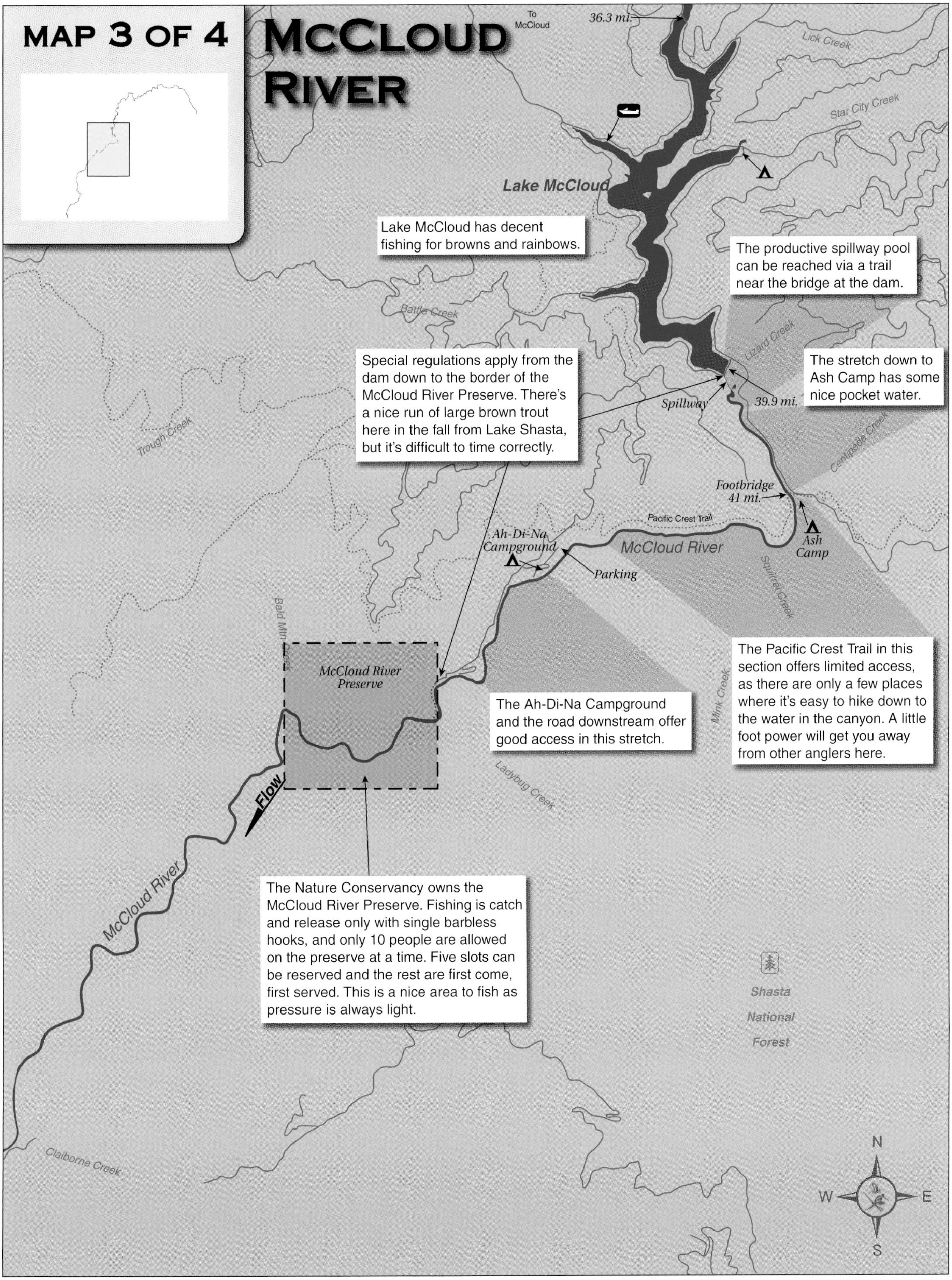

MAP 3 OF 4
McCLOUD RIVER
To McCloud
36.3 mi.
Lick Creek
Star City Creek
Lake McCloud
Lake McCloud has decent fishing for browns and rainbows.
The productive spillway pool can be reached via a trail near the bridge at the dam.
Battle Creek
Lizard Creek
Special regulations apply from the dam down to the border of the McCloud River Preserve. There's a nice run of large brown trout here in the fall from Lake Shasta, but it's difficult to time correctly.
The stretch down to Ash Camp has some nice pocket water.
Spillway
39.9 mi.
Trough Creek
Centipede Creek
Footbridge
41 mi.
Pacific Crest Trail
Ah-Di-Na Campground
McCloud River
Ash Camp
Parking
Squirrel Creek
Bald Mtn Creek
McCloud River Preserve
The Pacific Crest Trail in this section offers limited access, as there are only a few places where it's easy to hike down to the water in the canyon. A little foot power will get you away from other anglers here.
Mink Creek
The Ah-Di-Na Campground and the road downstream offer good access in this stretch.
Flow
Ladybug Creek
McCloud River
The Nature Conservancy owns the McCloud River Preserve. Fishing is catch and release only with single barbless hooks, and only 10 people are allowed on the preserve at a time. Five slots can be reserved and the rest are first come, first served. This is a nice area to fish as pressure is always light.
Shasta National Forest
N
W
E
S
Claiborne Creek

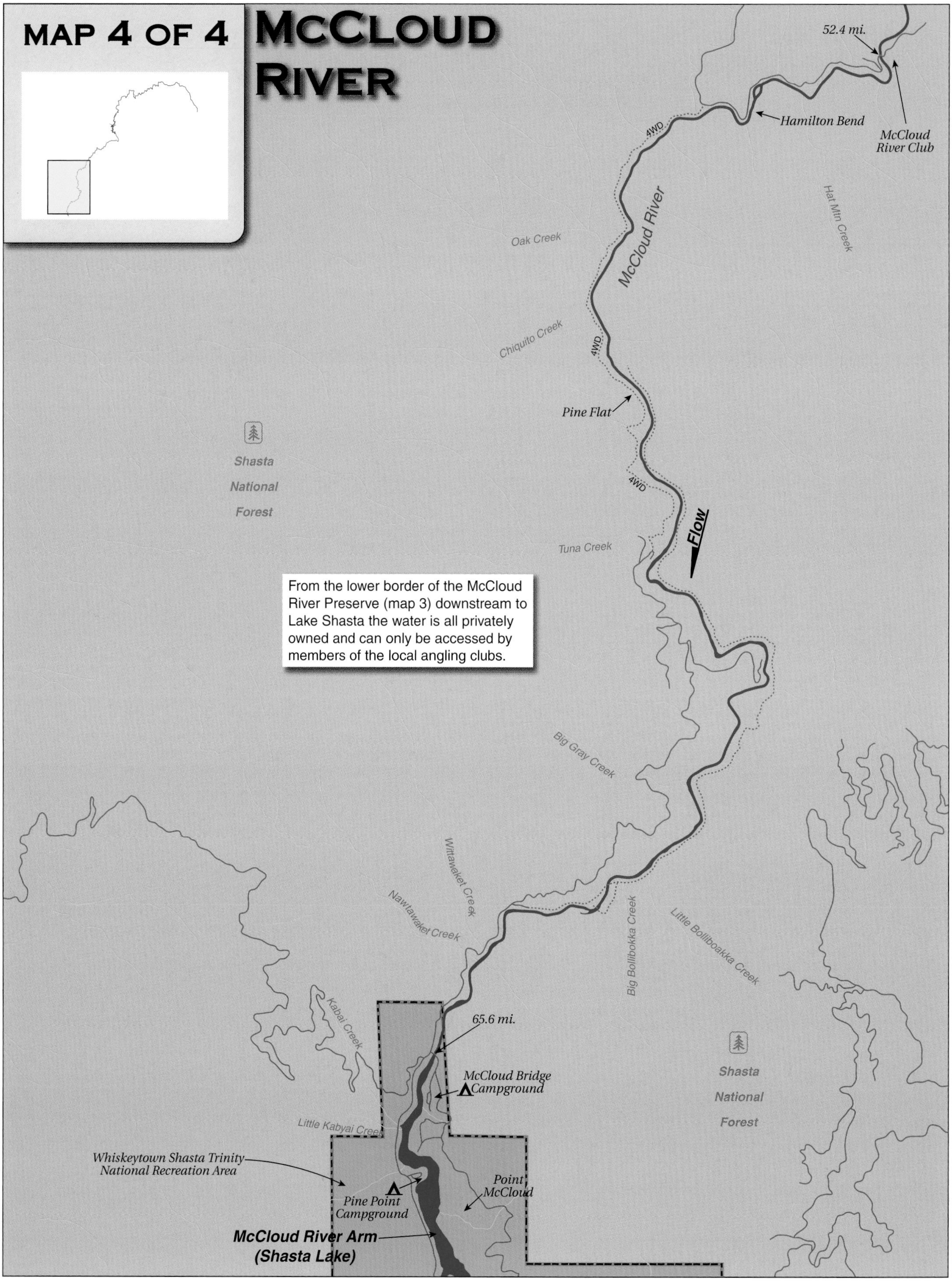
MAP 4 OF 4
McCLOUD RIVER
52.4 mi.
Hamilton Bend
McCloud River Club
4WD
McCloud River
Hat Mtn Creek
Oak Creek
Chiquito Creek
Pine Flat
Shasta National Forest
Flow
Tuna Creek
From the lower border of the McCloud River Preserve (map 3) downstream to Lake Shasta the water is all privately owned and can only be accessed by members of the local angling clubs.
Big Gray Creek
Wittawaket Creek
Nawtawaket Creek
Big Bollibokka Creek
Little Bolliboakka Creek
Kabai Creek
65.6 mi.
McCloud Bridge Campground
Little Kabyai Creek
Whiskeytown Shasta Trinity National Recreation Area
Pine Point Campground
Point McCloud
McCloud River Arm (Shasta Lake)

Merced River

The Merced rises in the backcountry of Yosemite National Park and flows all the way to the San Joaquin River. However, the best trout fishing (medium to small fish) is found from above Lake McClure up into the park. Most of the angling pressure occurs in the roadside section in the park, but there is good hike-in fishing above there and solid fishing in the national forest below the park boundary. Whitewater enthusiasts dominate the water below the park in spring, but by summer the lower flows are more conducive to angling.

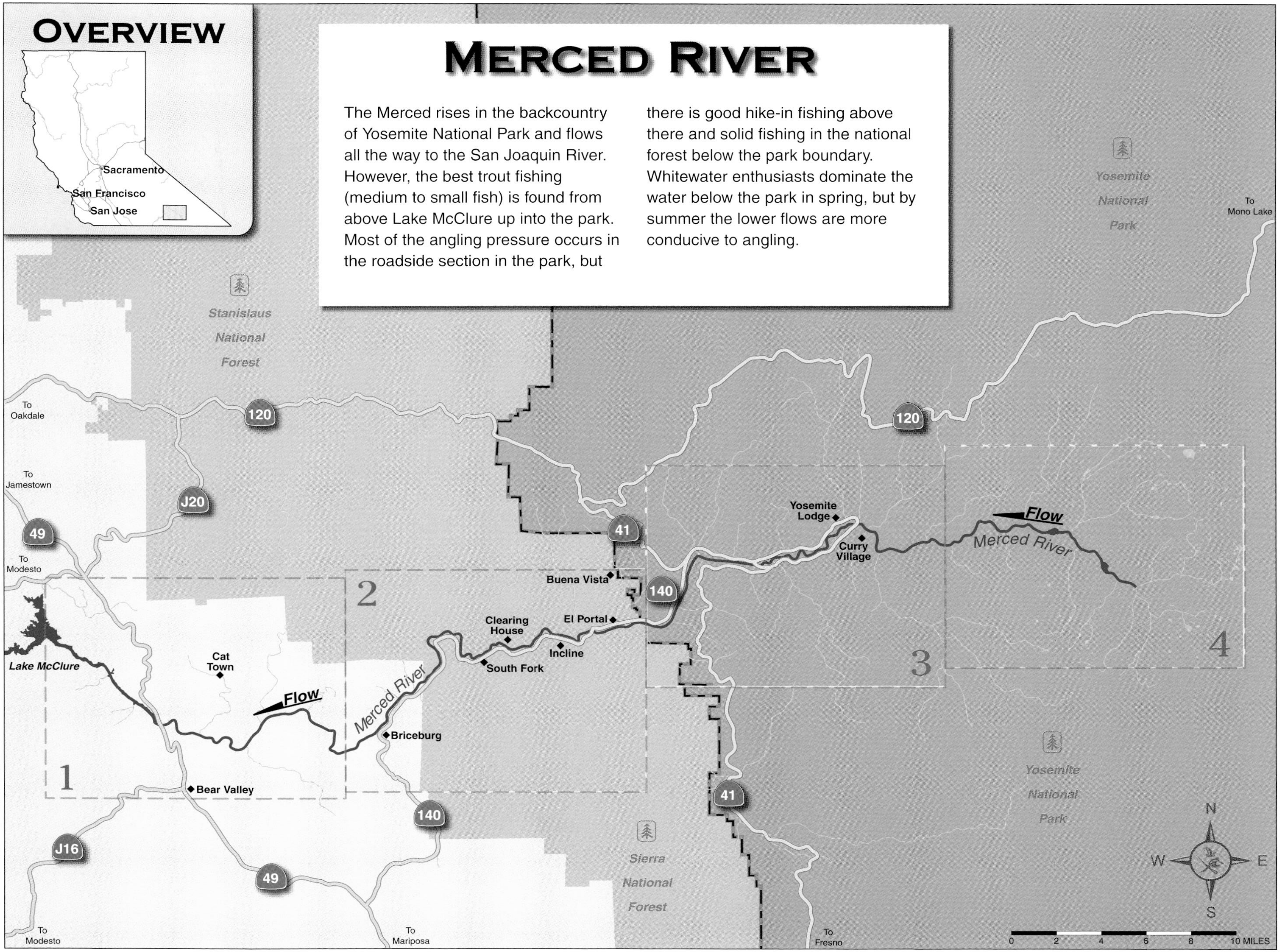

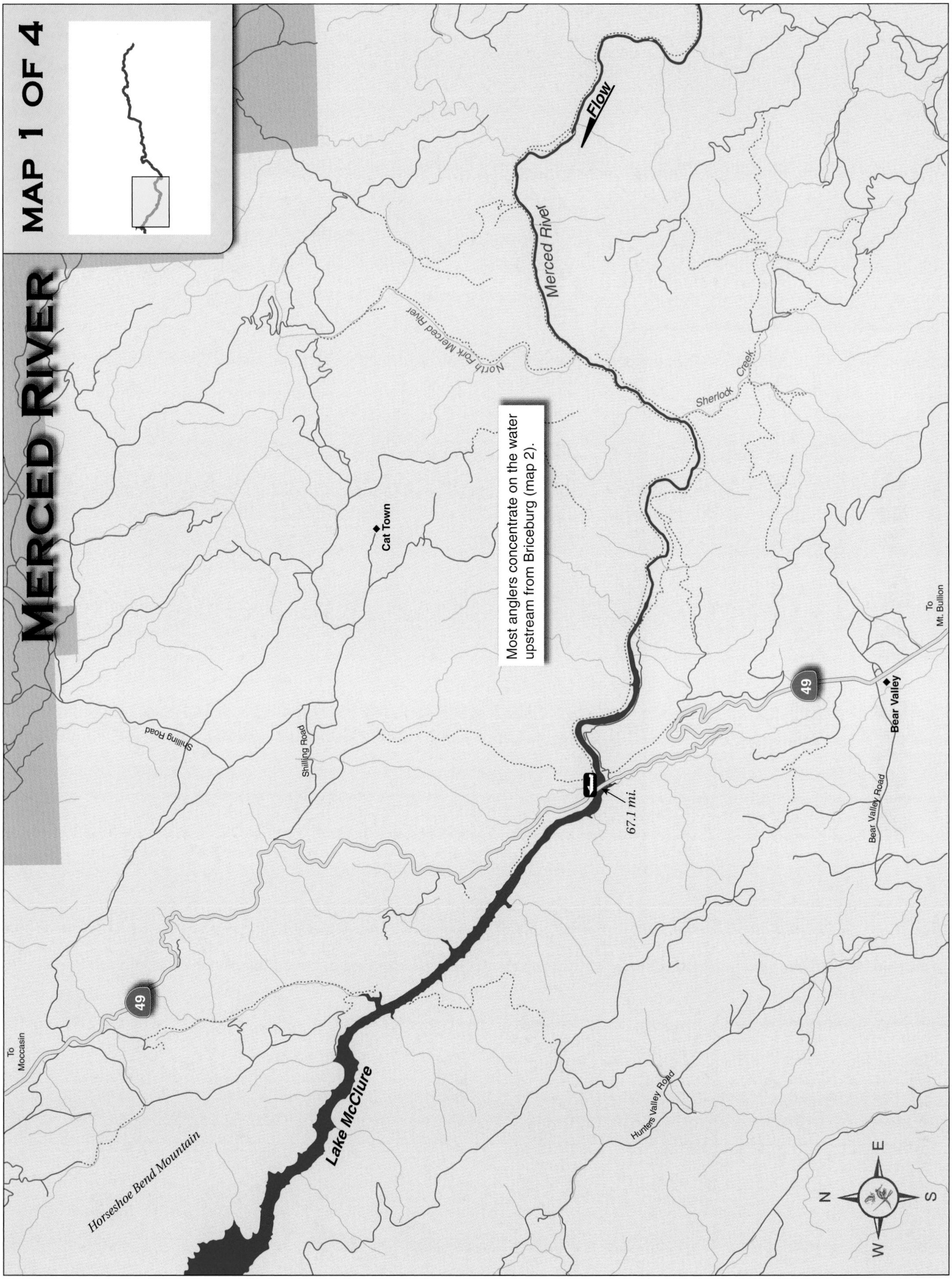
MERCED RIVER
MAP 1 OF 4
Flow
Merced River
North Fork Merced River
Sherlock Creek
Most anglers concentrate on the water upstream from Briceburg (map 2).
Cat Town
To Mt. Bullion
49
Bear Valley
Shilling Road
Shilling Road
67.1 mi.
Bear Valley Road
To Moccasin
49
Lake McClure
Hunters Valley Road
Horseshoe Bend Mountain
N
E
S
W

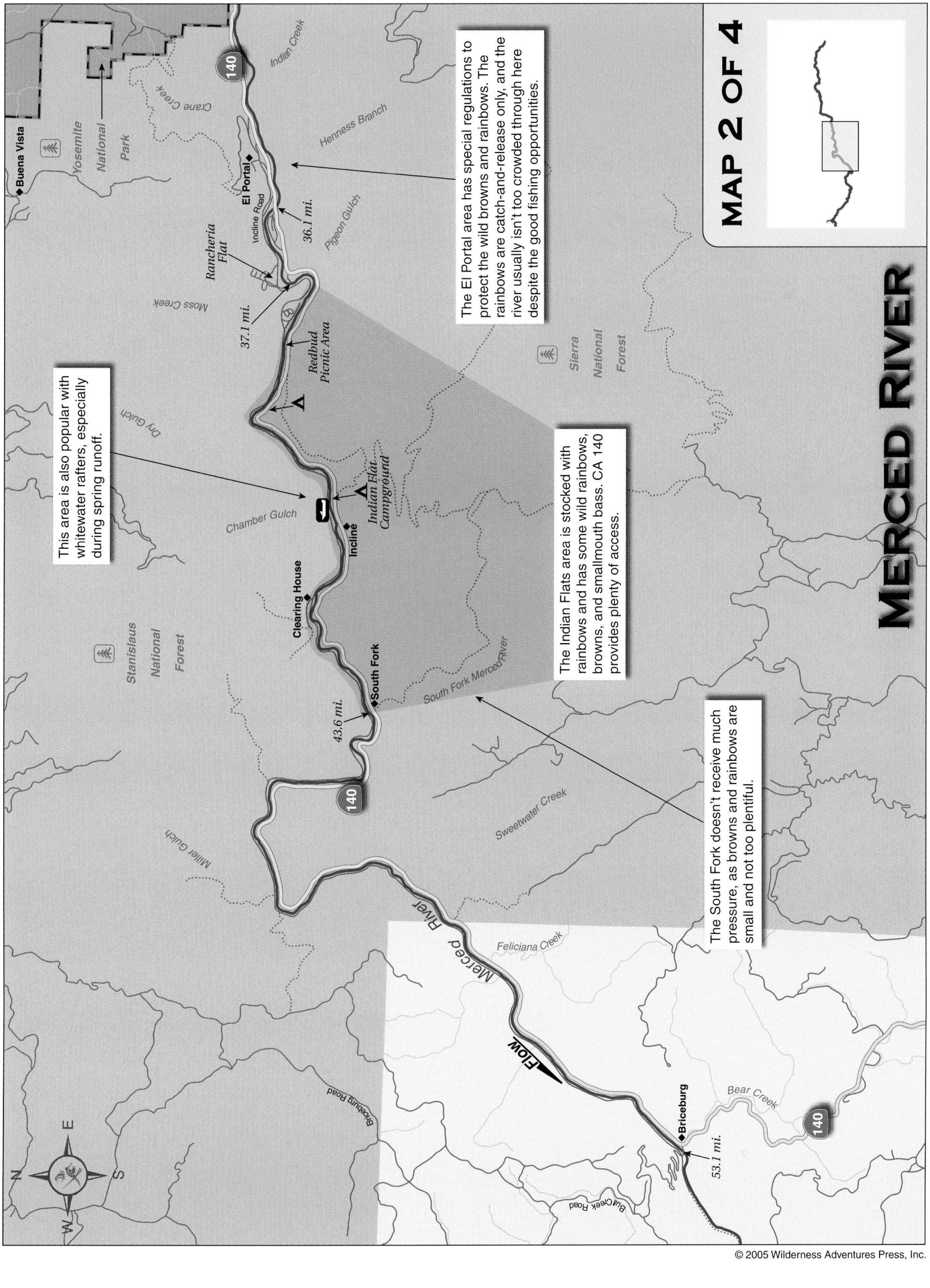

Merced River
Map 2 of 4
The El Portal area has special regulations to protect the wild browns and rainbows. The rainbows are catch-and-release only, and the river usually isn't too crowded through here despite the good fishing opportunities.
This area is also popular with whitewater rafters, especially during spring runoff.
The Indian Flats area is stocked with rainbows and has some wild rainbows, browns, and smallmouth bass. CA 140 provides plenty of access.
The South Fork doesn't receive much pressure, as browns and rainbows are small and not too plentiful.
Buena Vista
Yosemite National Park
Crane Creek
Indian Creek
Henness Branch
El Portal
Incline Road
36.1 mi.
Pigeon Gulch
Rancheria Flat
Moss Creek
37.1 mi.
Redbud Picnic Area
Dry Gulch
Indian Flat Campground
Chamber Gulch
Incline
Clearing House
Sierra National Forest
Stanislaus National Forest
South Fork
South Fork Merced River
43.6 mi.
140
Sweetwater Creek
Miller Gulch
Merced River
Feliciana Creek
Flow
Briceburg Road
Briceburg
Bear Creek
53.1 mi.
Bull Creek Road
N
E
S
W

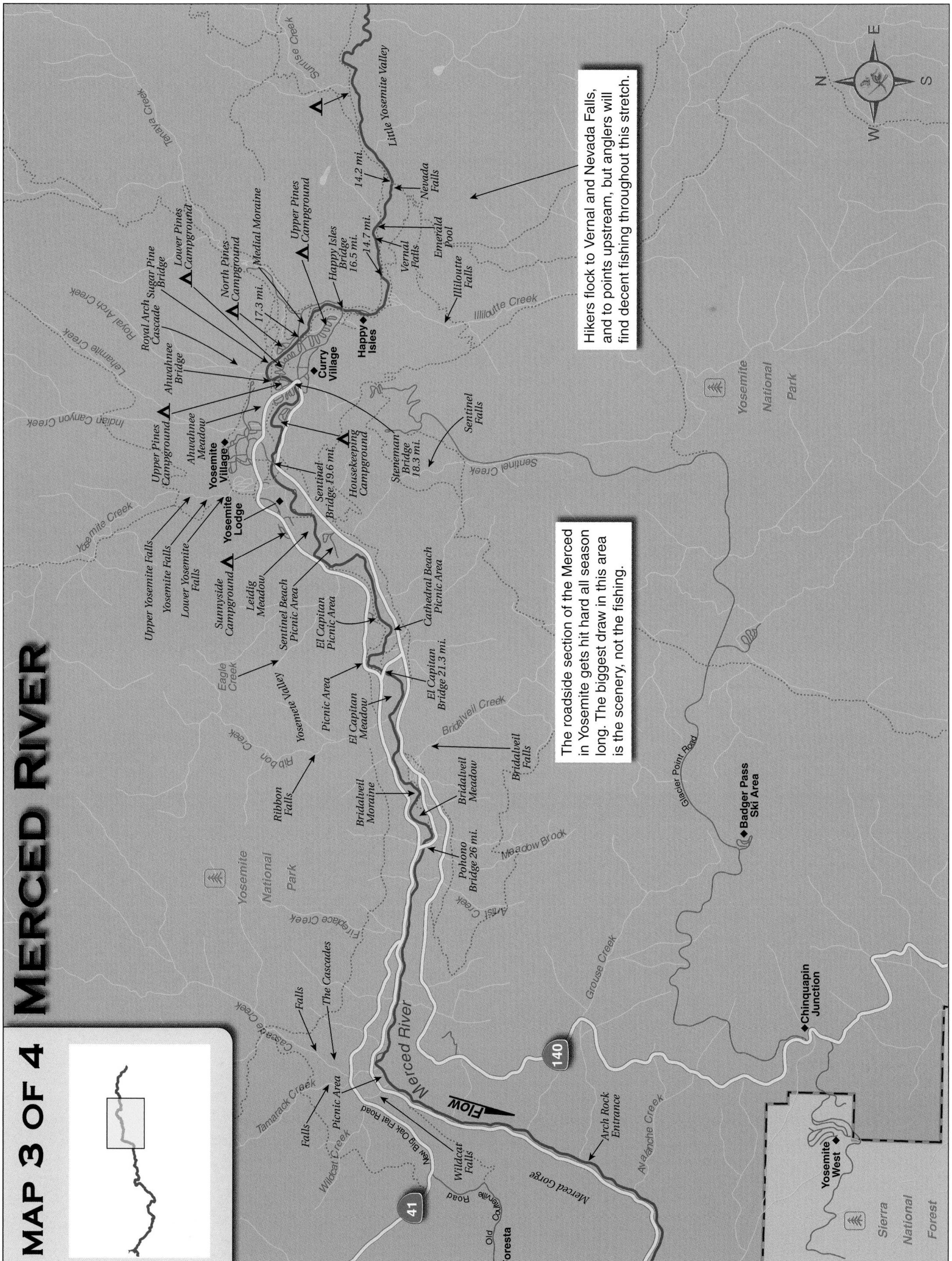
MAP 3 OF 4
MERCED RIVER
The roadside section of the Merced in Yosemite gets hit hard all season long. The biggest draw in this area is the scenery, not the fishing.
Hikers flock to Vernal and Nevada Falls, and to points upstream, but anglers will find decent fishing throughout this stretch.
Merced River
Flow
Merced Gorge
Arch Rock Entrance
Wildcat Falls
Picnic Area
Falls
The Cascades
Ribbon Falls
Yosemite Valley
El Capitan Meadow
El Capitan Bridge 21.3 mi.
El Capitan Picnic Area
Cathedral Beach Picnic Area
Bridalveil Moraine
Bridalveil Meadow
Bridalveil Falls
Pohono Bridge 26 mi.
Sentinel Beach Picnic Area
Leidig Meadow
Sunnyside Campground
Upper Yosemite Falls
Yosemite Falls
Lower Yosemite Falls
Yosemite Lodge
Yosemite Village
Sentinel Bridge 19.6 mi.
Housekeeping Campground
Stoneman Bridge 18.3 mi.
Sentinel Falls
Upper Pines Campground
Ahwahnee Meadow
Ahwahnee Bridge
Royal Arch Cascade
Sugar Pine Bridge
Lower Pines Campground
North Pines Campground
17.3 mi.
Medial Moraine
Upper Pines Campground
Curry Village
Happy Isles
Happy Isles Bridge 16.5 mi.
14.7 mi.
14.2 mi.
Vernal Falls
Emerald Pool
Nevada Falls
Illilouette Falls
Illilouette Creek
Little Yosemite Valley
Sunrise Creek
Tenaya Creek
Royal Arch Creek
Lehamite Creek
Indian Canyon Creek
Yosemite Creek
Eagle Creek
Ribbon Creek
Fireplace Creek
Cascade Creek
Tamarack Creek
Wildcat Creek
Bridalveil Creek
Meadow Brook
Artist Creek
Sentinel Creek
Grouse Creek
Avalanche Creek
Glacier Point Road
Badger Pass Ski Area
Chinquapin Junction
Yosemite West
New Big Oak Flat Road
Old Coulterville Road
Foresta
41
140
Yosemite National Park
Sierra National Forest
N
S
E
W

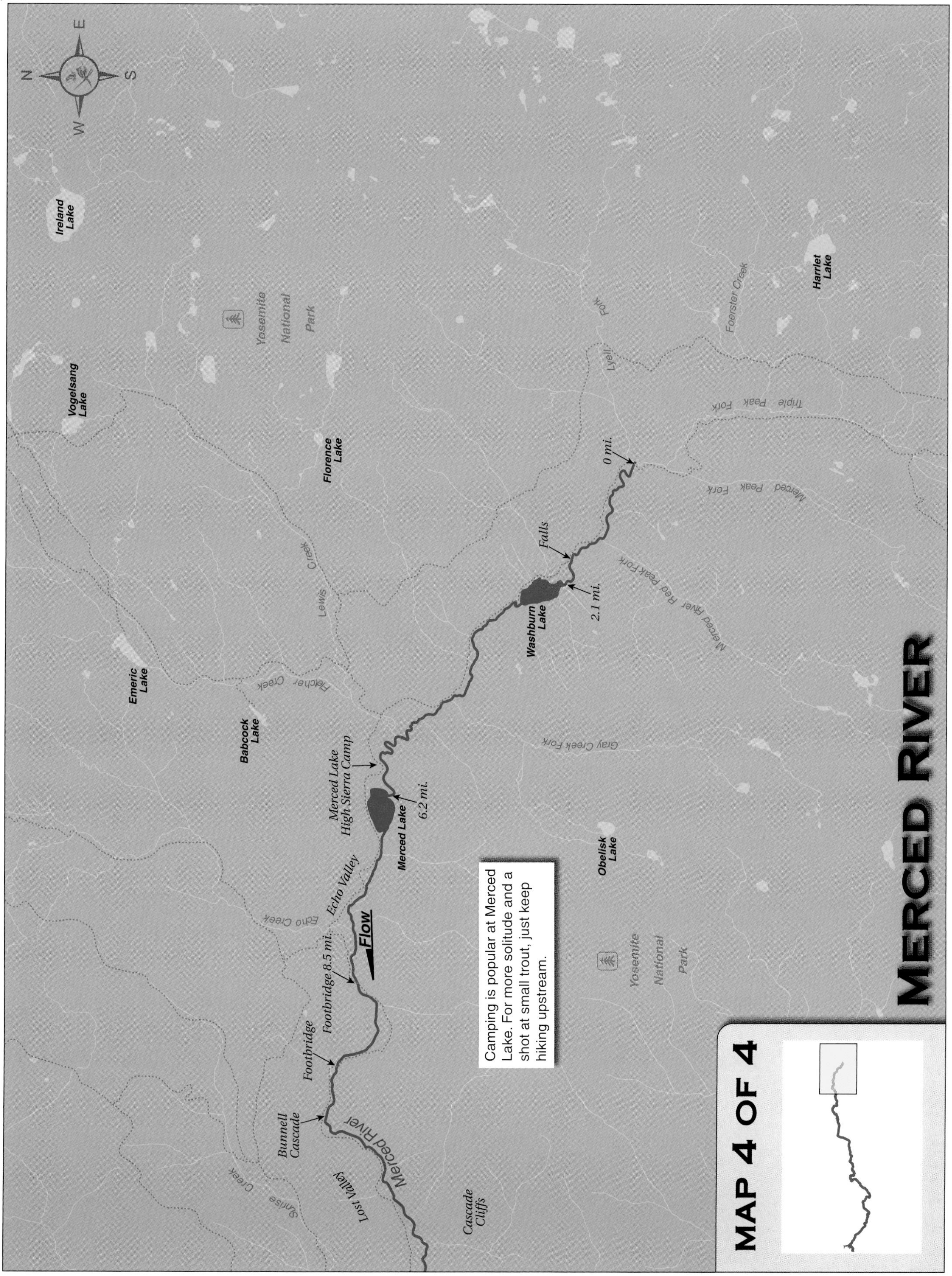
N
E
S
W
Ireland Lake
Vogelsang Lake
Emeric Lake
Babcock Lake
Florence Lake
Yosemite National Park
Lewis Creek
Fletcher Creek
Echo Creek
Echo Valley
Merced Lake High Sierra Camp
Merced Lake
6.2 mi.
Washburn Lake
2.1 mi.
Falls
0 mi.
Lyell Fork
Triple Peak Fork
Merced Peak Fork
Merced River Red Peak Fork
Gray Creek Fork
Foerster Creek
Harriet Lake
Obelisk Lake
Footbridge 8.5 mi.
Footbridge
Flow
Bunnell Cascade
Merced River
Lost Valley
Sunrise Creek
Cascade Cliffs
Camping is popular at Merced Lake. For more solitude and a shot at small trout, just keep hiking upstream.
MERCED RIVER
MAP 4 OF 4

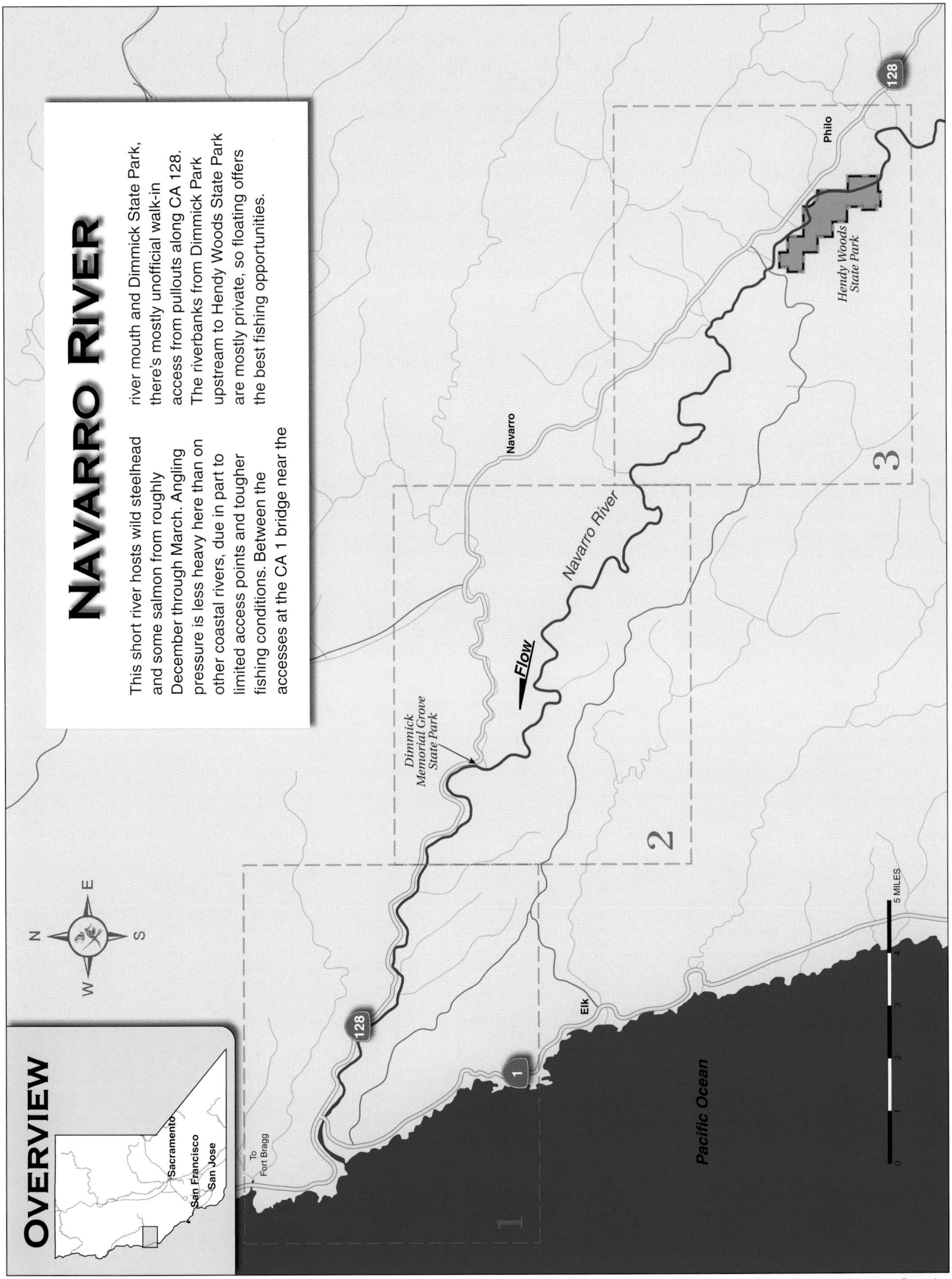
NAVARRO RIVER
This short river hosts wild steelhead and some salmon from roughly December through March. Angling pressure is less heavy here than on other coastal rivers, due in part to limited access points and tougher fishing conditions. Between the accesses at the CA 1 bridge near the river mouth and Dimmick State Park, there's mostly unofficial walk-in access from pullouts along CA 128. The riverbanks from Dimmick Park upstream to Hendy Woods State Park are mostly private, so floating offers the best fishing opportunities.
OVERVIEW
Sacramento
San Francisco
San Jose
N
E
S
W
To Fort Bragg
128
1
Elk
Pacific Ocean
Dimmick Memorial Grove State Park
Flow
Navarro River
Navarro
Hendy Woods State Park
Philo
128
1
2
3
5 MILES
0
1
2
3
4

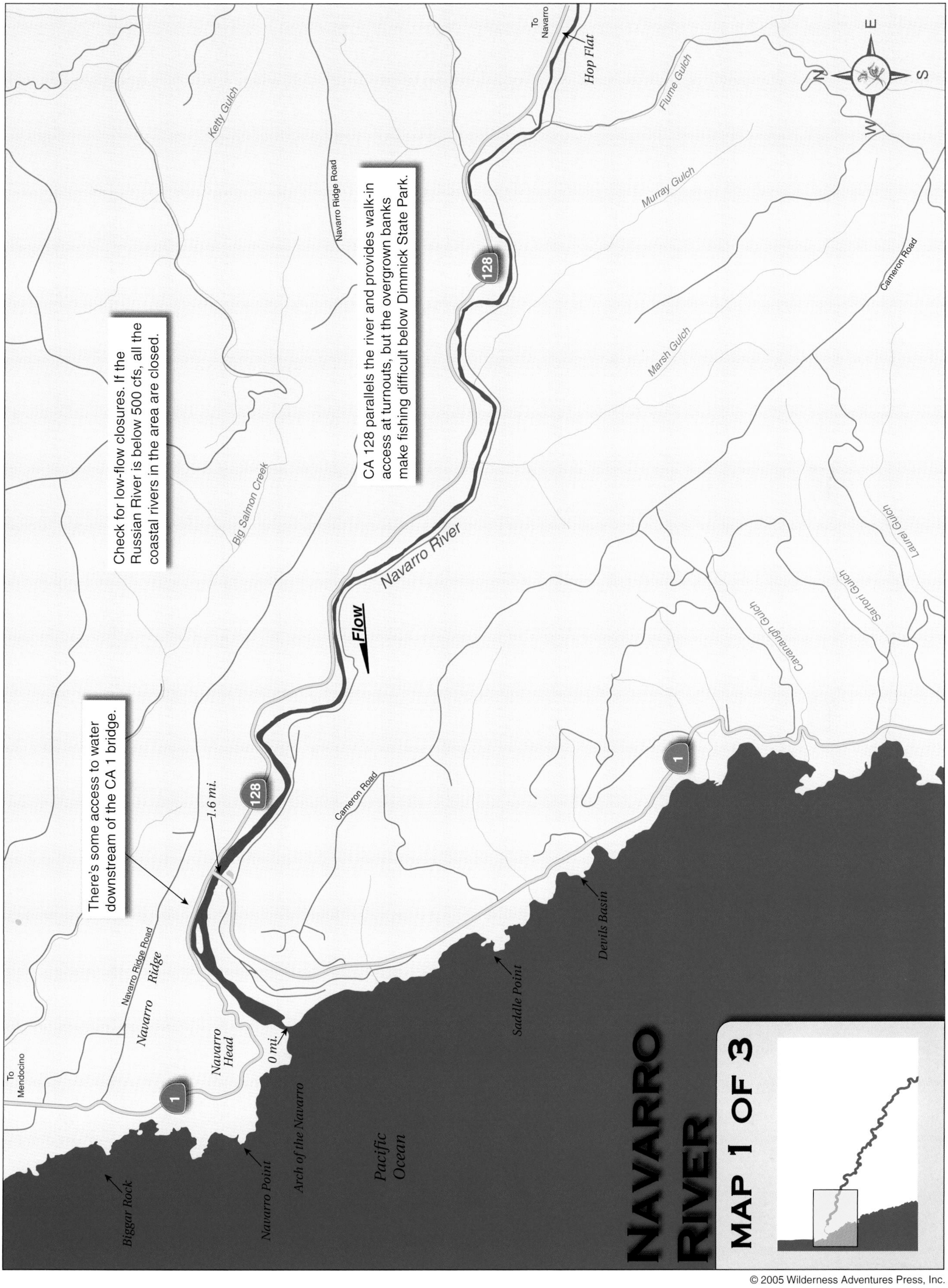
NAVARRO RIVER
MAP 1 OF 3
Check for low-flow closures. If the Russian River is below 500 cfs, all the coastal rivers in the area are closed.
CA 128 parallels the river and provides walk-in access at turnouts, but the overgrown banks make fishing difficult below Dimmick State Park.
There's some access to water downstream of the CA 1 bridge.
To Navarro
Hop Flat
Flume Gulch
Murray Gulch
Marsh Gulch
Cameron Road
Laurel Gulch
Sartori Gulch
Cavanaugh Gulch
Navarro Ridge Road
Kelty Gulch
Big Salmon Creek
Navarro River
Flow
128
1
1.6 mi.
0 mi.
Cameron Road
Navarro Ridge Road
Navarro Ridge
Navarro Head
To Mendocino
Devils Basin
Saddle Point
Arch of the Navarro
Navarro Point
Biggar Rock
Pacific Ocean
N
E
S
W

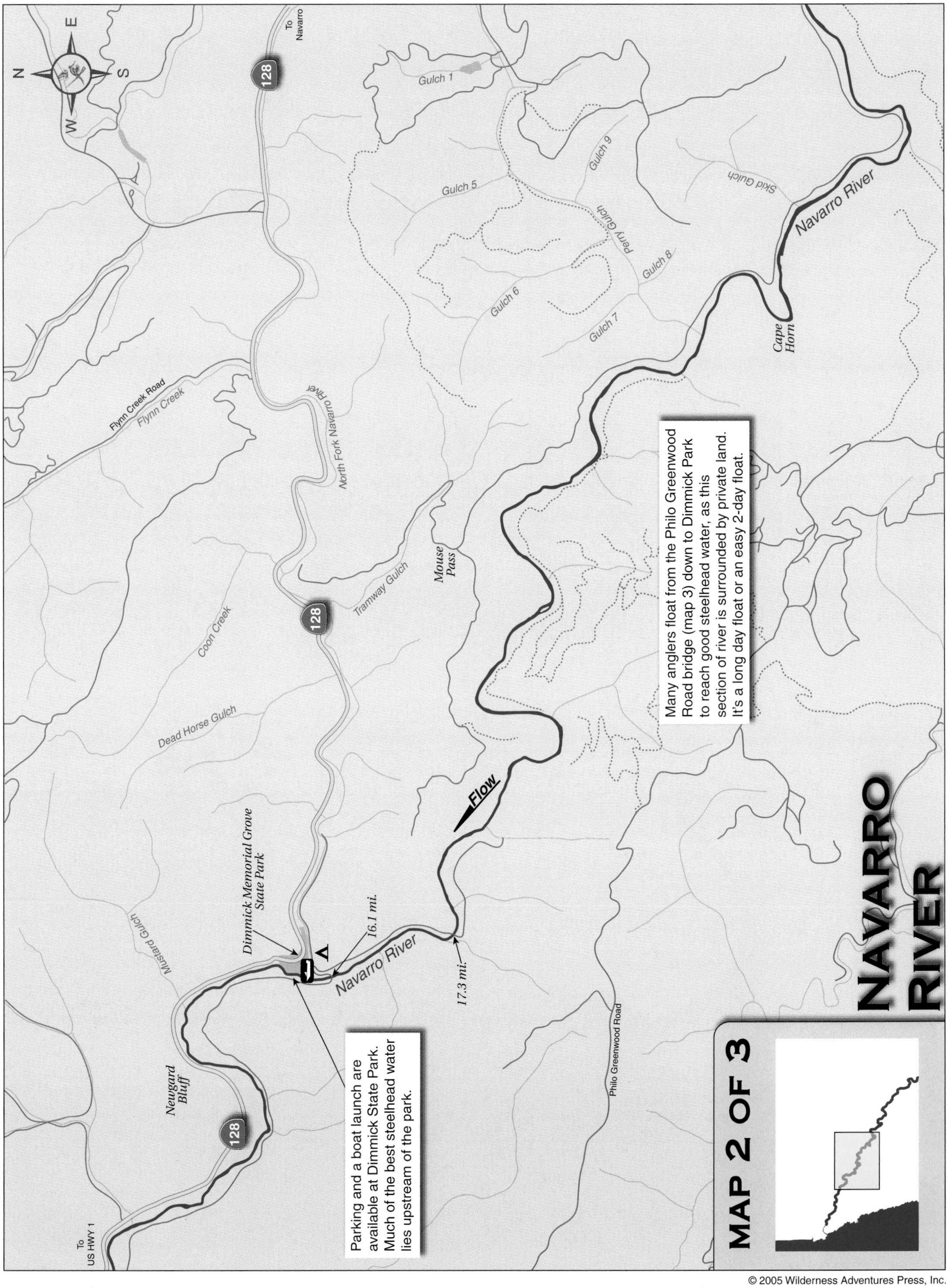
NAVARRO RIVER
MAP 2 OF 3
Many anglers float from the Philo Greenwood Road bridge (map 3) down to Dimmick Park to reach good steelhead water, as this section of river is surrounded by private land. It's a long day float or an easy 2-day float.
Parking and a boat launch are available at Dimmick State Park. Much of the best steelhead water lies upstream of the park.
Dimmick Memorial Grove State Park
16.1 mi.
17.3 mi.
Navarro River
Flow
Newgard Bluff
Mustard Gulch
Dead Horse Gulch
Coon Creek
Tramway Gulch
Mouse Pass
North Fork Navarro River
Flynn Creek Road
Flynn Creek
Philo Greenwood Road
Cape Horn
Gulch 1
Gulch 5
Gulch 6
Gulch 7
Gulch 8
Gulch 9
Perry Gulch
Skid Gulch
128
To US HWY 1
To Navarro
N
E
S
W

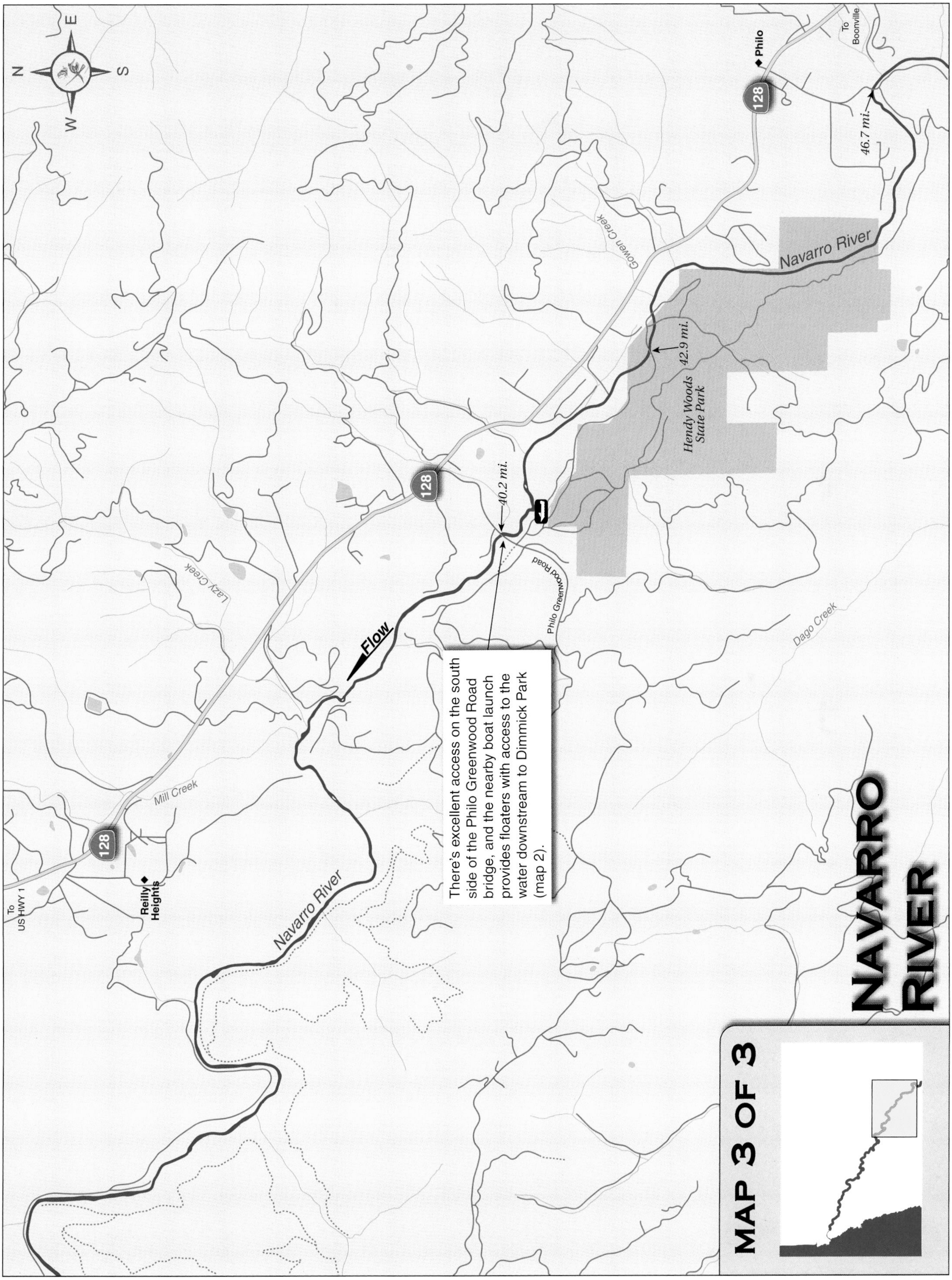
NAVARRO RIVER
MAP 3 OF 3
N
E
S
W
To Boonville
Philo
128
46.7 mi.
Navarro River
Gowen Creek
42.9 mi.
Hendy Woods State Park
40.2 mi.
Philo Greenwood Road
Dago Creek
Lazy Creek
Flow
There's excellent access on the south side of the Philo Greenwood Road bridge, and the nearby boat launch provides floaters with access to the water downstream to Dimmick Park (map 2).
Mill Creek
Reilly Heights
To US HWY 1
Navarro River

Owens River

The Owens River rises from Big Springs in the Inyo National Forest north of the town of Mammoth Lakes. The upper river—really a spring creek—has fantastic fishing for large trout, but access is limited above Crowley Lake. The water between Crowley and Pleasant Valley Reservoir once suffered greatly from dewatering but flows are now stabilized and the fishing is solid again. Access into the deep gorge here is tough, though, mostly due to the steepness of the canyon walls. The final stretch below Pleasant Valley has great access and fishing for wild brown trout. The entire Mammoth Lakes area has good fishing opportunities, as well as a host of other outdoor pursuits. Famous Hot Creek dumps into the Owens above Crowley Lake.

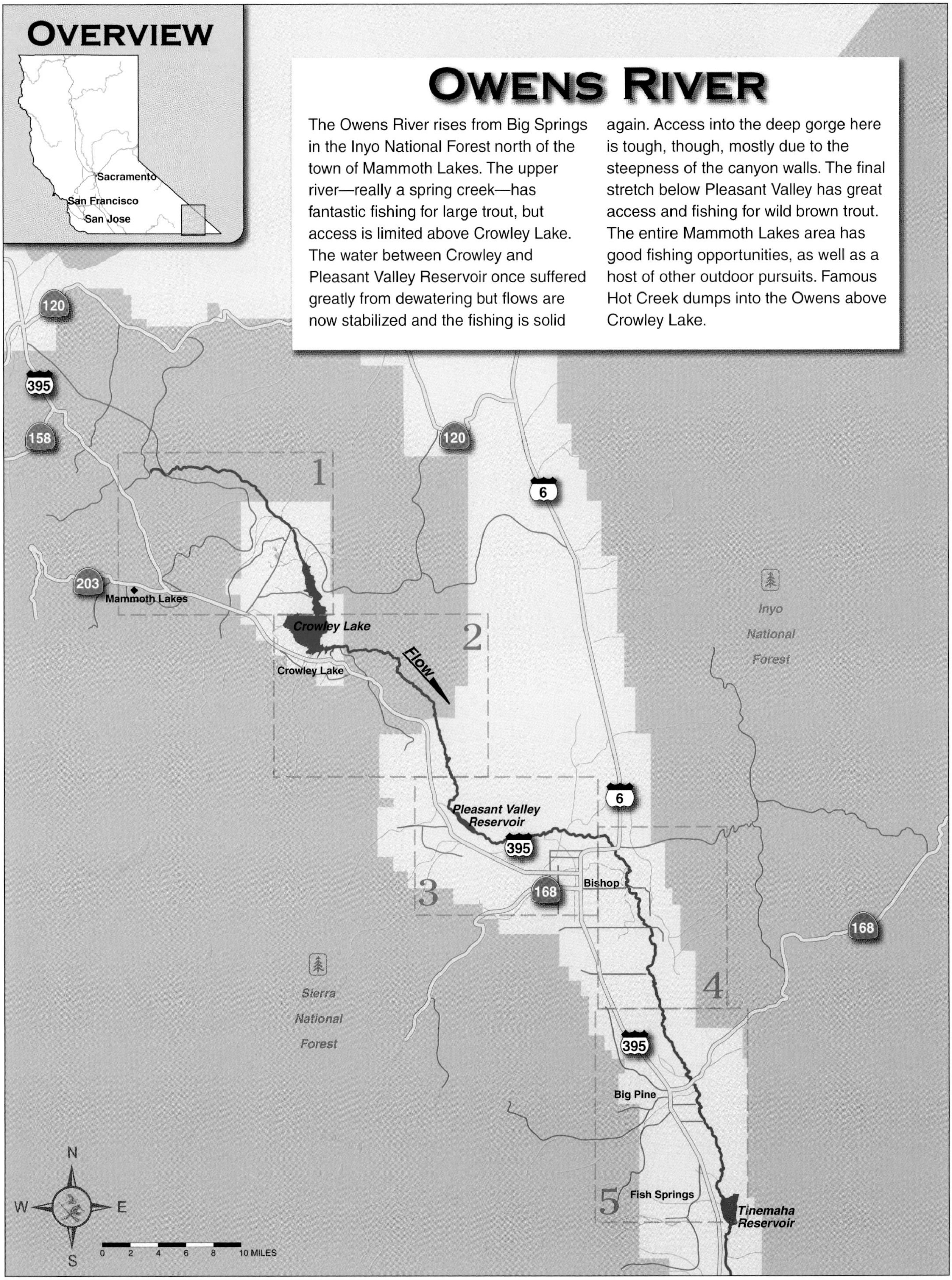

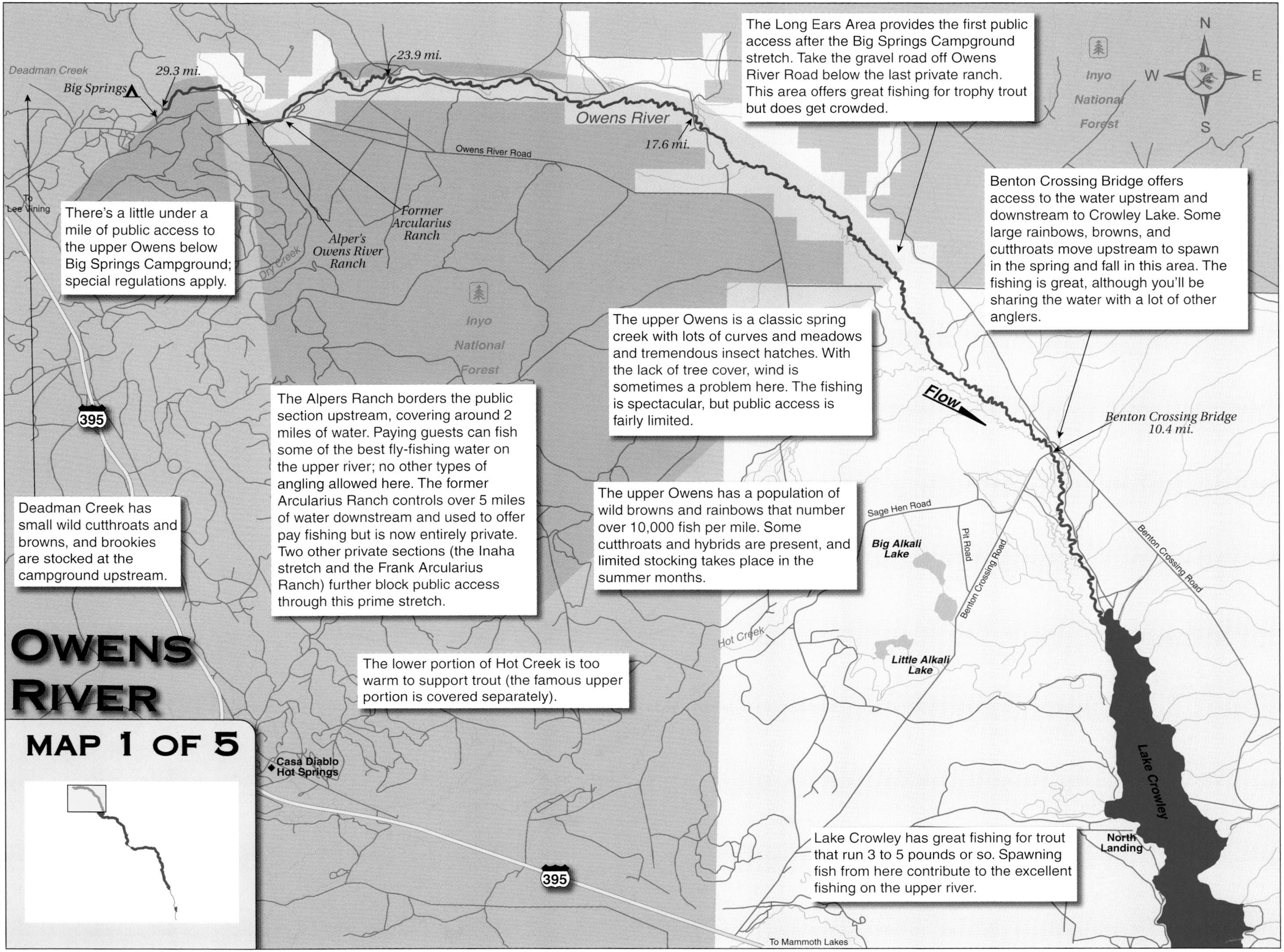
OWENS RIVER
MAP 1 OF 5
Deadman Creek
Big Springs
29.3 mi.
23.9 mi.
17.6 mi.
Owens River
Owens River Road
To Lee Vining
Alper's Owens River Ranch
Former Arcularius Ranch
Dry Creek
Inyo National Forest
N
W
E
S
The Long Ears Area provides the first public access after the Big Springs Campground stretch. Take the gravel road off Owens River Road below the last private ranch. This area offers great fishing for trophy trout but does get crowded.
Benton Crossing Bridge offers access to the water upstream and downstream to Crowley Lake. Some large rainbows, browns, and cutthroats move upstream to spawn in the spring and fall in this area. The fishing is great, although you'll be sharing the water with a lot of other anglers.
There's a little under a mile of public access to the upper Owens below Big Springs Campground; special regulations apply.
The upper Owens is a classic spring creek with lots of curves and meadows and tremendous insect hatches. With the lack of tree cover, wind is sometimes a problem here. The fishing is spectacular, but public access is fairly limited.
Flow
Benton Crossing Bridge 10.4 mi.
The Alpers Ranch borders the public section upstream, covering around 2 miles of water. Paying guests can fish some of the best fly-fishing water on the upper river; no other types of angling allowed here. The former Arcularius Ranch controls over 5 miles of water downstream and used to offer pay fishing but is now entirely private. Two other private sections (the Inaha stretch and the Frank Arcularius Ranch) further block public access through this prime stretch.
The upper Owens has a population of wild browns and rainbows that number over 10,000 fish per mile. Some cutthroats and hybrids are present, and limited stocking takes place in the summer months.
Deadman Creek has small wild cutthroats and browns, and brookies are stocked at the campground upstream.
395
Sage Hen Road
Pit Road
Benton Crossing Road
Big Alkali Lake
Little Alkali Lake
Hot Creek
The lower portion of Hot Creek is too warm to support trout (the famous upper portion is covered separately).
Casa Diablo Hot Springs
Lake Crowley
North Landing
Lake Crowley has great fishing for trout that run 3 to 5 pounds or so. Spawning fish from here contribute to the excellent fishing on the upper river.
To Mammoth Lakes

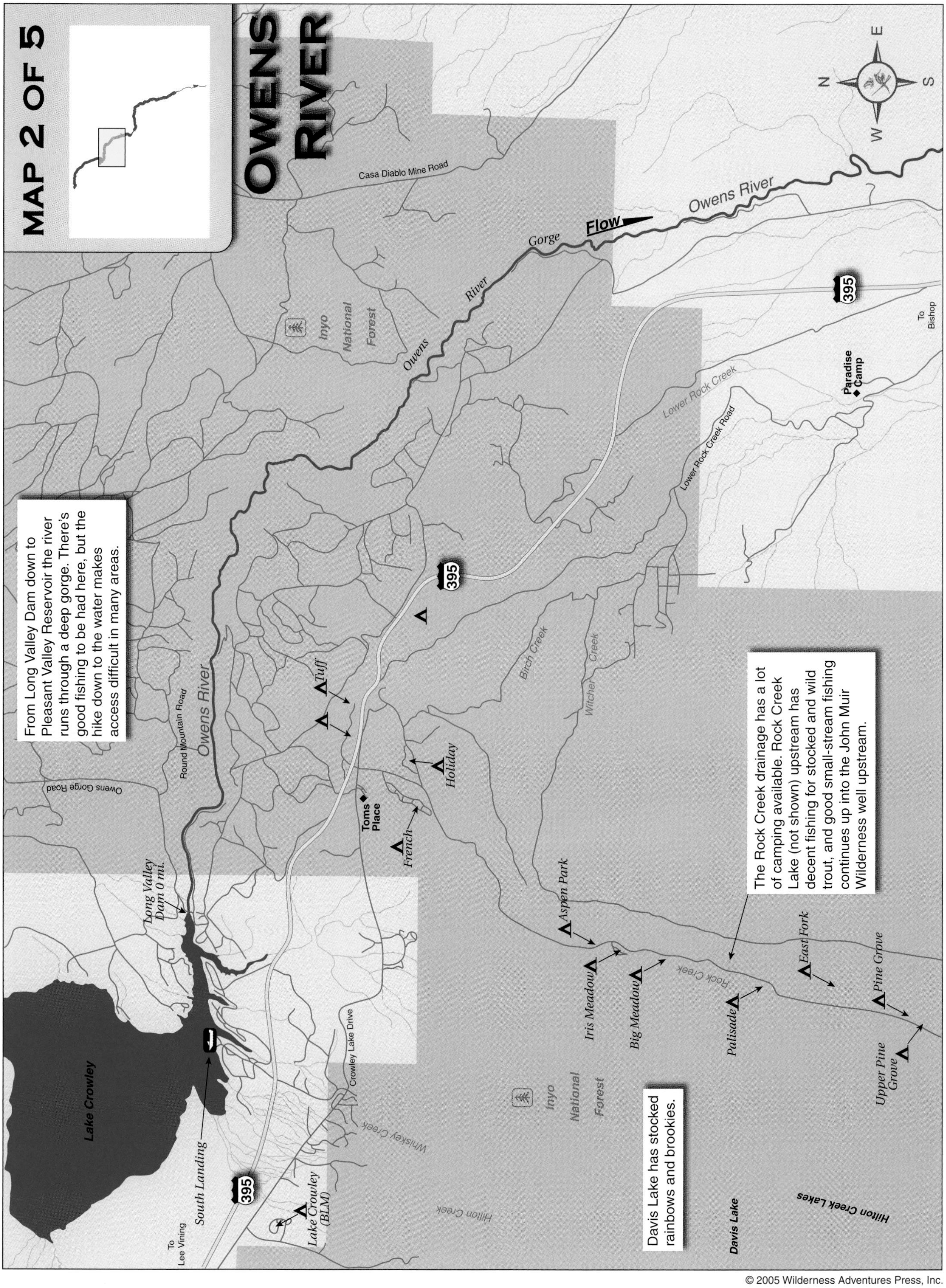
MAP 2 OF 5
OWENS RIVER
Casa Diablo Mine Road
Owens River
Flow
Gorge
River
Owens
Inyo National Forest
To Bishop
395
Paradise Camp
Lower Rock Creek
Lower Rock Creek Road
From Long Valley Dam down to Pleasant Valley Reservoir the river runs through a deep gorge. There's good fishing to be had here, but the hike down to the water makes access difficult in many areas.
Owens River
Round Mountain Road
Owens Gorge Road
Tuff
Holiday
Toms Place
French
Birch Creek
Witcher Creek
The Rock Creek drainage has a lot of camping available. Rock Creek Lake (not shown) upstream has decent fishing for stocked and wild trout, and good small-stream fishing continues up into the John Muir Wilderness well upstream.
Long Valley Dam 0 mi.
Aspen Park
Iris Meadow
Big Meadow
Rock Creek
East Fork
Palisade
Pine Grove
Upper Pine Grove
Lake Crowley
South Landing
Crowley Lake Drive
Whiskey Creek
Inyo National Forest
Davis Lake has stocked rainbows and brookies.
To Lee Vining
Lake Crowley (BLM)
Hilton Creek
Davis Lake
Hilton Creek Lakes
N
E
S
W

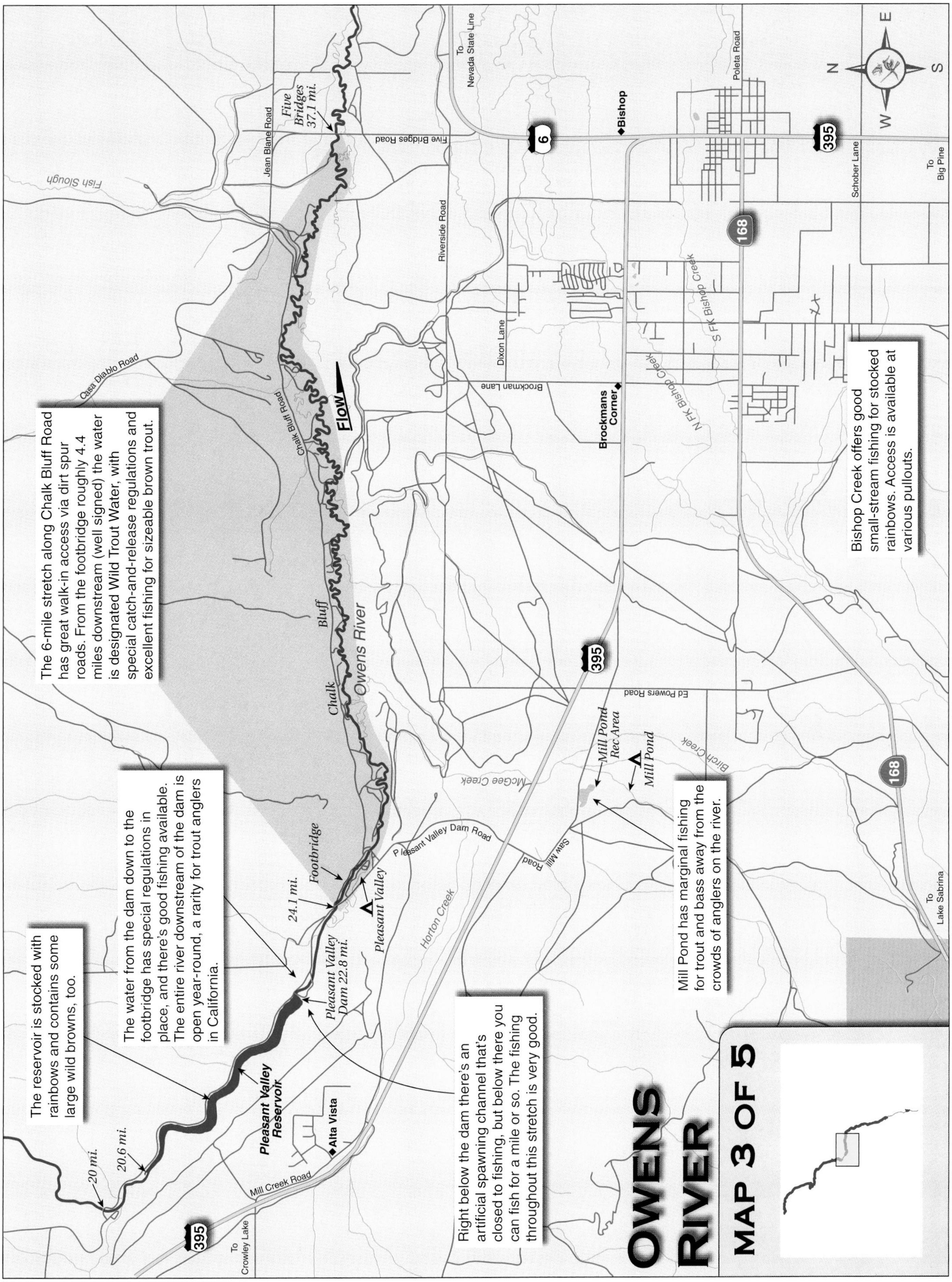
OWENS RIVER
MAP 3 OF 5
The reservoir is stocked with rainbows and contains some large wild browns, too.
The water from the dam down to the footbridge has special regulations in place, and there's good fishing available. The entire river downstream of the dam is open year-round, a rarity for trout anglers in California.
The 6-mile stretch along Chalk Bluff Road has great walk-in access via dirt spur roads. From the footbridge roughly 4.4 miles downstream (well signed) the water is designated Wild Trout Water, with special catch-and-release regulations and excellent fishing for sizeable brown trout.
Right below the dam there's an artificial spawning channel that's closed to fishing, but below there you can fish for a mile or so. The fishing throughout this stretch is very good.
Mill Pond has marginal fishing for trout and bass away from the crowds of anglers on the river.
Bishop Creek offers good small-stream fishing for stocked rainbows. Access is available at various pullouts.
20 mi.
20.6 mi.
Pleasant Valley Reservoir
Pleasant Valley Dam 22.8 mi.
24.1 mi.
Footbridge
Pleasant Valley
Chalk Bluff
Owens River
Flow
Five Bridges 37.1 mi.
Alta Vista
Mill Creek Road
To Crowley Lake
395
Pleasant Valley Dam Road
Saw Mill Road
Horton Creek
McGee Creek
Mill Pond Rec Area
Mill Pond
Birch Creek
Ed Powers Road
Casa Diablo Road
Chalk Bluff Road
Fish Slough
Jean Blanc Road
Five Bridges Road
Riverside Road
Dixon Lane
Brockman Lane
Brockmans Corner
N FK Bishop Creek
S FK Bishop Creek
168
6
Bishop
To Nevada State Line
Poleta Road
Schober Lane
To Big Pine
To Lake Sabrina
N
S
E
W

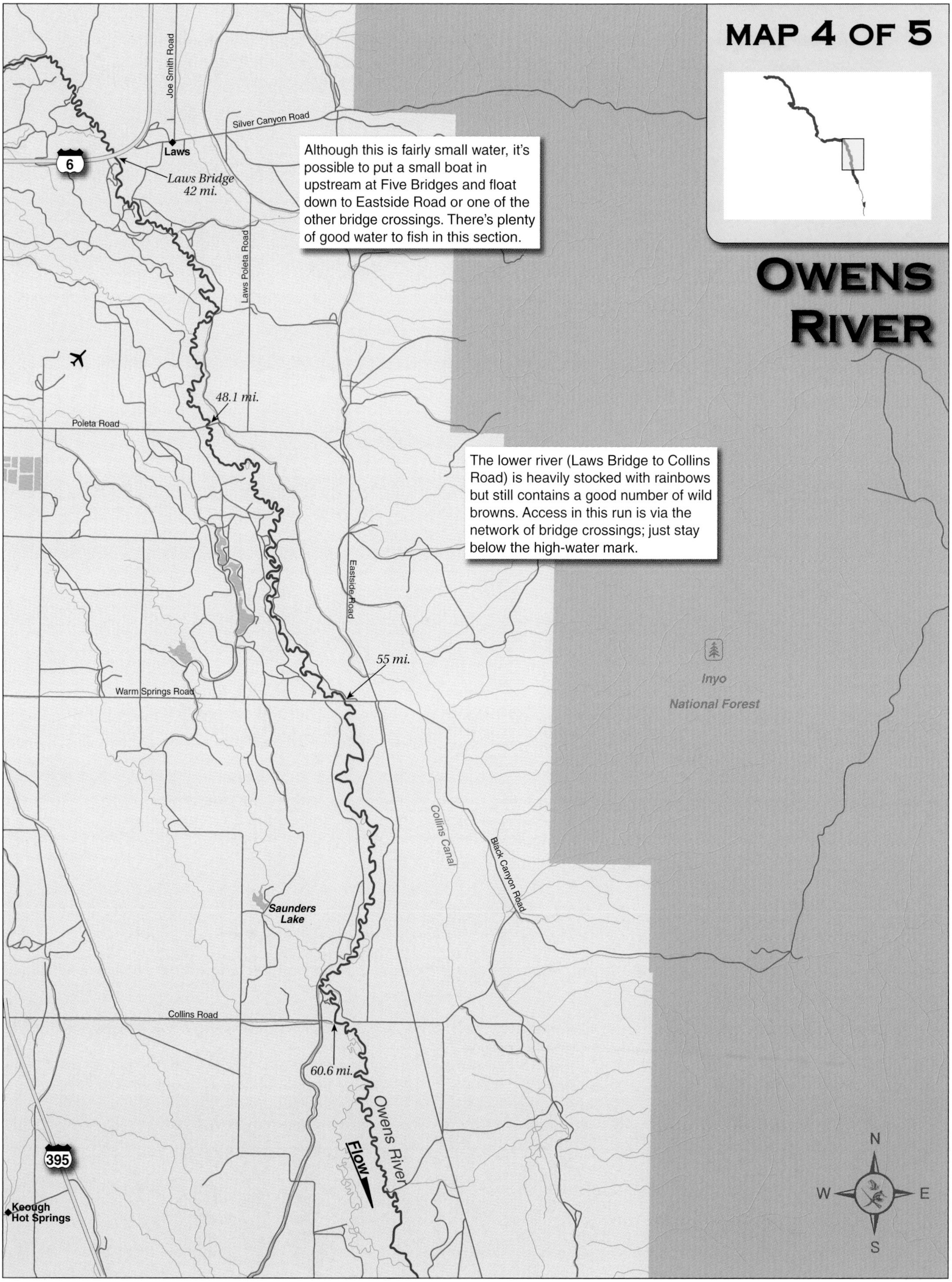

MAP 4 OF 5
OWENS RIVER
Although this is fairly small water, it's possible to put a small boat in upstream at Five Bridges and float down to Eastside Road or one of the other bridge crossings. There's plenty of good water to fish in this section.
The lower river (Laws Bridge to Collins Road) is heavily stocked with rainbows but still contains a good number of wild browns. Access in this run is via the network of bridge crossings; just stay below the high-water mark.
Joe Smith Road
Silver Canyon Road
Laws
6
Laws Bridge
42 mi.
Laws Poleta Road
48.1 mi.
Poleta Road
Eastside Road
55 mi.
Warm Springs Road
Inyo
National Forest
Collins Canal
Black Canyon Road
Saunders Lake
Collins Road
60.6 mi.
Owens River
Flow
395
Keough Hot Springs
N
W
E
S

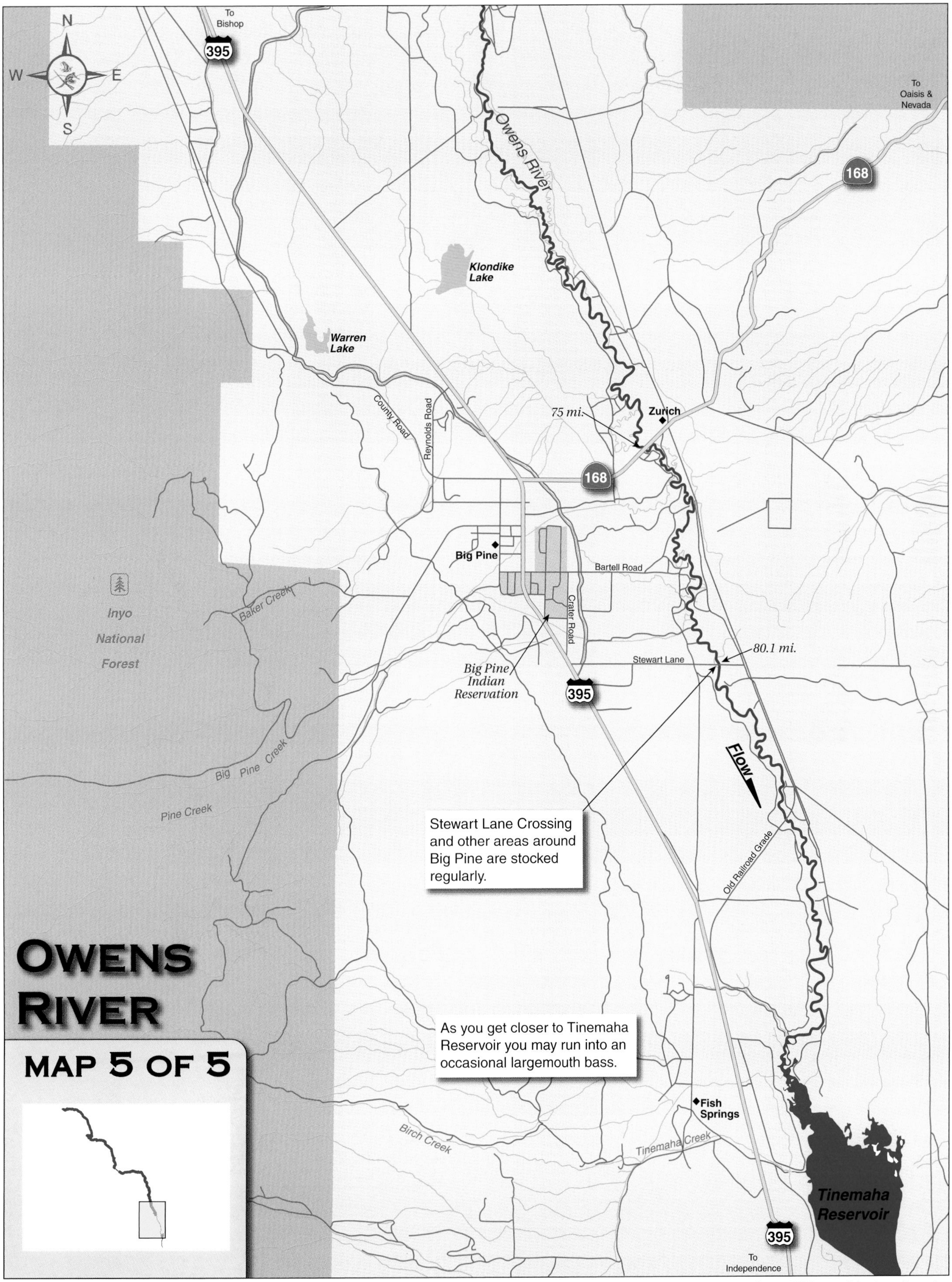
N
S
E
W
To Bishop
395
To Oaisis & Nevada
168
Owens River
Klondike Lake
Warren Lake
County Road
Reynolds Road
75 mi.
Zurich
168
Big Pine
Bartell Road
Crater Road
Baker Creek
Inyo National Forest
Stewart Lane
80.1 mi.
Big Pine Indian Reservation
395
Big Pine Creek
Pine Creek
Flow
Old Railroad Grade
Stewart Lane Crossing and other areas around Big Pine are stocked regularly.
OWENS RIVER
MAP 5 OF 5
As you get closer to Tinemaha Reservoir you may run into an occasional largemouth bass.
Fish Springs
Birch Creek
Tinemaha Creek
Tinemaha Reservoir
395
To Independence

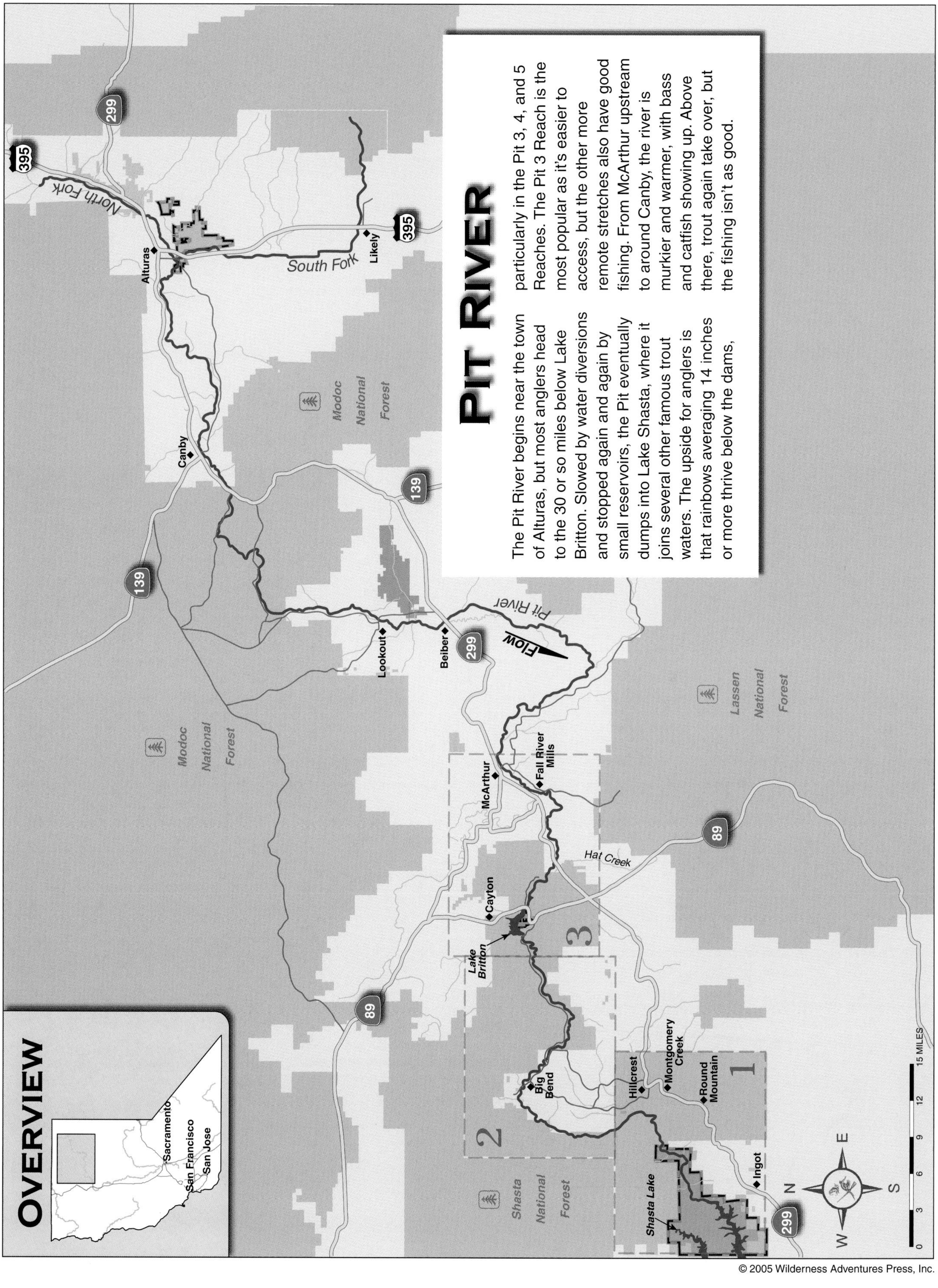

Pit River

The Pit River begins near the town of Alturas, but most anglers head to the 30 or so miles below Lake Britton. Slowed by water diversions and stopped again and again by small reservoirs, the Pit eventually dumps into Lake Shasta, where it joins several other famous trout waters. The upside for anglers is that rainbows averaging 14 inches or more thrive below the dams, particularly in the Pit 3, 4, and 5 Reaches. The Pit 3 Reach is the most popular as it's easier to access, but the other more remote stretches also have good fishing. From McArthur upstream to around Canby, the river is murkier and warmer, with bass and catfish showing up. Above there, trout again take over, but the fishing isn't as good.

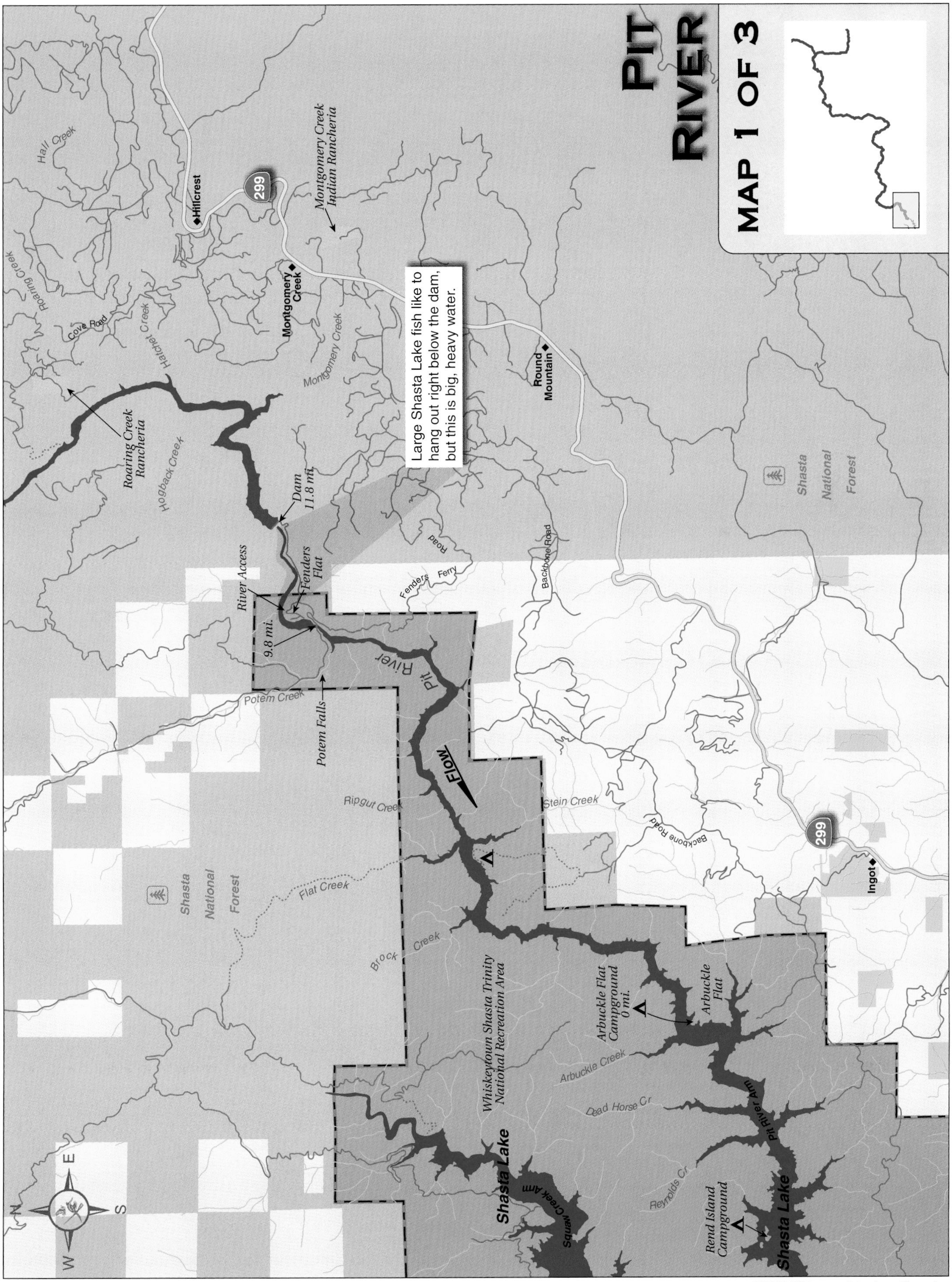
Pit River
Map 1 of 3
Large Shasta Lake fish like to hang out right below the dam, but this is big, heavy water.
Hall Creek
Hillcrest
299
Montgomery Creek Indian Rancheria
Roaring Creek
Montgomery Creek
Cove Road
Hatchet Creek
Montgomery Creek
Round Mountain
Roaring Creek Rancheria
Hogback Creek
Dam 11.8 mi.
River Access
Fenders Flat
9.8 mi.
Fenders Ferry Road
Backbone Road
Shasta National Forest
Pit River
Potem Creek
Potem Falls
Flow
Ripgut Creek
Stein Creek
Backbone Road
299
Ingot
Flat Creek
Shasta National Forest
Brock Creek
Whiskeytown Shasta Trinity National Recreation Area
Arbuckle Flat Campground 0 mi.
Arbuckle Flat
Arbuckle Creek
Dead Horse Cr
Pit River Arm
Shasta Lake
Squaw Creek Arm
Reynolds Cr
Rend Island Campground
Shasta Lake
N
E
S
W

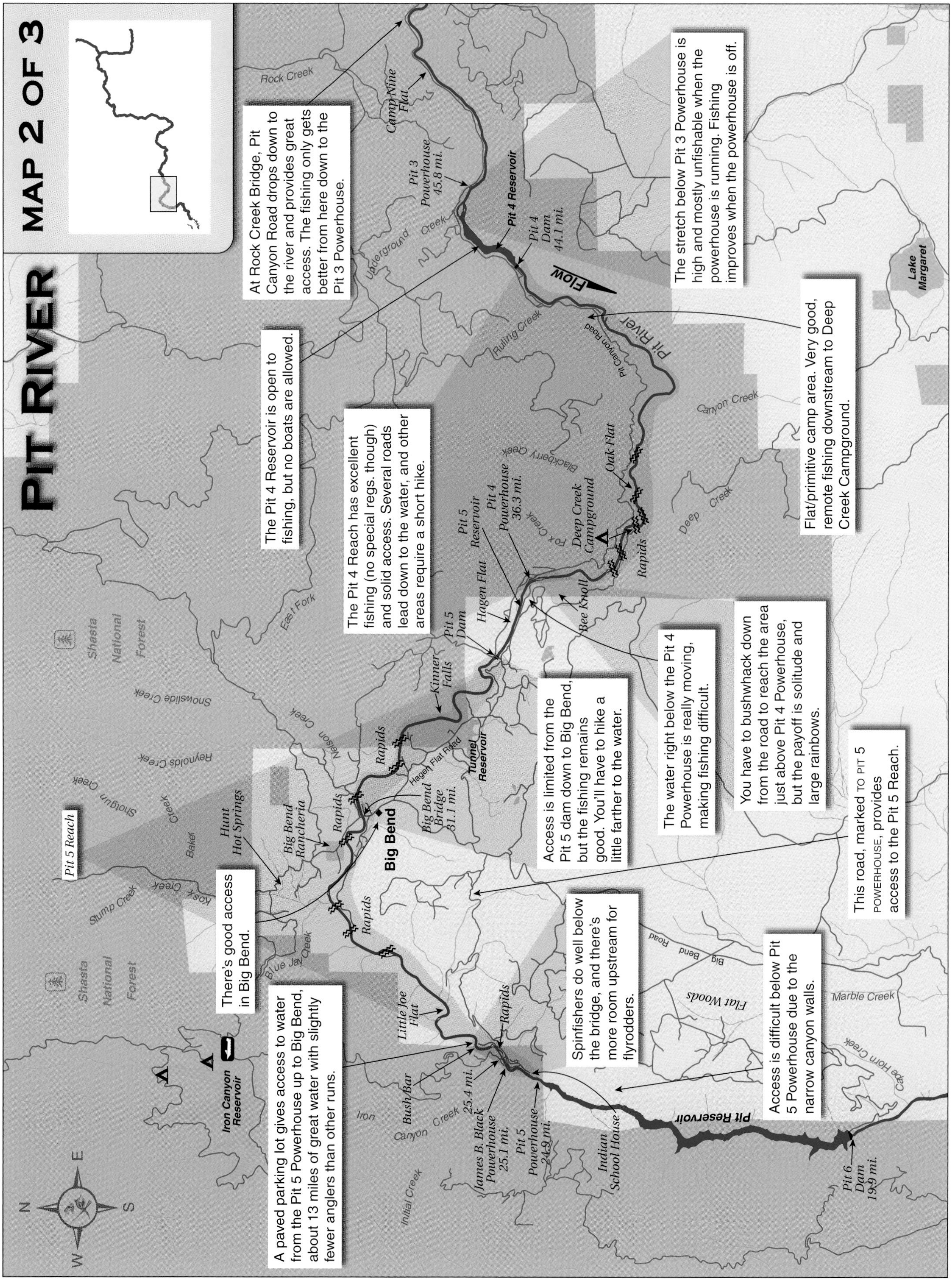
Pit River
Map 2 of 3
Flow
At Rock Creek Bridge, Pit Canyon Road drops down to the river and provides great access. The fishing only gets better from here down to the Pit 3 Powerhouse.
The Pit 4 Reservoir is open to fishing, but no boats are allowed.
The Pit 4 Reach has excellent fishing (no special regs. though) and solid access. Several roads lead down to the water, and other areas require a short hike.
The stretch below Pit 3 Powerhouse is high and mostly unfishable when the powerhouse is running. Fishing improves when the powerhouse is off.
Flat/primitive camp area. Very good, remote fishing downstream to Deep Creek Campground.
Access is limited from the Pit 5 dam down to Big Bend, but the fishing remains good. You'll have to hike a little farther to the water.
The water right below the Pit 4 Powerhouse is really moving, making fishing difficult.
You have to bushwhack down from the road to reach the area just above Pit 4 Powerhouse, but the payoff is solitude and large rainbows.
There's good access in Big Bend.
This road, marked TO PIT 5 POWERHOUSE, provides access to the Pit 5 Reach.
A paved parking lot gives access to water from the Pit 5 Powerhouse up to Big Bend, about 13 miles of great water with slightly fewer anglers than other runs.
Spinfishers do well below the bridge, and there's more room upstream for flyrodders.
Access is difficult below Pit 5 Powerhouse due to the narrow canyon walls.
Rock Creek
Camp Nine Flat
Pit 3 Powerhouse 45.8 mi.
Pit 4 Reservoir
Pit 4 Dam 44.1 mi.
Underground Creek
Ruling Creek
Pit Canyon Road
Pit River
Canyon Creek
Lake Margaret
Blackberry Creek
Oak Flat
Deep Creek
Pit 5 Reservoir
Pit 4 Powerhouse 36.3 mi.
Fox Creek
Deep Creek Campground
Rapids
Hagen Flat
Bee Knoll
Pit 5 Dam
East Fork
Shasta National Forest
Snowslide Creek
Nelson Creek
Kinner Falls
Reynolds Creek
Hagen Flat Road
Tunnel Reservoir
Shotgun Creek
Baker Creek
Hunt Hot Springs
Big Bend Rancheria
Big Bend
Big Bend Bridge 31.1 mi.
Pit 5 Reach
Kosk Creek
Stump Creek
Blue Jay Creek
Big Bend Road
Flat Woods
Marble Creek
Little Joe Flat
Iron Canyon Reservoir
Bush Bar
Iron Canyon Creek
James B. Black Powerhouse 25.1 mi.
25.4 mi.
Pit 5 Powerhouse 24.9 mi.
Indian School House
Pit Reservoir
Cove Horn Creek
Pit 6 Dam 19.9 mi.
Initial Creek
N
E
S
W

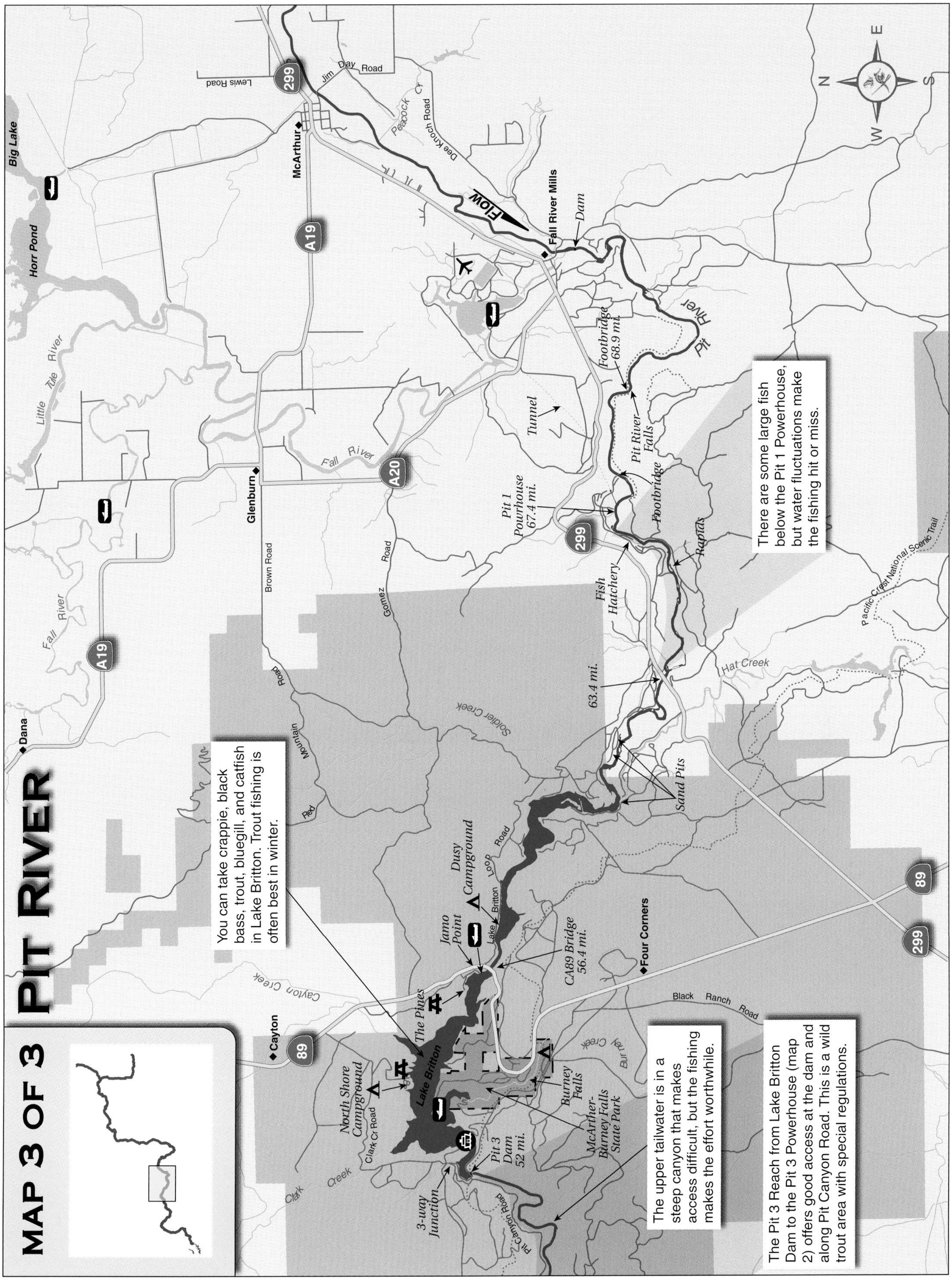
MAP 3 OF 3
PIT RIVER
You can take crappie, black bass, trout, bluegill, and catfish in Lake Britton. Trout fishing is often best in winter.
There are some large fish below the Pit 1 Powerhouse, but water fluctuations make the fishing hit or miss.
The upper tailwater is in a steep canyon that makes access difficult, but the fishing makes the effort worthwhile.
The Pit 3 Reach from Lake Britton Dam to the Pit 3 Powerhouse (map 2) offers good access at the dam and along Pit Canyon Road. This is a wild trout area with special regulations.
Big Lake
Horr Pond
McArthur
Fall River Mills
Dam
Flow
Jim Day Road
Lewis Road
Peacock Cr
Dee Knoch Road
Little Tule River
Fall River
Glenburn
Brown Road
Gomez Road
Tunnel
Footbridge 68.9 mi.
Pit River
Pit River Falls
Footbridge
Pit 1 Powerhouse 67.4 mi.
Rapids
Fish Hatchery
63.4 mi.
Hat Creek
Pacific Crest National Scenic Trail
Soldier Creek
Sand Pits
Dana
Mountain Road
Red
Dusy Campground
Lake Britton Loop Road
Jamo Point
CA89 Bridge 56.4 mi.
Four Corners
Cayton Creek
Cayton
The Pines
Black Ranch Road
Burney Creek
Lake Britton
Burney Falls
North Shore Campground
Clark Cr Road
McArthur-Burney Falls State Park
Pit 3 Dam 52 mi.
Clark Creek
3-way Junction
Pit Canyon Road
299
A19
A20
89
N
E
S
W

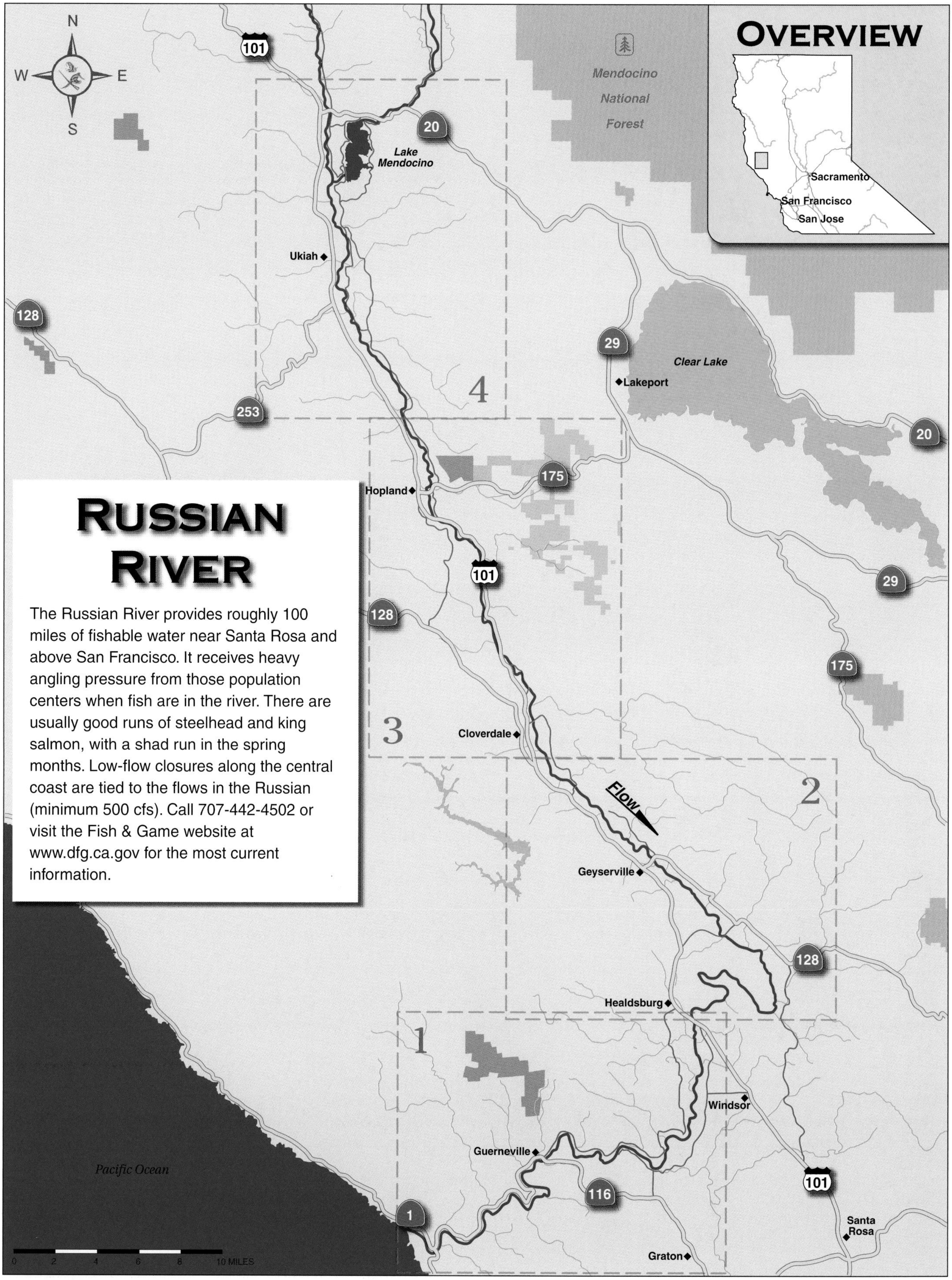

Russian River

The Russian River provides roughly 100 miles of fishable water near Santa Rosa and above San Francisco. It receives heavy angling pressure from those population centers when fish are in the river. There are usually good runs of steelhead and king salmon, with a shad run in the spring months. Low-flow closures along the central coast are tied to the flows in the Russian (minimum 500 cfs). Call 707-442-4502 or visit the Fish & Game website at www.dfg.ca.gov for the most current information.

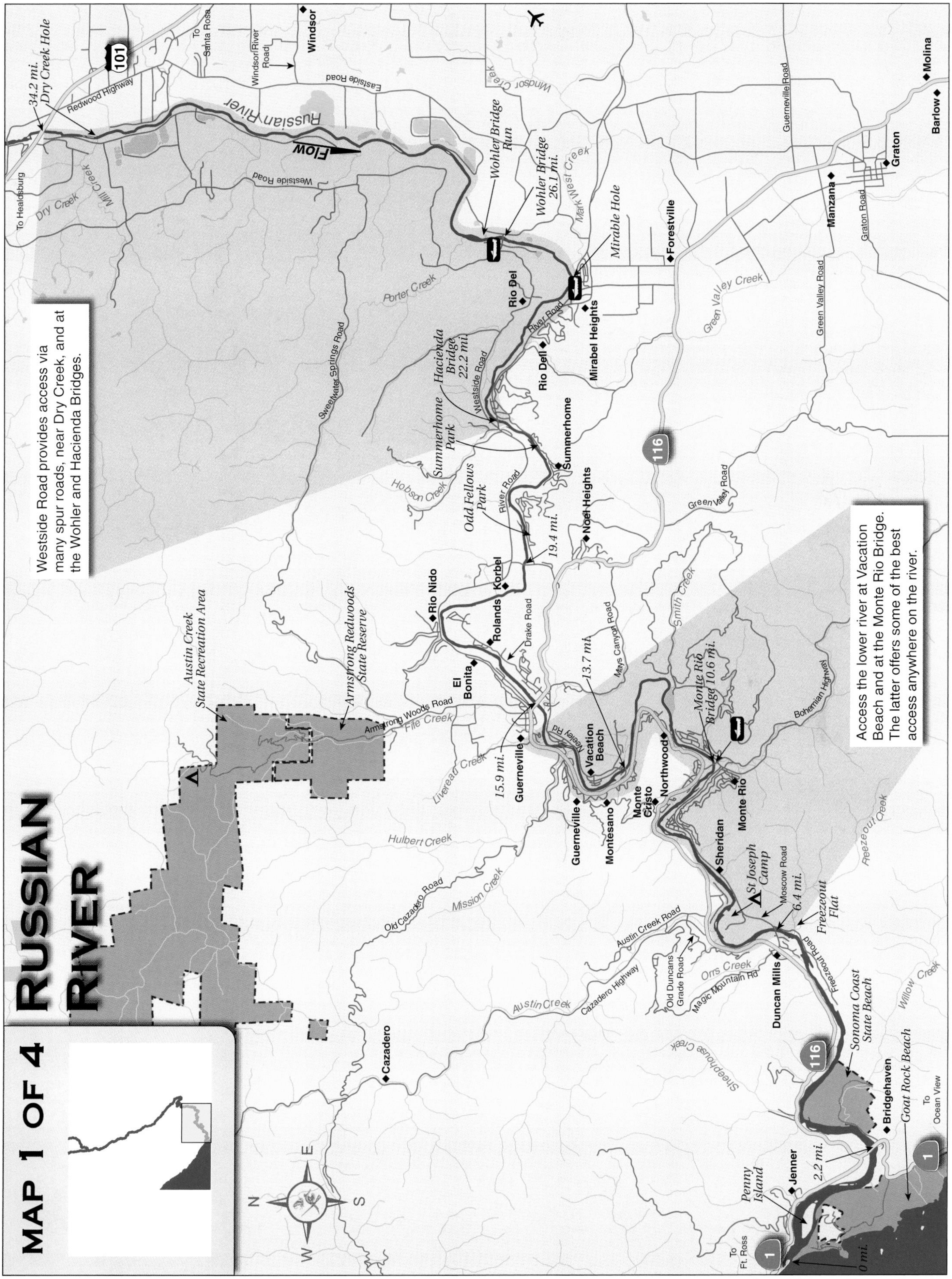
MAP 1 OF 4
RUSSIAN RIVER
Westside Road provides access via many spur roads, near Dry Creek, and at the Wohler and Hacienda Bridges.
Access the lower river at Vacation Beach and at the Monte Rio Bridge. The latter offers some of the best access anywhere on the river.
34.2 mi. Dry Creek Hole
Wohler Bridge Run
Wohler Bridge 26.1 mi.
Mirable Hole
Hacienda Bridge 22.2 mi.
Summerhome Park
Odd Fellows Park
19.4 mi.
15.9 mi.
13.7 mi.
Monte Rio Bridge 10.6 mi.
St Joseph Camp
6.4 mi.
Freezeout Flat
Sonoma Coast State Beach
Goat Rock Beach
2.2 mi.
Penny Island
0 mi.
Flow
Russian River
Austin Creek State Recreation Area
Armstrong Redwoods State Reserve
To Healdsburg
To Santa Rosa
To Ft. Ross
To Ocean View
Windsor
Windsor River Road
Redwood Highway
Eastside Road
Westside Road
Dry Creek
Mill Creek
Windsor Creek
Mark West Creek
Porter Creek
Sweetwater Springs Road
Hobson Creek
Green Valley Creek
Green Valley Road
Guerneville Road
Graton Road
Forestville
Manzana
Graton
Barlow
Molina
Rio Del
Rio Dell
Mirabel Heights
River Road
Summerhome
Noel Heights
Korbel
Rio Nido
Rolands
Drake Road
El Bonita
Armstrong Woods Road
Fife Creek
Livereau Creek
Guerneville
Vacation Beach
Neeley Rd
Mays Canyon Road
Smith Creek
Bohemian Highway
Montesano
Monte Cristo
Northwood
Monte Rio
Sheridan
Moscow Road
Freezeout Road
Freezeout Creek
Hulbert Creek
Mission Creek
Old Cazadero Road
Austin Creek Road
Old Duncans Grade Road
Orrs Creek
Magic Mountain Rd
Duncan Mills
Cazadero Highway
Austin Creek
Cazadero
Sheephouse Creek
Willow Creek
Bridgehaven
Jenner
101
116
1
N
E
S
W

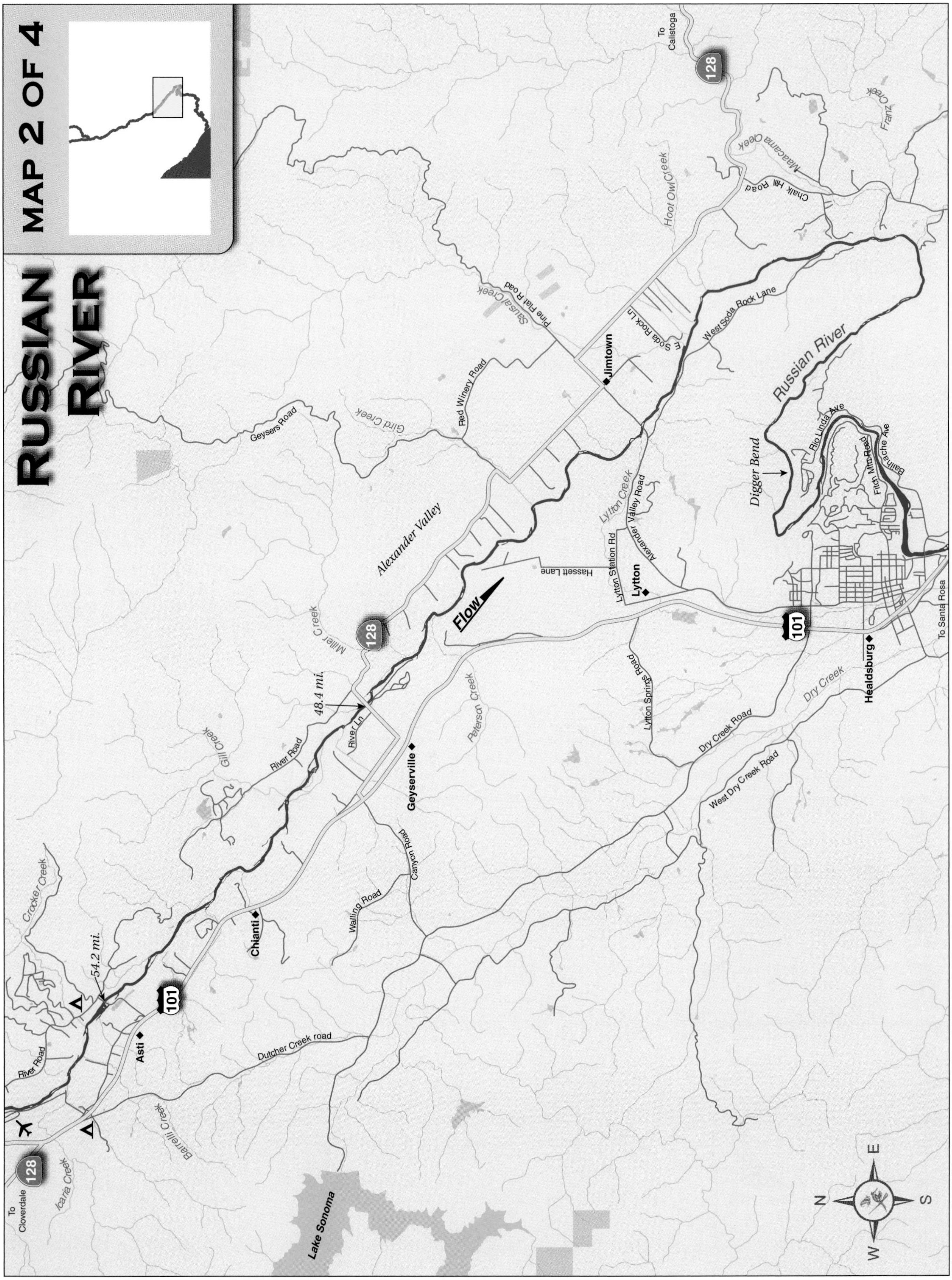
RUSSIAN RIVER
MAP 2 OF 4
To Calistoga
128
Franz Creek
Maacama Creek
Hoot Owl Creek
Chalk Hill Road
Sausal Creek
Pine Flat Road
E Soda Rock Ln
West Soda Rock Lane
Jimtown
Russian River
Red Winery Road
Gird Creek
Geysers Road
Rio Linda Ave
Digger Bend
Fitch Mtn Road
Bailhache Ave
Lytton Creek
Alexander Valley Road
Alexander Valley
Hassett Lane
Lytton Station Rd
Lytton
Flow
Miller Creek
101
To Santa Rosa
Healdsburg
48.4 mi.
Lytton Springs Road
Dry Creek
Peterson Creek
Gill Creek
River Road
River Ln
Geyserville
Dry Creek Road
West Dry Creek Road
Canyon Road
Walling Road
Crocker Creek
Chianti
54.2 mi.
Asti
Dutcher Creek road
River Road
Barrelli Creek
To Cloverdale
Icaria Creek
Lake Sonoma
N
E
S
W

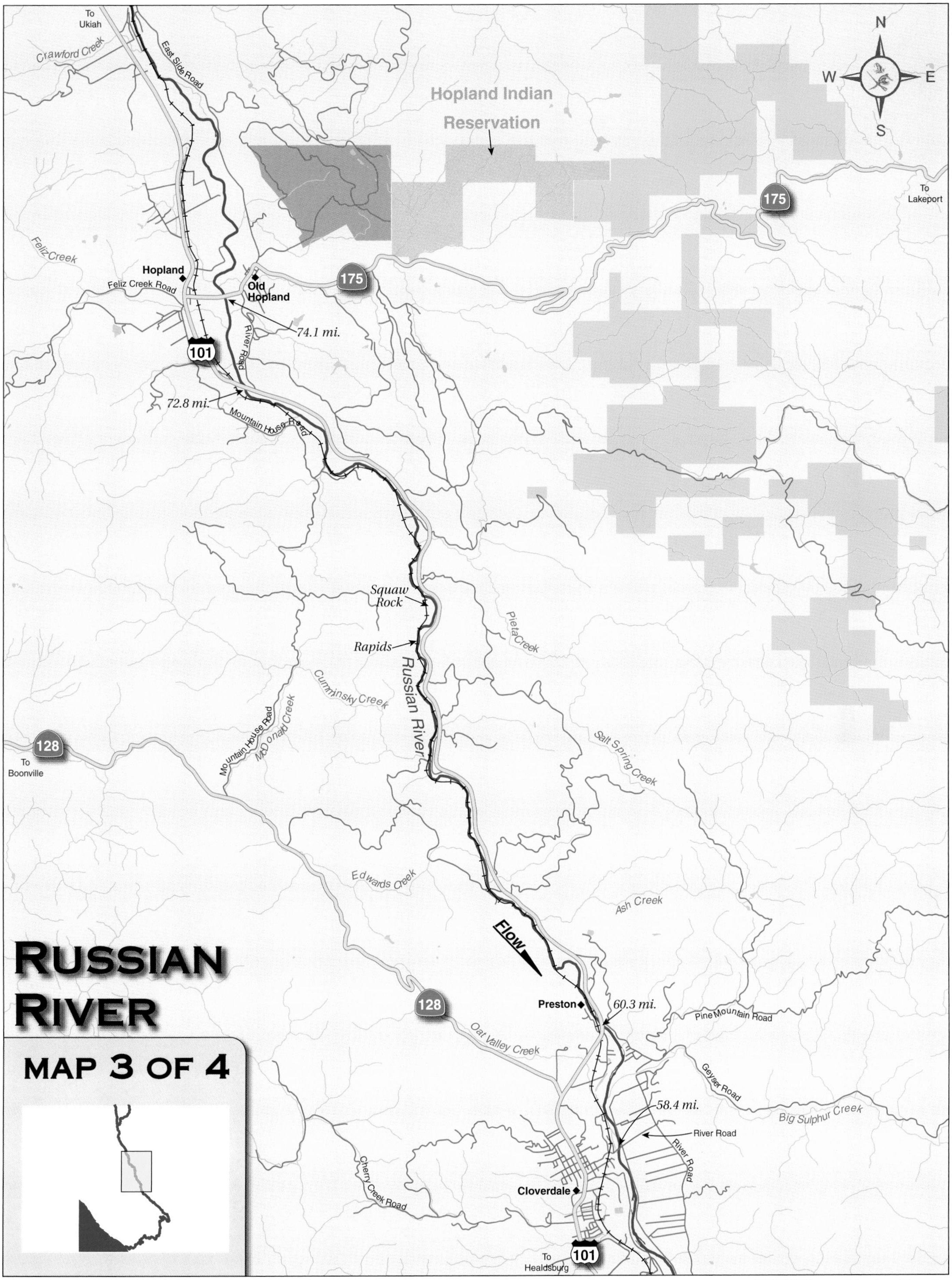
To Ukiah
Crawford Creek
East Side Road
Hopland Indian Reservation
N
W
E
S
175
To Lakeport
Feliz Creek
Hopland
Feliz Creek Road
Old Hopland
175
74.1 mi.
101
River Road
72.8 mi.
Mountain House Road
Squaw Rock
Rapids
Pieta Creek
Russian River
Cummisky Creek
McDonald Creek
Mountain House Road
128
To Boonville
Salt Spring Creek
Edwards Creek
Ash Creek
Flow
RUSSIAN RIVER
128
Preston
60.3 mi.
Pine Mountain Road
Oat Valley Creek
Geyser Road
MAP 3 OF 4
58.4 mi.
Big Sulphur Creek
River Road
River Road
Cherry Creek Road
Cloverdale
To Healdsburg
101

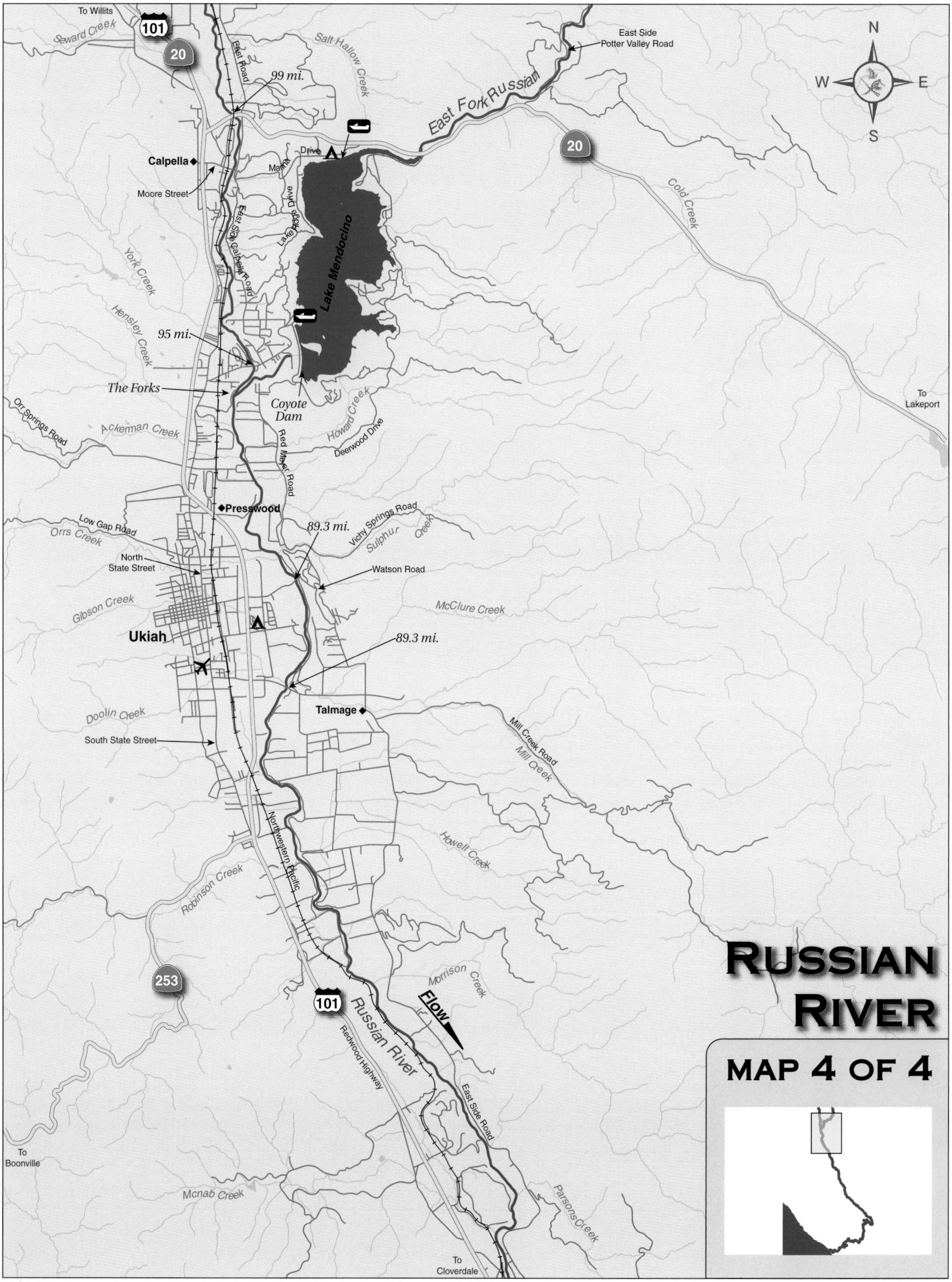

To Willits
101
20
Seward Creek
East Road
Salt Hallow Creek
East Side
Potter Valley Road
East Fork Russian
N
W
E
S
99 mi.
20
Drive
Marina
Calpella
Moore Street
Lake Ridge Drive
East Side Calpella Road
Lake Mendocino
Cold Creek
York Creek
Hensley Creek
95 mi.
The Forks
Coyote
Dam
Howard Creek
Deerwood Drive
Red Meyer Road
Orr Springs Road
Ackerman Creek
To
Lakeport
Presswood
Low Gap Road
Orrs Creek
Vichy Springs Road
Sulphur Creek
89.3 mi.
North
State Street
Watson Road
Gibson Creek
McClure Creek
Ukiah
89.3 mi.
Talmage
Doolin Creek
South State Street
Mill Creek Road
Mill Creek
Northwestern Pacific
Howell Creek
Robinson Creek
253
101
Russian River
Redwood Highway
Morrison Creek
Flow
East Side Road
RUSSIAN
RIVER
MAP 4 OF 4
To
Boonville
Mcnab Creek
Parsons Creek
To
Cloverdale

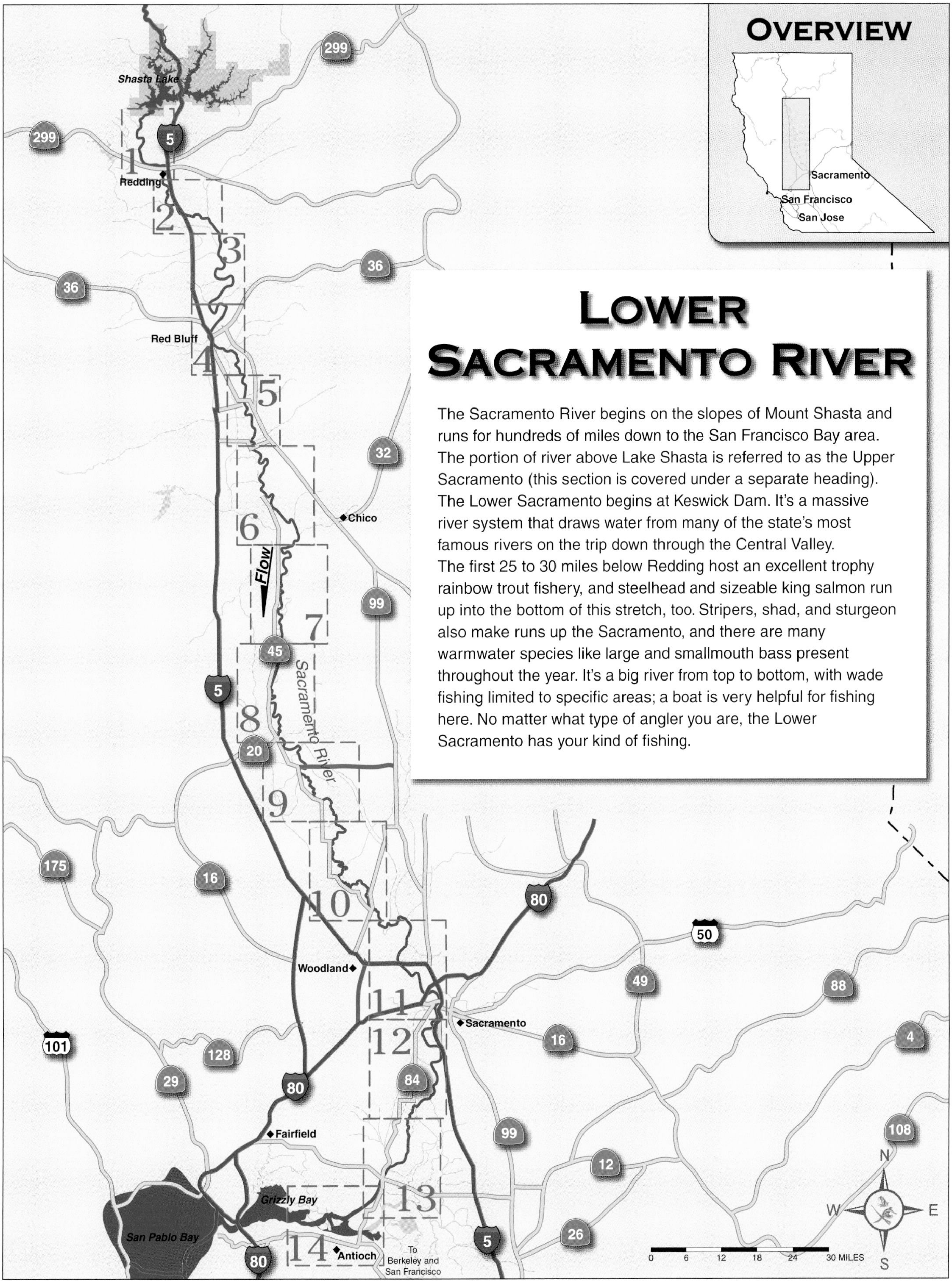

Lower Sacramento River

The Sacramento River begins on the slopes of Mount Shasta and runs for hundreds of miles down to the San Francisco Bay area. The portion of river above Lake Shasta is referred to as the Upper Sacramento (this section is covered under a separate heading). The Lower Sacramento begins at Keswick Dam. It's a massive river system that draws water from many of the state's most famous rivers on the trip down through the Central Valley. The first 25 to 30 miles below Redding host an excellent trophy rainbow trout fishery, and steelhead and sizeable king salmon run up into the bottom of this stretch, too. Stripers, shad, and sturgeon also make runs up the Sacramento, and there are many warmwater species like large and smallmouth bass present throughout the year. It's a big river from top to bottom, with wade fishing limited to specific areas; a boat is very helpful for fishing here. No matter what type of angler you are, the Lower Sacramento has your kind of fishing.

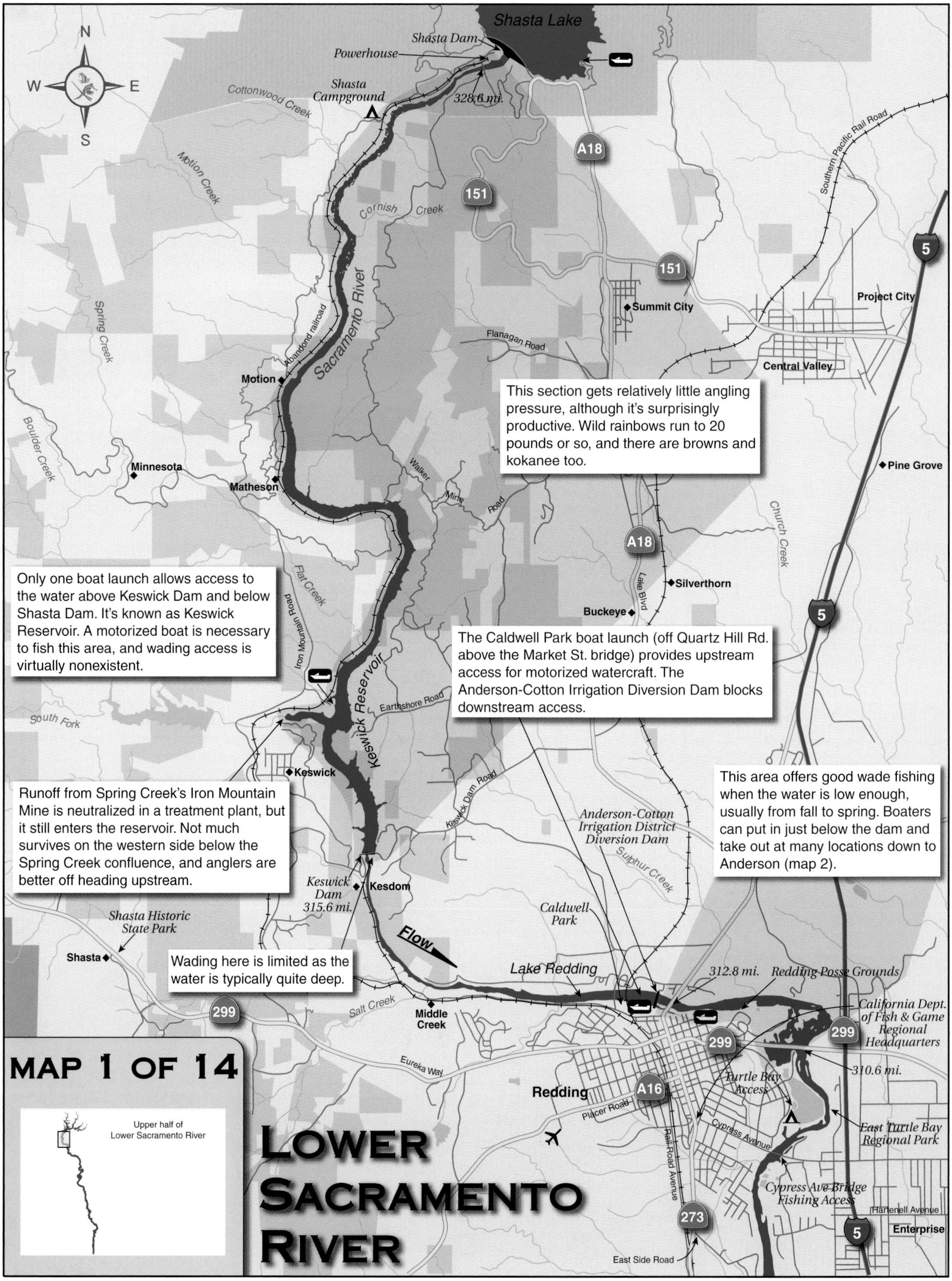
Shasta Lake
Shasta Dam
Powerhouse
Shasta Campground
328.6 mi.
Cottonwood Creek
Motion Creek
Cornish Creek
Sacramento River
Abandond railroad
Spring Creek
Flanagan Road
Summit City
Project City
Central Valley
Southern Pacific Rail Road
Motion
This section gets relatively little angling pressure, although it's surprisingly productive. Wild rainbows run to 20 pounds or so, and there are browns and kokanee too.
Boulder Creek
Minnesota
Matheson
Walker Mine Road
Pine Grove
Church Creek
Silverthorn
Buckeye
Lake Blvd
Only one boat launch allows access to the water above Keswick Dam and below Shasta Dam. It's known as Keswick Reservoir. A motorized boat is necessary to fish this area, and wading access is virtually nonexistent.
Flat Creek
Iron Mountain Road
Keswick Reservoir
Earthshore Road
The Caldwell Park boat launch (off Quartz Hill Rd. above the Market St. bridge) provides upstream access for motorized watercraft. The Anderson-Cotton Irrigation Diversion Dam blocks downstream access.
South Fork
Keswick
Keswick Dam Road
This area offers good wade fishing when the water is low enough, usually from fall to spring. Boaters can put in just below the dam and take out at many locations down to Anderson (map 2).
Runoff from Spring Creek's Iron Mountain Mine is neutralized in a treatment plant, but it still enters the reservoir. Not much survives on the western side below the Spring Creek confluence, and anglers are better off heading upstream.
Anderson-Cotton Irrigation District Diversion Dam
Sulphur Creek
Keswick Dam 315.6 mi.
Kesdom
Caldwell Park
Shasta Historic State Park
Shasta
Flow
Wading here is limited as the water is typically quite deep.
Lake Redding
312.8 mi.
Redding Posse Grounds
Salt Creek
Middle Creek
California Dept. of Fish & Game Regional Headquarters
MAP 1 OF 14
Eureka Way
310.6 mi.
Turtle Bay Access
Redding
Placer Road
Upper half of Lower Sacramento River
East Turtle Bay Regional Park
Cypress Avenue
Rail Road Avenue
Cypress Ave Bridge Fishing Access
Hartenell Avenue
Enterprise
East Side Road
LOWER SACRAMENTO RIVER

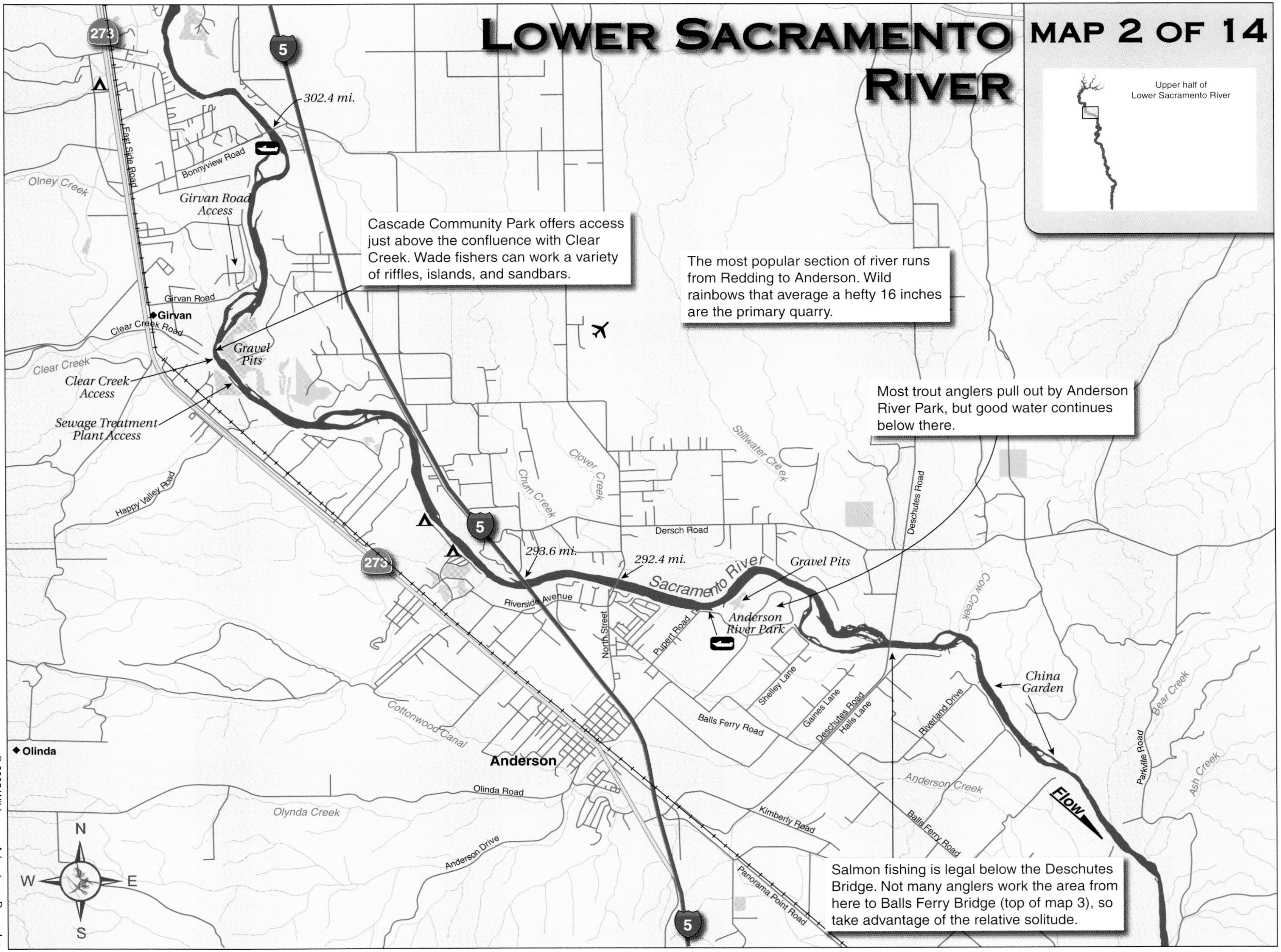
Lower Sacramento River
Map 2 of 14
Upper half of Lower Sacramento River
Cascade Community Park offers access just above the confluence with Clear Creek. Wade fishers can work a variety of riffles, islands, and sandbars.
The most popular section of river runs from Redding to Anderson. Wild rainbows that average a hefty 16 inches are the primary quarry.
Most trout anglers pull out by Anderson River Park, but good water continues below there.
Salmon fishing is legal below the Deschutes Bridge. Not many anglers work the area from here to Balls Ferry Bridge (top of map 3), so take advantage of the relative solitude.
302.4 mi.
293.6 mi.
292.4 mi.
Sacramento River
Girvan Road Access
Gravel Pits
Clear Creek Access
Sewage Treatment Plant Access
Anderson River Park
China Garden
Flow
Olney Creek
Clear Creek
Clear Creek Road
Girvan Road
Girvan
East Side Road
Bonnyview Road
Happy Valley Road
Chum Creek
Clover Creek
Stillwater Creek
Dersch Road
Deschutes Road
Cow Creek
Riverside Avenue
North Street
Pupert Road
Shelley Lane
Gaines Lane
Deschutes Road
Halls Lane
Riverland Drive
Balls Ferry Road
Kimberly Road
Panorama Point Road
Anderson Creek
Parkville Road
Bear Creek
Ash Creek
Cottonwood Canal
Anderson
Olinda Road
Olynda Creek
Anderson Drive
Olinda
N
S
E
W
5
273

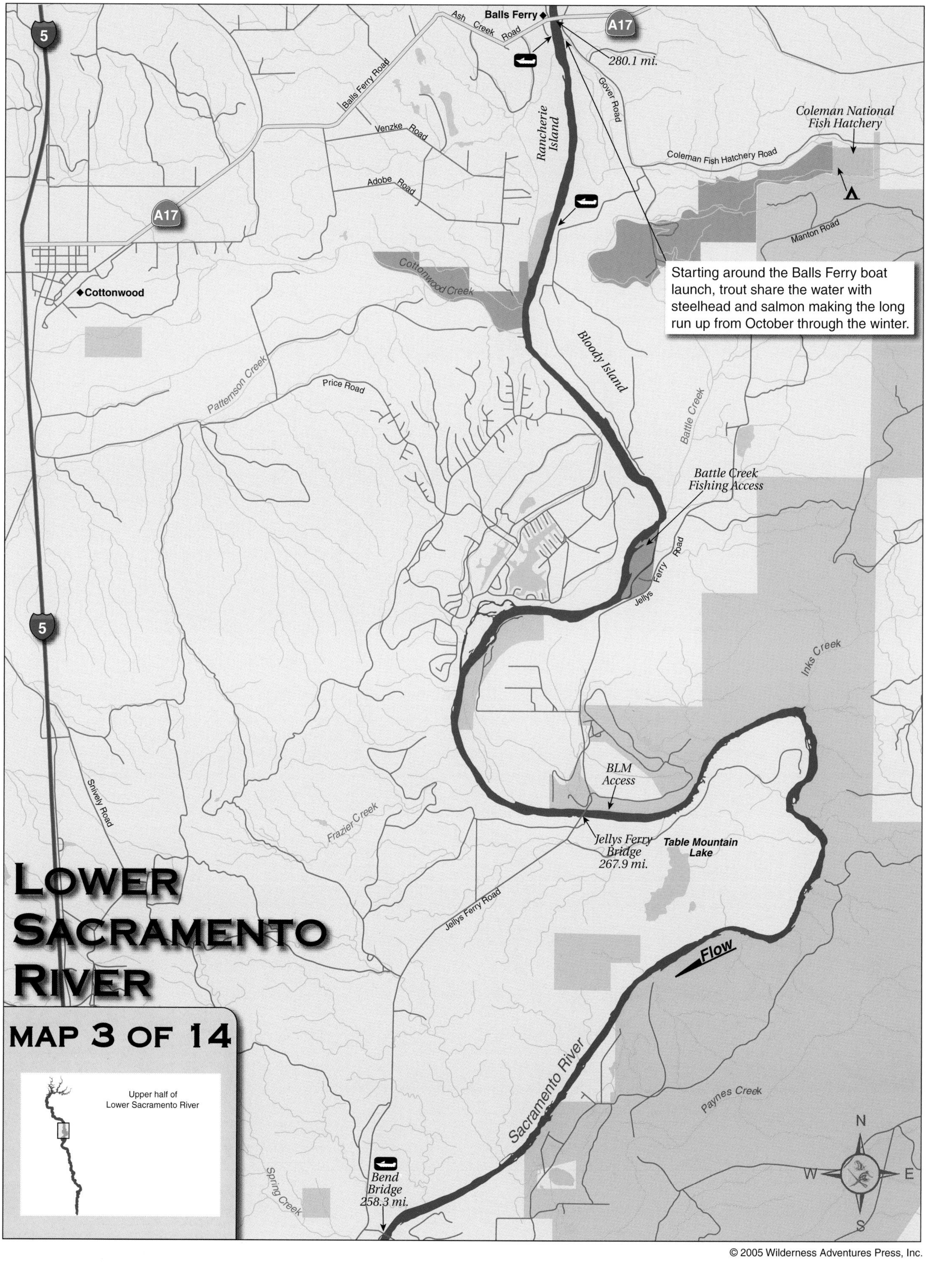

Balls Ferry
Ash Creek Road
A17
280.1 mi.
5
Balls Ferry Road
Gover Road
Rancherie Island
Coleman National Fish Hatchery
Venzke Road
Coleman Fish Hatchery Road
Adobe Road
A17
Manton Road
Cottonwood Creek
Starting around the Balls Ferry boat launch, trout share the water with steelhead and salmon making the long run up from October through the winter.
Cottonwood
Bloody Island
Patterson Creek
Price Road
Battle Creek
Battle Creek Fishing Access
Jellys Ferry Road
5
Inks Creek
BLM Access
Snively Road
Frazier Creek
Jellys Ferry Bridge 267.9 mi.
Table Mountain Lake
Jellys Ferry Road
Flow
Lower Sacramento River
Map 3 of 14
Upper half of Lower Sacramento River
Sacramento River
Paynes Creek
N
W
E
S
Spring Creek
Bend Bridge 258.3 mi.

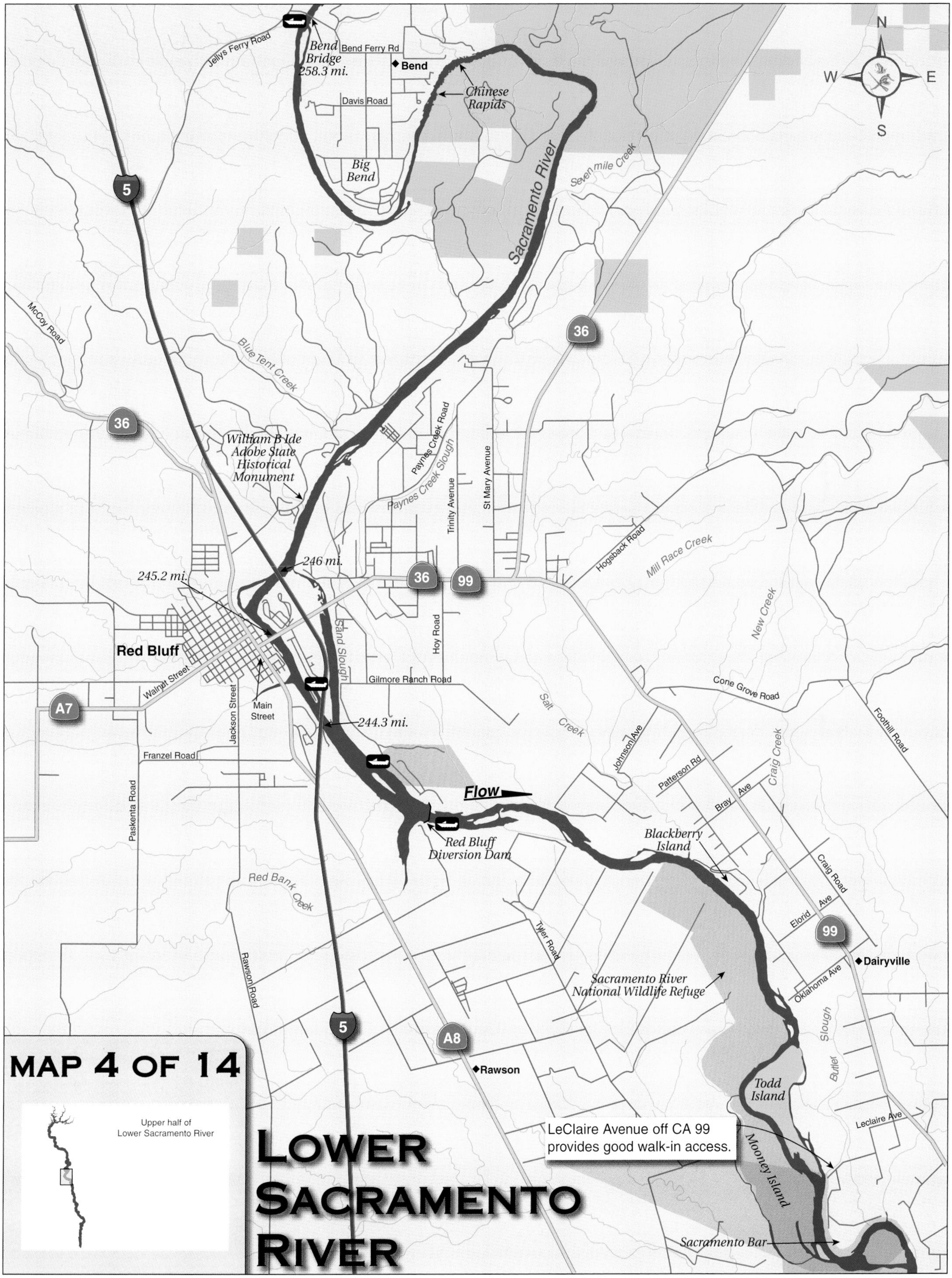
MAP 4 OF 14
Lower Sacramento River
Upper half of
Lower Sacramento River
Bend Bridge
258.3 mi.
Bend Ferry Rd
Bend
Jellys Ferry Road
Davis Road
Chinese Rapids
Big Bend
Sacramento River
Seven mile Creek
N
W
E
S
5
36
McCoy Road
Blue Tent Creek
William B Ide
Adobe State
Historical
Monument
Paynes Creek Road
Paynes Creek Slough
Trinity Avenue
St Mary Avenue
Hogsback Road
Mill Race Creek
246 mi.
245.2 mi.
99
Red Bluff
Sand Slough
Hoy Road
New Creek
Gilmore Ranch Road
Cone Grove Road
Walnut Street
Main Street
Jackson Street
A7
244.3 mi.
Salt Creek
Foothill Road
Johnson Ave
Franzel Road
Patterson Rd
Craig Creek
Bray Ave
Paskenta Road
Flow
Red Bluff
Diversion Dam
Blackberry
Island
Craig Road
Red Bank Creek
Elorid Ave
Tyler Road
Dairyville
Rawson Road
Sacramento River
National Wildlife Refuge
Oklahoma Ave
A8
Rawson
Slough
Butler
Todd
Island
Leclaire Ave
LeClaire Avenue off CA 99
provides good walk-in access.
Mooney Island
Sacramento Bar

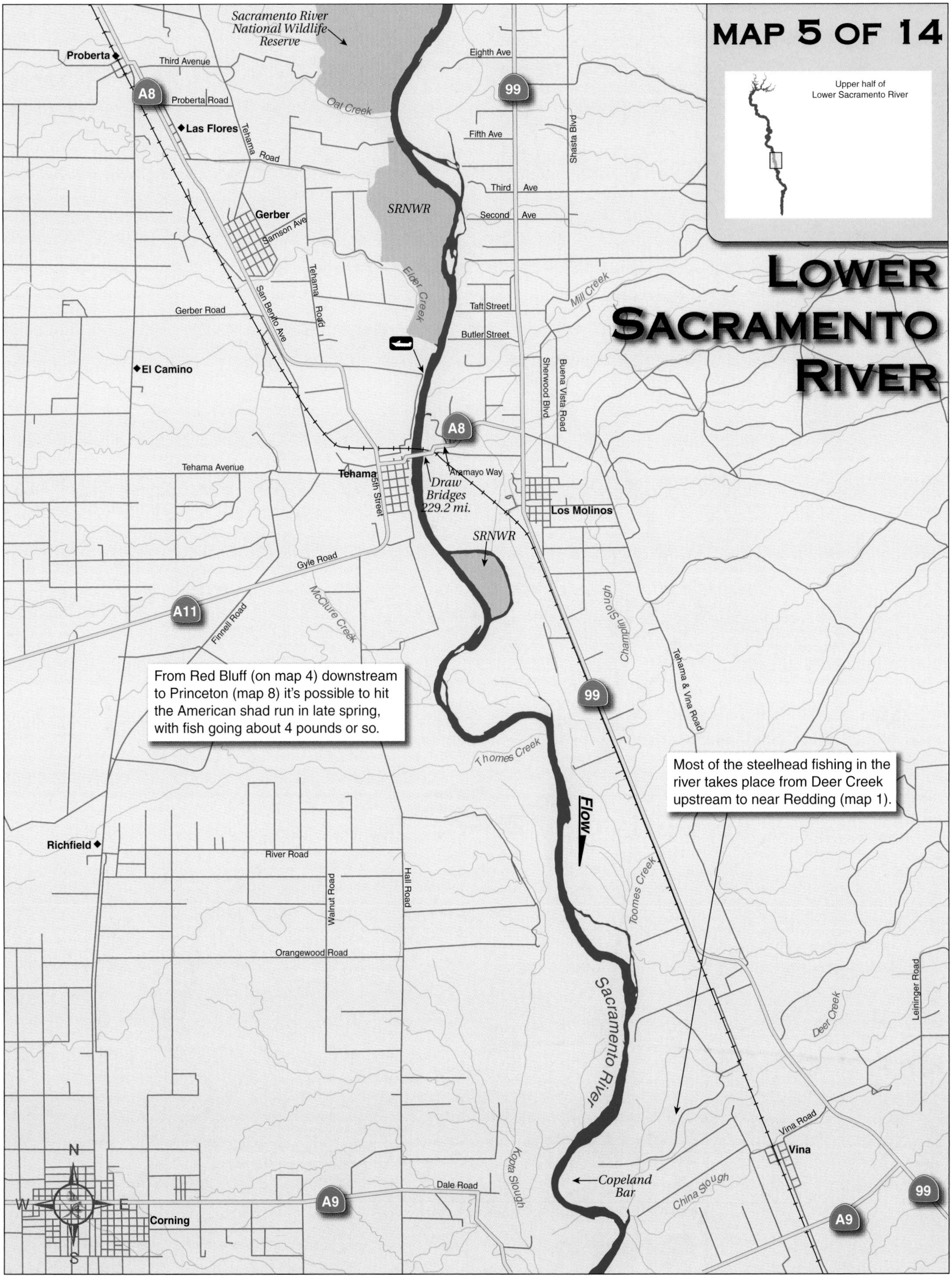

MAP 5 OF 14
Upper half of Lower Sacramento River
LOWER SACRAMENTO RIVER
Sacramento River National Wildlife Reserve
SRNWR
Proberta
Third Avenue
Proberta Road
Las Flores
Tehama Road
Oat Creek
Eighth Ave
Fifth Ave
Third Ave
Second Ave
Shasta Blvd
Gerber
Samson Ave
Tehama Road
San Benito Ave
Elder Creek
Gerber Road
Taft Street
Butler Street
Mill Creek
El Camino
Sherwood Blvd
Buena Vista Road
Tehama Avenue
Tehama
5th Street
Aramayo Way
Draw Bridges 229.2 mi.
Los Molinos
Gyle Road
McClure Creek
Finnell Road
Champlin Slough
Tehama & Vina Road
From Red Bluff (on map 4) downstream to Princeton (map 8) it's possible to hit the American shad run in late spring, with fish going about 4 pounds or so.
Thomes Creek
Flow
Most of the steelhead fishing in the river takes place from Deer Creek upstream to near Redding (map 1).
Richfield
River Road
Walnut Road
Hall Road
Toomes Creek
Orangewood Road
Sacramento River
Leininger Road
Deer Creek
Vina Road
Vina
Kopta Slough
Copeland Bar
Dale Road
China Slough
Corning
N
S
E
W
A8
A9
A11
99

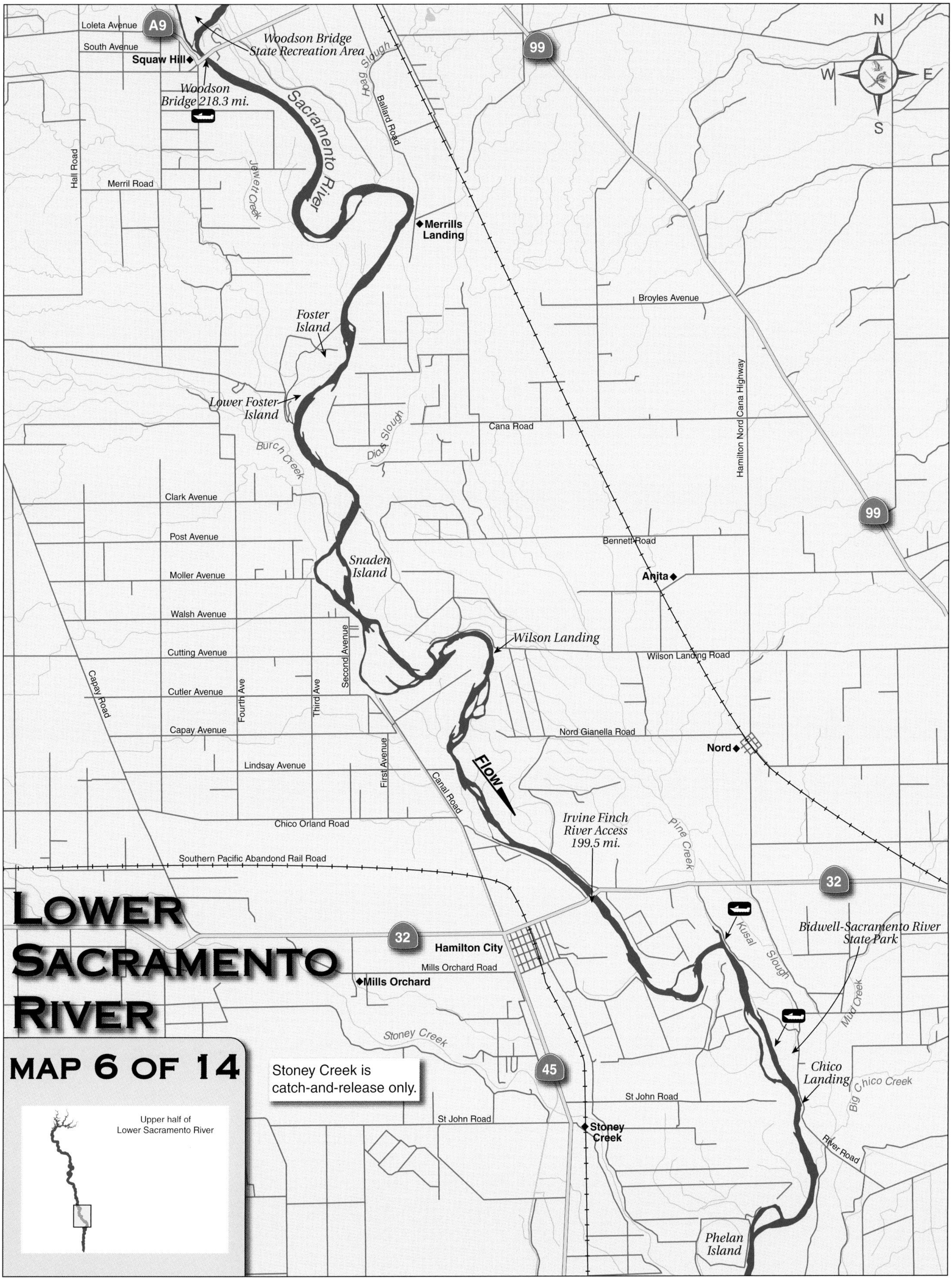
Lower Sacramento River
Map 6 of 14
Upper half of Lower Sacramento River
Stoney Creek is catch-and-release only.
Loleta Avenue
South Avenue
Squaw Hill
Woodson Bridge State Recreation Area
Woodson Bridge 218.3 mi.
Sacramento River
Hoag Slough
Ballard Road
Hall Road
Merril Road
Jewett Creek
Merrills Landing
Broyles Avenue
Foster Island
Lower Foster Island
Burch Creek
Dicus Slough
Cana Road
Hamilton Nord Cana Highway
Clark Avenue
Post Avenue
Moller Avenue
Walsh Avenue
Cutting Avenue
Cutler Avenue
Capay Avenue
Capay Road
Lindsay Avenue
Fourth Ave
Third Ave
Second Avenue
First Avenue
Snaden Island
Bennett Road
Anita
Wilson Landing
Wilson Landing Road
Nord Gianella Road
Nord
Flow
Canal Road
Chico Orland Road
Irvine Finch River Access 199.5 mi.
Pine Creek
Southern Pacific Abandond Rail Road
Hamilton City
Mills Orchard Road
Mills Orchard
Kusal Slough
Bidwell-Sacramento River State Park
Mud Creek
Stoney Creek
Chico Landing
Big Chico Creek
St John Road
Stoney Creek
River Road
Phelan Island
N
S
E
W
A9
99
32
45

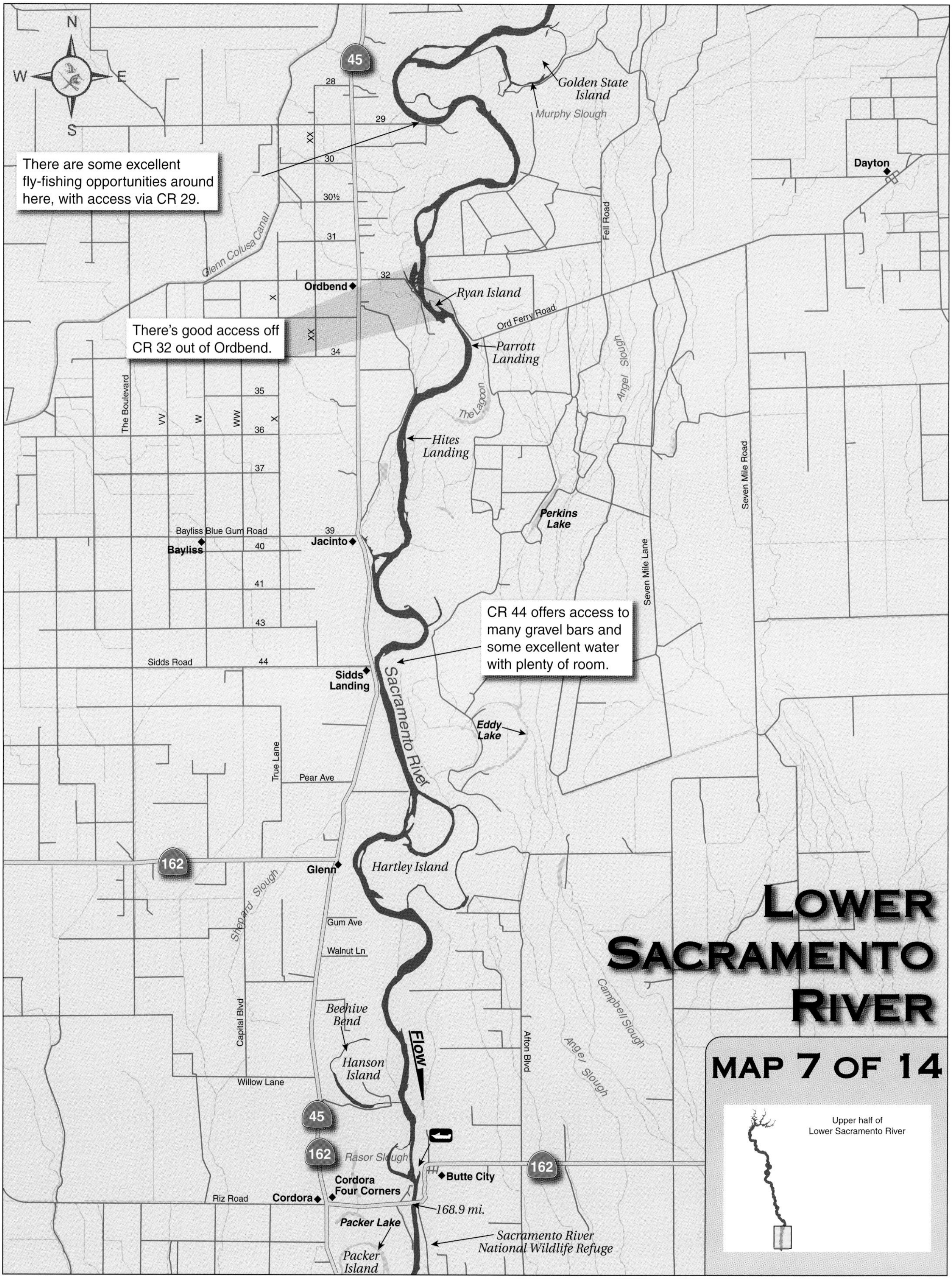

LOWER SACRAMENTO RIVER
MAP 7 OF 14
There are some excellent fly-fishing opportunities around here, with access via CR 29.
There's good access off CR 32 out of Ordbend.
CR 44 offers access to many gravel bars and some excellent water with plenty of room.
Golden State Island
Murphy Slough
Dayton
Ryan Island
Ordbend
Ord Ferry Road
Parrott Landing
Angel Slough
The Lagoon
Hites Landing
Fell Road
Seven Mile Road
Seven Mile Lane
Perkins Lake
Glenn Colusa Canal
The Boulevard
Bayliss Blue Gum Road
Bayliss
Jacinto
Sidds Road
Sidds Landing
Sacramento River
Eddy Lake
True Lane
Pear Ave
Glenn
Hartley Island
Shepard Slough
Gum Ave
Walnut Ln
Capital Blvd
Beehive Bend
Hanson Island
Willow Lane
Flow
Afton Blvd
Angel Slough
Campbell Slough
Rasor Slough
Butte City
Cordora Four Corners
Cordora
Riz Road
168.9 mi.
Packer Lake
Packer Island
Sacramento River National Wildlife Refuge
Upper half of Lower Sacramento River
45
162

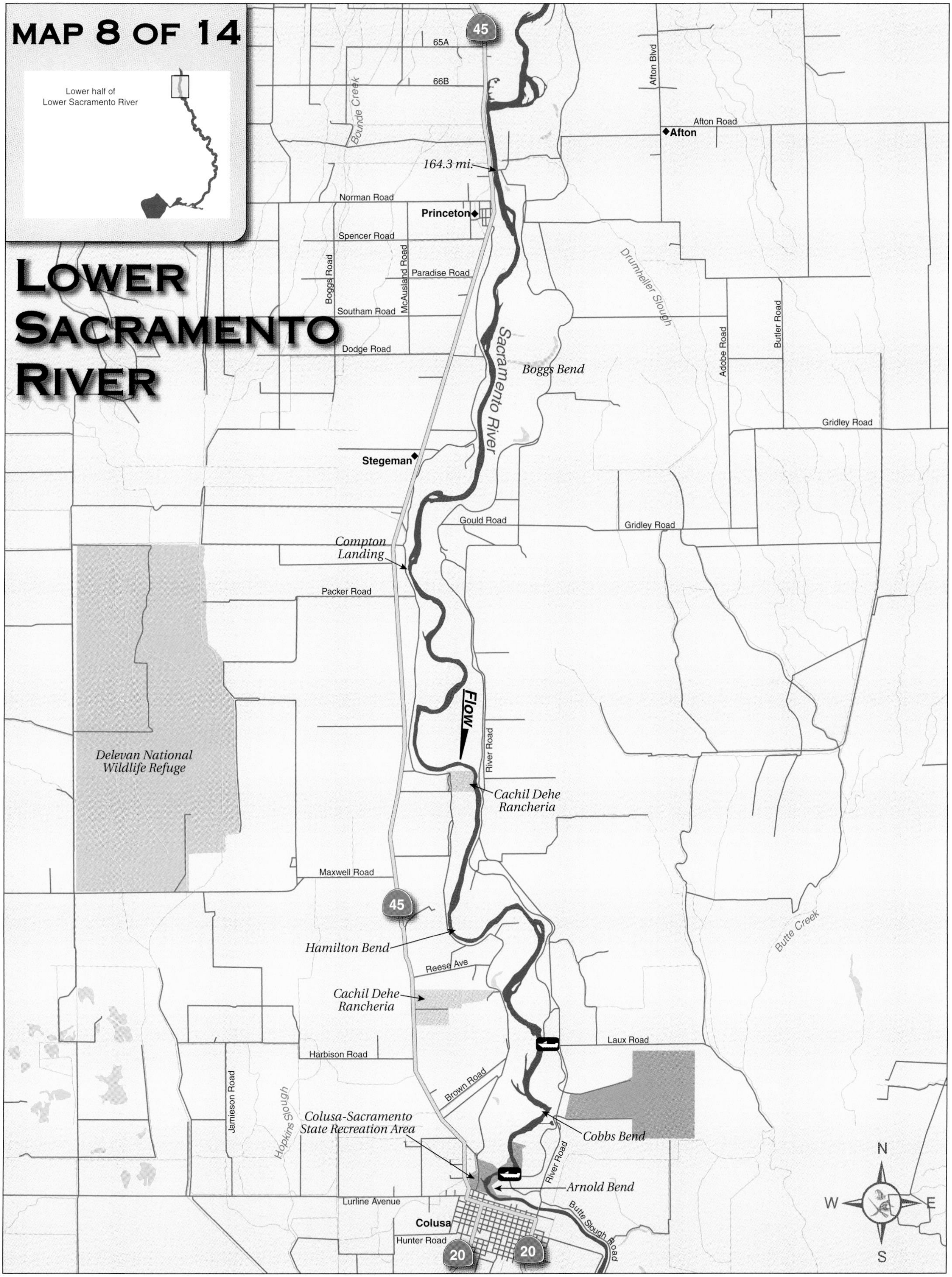
MAP 8 OF 14
Lower half of
Lower Sacramento River
LOWER SACRAMENTO RIVER
45
65A
66B
Bounde Creek
Afton Blvd
Afton Road
Afton
164.3 mi.
Norman Road
Princeton
Spencer Road
Boggs Road
McAusland Road
Paradise Road
Southam Road
Dodge Road
Drumheller Slough
Adobe Road
Butler Road
Sacramento River
Boggs Bend
Gridley Road
Stegeman
Gould Road
Gridley Road
Compton Landing
Packer Road
Flow
River Road
Delevan National Wildlife Refuge
Cachil Dehe Rancheria
Maxwell Road
45
Butte Creek
Hamilton Bend
Reese Ave
Cachil Dehe Rancheria
Laux Road
Harbison Road
Jamieson Road
Hopkins Slough
Brown Road
Colusa-Sacramento State Recreation Area
Cobbs Bend
River Road
Arnold Bend
Lurline Avenue
Colusa
Butte Slough Road
Hunter Road
20
20
N
W
E
S

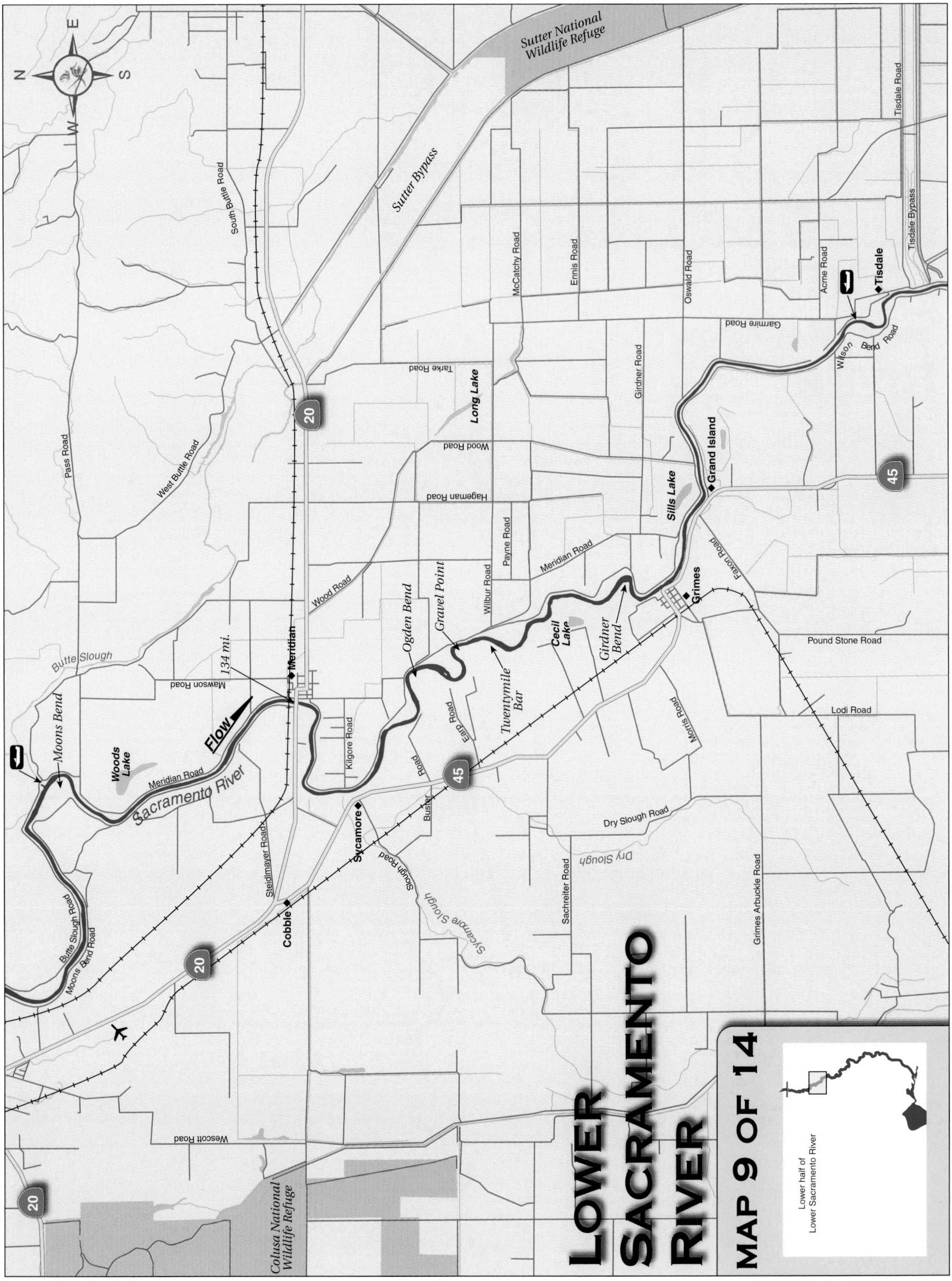
LOWER SACRAMENTO RIVER
MAP 9 OF 14
Lower half of Lower Sacramento River
N
E
S
W
Sutter National Wildlife Refuge
Sutter Bypass
Colusa National Wildlife Refuge
Sacramento River
Flow
134 mi.
Moons Bend
Woods Lake
Meridian Road
Butte Slough
Butte Slough Road
Moons Bend Road
Pass Road
West Buttle Road
South Buttle Road
Mawson Road
Meridian
Steidlmayer Road
Cobble
Sycamore
Slough Road
Sycamore Slough
Kilgore Road
Buster Road
Earp Road
Wood Road
Ogden Bend
Gravel Point
Twentymile Bar
Cecil Lake
Girdner Bend
Grimes
Morris Road
Sachreiter Road
Dry Slough
Dry Slough Road
Grimes Arbuckle Road
Pound Stone Road
Lodi Road
Faxon Road
Wilbur Road
Payne Road
Hageman Road
Wood Road
Long Lake
Take Road
McCatchy Road
Ennis Road
Oswald Road
Girdner Road
Sills Lake
Grand Island
Garmire Road
Acme Road
Tisdale
Wilson Bend Road
Tisdale Road
Tisdale Bypass
Wescott Road
20
45

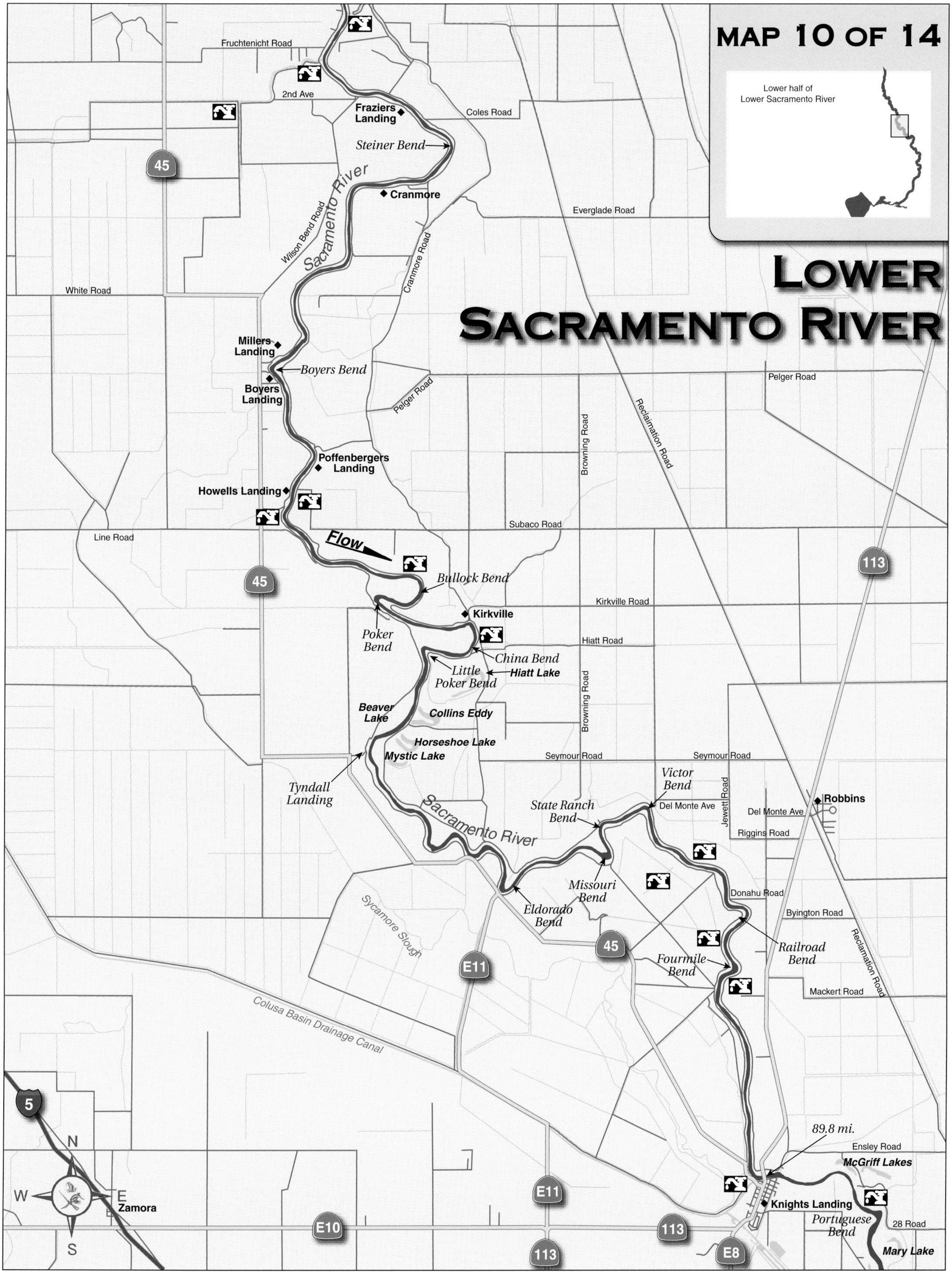
MAP 10 OF 14
Lower half of
Lower Sacramento River
LOWER
SACRAMENTO RIVER
Fruchtenicht Road
2nd Ave
Fraziers Landing
Coles Road
Steiner Bend
Sacramento River
Cranmore
Everglade Road
Wilson Bend Road
Cranmore Road
White Road
Millers Landing
Boyers Bend
Boyers Landing
Pelger Road
Pelger Road
Browning Road
Reclamation Road
Poffenbergers Landing
Howells Landing
Subaco Road
Line Road
Flow
Bullock Bend
Kirkville Road
Kirkville
Poker Bend
Hiatt Road
China Bend
Little Poker Bend
Hiatt Lake
Browning Road
Beaver Lake
Collins Eddy
Horseshoe Lake
Mystic Lake
Seymour Road
Seymour Road
Tyndall Landing
Victor Bend
Jewett Road
Robbins
State Ranch Bend
Del Monte Ave
Del Monte Ave
Riggins Road
Sacramento River
Missouri Bend
Donahu Road
Eldorado Bend
Byington Road
Sycamore Slough
Railroad Bend
Reclamation Road
Fourmile Bend
Mackert Road
Colusa Basin Drainage Canal
89.8 mi.
Ensley Road
McGriff Lakes
Knights Landing
Portuguese Bend
28 Road
Mary Lake
Zamora
N
S
E
W
45
45
45
113
113
113
E11
E11
E10
E8
5

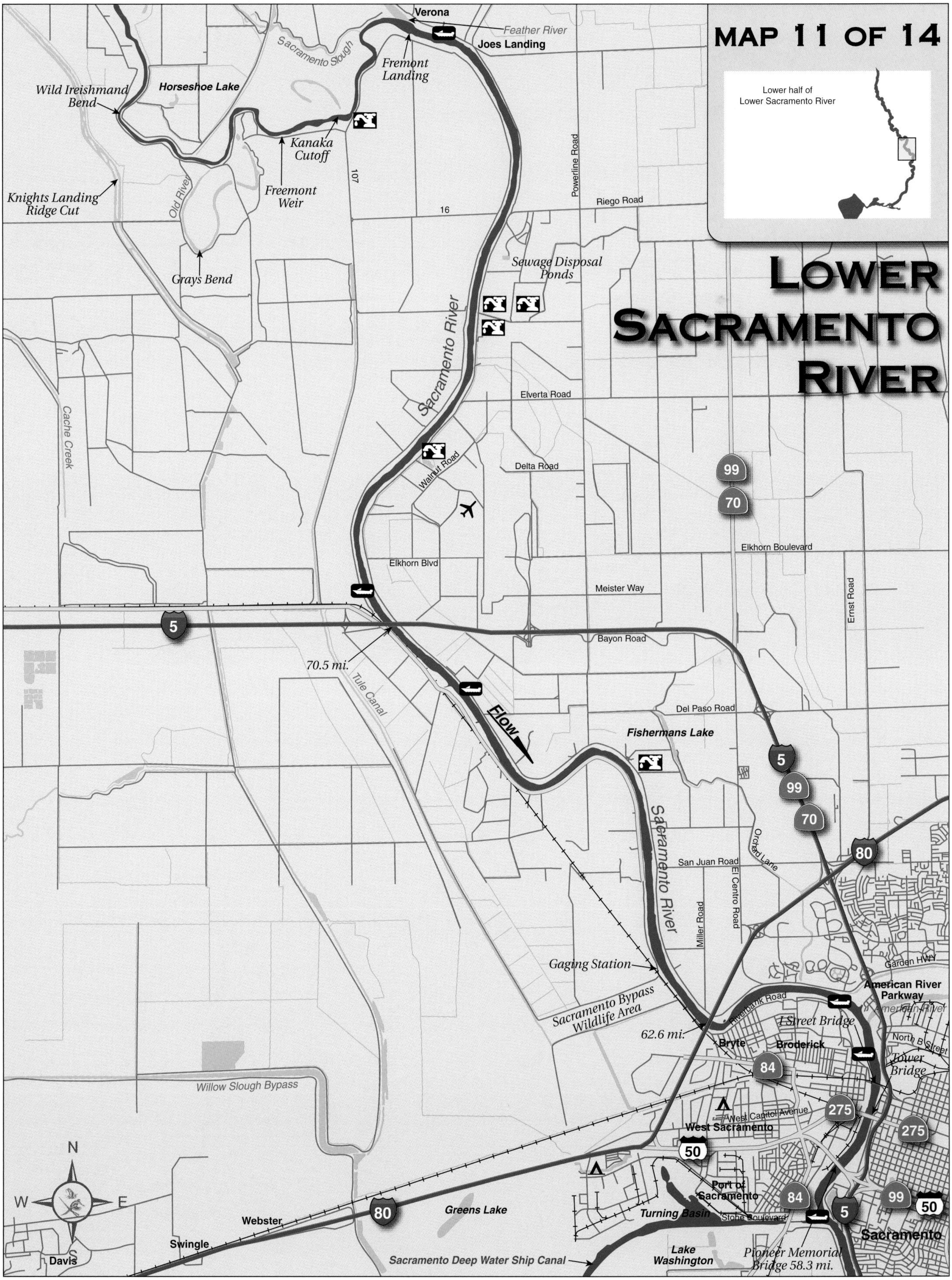
MAP 11 OF 14
Lower half of
Lower Sacramento River
LOWER SACRAMENTO RIVER
Verona
Feather River
Joes Landing
Sacramento Slough
Fremont Landing
Wild Ireishmand Bend
Horseshoe Lake
Kanaka Cutoff
Freemont Weir
Knights Landing Ridge Cut
Old River
Grays Bend
107
16
Powerline Road
Riego Road
Sewage Disposal Ponds
Sacramento River
Elverta Road
Cache Creek
Walnut Road
Delta Road
99
70
Elkhorn Blvd
Elkhorn Boulevard
Ernst Road
Meister Way
5
Bayon Road
70.5 mi.
Tule Canal
Flow
Del Paso Road
Fishermans Lake
Orchard Lane
80
San Juan Road
El Centro Road
Miller Road
Gaging Station
Garden HWY
American River Parkway
American River
Sacramento Bypass Wildlife Area
Riverbank Road
I Street Bridge
62.6 mi.
Bryte
Broderick
North B Street
Tower Bridge
84
Willow Slough Bypass
West Capitol Avenue
275
West Sacramento
50
Port of Sacramento
Turning Basin
Stone Boulevard
Greens Lake
Webster
Swingle
Davis
Lake Washington
Sacramento Deep Water Ship Canal
Pioneer Memorial Bridge 58.3 mi.
Sacramento
N
W
E
S

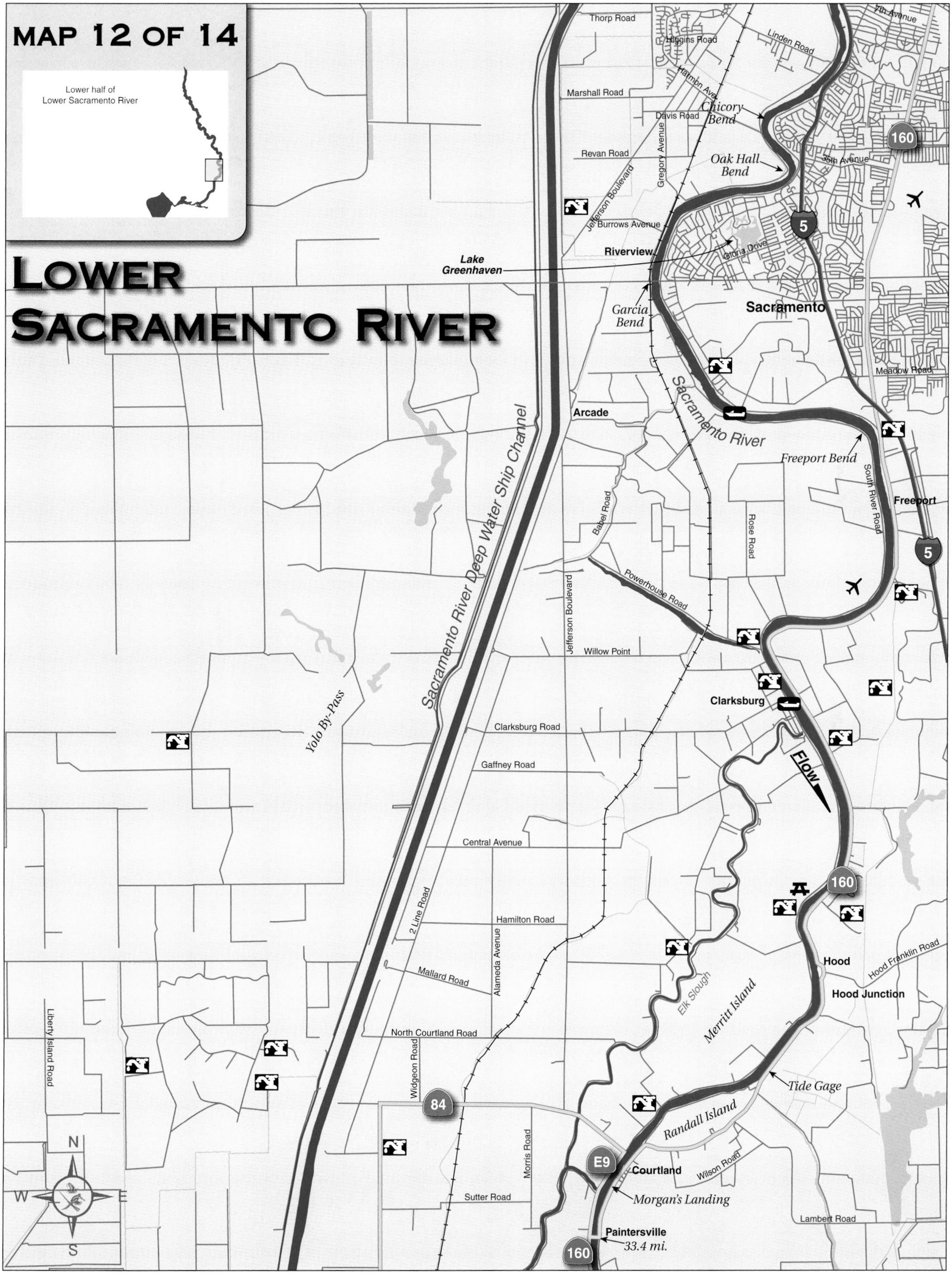
MAP 12 OF 14
Lower half of
Lower Sacramento River
LOWER
SACRAMENTO RIVER
Thorp Road
Higgins Road
Linden Road
7th Avenue
Marshall Road
Hamlin Ave.
Chicory Bend
Davis Road
160
Revan Road
Oak Hall Bend
35th Avenue
Gregory Avenue
Jefferson Boulevard
Burrows Avenue
5
Riverview
Gloria Drive
Lake Greenhaven
Garcia Bend
Sacramento
Meadow Road
Arcade
Sacramento River
Freeport Bend
Sacramento River Deep Water Ship Channel
South River Road
Freeport
Babel Road
Rose Road
Powerhouse Road
Jefferson Boulevard
Willow Point
Clarksburg
Yolo By-Pass
Clarksburg Road
Gaffney Road
Flow
Central Avenue
2 Line Road
Hamilton Road
Alameda Avenue
Mallard Road
Hood
Hood Franklin Road
Elk Slough
Merritt Island
Hood Junction
Liberty Island Road
North Courtland Road
Widgeon Road
Tide Gage
84
Randall Island
Morris Road
E9
Courtland
Wilson Road
Sutter Road
Morgan's Landing
Lambert Road
Paintersville
33.4 mi.
N
W
E
S

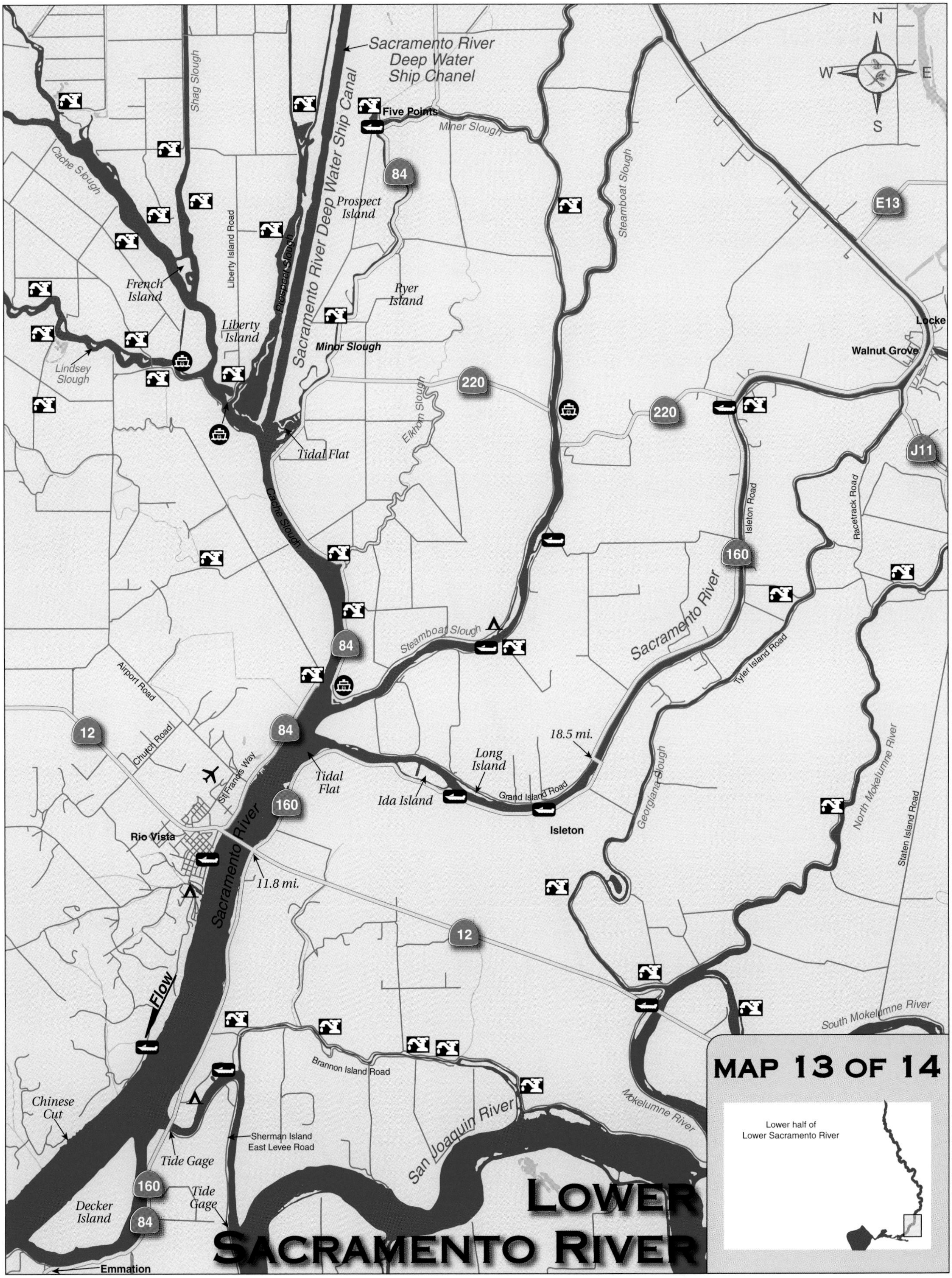
Sacramento River Deep Water Ship Chanel
Sacramento River Deep Water Ship Canal
Five Points
Miner Slough
Shag Slough
Cache Slough
Prospect Island
Liberty Island Road
Prospect Slough
French Island
Liberty Island
Ryer Island
Minor Slough
Lindsey Slough
Tidal Flat
Elkhorn Slough
Steamboat Slough
Locke
Walnut Grove
Isleton Road
Racetrack Road
Sacramento River
Tyler Island Road
Airport Road
Church Road
St. Francis Way
Rio Vista
18.5 mi.
Long Island
Ida Island
Grand Island Road
Isleton
Georgiana Slough
North Mokelumne River
Staten Island Road
11.8 mi.
Flow
South Mokelumne River
Brannon Island Road
Mokelumne River
San Joaquin River
Chinese Cut
Sherman Island East Levee Road
Tide Gage
Decker Island
Emmation
MAP 13 OF 14
Lower half of Lower Sacramento River
LOWER SACRAMENTO RIVER

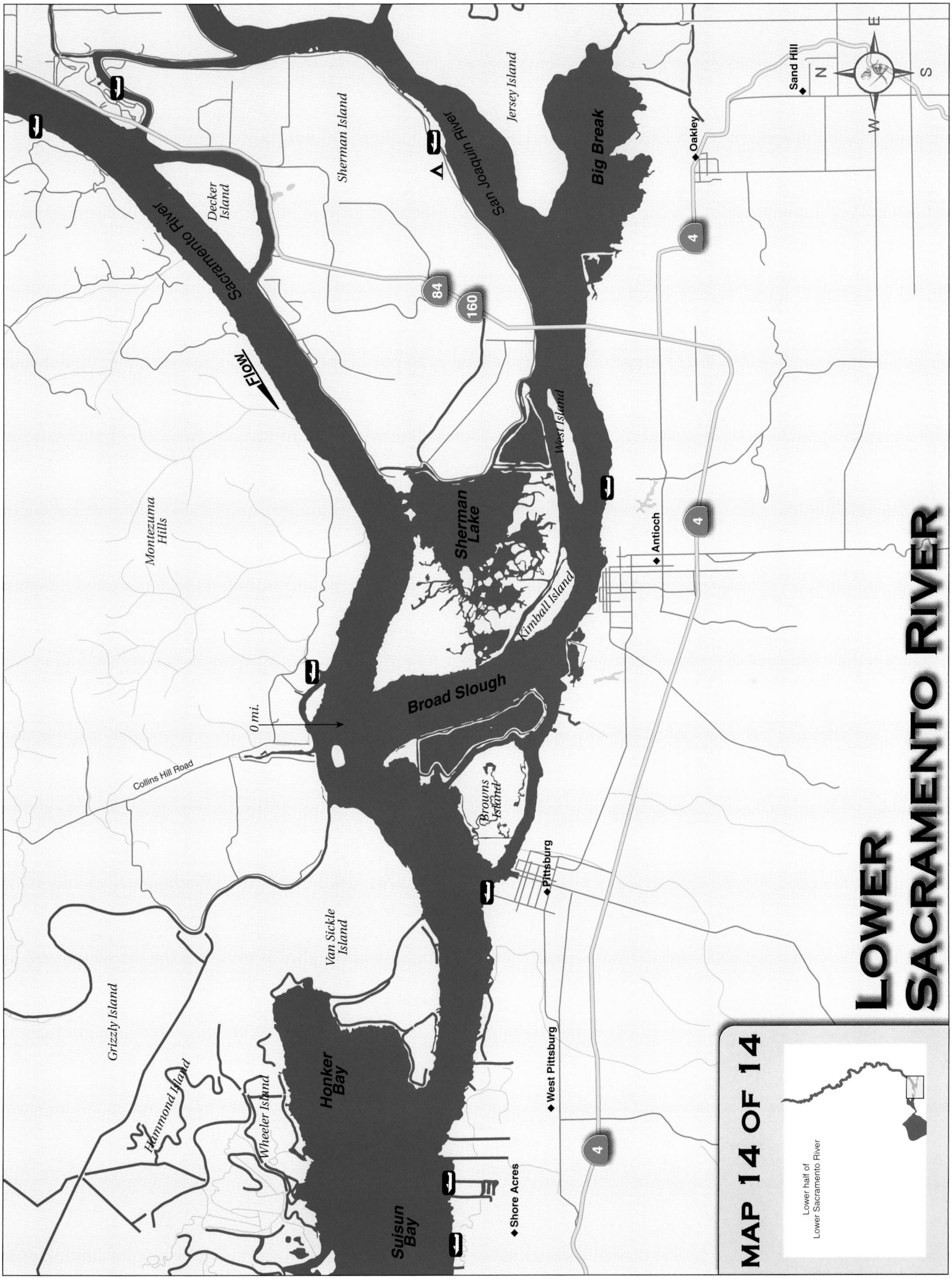

Lower Sacramento River
Map 14 of 14
Lower half of Lower Sacramento River
Sacramento River
San Joaquin River
Sherman Island
Jersey Island
Decker Island
Big Break
Oakley
Sand Hill
N
E
S
W
84
160
4
Flow
Montezuma Hills
West Island
Sherman Lake
Antioch
Kimball Island
Broad Slough
0 mi.
Collins Hill Road
Browns Island
Pittsburg
Van Sickle Island
Grizzly Island
Hammond Island
Wheeler Island
Honker Bay
West Pittsburg
Shore Acres
Suisun Bay

UPPER SACRAMENTO RIVER

The Upper Sacramento is everything a freestone trout stream should be, with riffles, pocket water, long runs, and deep pools. Gathering its water from the slopes of Mount Shasta, the upper river flows roughly 37 miles from Lake Siskiyou to Lake Shasta. The river has recovered surprisingly well from the chemical spill that decimated its trout population over a decade ago. These days you'll find wild rainbows throughout the river, and although they only average 12 inches or so, it's possible to hook up with one of the 20-inchers present. Some of those larger fish run up from Lake Shasta. Special regulations (catch-and-release only) protect these fish everywhere but in the 6-mile stretch around Dunsmuir, where hatchery rainbows are stocked. Access is excellent along the entire river, with I-5 running close to the water and a railroad bed providing hike-in access almost everywhere. When you hit a crowded area, just use the tracks to reach open water.

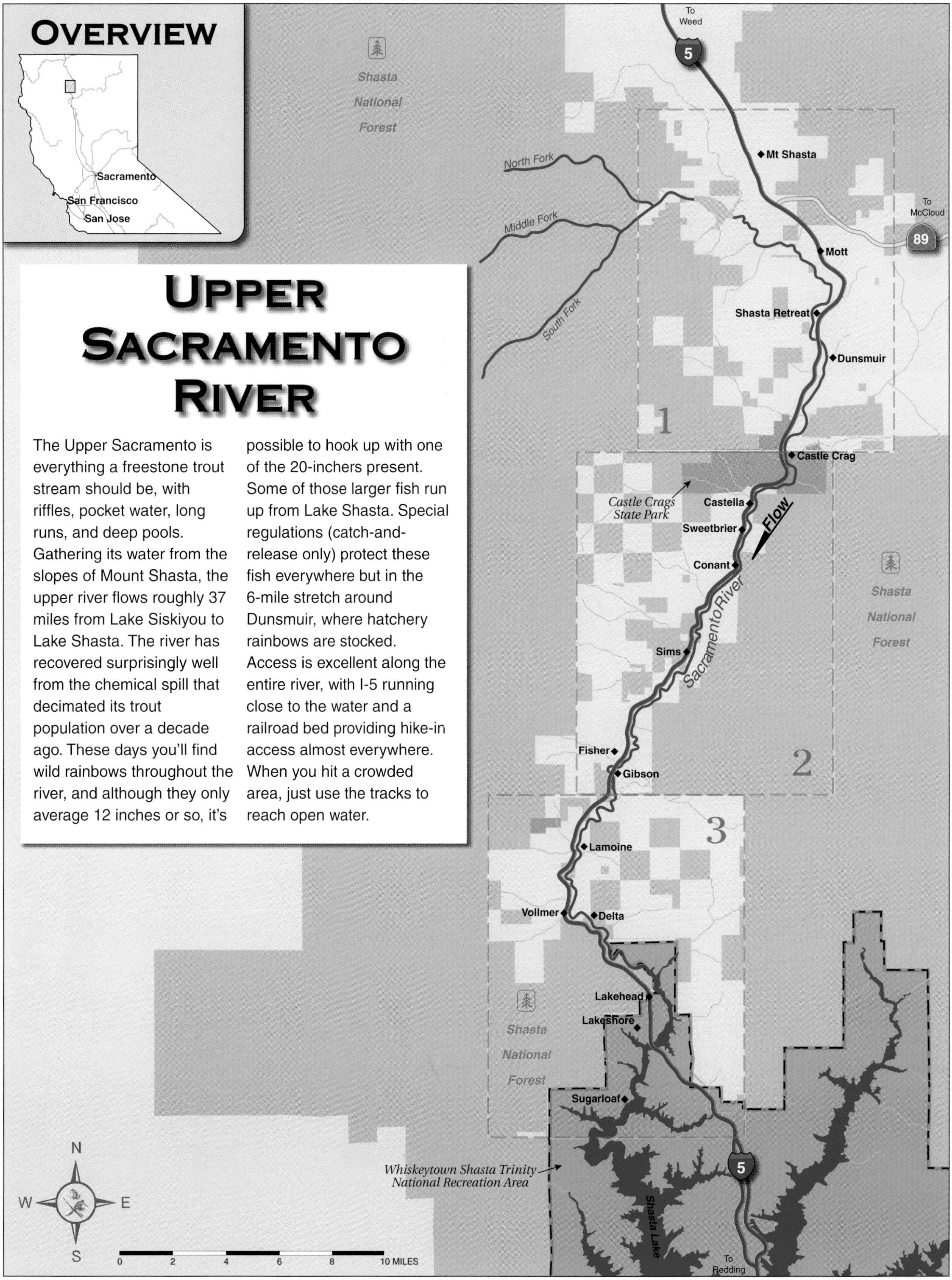

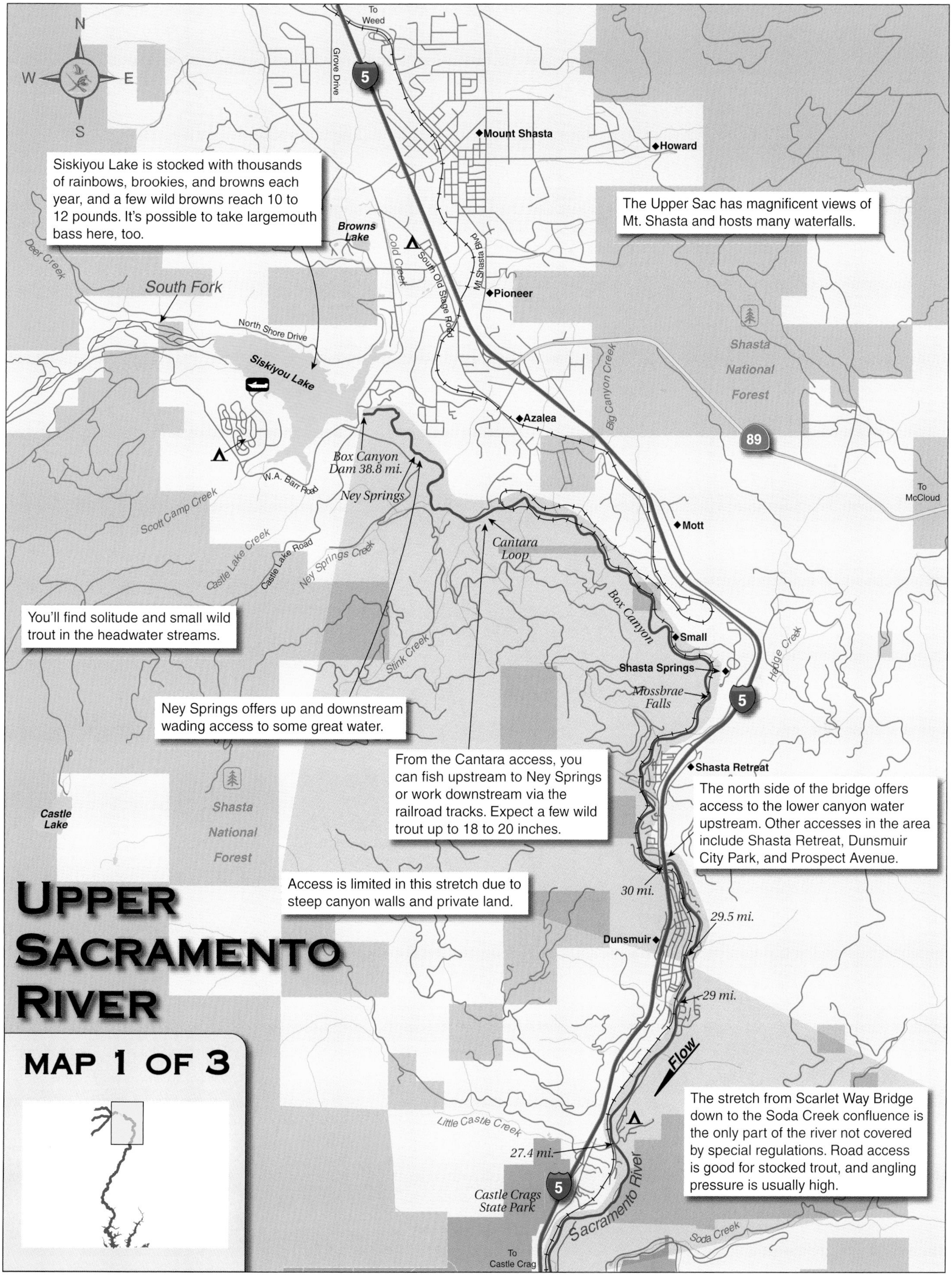
Siskiyou Lake is stocked with thousands of rainbows, brookies, and browns each year, and a few wild browns reach 10 to 12 pounds. It's possible to take largemouth bass here, too.
The Upper Sac has magnificent views of Mt. Shasta and hosts many waterfalls.
You'll find solitude and small wild trout in the headwater streams.
Ney Springs offers up and downstream wading access to some great water.
From the Cantara access, you can fish upstream to Ney Springs or work downstream via the railroad tracks. Expect a few wild trout up to 18 to 20 inches.
The north side of the bridge offers access to the lower canyon water upstream. Other accesses in the area include Shasta Retreat, Dunsmuir City Park, and Prospect Avenue.
Access is limited in this stretch due to steep canyon walls and private land.
The stretch from Scarlet Way Bridge down to the Soda Creek confluence is the only part of the river not covered by special regulations. Road access is good for stocked trout, and angling pressure is usually high.
UPPER SACRAMENTO RIVER
MAP 1 OF 3
N
S
E
W
To Weed
Grove Drive
Mount Shasta
Howard
Browns Lake
Cold Creek
South Old Stage Road
Mt Shasta Blvd
Pioneer
Deer Creek
South Fork
North Shore Drive
Siskiyou Lake
Shasta National Forest
Big Canyon Creek
Azalea
89
To McCloud
Box Canyon Dam 38.8 mi.
W.A. Barr Road
Ney Springs
Scott Camp Creek
Castle Lake Creek
Castle Lake Road
Ney Springs Creek
Cantara Loop
Mott
Box Canyon
Small
Stink Creek
Shasta Springs
Mossbrae Falls
Hedge Creek
5
Shasta Retreat
Castle Lake
Shasta National Forest
30 mi.
29.5 mi.
Dunsmuir
29 mi.
Flow
Little Castle Creek
27.4 mi.
Castle Crags State Park
Sacramento River
Soda Creek
To Castle Crag

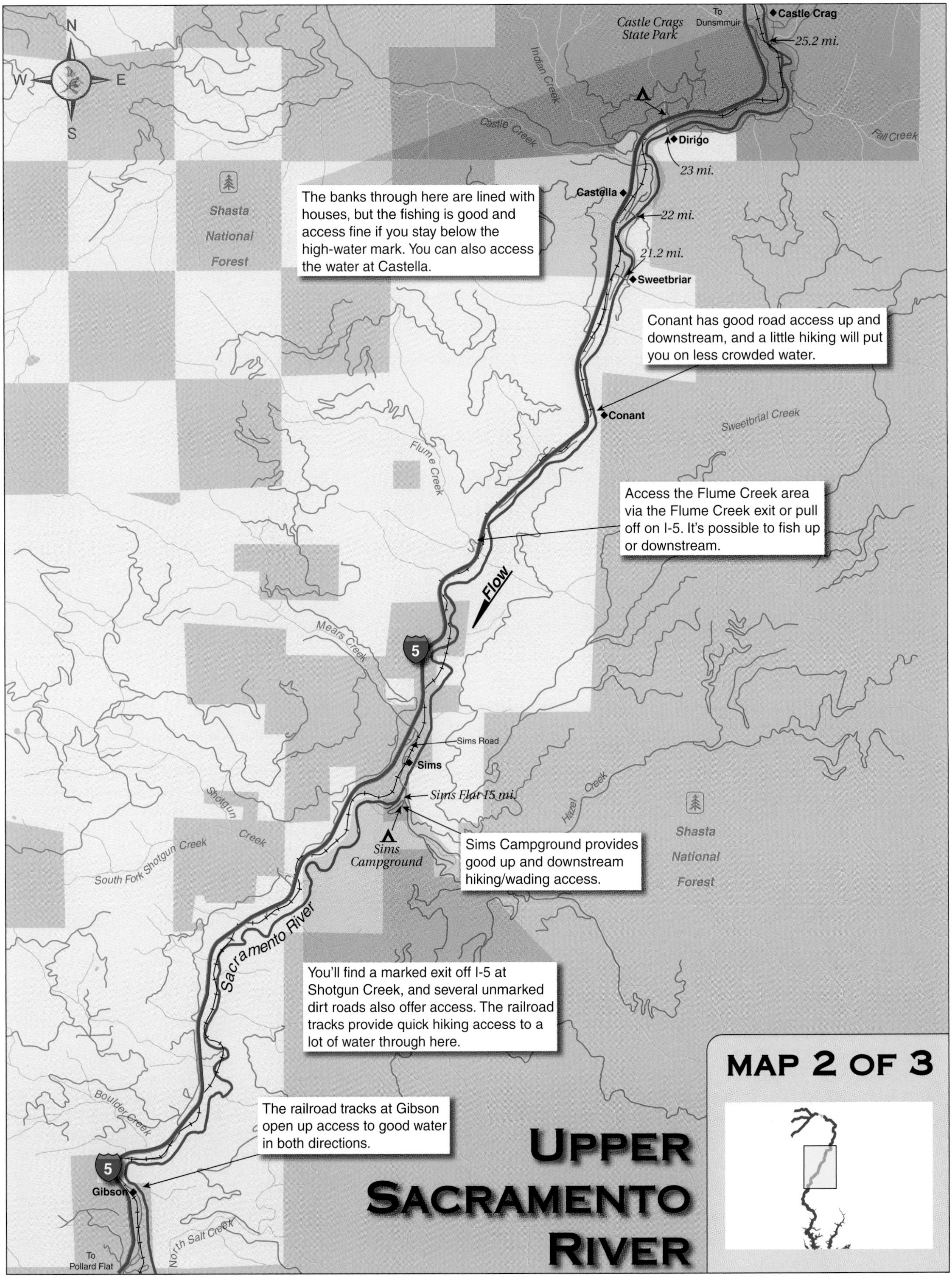
N
S
W
E
To Dunsmuir
Castle Crag
Castle Crags State Park
25.2 mi.
Indian Creek
Castle Creek
Fall Creek
Dirigo
23 mi.
Castella
22 mi.
21.2 mi.
Sweetbriar
Shasta National Forest
The banks through here are lined with houses, but the fishing is good and access fine if you stay below the high-water mark. You can also access the water at Castella.
Conant has good road access up and downstream, and a little hiking will put you on less crowded water.
Conant
Sweetbrial Creek
Flume Creek
Access the Flume Creek area via the Flume Creek exit or pull off on I-5. It's possible to fish up or downstream.
Flow
Mears Creek
5
Sims Road
Sims
Sims Flat 15 mi.
Hazel Creek
Shotgun Creek
South Fork Shotgun Creek
Sims Campground
Sims Campground provides good up and downstream hiking/wading access.
Shasta National Forest
Sacramento River
You'll find a marked exit off I-5 at Shotgun Creek, and several unmarked dirt roads also offer access. The railroad tracks provide quick hiking access to a lot of water through here.
Boulder Creek
The railroad tracks at Gibson open up access to good water in both directions.
Gibson
North Salt Creek
To Pollard Flat
MAP 2 OF 3
UPPER SACRAMENTO RIVER

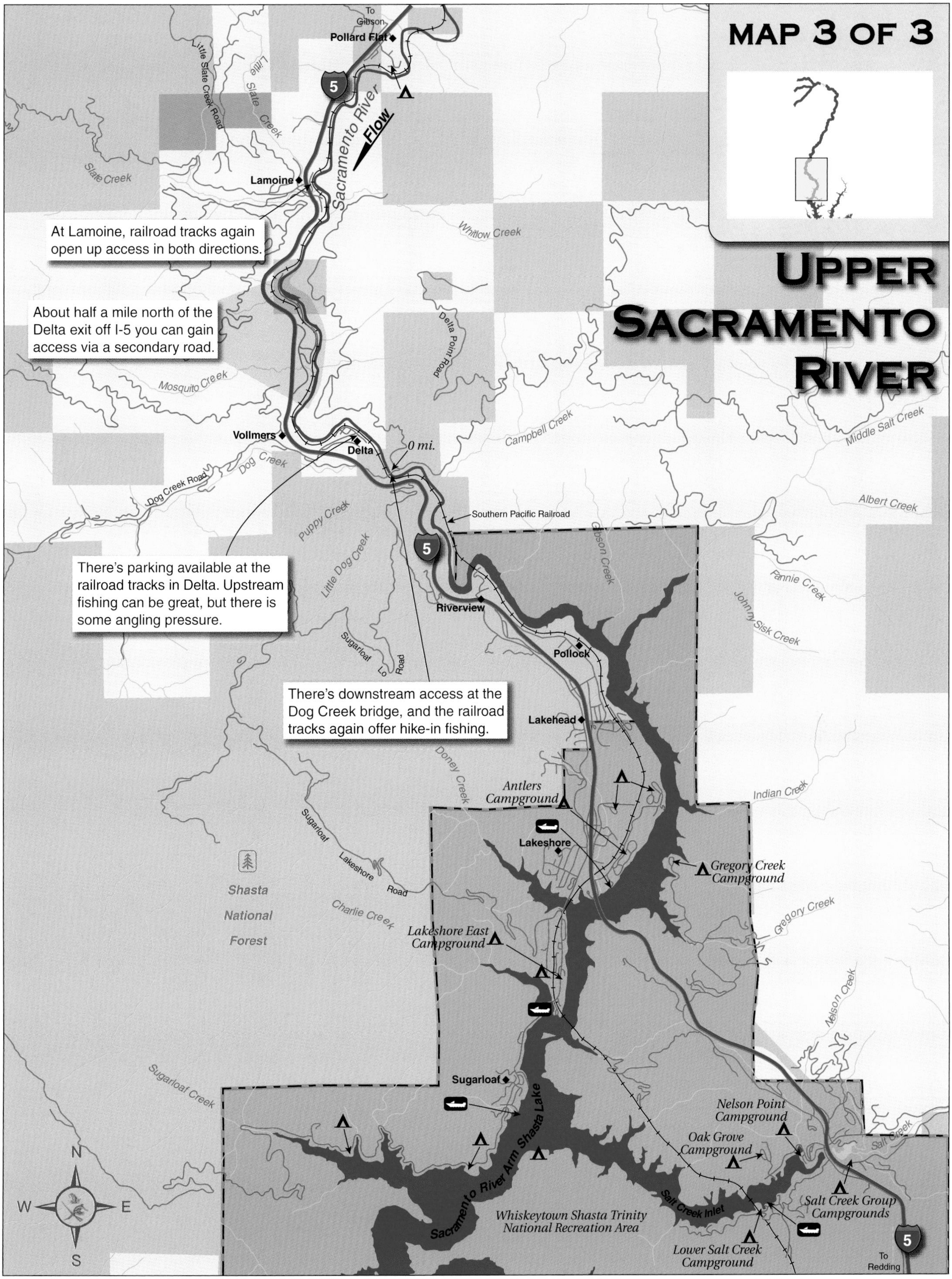

MAP 3 OF 3
UPPER SACRAMENTO RIVER
To Gibson
Pollard Flat
Little Slate Creek Road
Little Slate Creek
Sacramento River
Flow
Slate Creek
Lamoine
At Lamoine, railroad tracks again open up access in both directions.
Whitlow Creek
About half a mile north of the Delta exit off I-5 you can gain access via a secondary road.
Delta Point Road
Mosquito Creek
Vollmers
Delta
0 mi.
Campbell Creek
Middle Salt Creek
Dog Creek Road
Dog Creek
Albert Creek
Southern Pacific Railroad
Puppy Creek
Gibson Creek
There's parking available at the railroad tracks in Delta. Upstream fishing can be great, but there is some angling pressure.
Little Dog Creek
Fannie Creek
Johnny Sisk Creek
Riverview
Pollock
Sugarloaf Lo Road
There's downstream access at the Dog Creek bridge, and the railroad tracks again offer hike-in fishing.
Lakehead
Doney Creek
Antlers Campground
Indian Creek
Lakeshore
Sugarloaf Lakeshore Road
Gregory Creek Campground
Shasta National Forest
Charlie Creek
Gregory Creek
Lakeshore East Campground
Nelson Creek
Sugarloaf
Sugarloaf Creek
Nelson Point Campground
Oak Grove Campground
Salt Creek
Sacramento River Arm Shasta Lake
Salt Creek Inlet
Salt Creek Group Campgrounds
Whiskeytown Shasta Trinity National Recreation Area
Lower Salt Creek Campground
To Redding
N
W
E
S

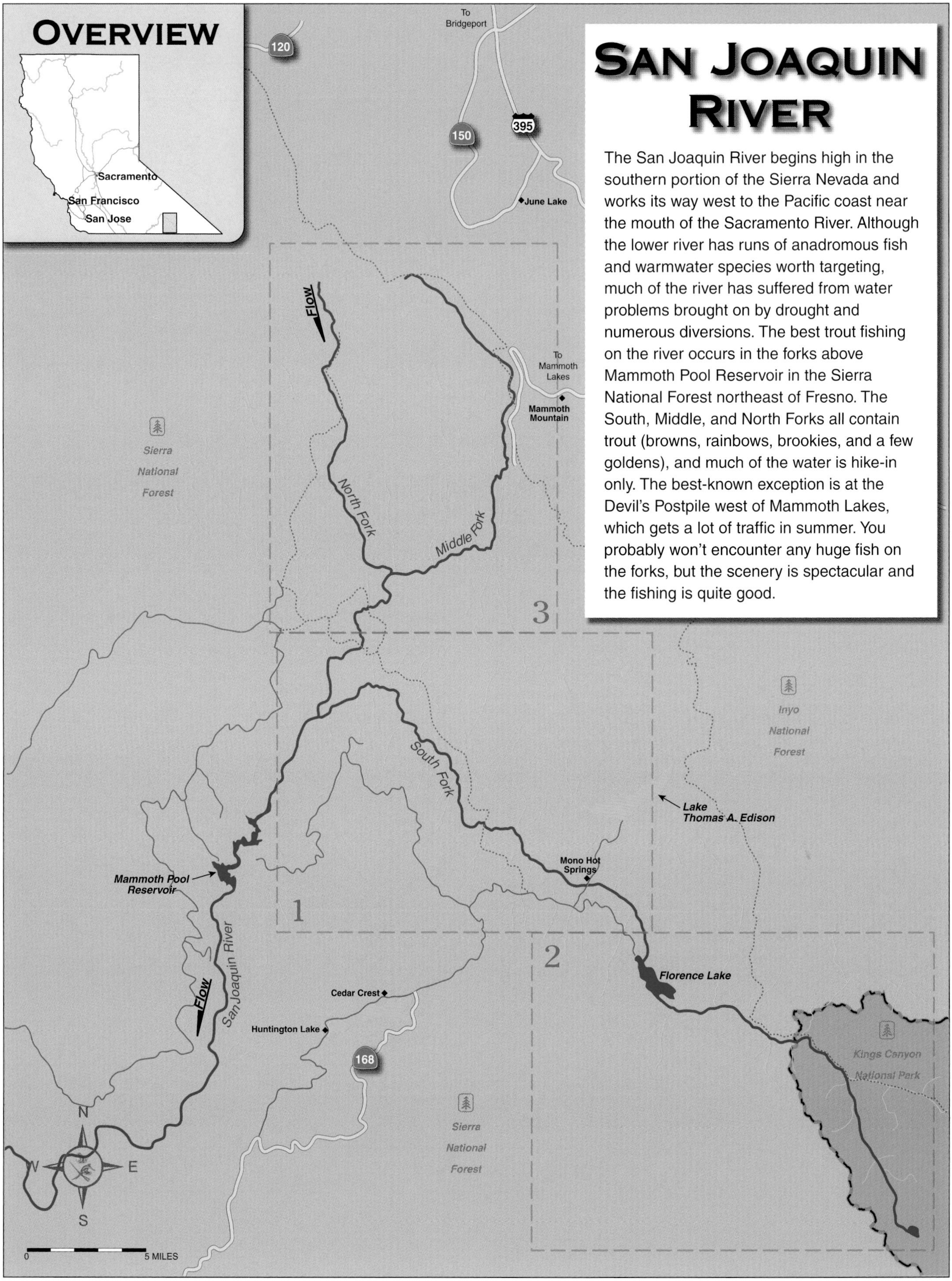

San Joaquin River

The San Joaquin River begins high in the southern portion of the Sierra Nevada and works its way west to the Pacific coast near the mouth of the Sacramento River. Although the lower river has runs of anadromous fish and warmwater species worth targeting, much of the river has suffered from water problems brought on by drought and numerous diversions. The best trout fishing on the river occurs in the forks above Mammoth Pool Reservoir in the Sierra National Forest northeast of Fresno. The South, Middle, and North Forks all contain trout (browns, rainbows, brookies, and a few goldens), and much of the water is hike-in only. The best-known exception is at the Devil's Postpile west of Mammoth Lakes, which gets a lot of traffic in summer. You probably won't encounter any huge fish on the forks, but the scenery is spectacular and the fishing is quite good.

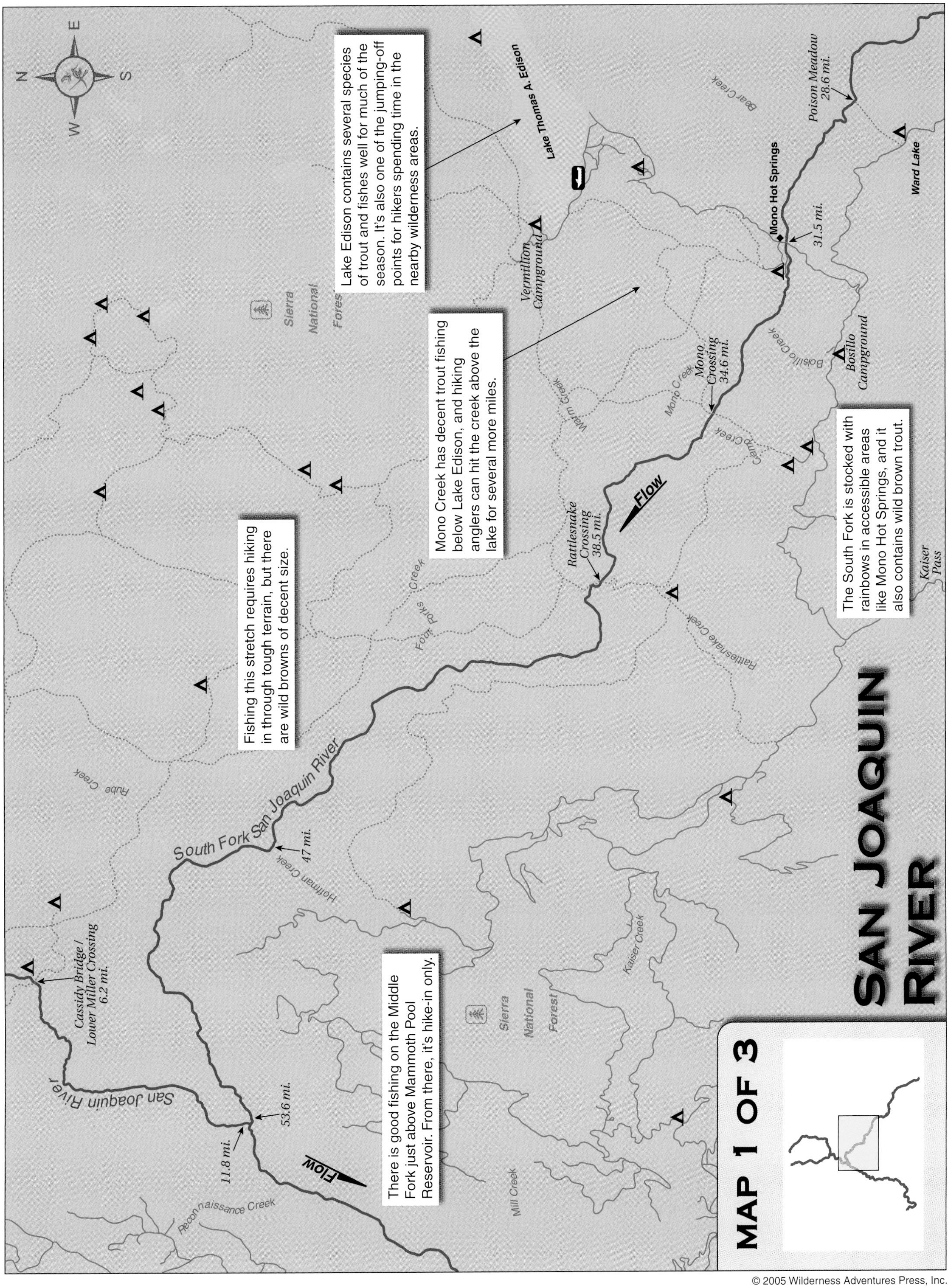
San Joaquin River
Map 1 of 3
Flow
Lake Edison contains several species of trout and fishes well for much of the season. It's also one of the jumping-off points for hikers spending time in the nearby wilderness areas.
Mono Creek has decent trout fishing below Lake Edison, and hiking anglers can hit the creek above the lake for several more miles.
Fishing this stretch requires hiking in through tough terrain, but there are wild browns of decent size.
The South Fork is stocked with rainbows in accessible areas like Mono Hot Springs, and it also contains wild brown trout.
There is good fishing on the Middle Fork just above Mammoth Pool Reservoir. From there, it's hike-in only.
Lake Thomas A. Edison
Vermillion Campground
Sierra National Forest
Bear Creek
Poison Meadow 28.6 mi.
Mono Hot Springs
31.5 mi.
Ward Lake
Mono Creek
Mono Crossing 34.6 mi.
Warm Creek
Bolsillo Creek
Bosillo Campground
Camp Creek
Rattlesnake Crossing 38.5 mi.
Kaiser Pass
Four Forks Creek
Rattlesnake Creek
South Fork San Joaquin River
47 mi.
Rube Creek
Hoffman Creek
Kaiser Creek
Cassidy Bridge / Lower Miller Crossing 6.2 mi.
San Joaquin River
53.6 mi.
11.8 mi.
Mill Creek
Reconnaissance Creek
N
S
E
W

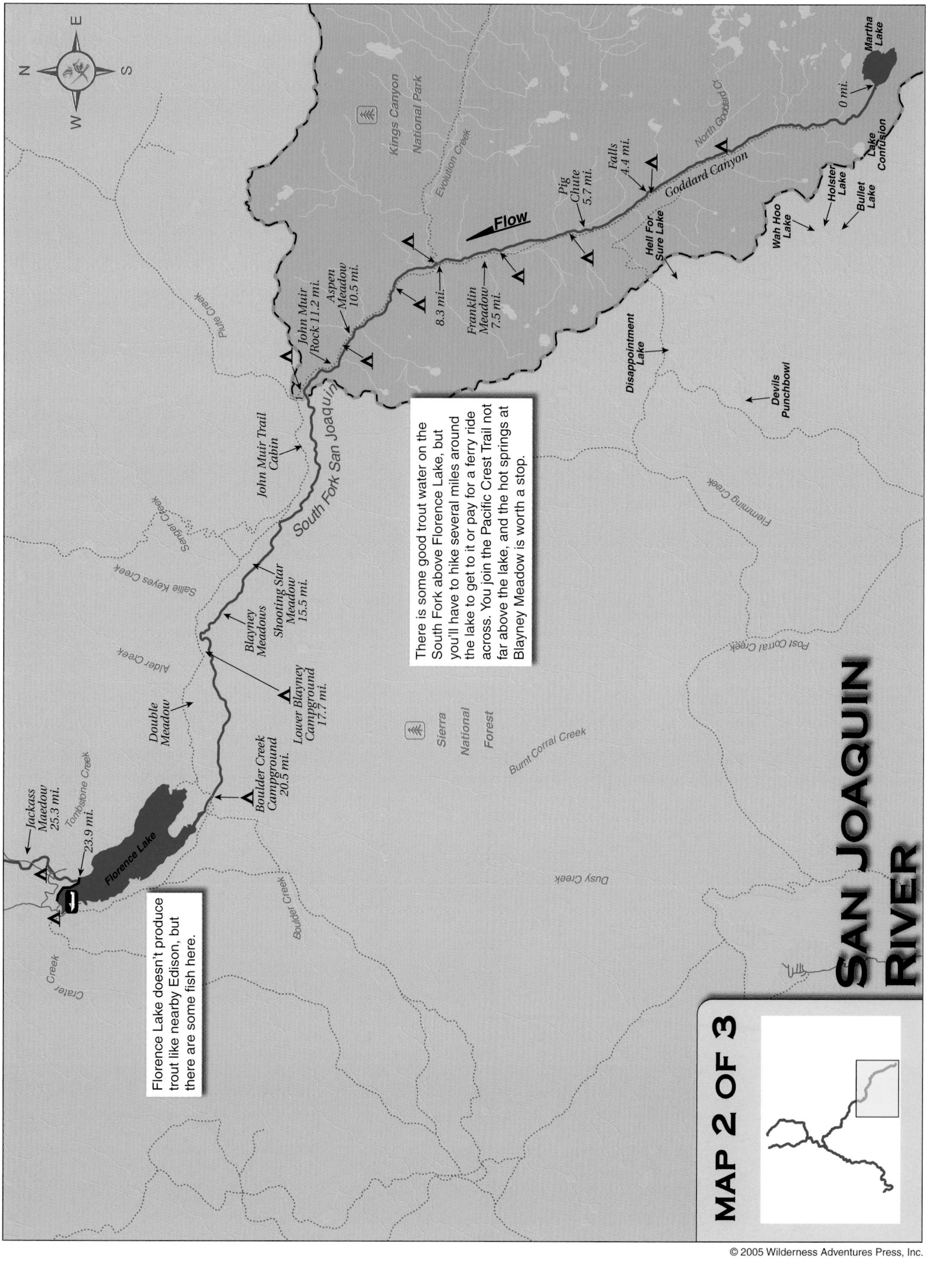
San Joaquin River
Map 2 of 3
N
E
S
W
Kings Canyon National Park
Sierra National Forest
Martha Lake
0 mi.
Lake Confusion
Holster Lake
Bullet Lake
Wah Hoo Lake
Hell For Sure Lake
North Goddard Cr
Goddard Canyon
Falls 4.4 mi.
Pig Chute 5.7 mi.
Flow
Evolution Creek
Franklin Meadow 7.5 mi.
8.3 mi.
Aspen Meadow 10.5 mi.
John Muir Rock 11.2 mi.
Piute Creek
John Muir Trail Cabin
South Fork San Joaquin
Disappointment Lake
Devils Punchbowl
Flemming Creek
Sanger Creek
Sallie Keyes Creek
Shooting Star Meadow 15.5 mi.
Blayney Meadows
Lower Blayney Campground 17.7 mi.
Alder Creek
Post Corral Creek
Double Meadow
Boulder Creek Campground 20.5 mi.
Burnt Corral Creek
Jackass Maedow 25.3 mi.
Tombstone Creek
23.9 mi.
Florence Lake
Dusy Creek
Boulder Creek
Crater Creek
There is some good trout water on the South Fork above Florence Lake, but you'll have to hike several miles around the lake to get to it or pay for a ferry ride across. You join the Pacific Crest Trail not far above the lake, and the hot springs at Blayney Meadow is worth a stop.
Florence Lake doesn't produce trout like nearby Edison, but there are some fish here.

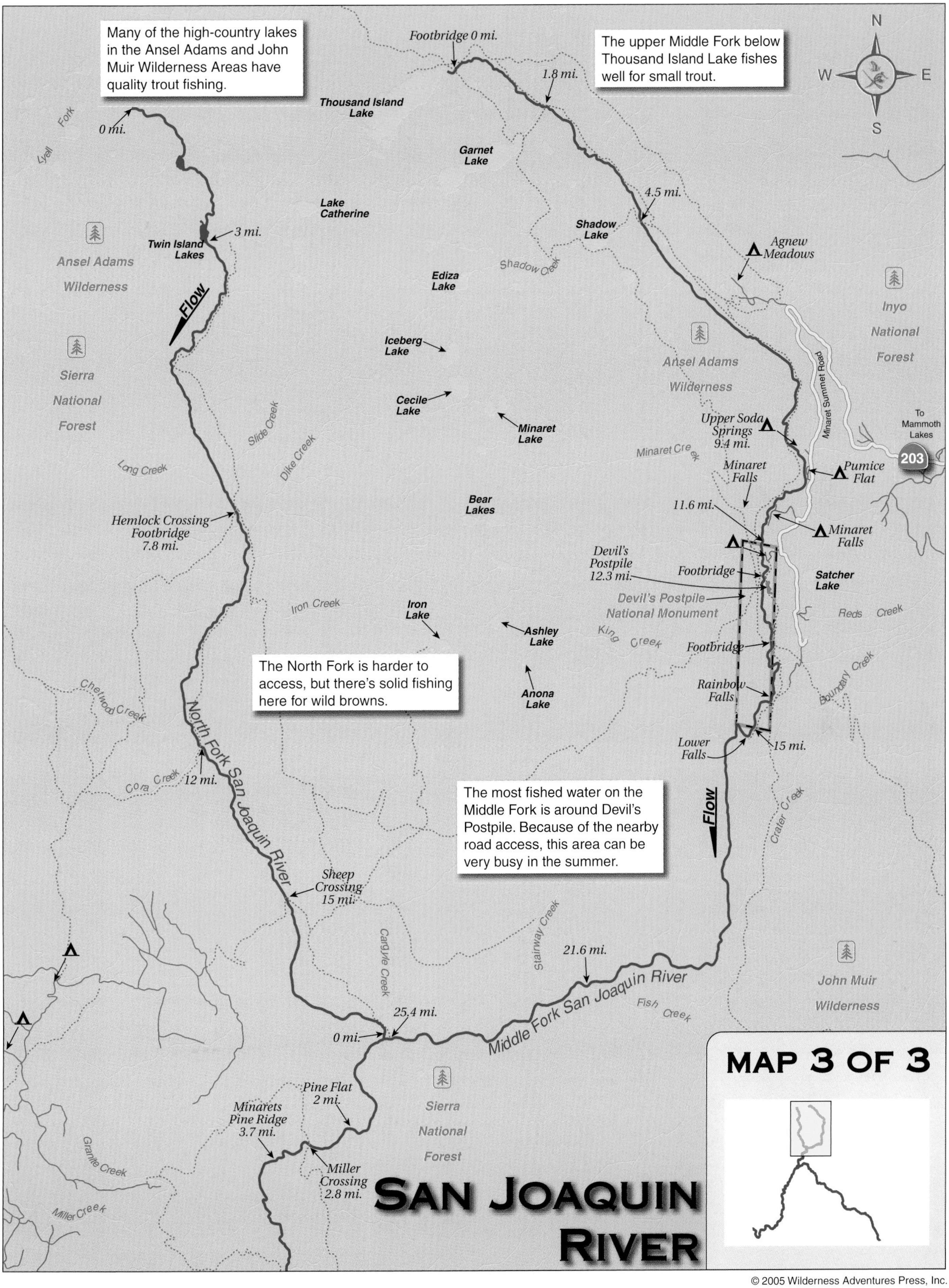
Many of the high-country lakes in the Ansel Adams and John Muir Wilderness Areas have quality trout fishing.
The upper Middle Fork below Thousand Island Lake fishes well for small trout.
The North Fork is harder to access, but there's solid fishing here for wild browns.
The most fished water on the Middle Fork is around Devil's Postpile. Because of the nearby road access, this area can be very busy in the summer.
Footbridge 0 mi.
1.8 mi.
4.5 mi.
Thousand Island Lake
Garnet Lake
Lake Catherine
Shadow Lake
Shadow Creek
Ediza Lake
Iceberg Lake
Cecile Lake
Minaret Lake
Bear Lakes
Iron Lake
Ashley Lake
Anona Lake
Iron Creek
King Creek
Lyell Fork
0 mi.
3 mi.
Twin Island Lakes
Ansel Adams Wilderness
Sierra National Forest
Flow
Slide Creek
Dike Creek
Long Creek
Hemlock Crossing Footbridge 7.8 mi.
Chetwood Creek
Cora Creek
12 mi.
North Fork San Joaquin River
Sheep Crossing 15 mi.
Carlyle Creek
Stairway Creek
21.6 mi.
Middle Fork San Joaquin River
Fish Creek
25.4 mi.
0 mi.
Pine Flat 2 mi.
Minarets Pine Ridge 3.7 mi.
Miller Crossing 2.8 mi.
Granite Creek
Miller Creek
Agnew Meadows
Inyo National Forest
Minaret Summit Road
To Mammoth Lakes
203
Upper Soda Springs 9.4 mi.
Minaret Creek
Pumice Flat
Minaret Falls
11.6 mi.
Devil's Postpile 12.3 mi.
Footbridge
Devil's Postpile National Monument
Satcher Lake
Reds Creek
Footbridge
Rainbow Falls
Boundary Creek
Lower Falls
15 mi.
Crater Creek
John Muir Wilderness
MAP 3 OF 3
SAN JOAQUIN RIVER
N
S
E
W

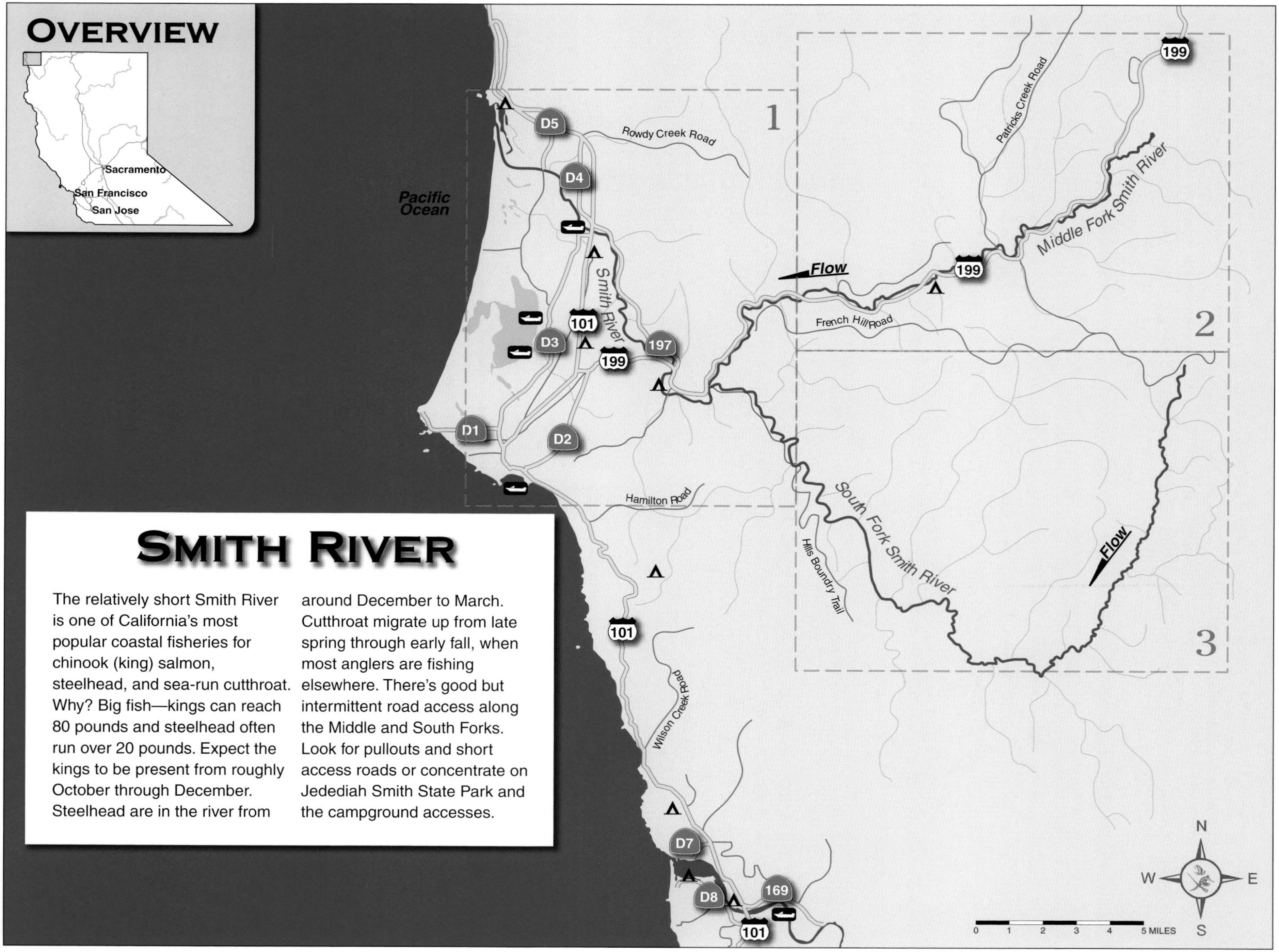

Smith River

The relatively short Smith River is one of California's most popular coastal fisheries for chinook (king) salmon, steelhead, and sea-run cutthroat. Why? Big fish—kings can reach 80 pounds and steelhead often run over 20 pounds. Expect the kings to be present from roughly October through December. Steelhead are in the river from around December to March. Cutthroat migrate up from late spring through early fall, when most anglers are fishing elsewhere. There's good but intermittent road access along the Middle and South Forks. Look for pullouts and short access roads or concentrate on Jedediah Smith State Park and the campground accesses.

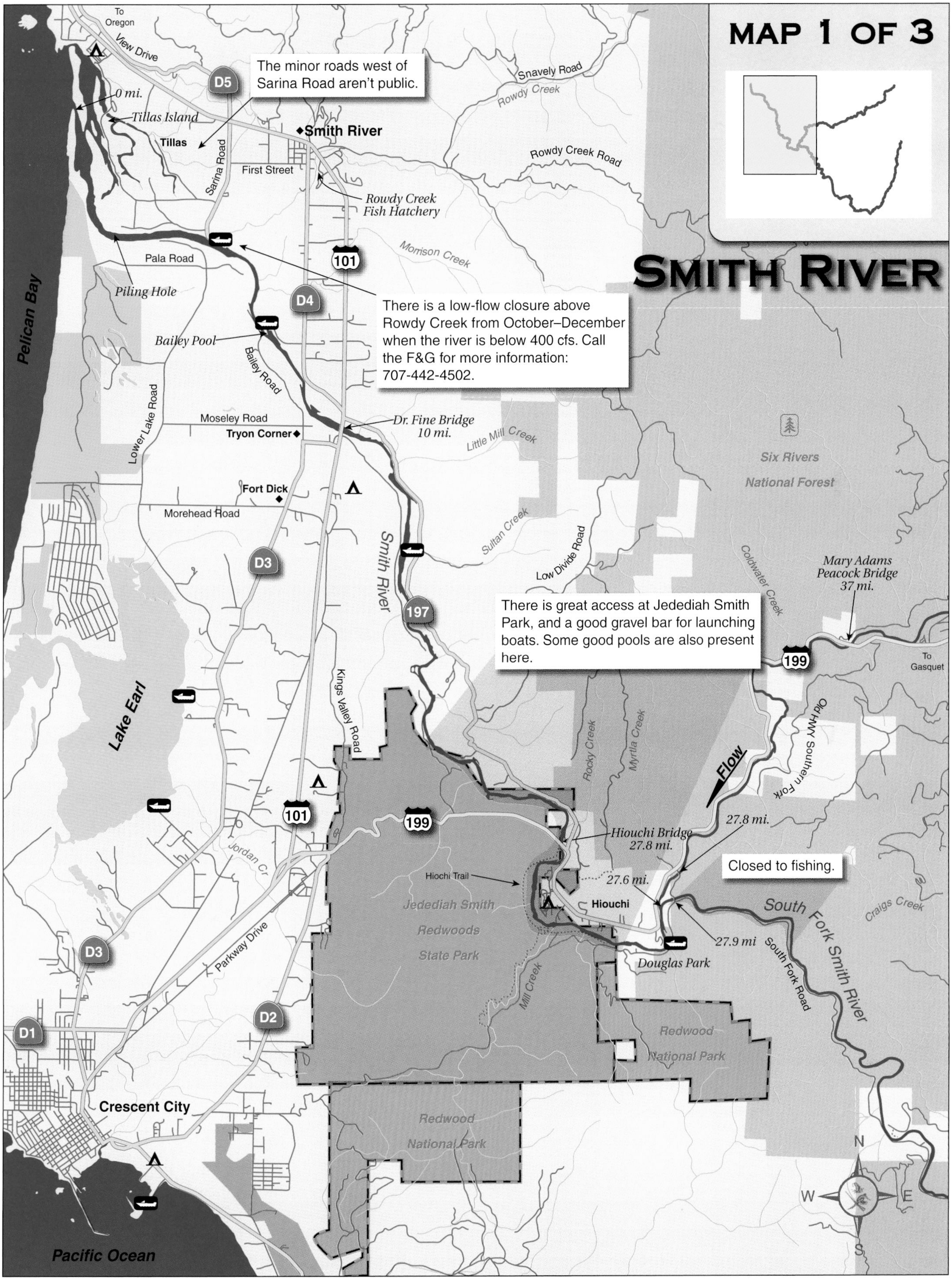
MAP 1 OF 3
SMITH RIVER
The minor roads west of Sarina Road aren't public.
There is a low-flow closure above Rowdy Creek from October–December when the river is below 400 cfs. Call the F&G for more information: 707-442-4502.
There is great access at Jedediah Smith Park, and a good gravel bar for launching boats. Some good pools are also present here.
Closed to fishing.
To Oregon
View Drive
0 mi.
Tillas Island
Tillas
Smith River
Sarina Road
First Street
Rowdy Creek Fish Hatchery
Snavely Road
Rowdy Creek
Rowdy Creek Road
Morrison Creek
Pala Road
Piling Hole
Pelican Bay
Bailey Pool
Bailey Road
Lower Lake Road
Moseley Road
Tryon Corner
Dr. Fine Bridge 10 mi.
Little Mill Creek
Six Rivers National Forest
Fort Dick
Morehead Road
Sultan Creek
Low Divide Road
Smith River
Coldwater Creek
Mary Adams Peacock Bridge 37 mi.
To Gasquet
Lake Earl
Kings Valley Road
Rocky Creek
Myrtle Creek
Old HWY Southern Fork
Flow
Hiouchi Bridge 27.8 mi.
27.8 mi.
Jordan Cr
Hiochi Trail
27.6 mi.
Hiouchi
Jedediah Smith Redwoods State Park
27.9 mi
Douglas Park
South Fork Smith River
South Fork Road
Craigs Creek
Parkway Drive
Mill Creek
Redwood National Park
Crescent City
Pacific Ocean
N
W
E
S

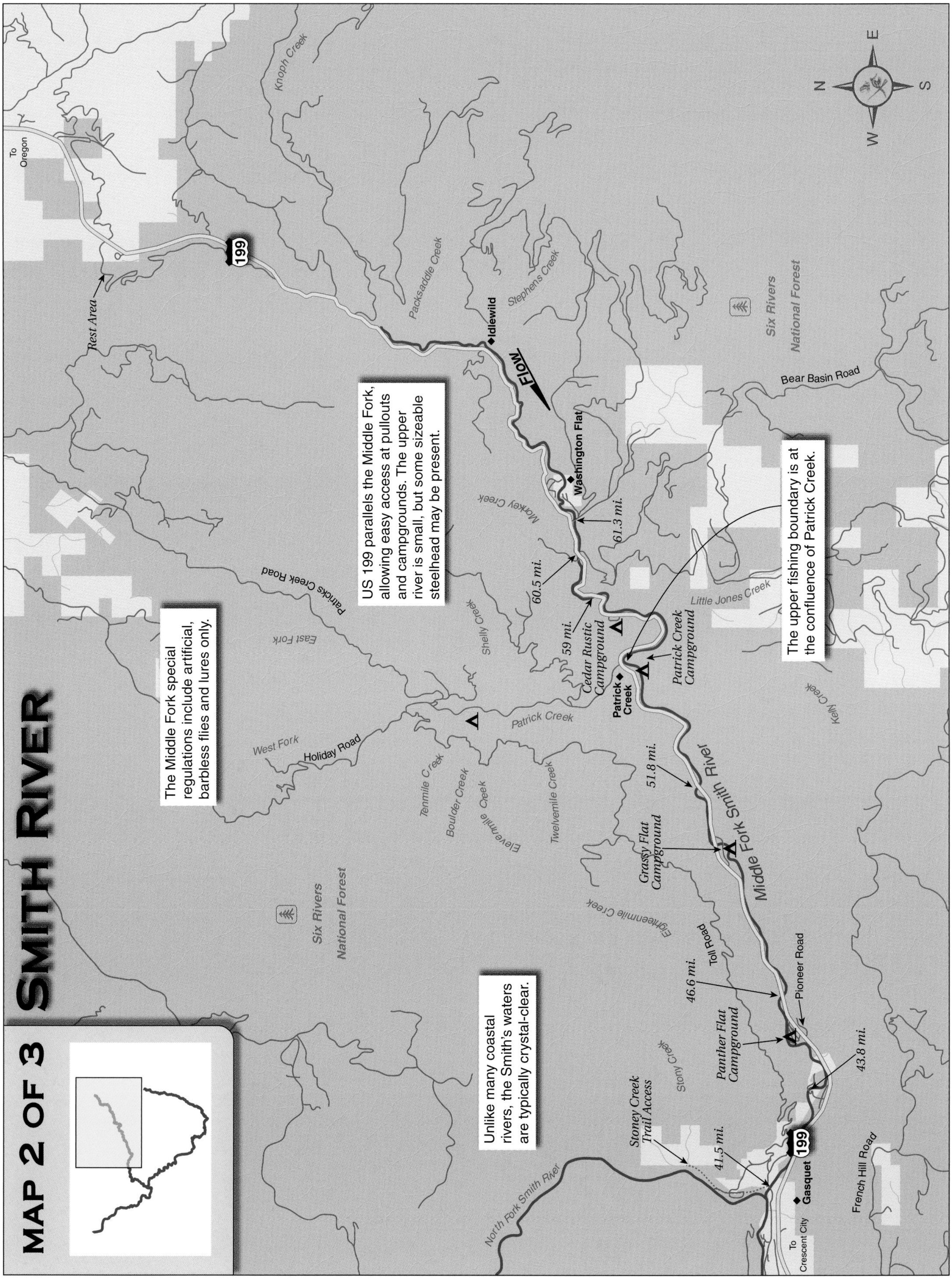

MAP 2 OF 3
SMITH RIVER
The Middle Fork special regulations include artificial, barbless flies and lures only.
US 199 parallels the Middle Fork, allowing easy access at pullouts and campgrounds. The upper river is small, but some sizeable steelhead may be present.
The upper fishing boundary is at the confluence of Patrick Creek.
Unlike many coastal rivers, the Smith's waters are typically crystal-clear.
To Oregon
199
Rest Area
Knoph Creek
Packsaddle Creek
Stephens Creek
Idlewild
Flow
Washington Flat
Monkey Creek
61.3 mi.
60.5 mi.
59 mi.
Six Rivers National Forest
Bear Basin Road
Little Jones Creek
Patricks Creek Road
East Fork
Shelly Creek
Cedar Rustic Campground
Patrick Creek Campground
Patrick Creek
Kelly Creek
West Fork
Holiday Road
Patrick Creek
Tenmile Creek
Boulder Creek
Elevenmile Creek
Twelvemile Creek
51.8 mi.
Middle Fork Smith River
Grassy Flat Campground
Eighteenmile Creek
Six Rivers National Forest
Toll Road
Pioneer Road
46.6 mi.
Panther Flat Campground
43.8 mi.
Stony Creek
Stoney Creek Trail Access
41.5 mi.
199
Gasquet
French Hill Road
North Fork Smith River
To Crescent City
N
S
E
W

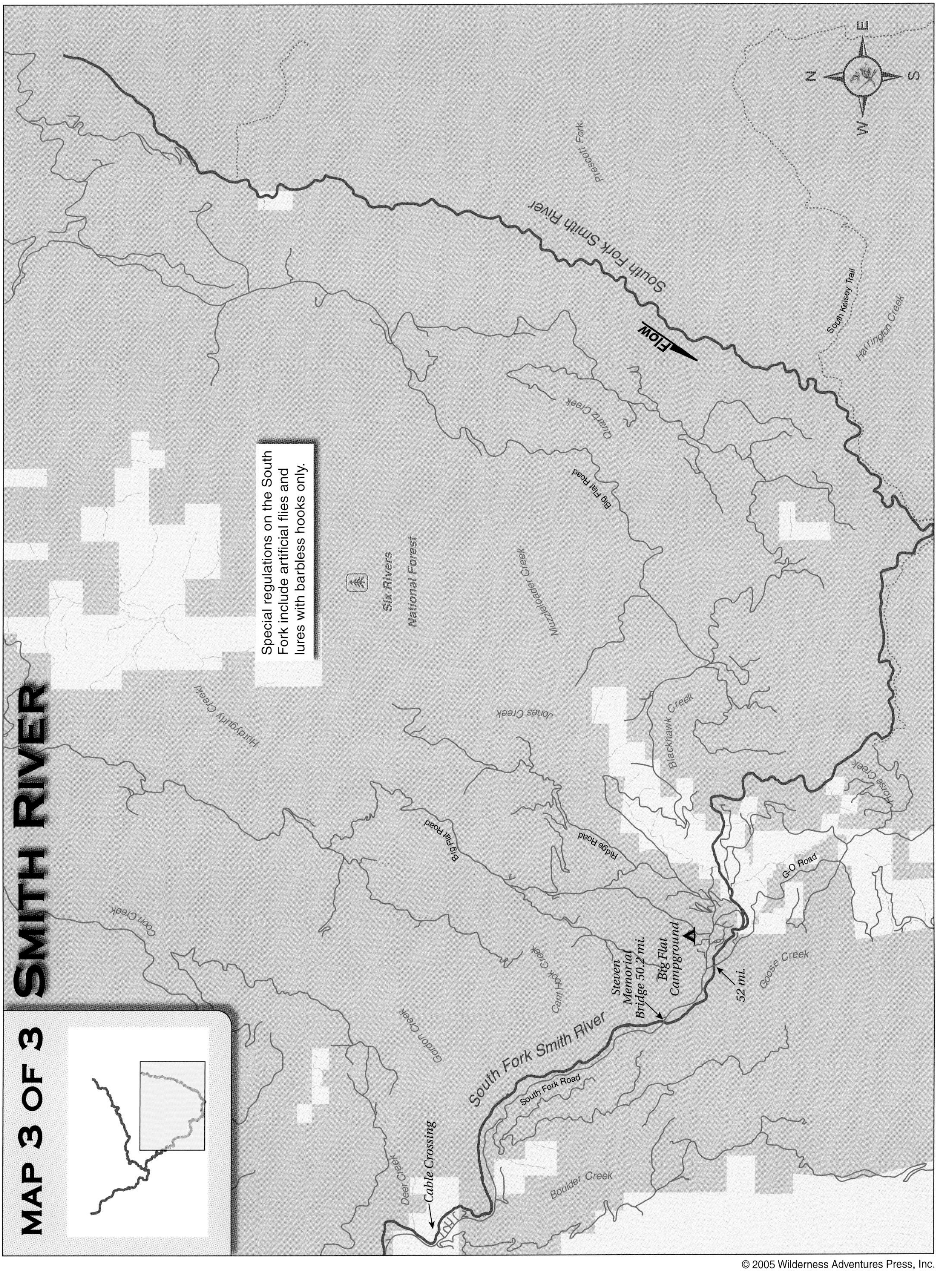

MAP 3 OF 3
SMITH RIVER
Special regulations on the South Fork include artificial flies and lures with barbless hooks only.
Six Rivers National Forest
South Fork Smith River
Flow
Prescott Fork
South Kelsey Trail
Harrington Creek
Quartz Creek
Big Flat Road
Muzzleloader Creek
Jones Creek
Blackhawk Creek
Hurdygurdy Creek
Horse Creek
Ridge Road
G-O Road
Coon Creek
Cant Hook Creek
Gordon Creek
Steven Memorial Bridge 50.2 mi.
Big Flat Campground
52 mi.
Goose Creek
South Fork Road
Boulder Creek
Deer Creek
Cable Crossing
N
E
S
W

Stanislaus River

The Stanislaus River covers a lot of ground from where its forks rise in the Sierra Nevada to where it dumps into the San Joaquin. The lower river has solid fishing for stocked rainbows and smallmouth bass, along with salmon and striped bass when they're running. New Melones Reservoir gathers the flows of the North, Middle, and South Forks. Trout fishing, particularly in the North and Middle Forks, can be very good, although access is sporadic in some areas. You'll find stocked fish around many bridge crossings and campgrounds, but wild fish are often a short hike away. This is beautiful country, and the Stanislaus is well worth a visit.

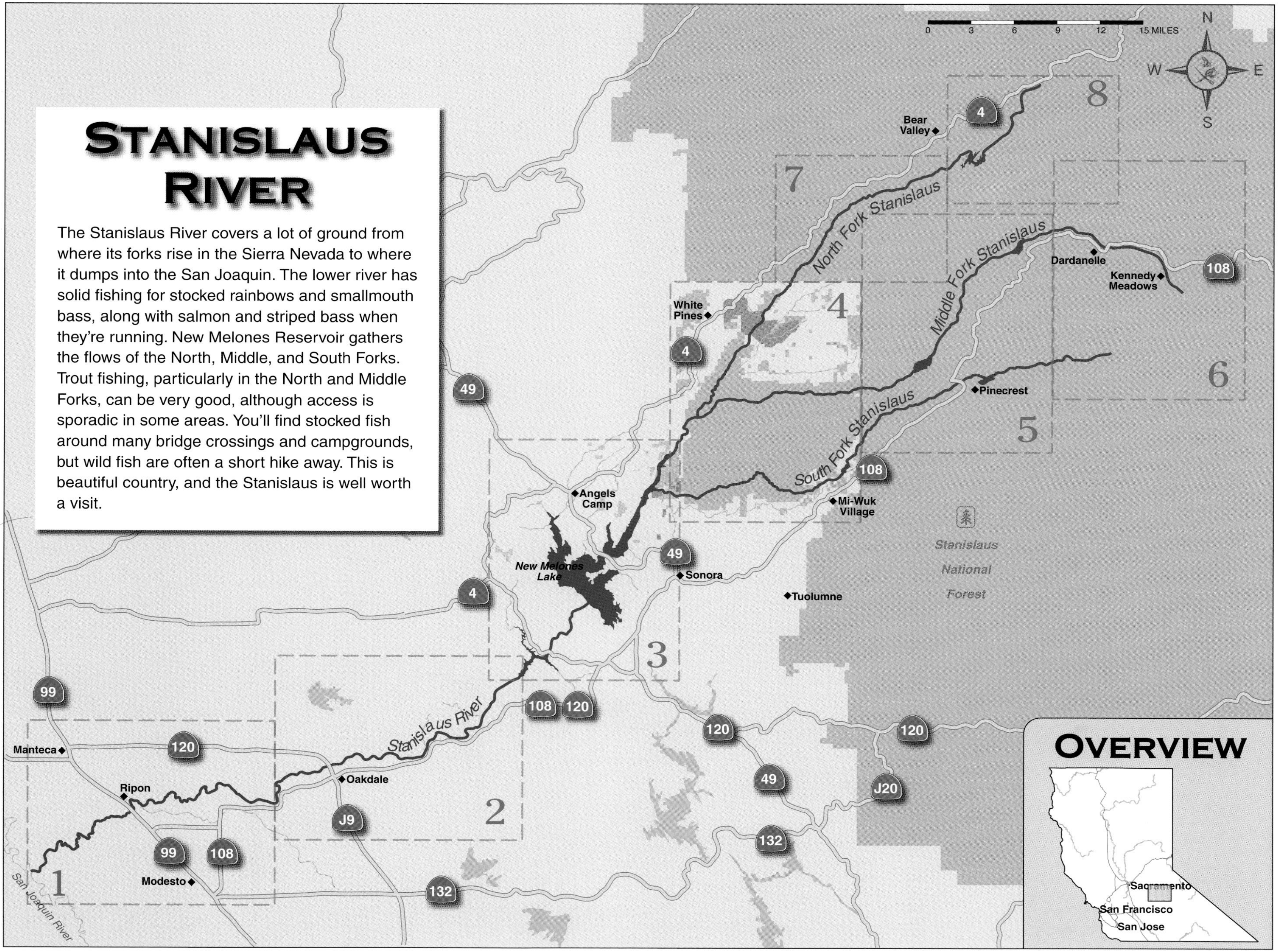

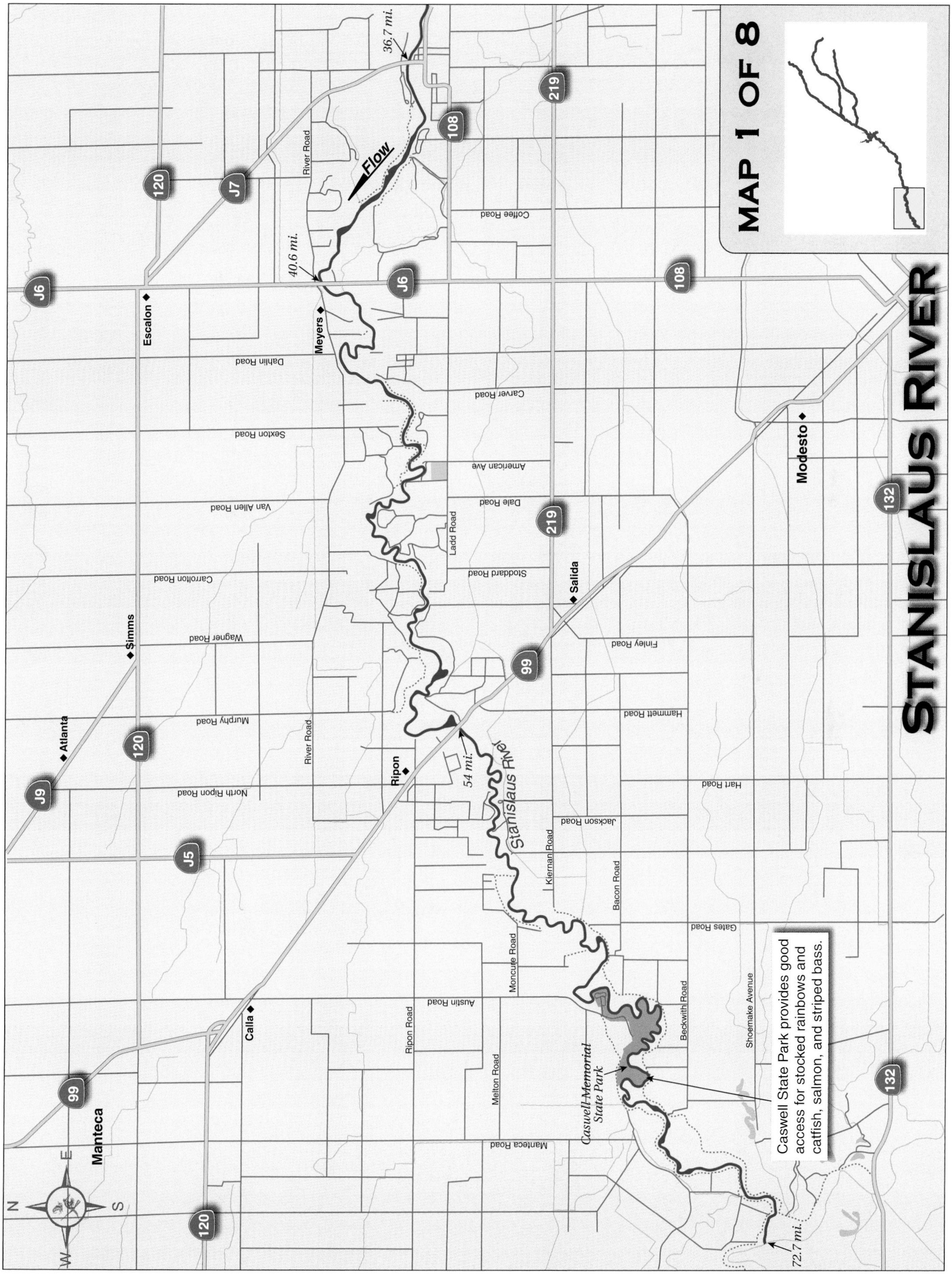
Stanislaus River
Map 1 of 8
Flow
36.7 mi.
40.6 mi.
54 mi.
72.7 mi.
Stanislaus River
Caswell Memorial State Park
Caswell State Park provides good access for stocked rainbows and catfish, salmon, and striped bass.
Manteca
Calla
Ripon
Atlanta
Simms
Escalon
Meyers
Salida
Modesto
River Road
Coffee Road
Dahlin Road
Carver Road
Sexton Road
American Ave
Van Allen Road
Dale Road
Ladd Road
Carrolton Road
Stoddard Road
Wagner Road
Finley Road
Murphy Road
Hammett Road
North Ripon Road
Hart Road
Jackson Road
Kiernan Road
Bacon Road
Gates Road
Moncure Road
Austin Road
Ripon Road
Beckwith Road
Shoemake Avenue
Melton Road
Manteca Road
120
J7
108
219
J6
99
J9
J5
132
N
E
S
W

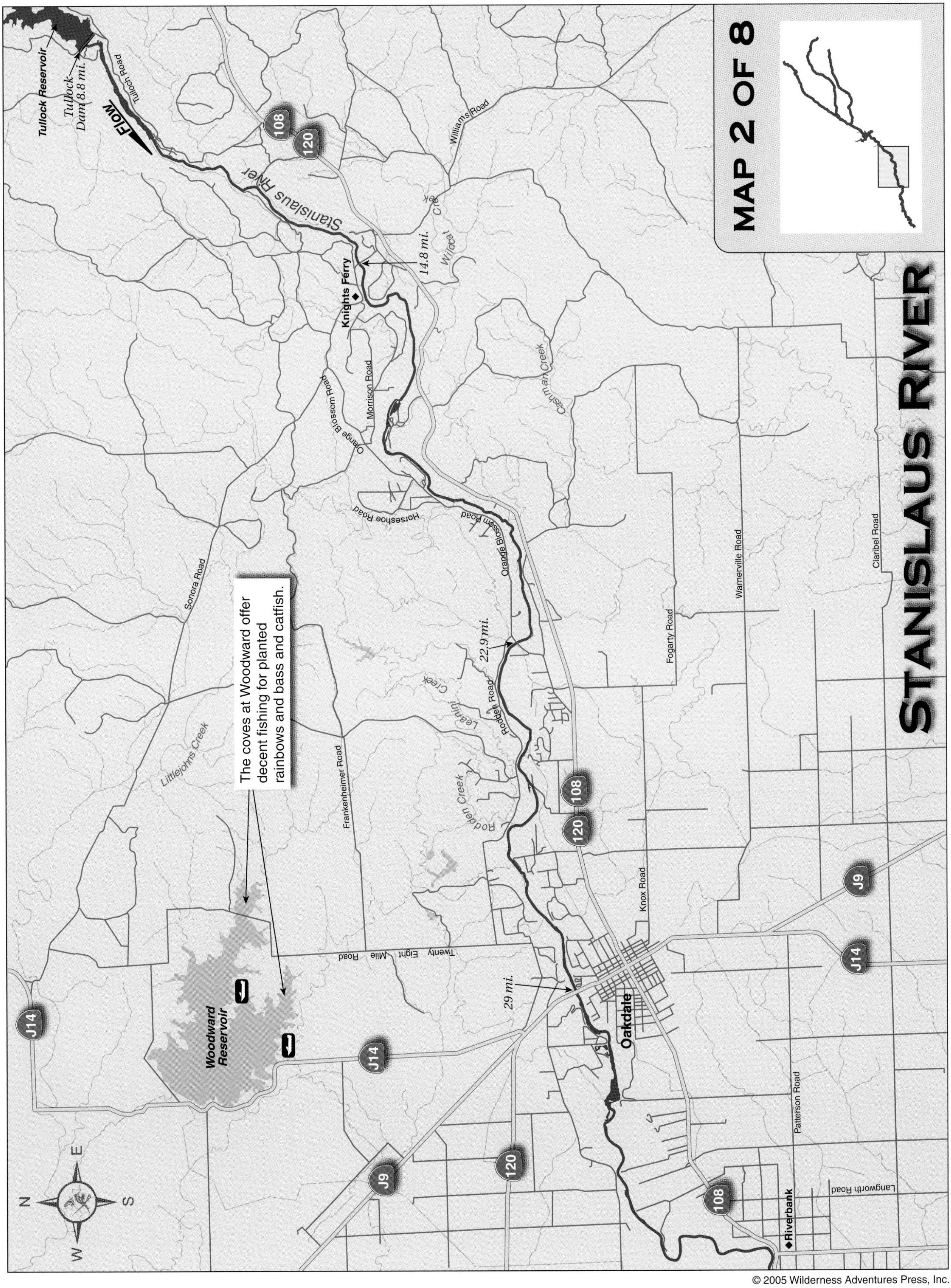
MAP 2 OF 8
STANISLAUS RIVER
Tullock Reservoir
Tullock Dam 8.8 mi.
Tulloch Road
FLOW
Stanislaus River
Williams Road
Wildcat Creek
14.8 mi.
Knights Ferry
Morrison Road
Orange Blossom Road
Horseshoe Road
Cashman Creek
Orange Blossom Road
22.9 mi.
Rodden Road
Lesnini Creek
Rodden Creek
Sonora Road
Littlejohns Creek
The coves at Woodward offer decent fishing for planted rainbows and bass and catfish.
Frankenheimer Road
Twenty Eight Mile Road
Woodward Reservoir
29 mi.
Oakdale
Knox Road
Fogarty Road
Warnerville Road
Claribel Road
Patterson Road
Langworth Road
Riverbank
108
120
J9
J14
N
E
S
W

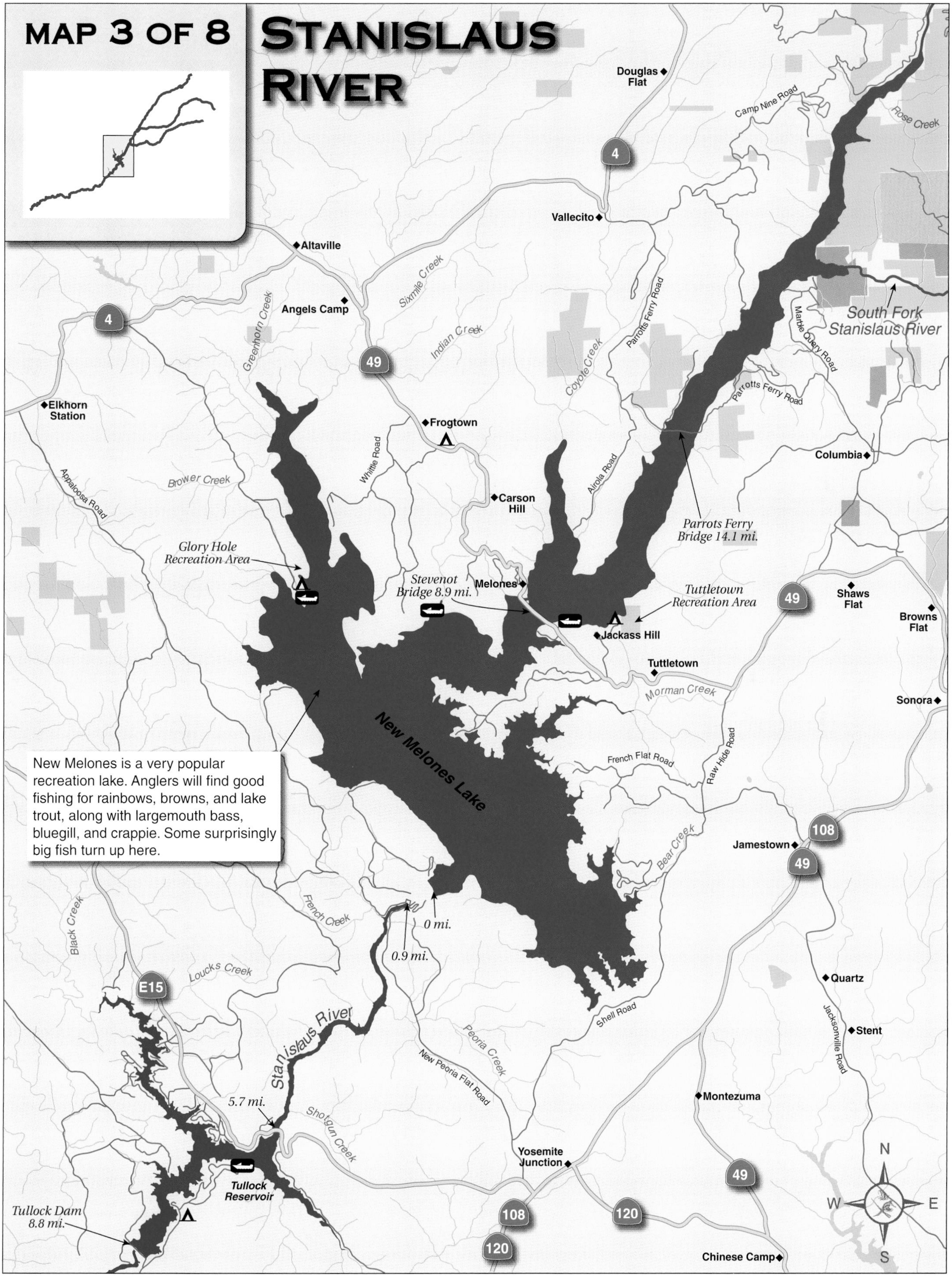
Map 3 of 8
Stanislaus River
New Melones is a very popular recreation lake. Anglers will find good fishing for rainbows, browns, and lake trout, along with largemouth bass, bluegill, and crappie. Some surprisingly big fish turn up here.
New Melones Lake
Glory Hole Recreation Area
Stevenot Bridge 8.9 mi.
Tuttletown Recreation Area
Parrots Ferry Bridge 14.1 mi.
South Fork Stanislaus River
Tullock Dam 8.8 mi.
Tullock Reservoir
5.7 mi.
0 mi.
0.9 mi.
Stanislaus River
Douglas Flat
Vallecito
Altaville
Angels Camp
Elkhorn Station
Frogtown
Carson Hill
Melones
Jackass Hill
Tuttletown
Columbia
Shaws Flat
Browns Flat
Sonora
Jamestown
Quartz
Stent
Montezuma
Yosemite Junction
Chinese Camp
Camp Nine Road
Rose Creek
Sixmile Creek
Indian Creek
Greenhorn Creek
Coyote Creek
Parrotts Ferry Road
Marble Quarry Road
Whittle Road
Airola Road
Brower Creek
Appaloosa Road
Morman Creek
French Flat Road
Raw Hide Road
Bear Creek
French Creek
Black Creek
Loucks Creek
Peoria Creek
New Peoria Flat Road
Shell Road
Shotgun Creek
Jacksonville Road
4
49
108
120
E15
N
S
E
W

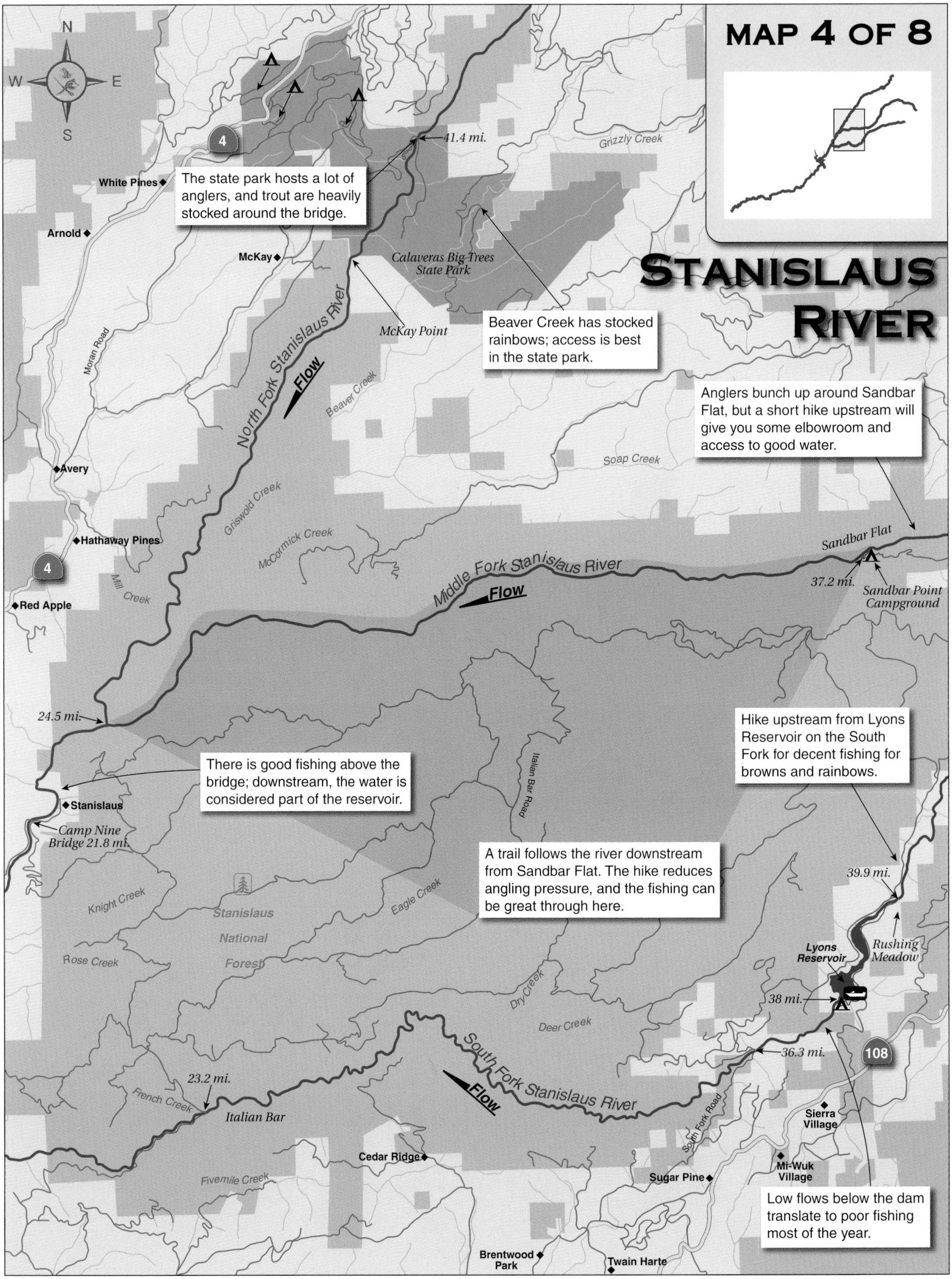
MAP 4 OF 8
STANISLAUS RIVER
N
S
E
W
The state park hosts a lot of anglers, and trout are heavily stocked around the bridge.
Beaver Creek has stocked rainbows; access is best in the state park.
Anglers bunch up around Sandbar Flat, but a short hike upstream will give you some elbowroom and access to good water.
Hike upstream from Lyons Reservoir on the South Fork for decent fishing for browns and rainbows.
There is good fishing above the bridge; downstream, the water is considered part of the reservoir.
A trail follows the river downstream from Sandbar Flat. The hike reduces angling pressure, and the fishing can be great through here.
Low flows below the dam translate to poor fishing most of the year.
41.4 mi.
Grizzly Creek
White Pines
Arnold
McKay
Calaveras Big Trees State Park
McKay Point
North Fork Stanislaus River
Flow
Moran Road
Beaver Creek
Soap Creek
Avery
Griswold Creek
McCormick Creek
Hathaway Pines
Mill Creek
Red Apple
Sandbar Flat
Middle Fork Stanislaus River
37.2 mi.
Sandbar Point Campground
24.5 mi.
Stanislaus
Camp Nine Bridge 21.8 mi.
Italian Bar Road
Knight Creek
Stanislaus National Forest
Eagle Creek
Rose Creek
39.9 mi.
Lyons Reservoir
Rushing Meadow
38 mi.
Dry Creek
Deer Creek
36.3 mi.
108
4
23.2 mi.
French Creek
Italian Bar
South Fork Stanislaus River
South Fork Road
Sierra Village
Mi-Wuk Village
Cedar Ridge
Sugar Pine
Fivemile Creek
Brentwood Park
Twain Harte

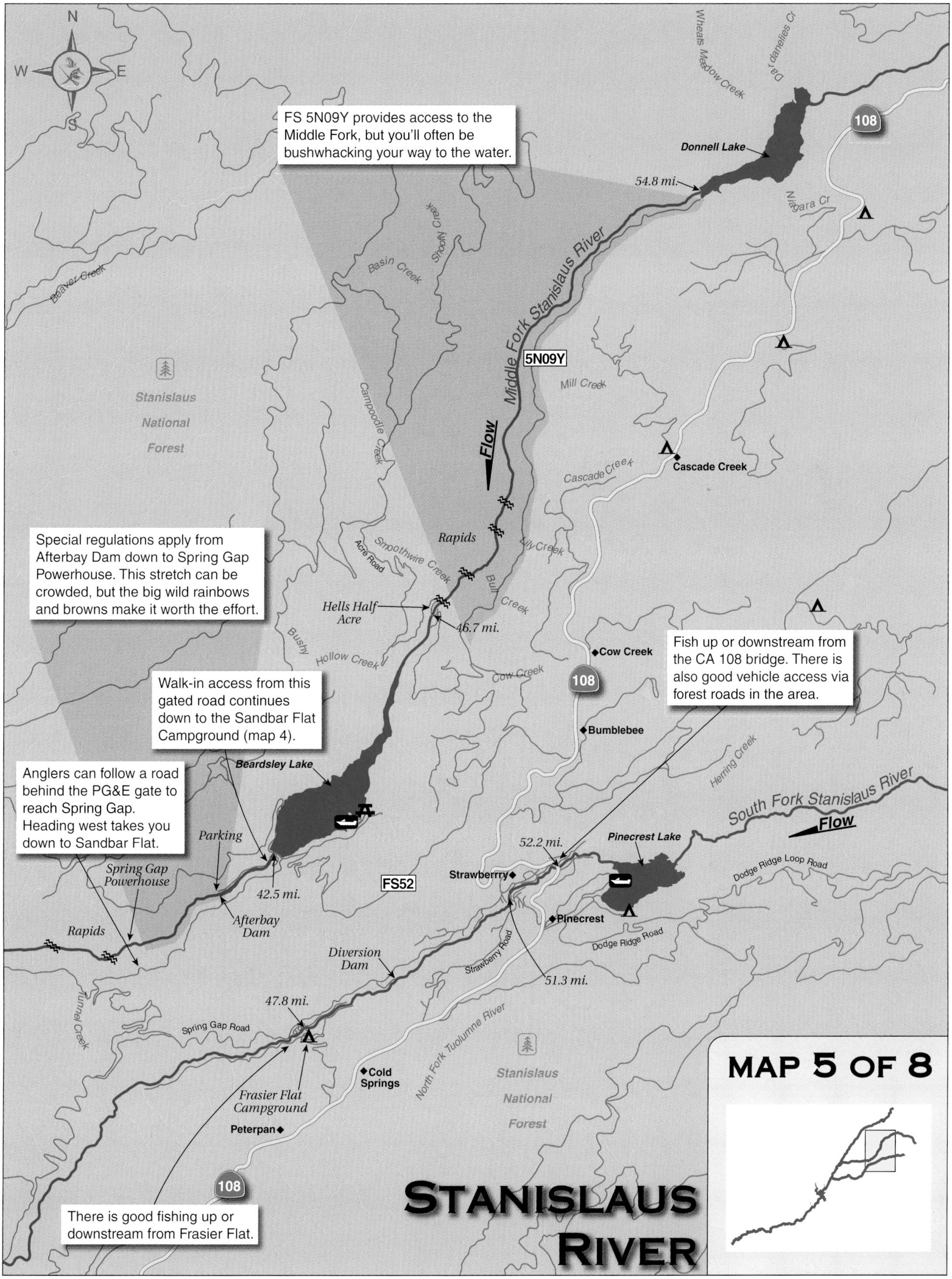
FS 5N09Y provides access to the Middle Fork, but you'll often be bushwhacking your way to the water.
Special regulations apply from Afterbay Dam down to Spring Gap Powerhouse. This stretch can be crowded, but the big wild rainbows and browns make it worth the effort.
Walk-in access from this gated road continues down to the Sandbar Flat Campground (map 4).
Anglers can follow a road behind the PG&E gate to reach Spring Gap. Heading west takes you down to Sandbar Flat.
Fish up or downstream from the CA 108 bridge. There is also good vehicle access via forest roads in the area.
There is good fishing up or downstream from Frasier Flat.
Donnell Lake
54.8 mi.
Middle Fork Stanislaus River
5N09Y
Flow
Rapids
Hells Half Acre
46.7 mi.
Beardsley Lake
Parking
Spring Gap Powerhouse
42.5 mi.
Afterbay Dam
FS52
Diversion Dam
47.8 mi.
Spring Gap Road
Frasier Flat Campground
Cold Springs
Peterpan
Strawberry
Pinecrest
Pinecrest Lake
52.2 mi.
51.3 mi.
South Fork Stanislaus River
Dodge Ridge Loop Road
Dodge Ridge Road
Strawberry Road
North Fork Tuolumne River
Cascade Creek
Cow Creek
Bumblebee
Stanislaus National Forest
Wheats Meadow Creek
Dardanelles Cr
Niagara Cr
Basin Creek
Shoofly Creek
Beaver Creek
Campoodle Creek
Mill Creek
Lily Creek
Bull Creek
Smoothwire Creek
Acre Road
Bushy Hollow Creek
Herring Creek
Tunnel Creek
108
MAP 5 OF 8
STANISLAUS RIVER

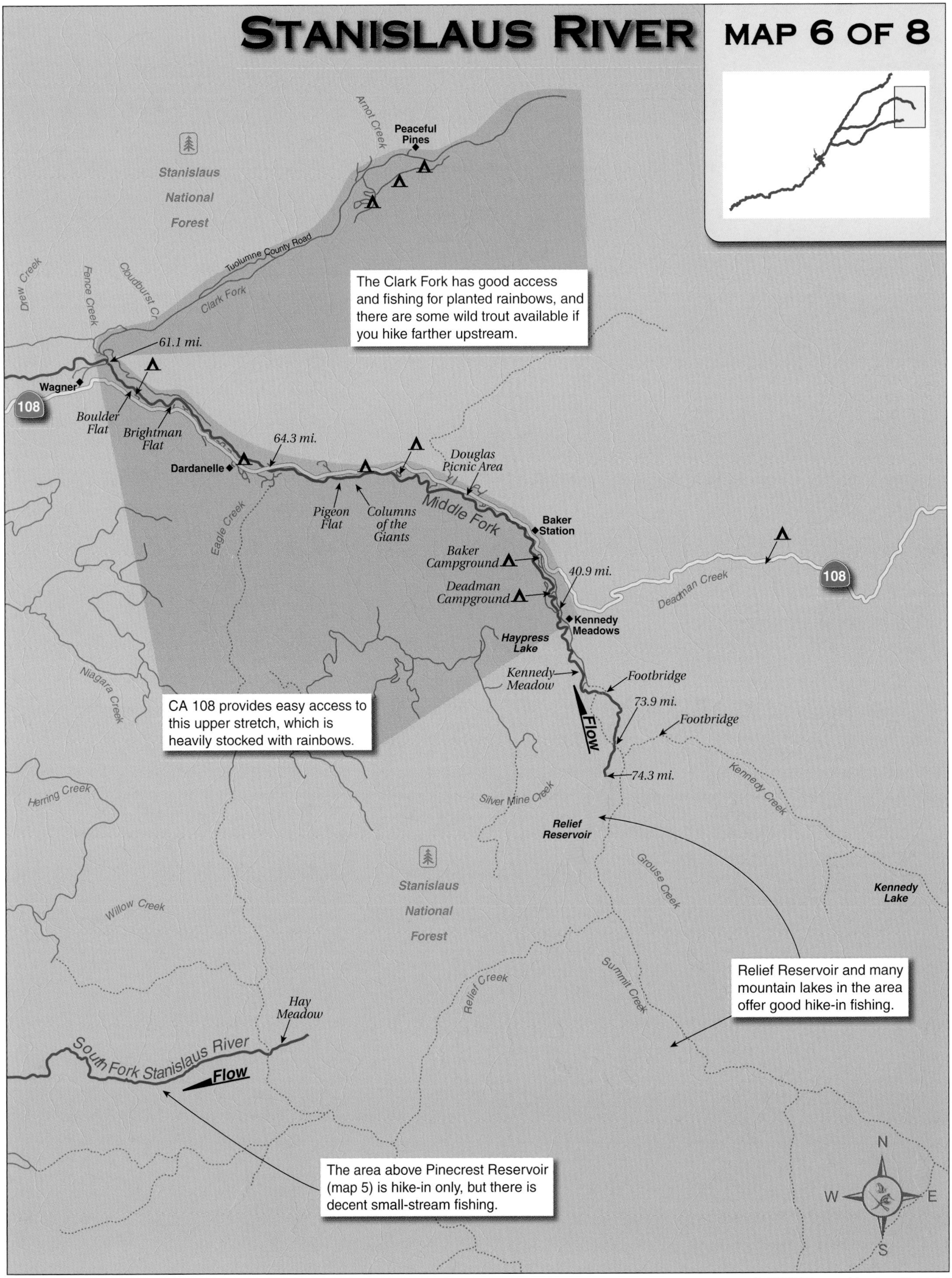
Stanislaus River
Map 6 of 8
Peaceful Pines
Arnot Creek
Stanislaus National Forest
Tuolumne County Road
Clark Fork
Drew Creek
Fence Creek
Cloudburst Cr
The Clark Fork has good access and fishing for planted rainbows, and there are some wild trout available if you hike farther upstream.
61.1 mi.
Wagner
108
Boulder Flat
Brightman Flat
64.3 mi.
Dardanelle
Douglas Picnic Area
Pigeon Flat
Columns of the Giants
Middle Fork
Eagle Creek
Baker Station
Baker Campground
40.9 mi.
Deadman Campground
Deadman Creek
108
Kennedy Meadows
Haypress Lake
Kennedy Meadow
Footbridge
73.9 mi.
Footbridge
Flow
74.3 mi.
Niagara Creek
CA 108 provides easy access to this upper stretch, which is heavily stocked with rainbows.
Herring Creek
Silver Mine Creek
Relief Reservoir
Kennedy Creek
Stanislaus National Forest
Grouse Creek
Kennedy Lake
Willow Creek
Relief Creek
Summit Creek
Relief Reservoir and many mountain lakes in the area offer good hike-in fishing.
Hay Meadow
South Fork Stanislaus River
Flow
The area above Pinecrest Reservoir (map 5) is hike-in only, but there is decent small-stream fishing.
N
W
E
S

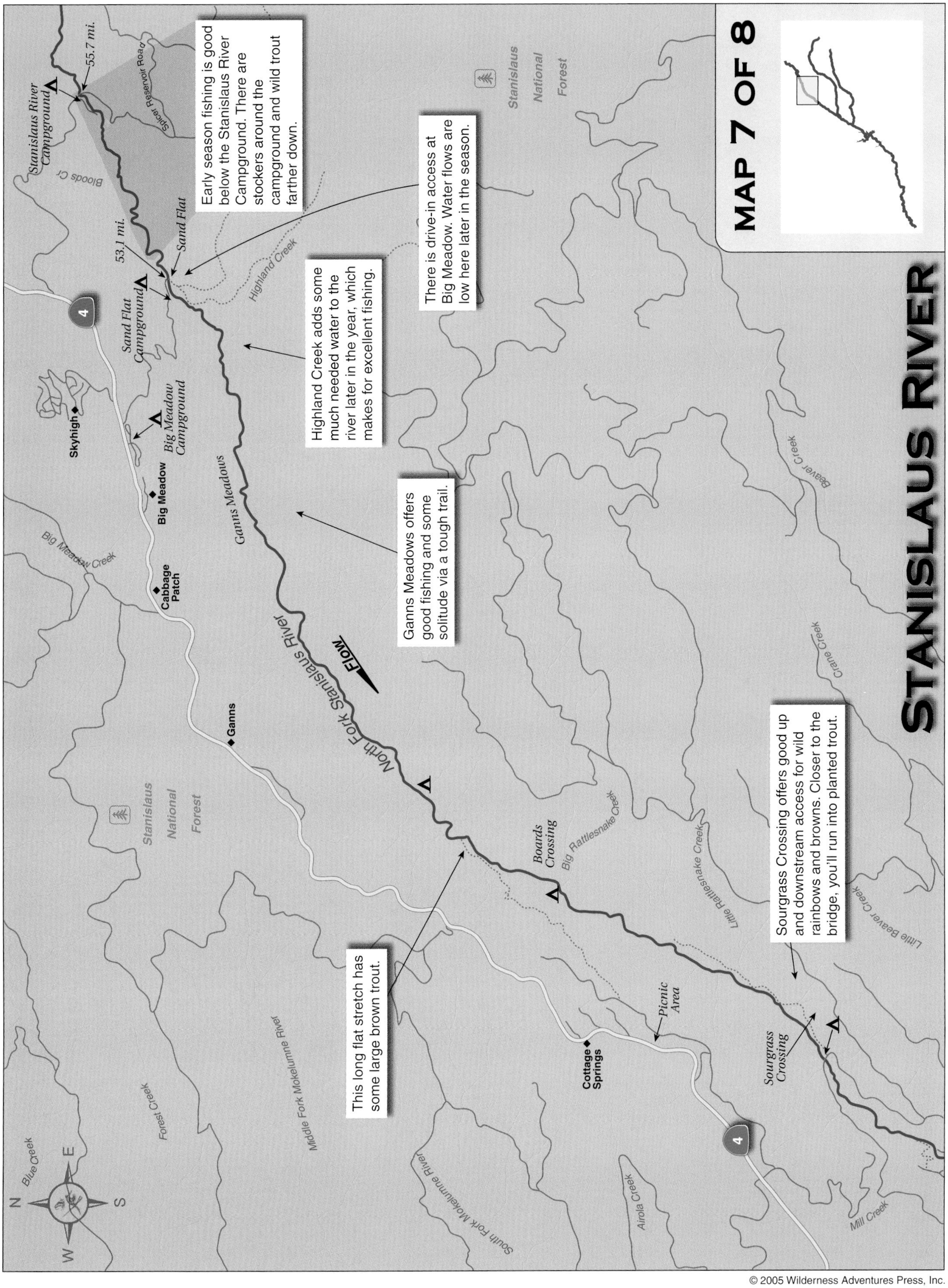
Stanislaus River
Map 7 of 8
Early season fishing is good below the Stanislaus River Campground. There are stockers around the campground and wild trout farther down.
There is drive-in access at Big Meadow. Water flows are low here later in the season.
Highland Creek adds some much needed water to the river later in the year, which makes for excellent fishing.
Ganns Meadows offers good fishing and some solitude via a tough trail.
This long flat stretch has some large brown trout.
Sourgrass Crossing offers good up and downstream access for wild rainbows and browns. Closer to the bridge, you'll run into planted trout.
Stanislaus River Campground
55.7 mi.
53.1 mi.
Spicer Reservoir Road
Bloods Cr
Sand Flat
Sand Flat Campground
Highland Creek
Big Meadow Campground
Skyhigh
Big Meadow
Ganns Meadows
Big Meadow Creek
Cabbage Patch
North Fork Stanislaus River
Flow
Ganns
Stanislaus National Forest
Boards Crossing
Big Rattlesnake Creek
Little Rattlesnake Creek
Beaver Creek
Crane Creek
Little Beaver Creek
Picnic Area
Cottage Springs
Sourgrass Crossing
Middle Fork Mokelumne River
South Fork Mokelumne River
Forest Creek
Blue Creek
Airola Creek
Mill Creek
4
N
E
S
W

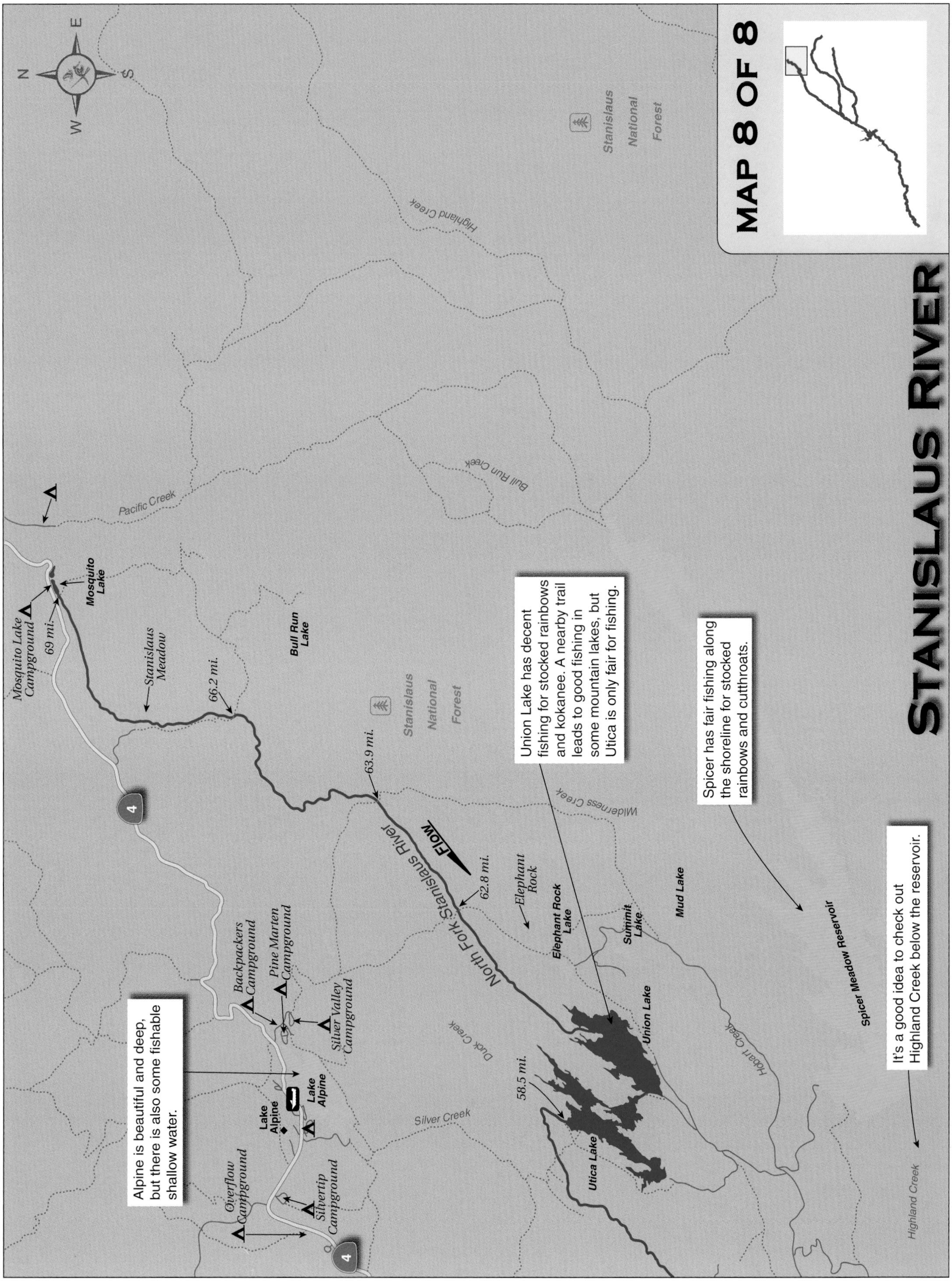
Stanislaus River
Map 8 of 8
N
E
S
W
Stanislaus National Forest
Highland Creek
Pacific Creek
Bull Run Creek
Mosquito Lake Campground
69 mi.
Mosquito Lake
Stanislaus Meadow
66.2 mi.
Bull Run Lake
Stanislaus National Forest
63.9 mi.
4
Wilderness Creek
North Fork Stanislaus River
Flow
62.8 mi.
Elephant Rock
Elephant Rock Lake
Summit Lake
Mud Lake
Union Lake has decent fishing for stocked rainbows and kokanee. A nearby trail leads to good fishing in some mountain lakes, but Utica is only fair for fishing.
Spicer has fair fishing along the shoreline for stocked rainbows and cutthroats.
Spicer Meadow Reservoir
It's a good idea to check out Highland Creek below the reservoir.
Hobart Creek
Union Lake
Utica Lake
58.5 mi.
Duck Creek
Silver Creek
Highland Creek
Backpackers Campground
Pine Marten Campground
Silver Valley Campground
Lake Alpine
Alpine is beautiful and deep, but there is also some fishable shallow water.
Overflow Campground
Silvertip Campground
4

Trinity River

From its headwaters in the Trinity Alps Wilderness the once wild Trinity River flows well over 100 miles down to its confluence with the Klamath River at the town of Weitchpec. Lewiston and Clair Engle (Trinity) Dams block steelhead and salmon from reaching spawning grounds upstream, but a tailwater fishery for brown trout and anadromous hatchery fish now exists below Lewiston. Upstream of the big lakes there's still fishing for small trout, but most anglers concentrate their trout fishing on the 20 or so miles below the Lewiston Dam. There are some huge browns in here, although not large numbers of fish. Good steelhead and salmon fishing continues all the way downstream to the Klamath when the fish are running. For anglers willing to strap on hiking boots, this area has a wealth of high-mountain lakes and streams worth exploring. Lewiston and Clair Engle also offer great trout and bass fishing.

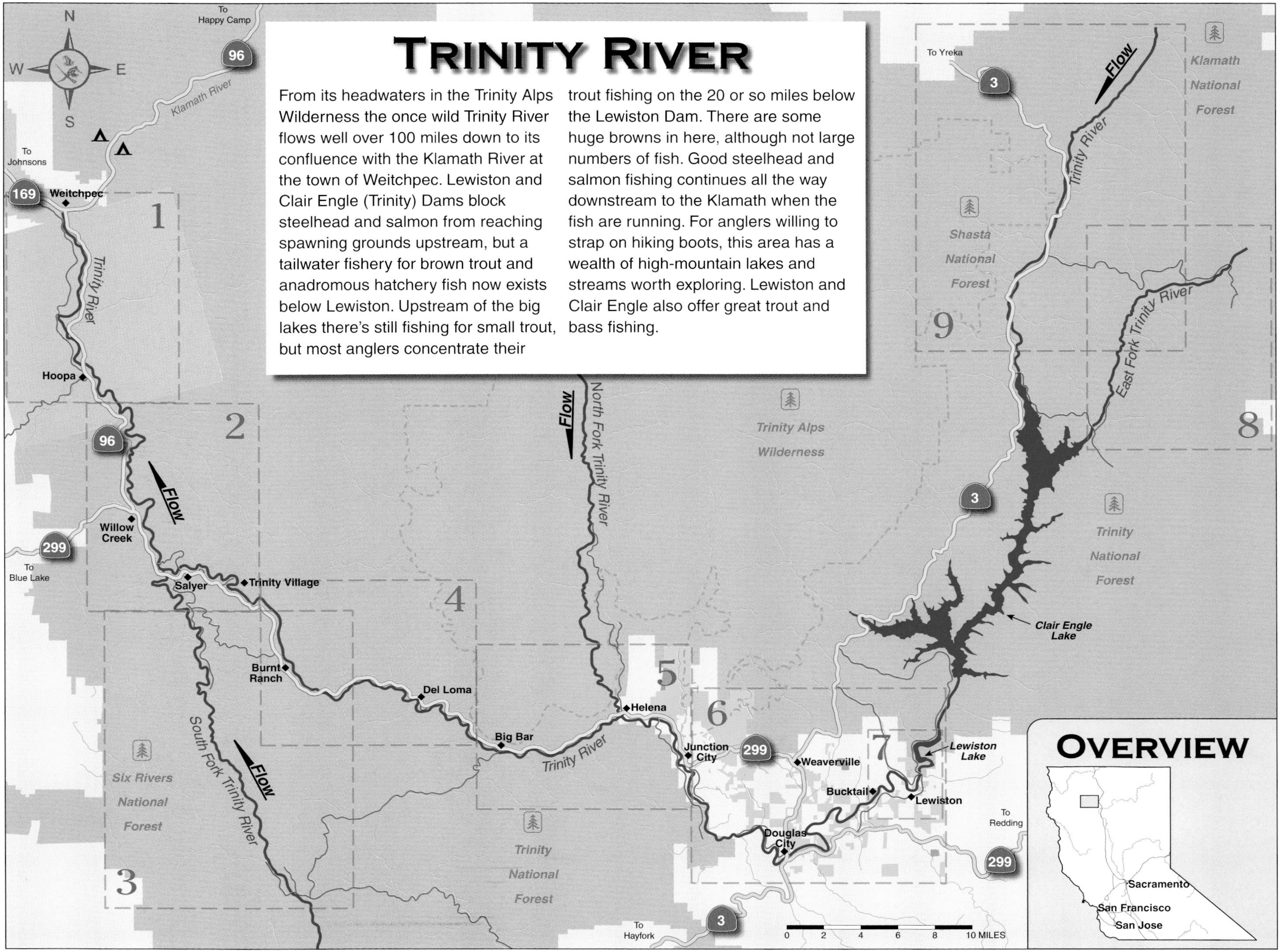

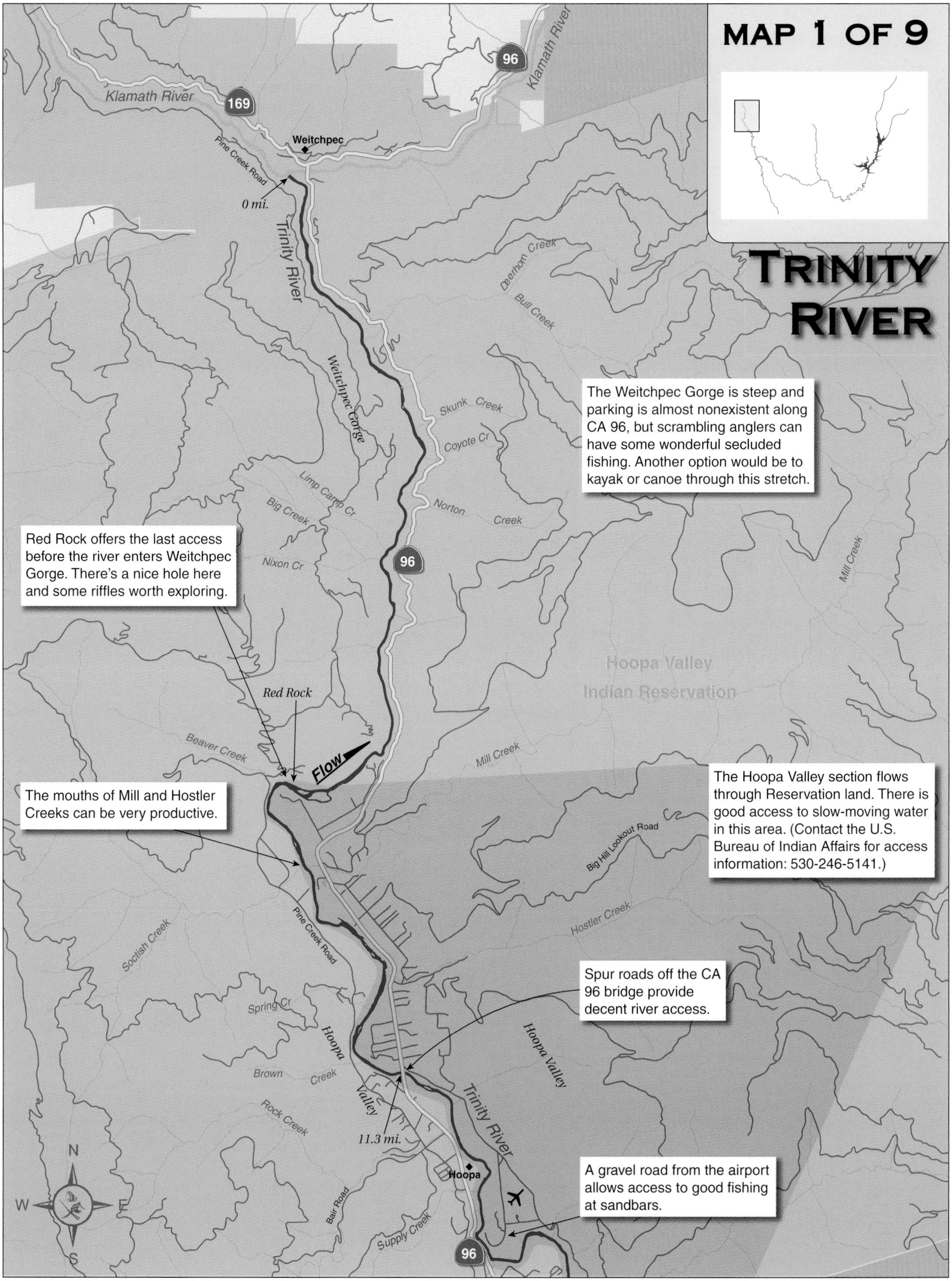
MAP 1 OF 9
TRINITY RIVER
The Weitchpec Gorge is steep and parking is almost nonexistent along CA 96, but scrambling anglers can have some wonderful secluded fishing. Another option would be to kayak or canoe through this stretch.
Red Rock offers the last access before the river enters Weitchpec Gorge. There's a nice hole here and some riffles worth exploring.
The mouths of Mill and Hostler Creeks can be very productive.
The Hoopa Valley section flows through Reservation land. There is good access to slow-moving water in this area. (Contact the U.S. Bureau of Indian Affairs for access information: 530-246-5141.)
Spur roads off the CA 96 bridge provide decent river access.
A gravel road from the airport allows access to good fishing at sandbars.
Klamath River
169
96
Weitchpec
Pine Creek Road
0 mi.
Trinity River
Weitchpec Gorge
Skunk Creek
Coyote Cr
Norton Creek
Limp Camp Cr
Big Creek
Nixon Cr
Bull Creek
Mill Creek
Hoopa Valley Indian Reservation
Red Rock
Beaver Creek
Flow
Big Hill Lookout Road
Hostler Creek
Soctish Creek
Spring Cr
Hoopa Valley
Brown Creek
Rock Creek
11.3 mi.
Hoopa
Bair Road
Supply Creek
N
S
E
W

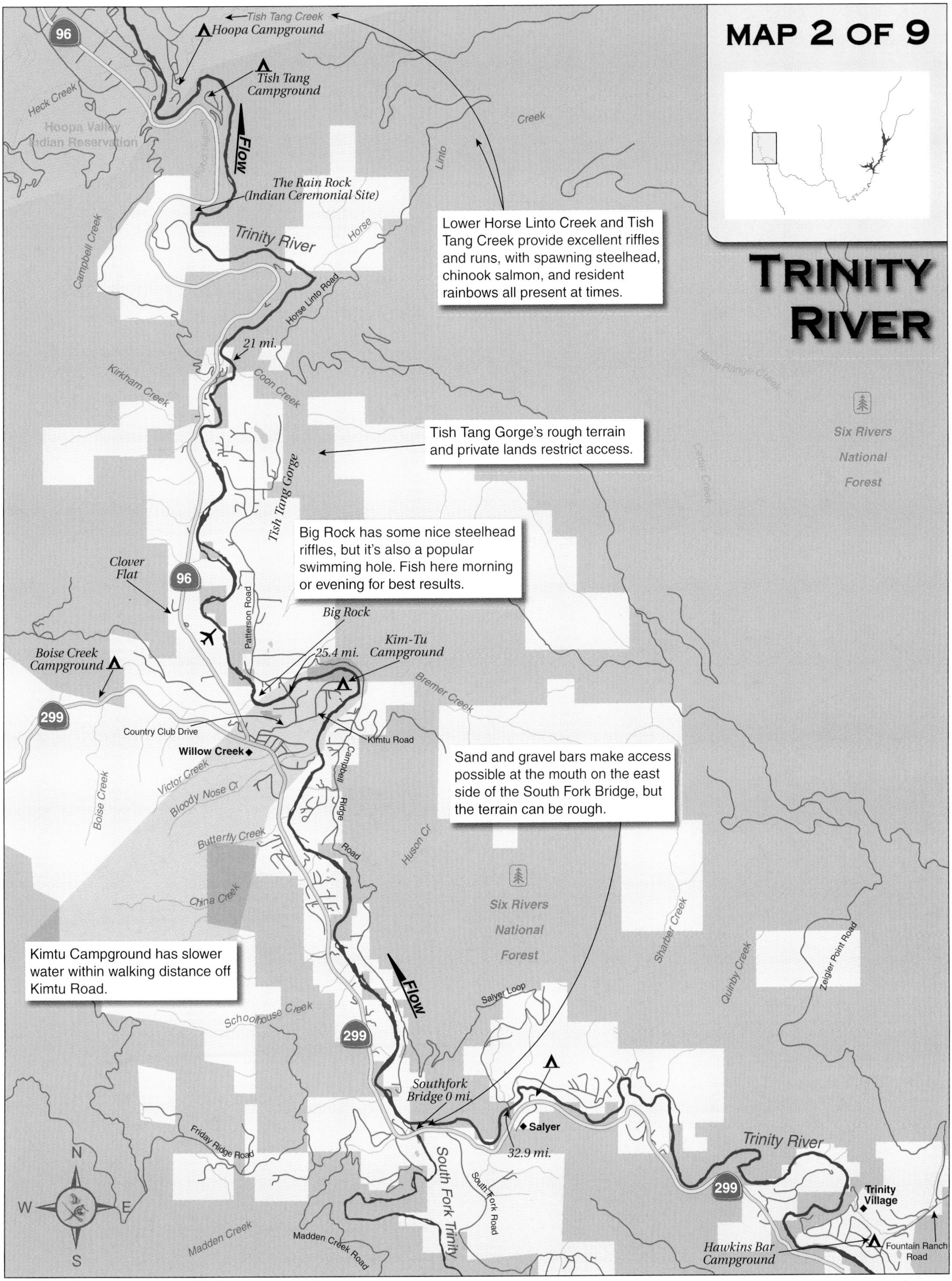
MAP 2 OF 9
TRINITY RIVER
Tish Tang Creek
Hoopa Campground
Tish Tang Campground
Heck Creek
Hoopa Valley Indian Reservation
Flow
The Rain Rock (Indian Ceremonial Site)
Trinity River
Horse
Linto
Creek
Campbell Creek
Horse Linto Road
Lower Horse Linto Creek and Tish Tang Creek provide excellent riffles and runs, with spawning steelhead, chinook salmon, and resident rainbows all present at times.
21 mi.
Kirkham Creek
Coon Creek
Horse Range Creek
Six Rivers National Forest
Tish Tang Gorge's rough terrain and private lands restrict access.
Cedar Creek
Tish Tang Gorge
Big Rock has some nice steelhead riffles, but it's also a popular swimming hole. Fish here morning or evening for best results.
Clover Flat
96
Patterson Road
Big Rock
Kim-Tu Campground
25.4 mi.
Boise Creek Campground
299
Bremer Creek
Country Club Drive
Kimtu Road
Willow Creek
Campbell Ridge Road
Sand and gravel bars make access possible at the mouth on the east side of the South Fork Bridge, but the terrain can be rough.
Victor Creek
Bloody Nose Cr
Boise Creek
Butterfly Creek
Huson Cr
China Creek
Six Rivers National Forest
Sharber Creek
Zeigler Point Road
Quinby Creek
Kimtu Campground has slower water within walking distance off Kimtu Road.
Flow
Salyer Loop
Schoolhouse Creek
Southfork Bridge 0 mi.
Salyer
32.9 mi.
Trinity River
Friday Ridge Road
South Fork Trinity
South Fork Road
Trinity Village
Fountain Ranch Road
Hawkins Bar Campground
Madden Creek
Madden Creek Road
N
W
E
S

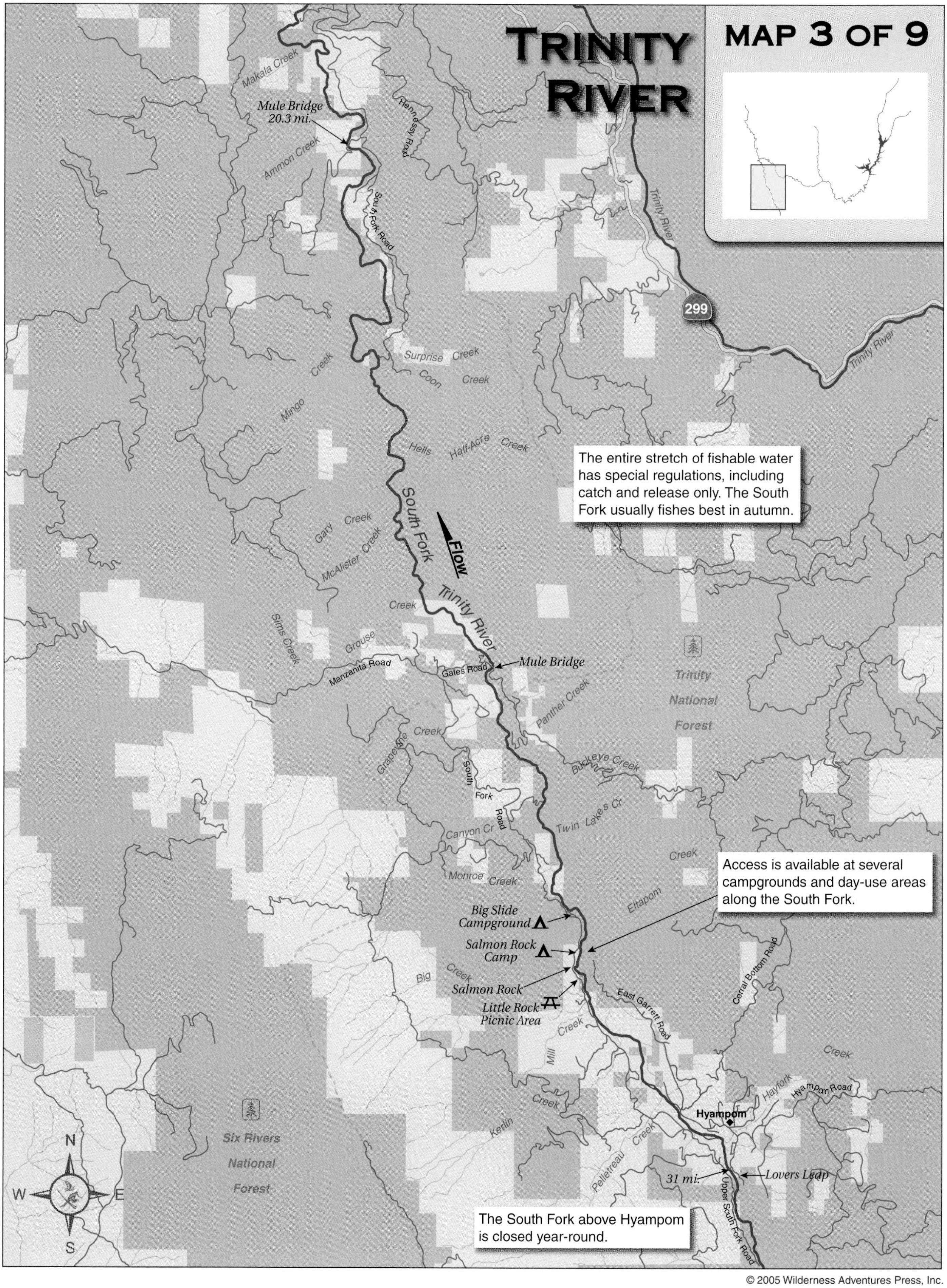
TRINITY RIVER
MAP 3 OF 9
Makala Creek
Mule Bridge 20.3 mi.
Ammon Creek
Hennessy Road
South Fork Road
Trinity River
299
Trinity River
Surprise Creek
Coon Creek
Mingo Creek
Hells
Half-Acre Creek
The entire stretch of fishable water has special regulations, including catch and release only. The South Fork usually fishes best in autumn.
South Fork Trinity River
Flow
Gary Creek
McAlister Creek
Creek
Sims Creek
Grouse
Manzanita Road
Gates Road
Mule Bridge
Trinity National Forest
Panther Creek
Grapevine Creek
South Fork Road
Buckeye Creek
Twin Lakes Cr
Canyon Cr
Creek
Monroe Creek
Eltapom
Access is available at several campgrounds and day-use areas along the South Fork.
Big Slide Campground
Salmon Rock Camp
Big Creek
Salmon Rock
Little Rock Picnic Area
Corral Bottom Road
East Garrett Road
Mill Creek
Creek
Hayfork
Hyampom Road
Creek
Kerlin
Hyampom
Six Rivers National Forest
Pelletreau Creek
31 mi.
Lovers Leap
Upper South Fork Road
The South Fork above Hyampom is closed year-round.
N
W
E
S

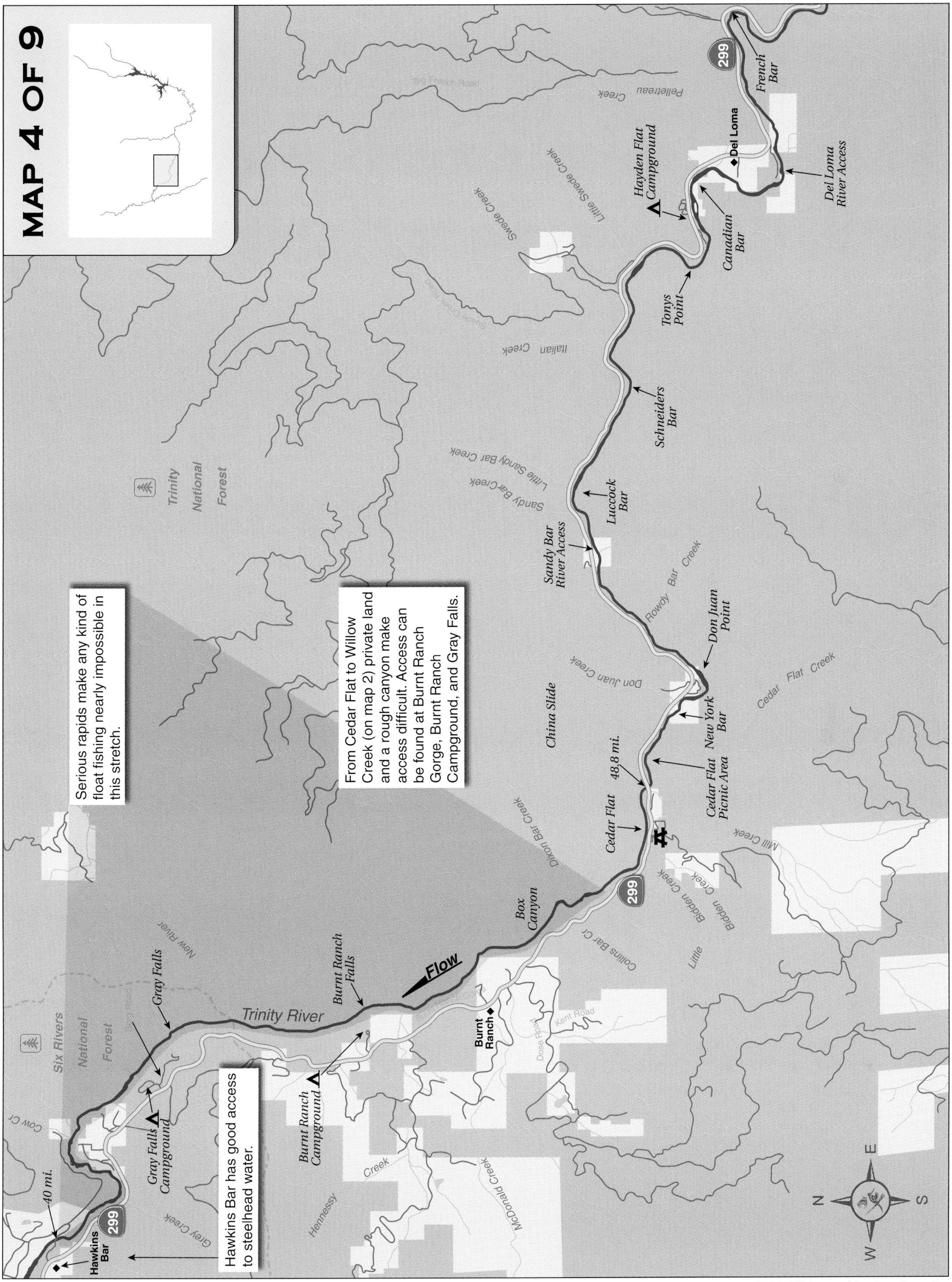
MAP 4 OF 9
Serious rapids make any kind of float fishing nearly impossible in this stretch.
From Cedar Flat to Willow Creek (on map 2) private land and a rough canyon make access difficult. Access can be found at Burnt Ranch Gorge, Burnt Ranch Campground, and Gray Falls.
Hawkins Bar has good access to steelhead water.
Trinity National Forest
Six Rivers National Forest
Trinity River
Flow
299
French Bar
Del Loma
Del Loma River Access
Hayden Flat Campground
Canadian Bar
Tonys Point
Schneiders Bar
Luccock Bar
Sandy Bar River Access
Don Juan Point
New York Bar
Cedar Flat Picnic Area
48.8 mi.
Cedar Flat
China Slide
Box Canyon
Burnt Ranch Falls
Gray Falls
Gray Falls Campground
Burnt Ranch Campground
Burnt Ranch
40 mi.
Hawkins Bar
Pelletreau Creek
Swede Creek
Little Swede Creek
Italian Creek
Little Sandy Bar Creek
Sandy Bar Creek
Rowdy Bar Creek
Don Juan Creek
Cedar Flat Creek
Mill Creek
Dixon Bar Creek
Bidden Creek
Little Bidden Creek
Collins Bar Cr
New River
Cow Cr
Grey Creek
Hennessy Creek
McDonald Creek
Big French Road
Kent Road
Dose Road
N
E
S
W

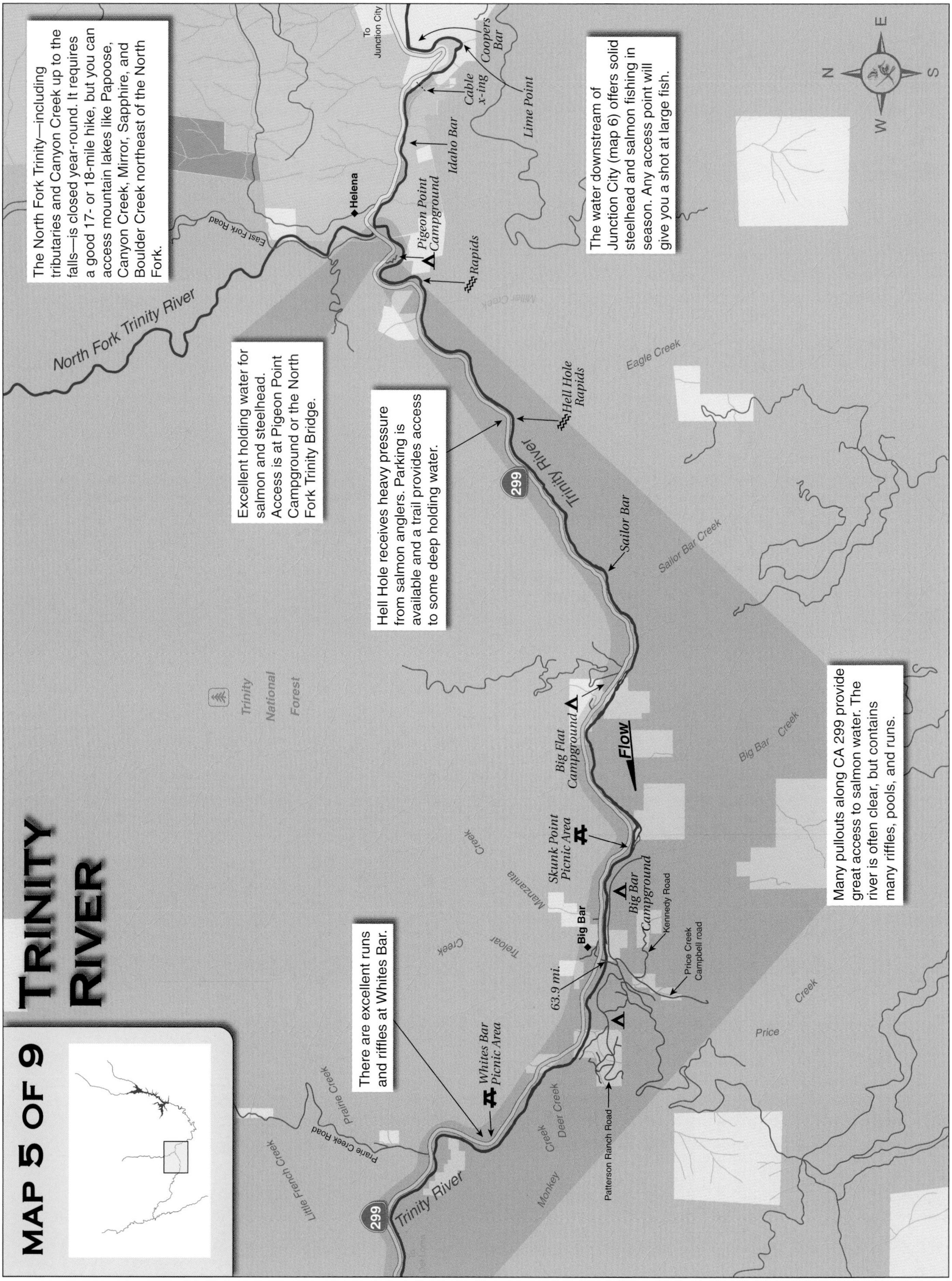
MAP 5 OF 9
TRINITY RIVER
The North Fork Trinity—including tributaries and Canyon Creek up to the falls—is closed year-round. It requires a good 17- or 18-mile hike, but you can access mountain lakes like Papoose, Canyon Creek, Mirror, Sapphire, and Boulder Creek northeast of the North Fork.
Excellent holding water for salmon and steelhead. Access is at Pigeon Point Campground or the North Fork Trinity Bridge.
Hell Hole receives heavy pressure from salmon anglers. Parking is available and a trail provides access to some deep holding water.
The water downstream of Junction City (map 6) offers solid steelhead and salmon fishing in season. Any access point will give you a shot at large fish.
Many pullouts along CA 299 provide great access to salmon water. The river is often clear, but contains many riffles, pools, and runs.
There are excellent runs and riffles at Whites Bar.
To Junction City
Coopers Bar
Cable x-ing
Lime Point
Idaho Bar
Helena
Pigeon Point Campground
Rapids
East Fork Road
North Fork Trinity River
Miller Creek
Eagle Creek
Hell Hole Rapids
Trinity River
299
Sailor Bar
Sailor Bar Creek
Trinity National Forest
Big Flat Campground
Flow
Big Bar Creek
Skunk Point Picnic Area
Manzanita Creek
Big Bar Campground
Kennedy Road
Big Bar
Treloar Creek
Price Creek Campbell road
63.9 mi.
Price Creek
Whites Bar Picnic Area
Prairie Creek
Prarie Creek Road
Little French Creek
Deer Creek
Monkey Creek
Patterson Ranch Road
N
E
S
W

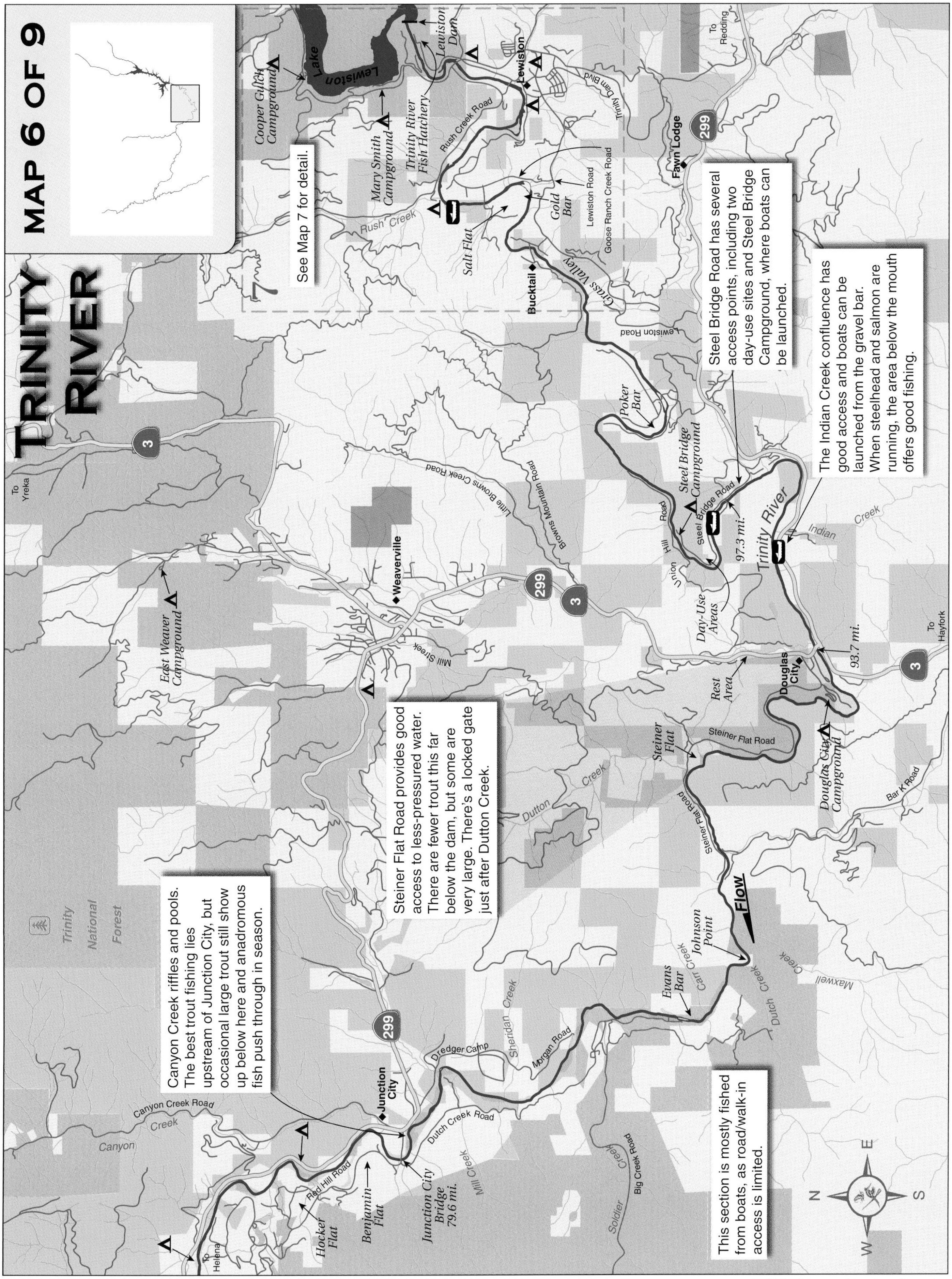
Trinity River
Map 6 of 9
See Map 7 for detail.
Steel Bridge Road has several access points, including two day-use sites and Steel Bridge Campground, where boats can be launched.
The Indian Creek confluence has good access and boats can be launched from the gravel bar. When steelhead and salmon are running, the area below the mouth offers good fishing.
Steiner Flat Road provides good access to less-pressured water. There are fewer trout this far below the dam, but some are very large. There's a locked gate just after Dutton Creek.
Canyon Creek riffles and pools. The best trout fishing lies upstream of Junction City, but occasional large trout still show up below here and anadromous fish push through in season.
This section is mostly fished from boats, as road/walk-in access is limited.
Cooper Gulch Campground
Lewiston Lake
Lewiston Dam
Mary Smith Campground
Trinity River Fish Hatchery
Lewiston
Rush Creek Road
Rush Creek
Trinity Dam Blvd
To Redding
Fawn Lodge
299
Salt Flat
Gold Bar
Lewiston Road
Goose Ranch Creek Road
Bucktail
Grass Valley
Poker Bar
Steel Bridge Campground
Steel Bridge Road
Union Hill Road
97.3 mi.
Trinity River
Indian Creek
Day-Use Areas
To Yreka
3
Weaverville
Little Browns Creek Road
Browns Mountain Road
East Weaver Campground
Mill Street
To Hayfork
93.7 mi.
Douglas City
Rest Area
Steiner Flat
Steiner Flat Road
Douglas City Campground
Bar K Road
Dutton Creek
Flow
Johnson Point
Evans Bar
Carr Creek
Dutch Creek
Maxwell Creek
Trinity National Forest
Sheridan Creek
Morgan Road
Dredger Camp
Junction City
Canyon Creek Road
Canyon Creek
Dutch Creek Road
Junction City Bridge 79.6 mi.
Mill Creek
Big Creek Road
Soldier Creek
Benjamin Flat
Red Hill Road
Hocker Flat
To Helena
N
E
S
W

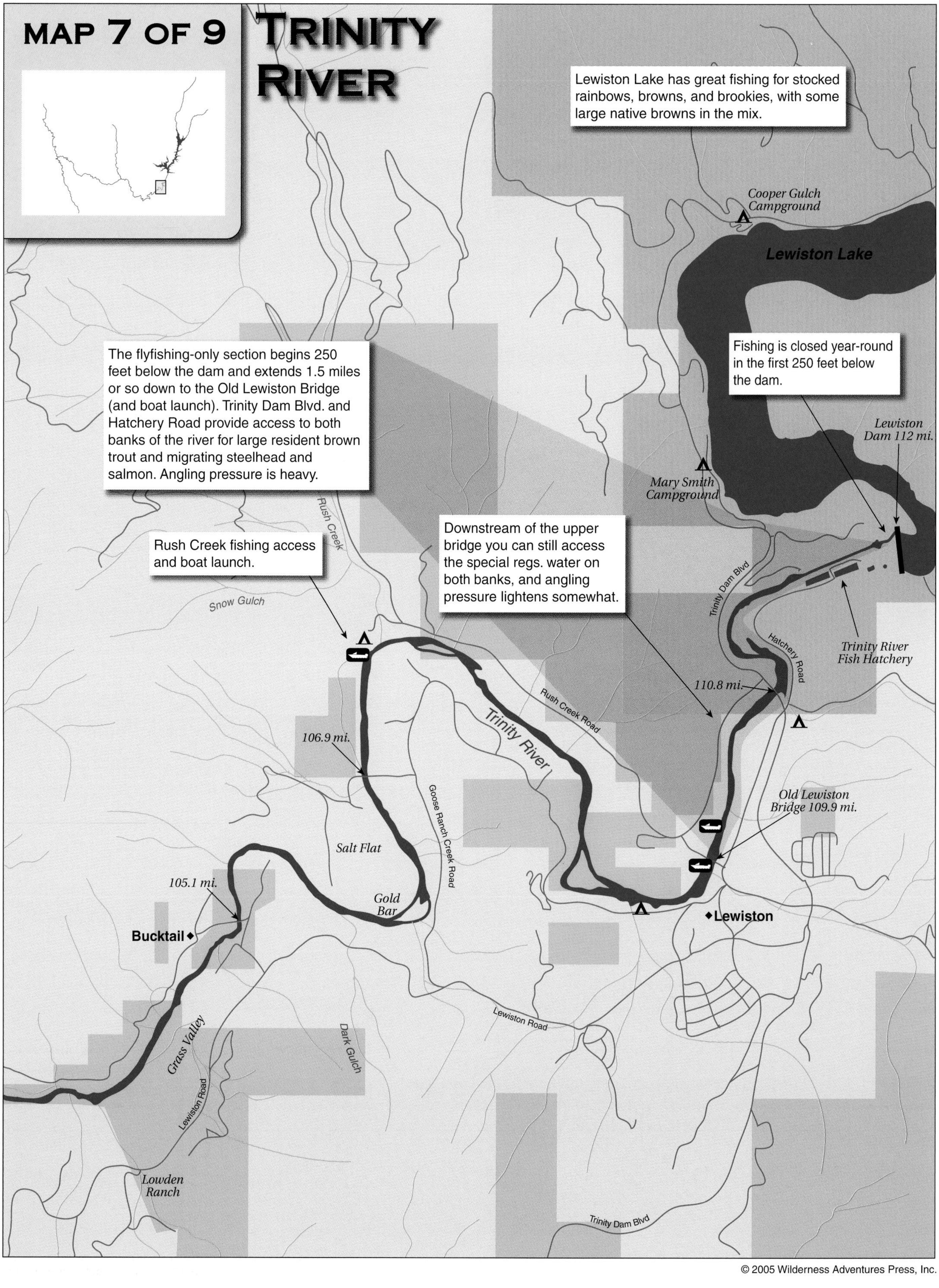
MAP 7 OF 9
TRINITY RIVER
Lewiston Lake has great fishing for stocked rainbows, browns, and brookies, with some large native browns in the mix.
Cooper Gulch Campground
Lewiston Lake
Fishing is closed year-round in the first 250 feet below the dam.
Lewiston Dam 112 mi.
The flyfishing-only section begins 250 feet below the dam and extends 1.5 miles or so down to the Old Lewiston Bridge (and boat launch). Trinity Dam Blvd. and Hatchery Road provide access to both banks of the river for large resident brown trout and migrating steelhead and salmon. Angling pressure is heavy.
Mary Smith Campground
Rush Creek
Rush Creek fishing access and boat launch.
Downstream of the upper bridge you can still access the special regs. water on both banks, and angling pressure lightens somewhat.
Trinity Dam Blvd
Snow Gulch
Hatchery Road
Trinity River Fish Hatchery
110.8 mi.
Rush Creek Road
Trinity River
106.9 mi.
Goose Ranch Creek Road
Old Lewiston Bridge 109.9 mi.
Salt Flat
105.1 mi.
Gold Bar
Lewiston
Bucktail
Lewiston Road
Grass Valley
Dark Gulch
Lewiston Road
Lowden Ranch
Trinity Dam Blvd

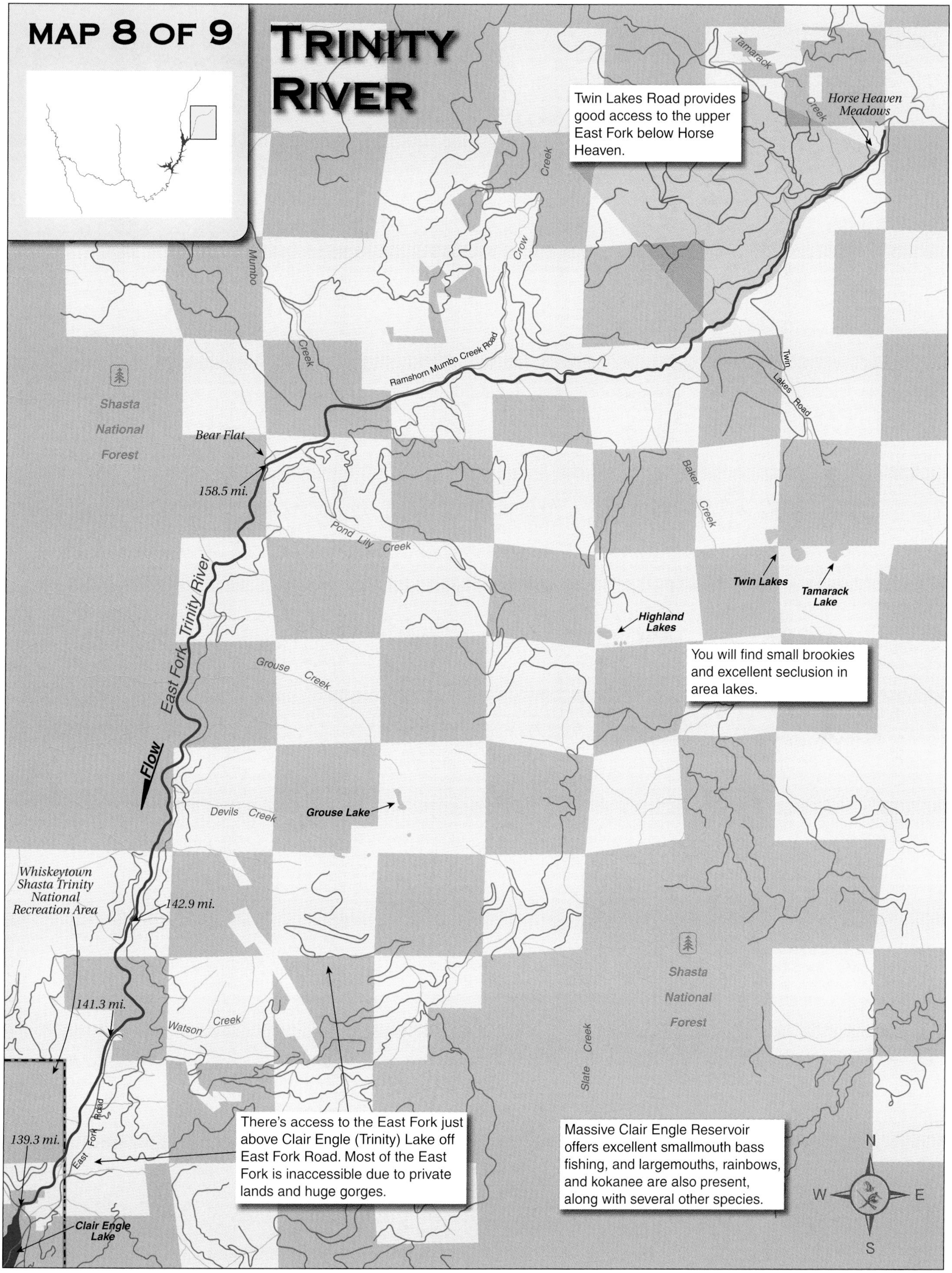
MAP 8 OF 9
TRINITY RIVER
Twin Lakes Road provides good access to the upper East Fork below Horse Heaven.
Horse Heaven Meadows
Tamarack Creek
Creek
Crow
Mumbo Creek
Ramshorn Mumbo Creek Road
Twin Lakes Road
Shasta National Forest
Bear Flat
158.5 mi.
Baker Creek
Pond Lily Creek
Twin Lakes
Tamarack Lake
Highland Lakes
East Fork Trinity River
Grouse Creek
You will find small brookies and excellent seclusion in area lakes.
Flow
Devils Creek
Grouse Lake
Whiskeytown Shasta Trinity National Recreation Area
142.9 mi.
Shasta National Forest
141.3 mi.
Watson Creek
Slate Creek
East Fork Road
139.3 mi.
There's access to the East Fork just above Clair Engle (Trinity) Lake off East Fork Road. Most of the East Fork is inaccessible due to private lands and huge gorges.
Massive Clair Engle Reservoir offers excellent smallmouth bass fishing, and largemouths, rainbows, and kokanee are also present, along with several other species.
N
W
E
S
Clair Engle Lake

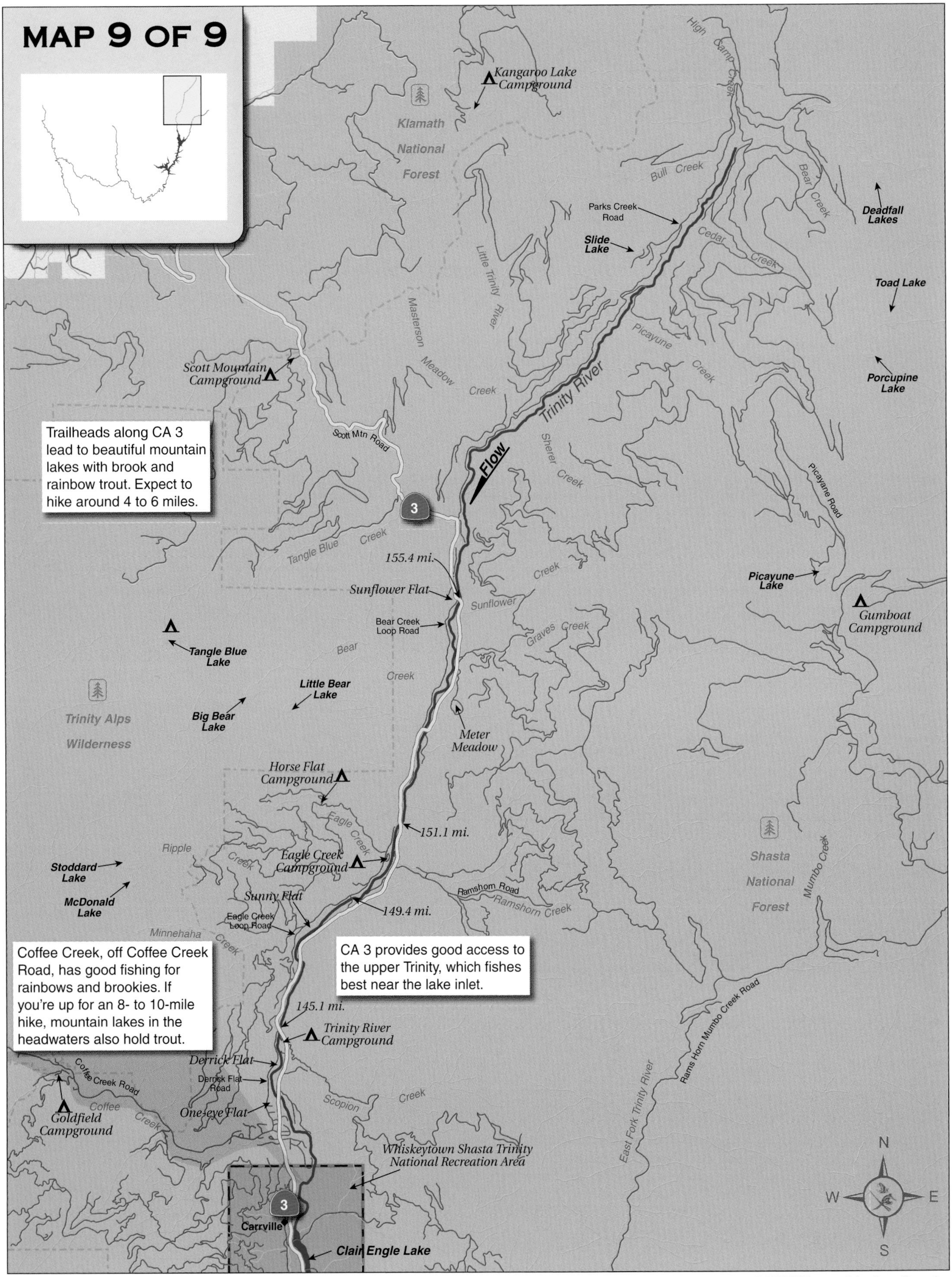
MAP 9 OF 9
Kangaroo Lake Campground
Klamath National Forest
High Camp Creek
Bull Creek
Bear Creek
Parks Creek Road
Slide Lake
Deadfall Lakes
Cedar Creek
Little Trinity River
Masterson Meadow Creek
Toad Lake
Picayune Creek
Porcupine Lake
Scott Mountain Campground
Trinity River
Flow
Scott Mtn Road
Sherer Creek
Picayane Road
Trailheads along CA 3 lead to beautiful mountain lakes with brook and rainbow trout. Expect to hike around 4 to 6 miles.
3
Tangle Blue Creek
155.4 mi.
Sunflower Flat
Sunflower Creek
Picayune Lake
Gumboat Campground
Bear Creek Loop Road
Graves Creek
Tangle Blue Lake
Bear Creek
Little Bear Lake
Big Bear Lake
Trinity Alps Wilderness
Meter Meadow
Horse Flat Campground
Eagle Creek
151.1 mi.
Ripple Creek
Eagle Creek Campground
Stoddard Lake
McDonald Lake
Sunny Flat
Ramshorn Road
Ramshorn Creek
149.4 mi.
Shasta National Forest
Mumbo Creek
Eagle Creek Loop Road
Minnehaha Creek
Coffee Creek, off Coffee Creek Road, has good fishing for rainbows and brookies. If you're up for an 8- to 10-mile hike, mountain lakes in the headwaters also hold trout.
CA 3 provides good access to the upper Trinity, which fishes best near the lake inlet.
145.1 mi.
Trinity River Campground
Rams Horn Mumbo Creek Road
Derrick Flat
Derrick Flat Road
Coffee Creek Road
East Fork Trinity River
Scopion Creek
Coffee Creek
One-eye Flat
Goldfield Campground
Whiskeytown Shasta Trinity National Recreation Area
N
W
E
S
Carrville
Clair Engle Lake

TRUCKEE RIVER

The scenic Truckee River is the only outlet for massive Lake Tahoe. It flows 88 miles through a series of canyons down to Pyramid Lake in Nevada. Access is good along most of the river and the fishing can be excellent for wild browns and stocked rainbows. There's a variety of water types here, from shallow riffles that hold small fish to deep holes harboring surprisingly large browns. The river and the area around Lake Tahoe play host to a huge influx of skiers in winter and anglers, hikers, and rafters the rest of the year.

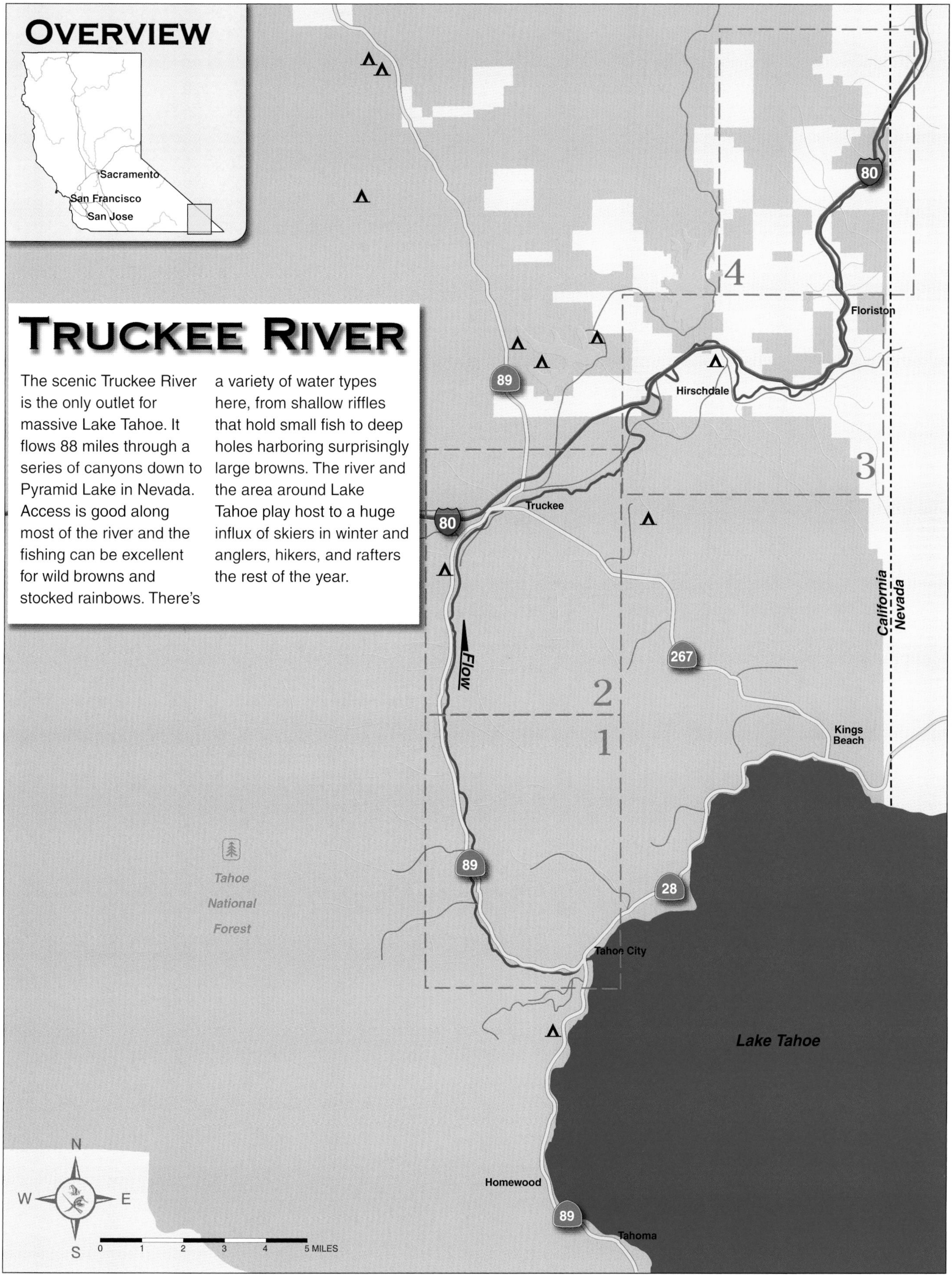

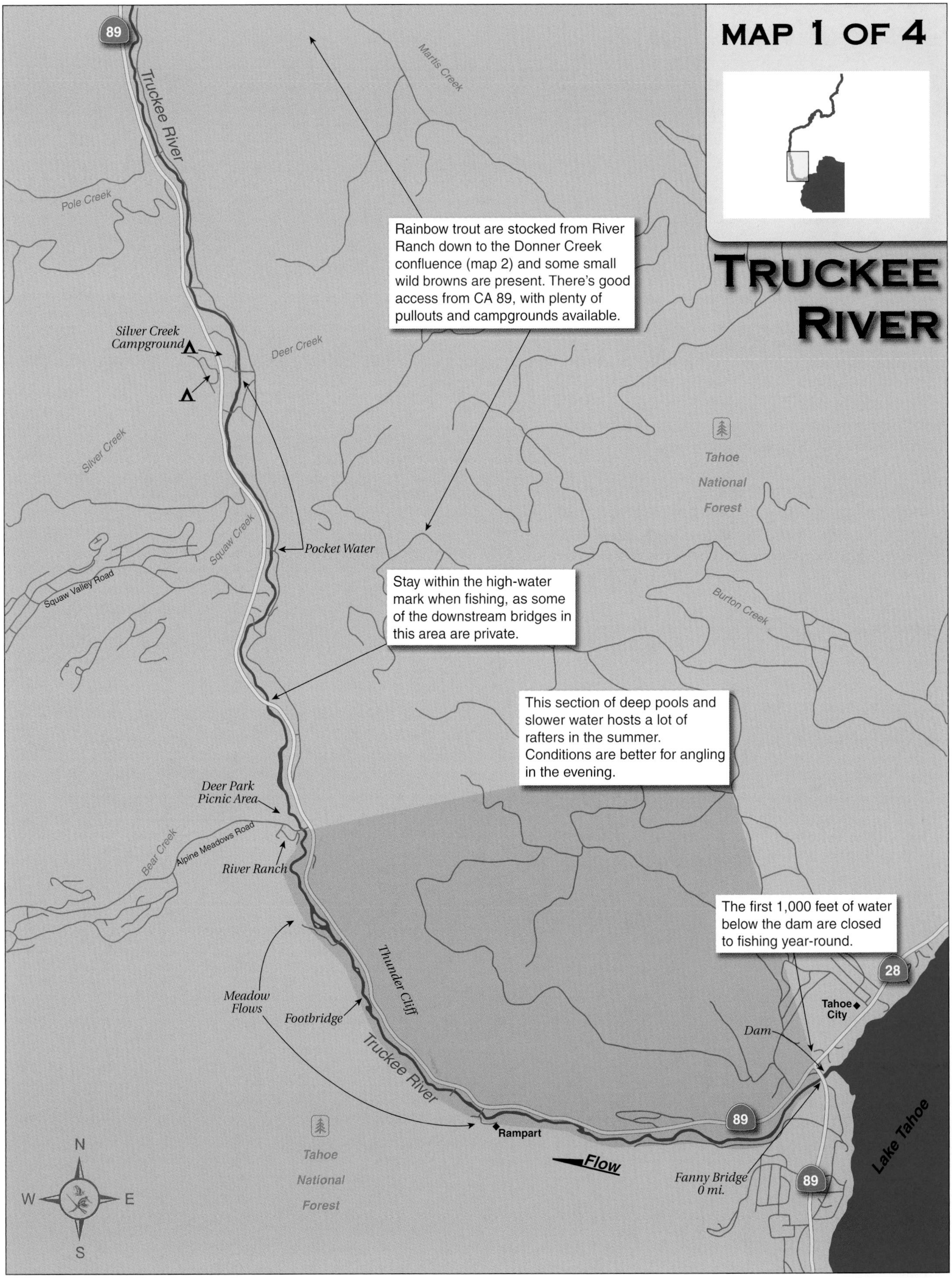
MAP 1 OF 4
TRUCKEE RIVER
Rainbow trout are stocked from River Ranch down to the Donner Creek confluence (map 2) and some small wild browns are present. There's good access from CA 89, with plenty of pullouts and campgrounds available.
Stay within the high-water mark when fishing, as some of the downstream bridges in this area are private.
This section of deep pools and slower water hosts a lot of rafters in the summer. Conditions are better for angling in the evening.
The first 1,000 feet of water below the dam are closed to fishing year-round.
89
Truckee River
Martis Creek
Pole Creek
Silver Creek Campground
Deer Creek
Silver Creek
Squaw Creek
Pocket Water
Squaw Valley Road
Tahoe National Forest
Burton Creek
Deer Park Picnic Area
Alpine Meadows Road
Bear Creek
River Ranch
Thunder Cliff
Meadow Flows
Footbridge
Rampart
Flow
28
Tahoe City
Dam
Fanny Bridge 0 mi.
Lake Tahoe
N
W
E
S

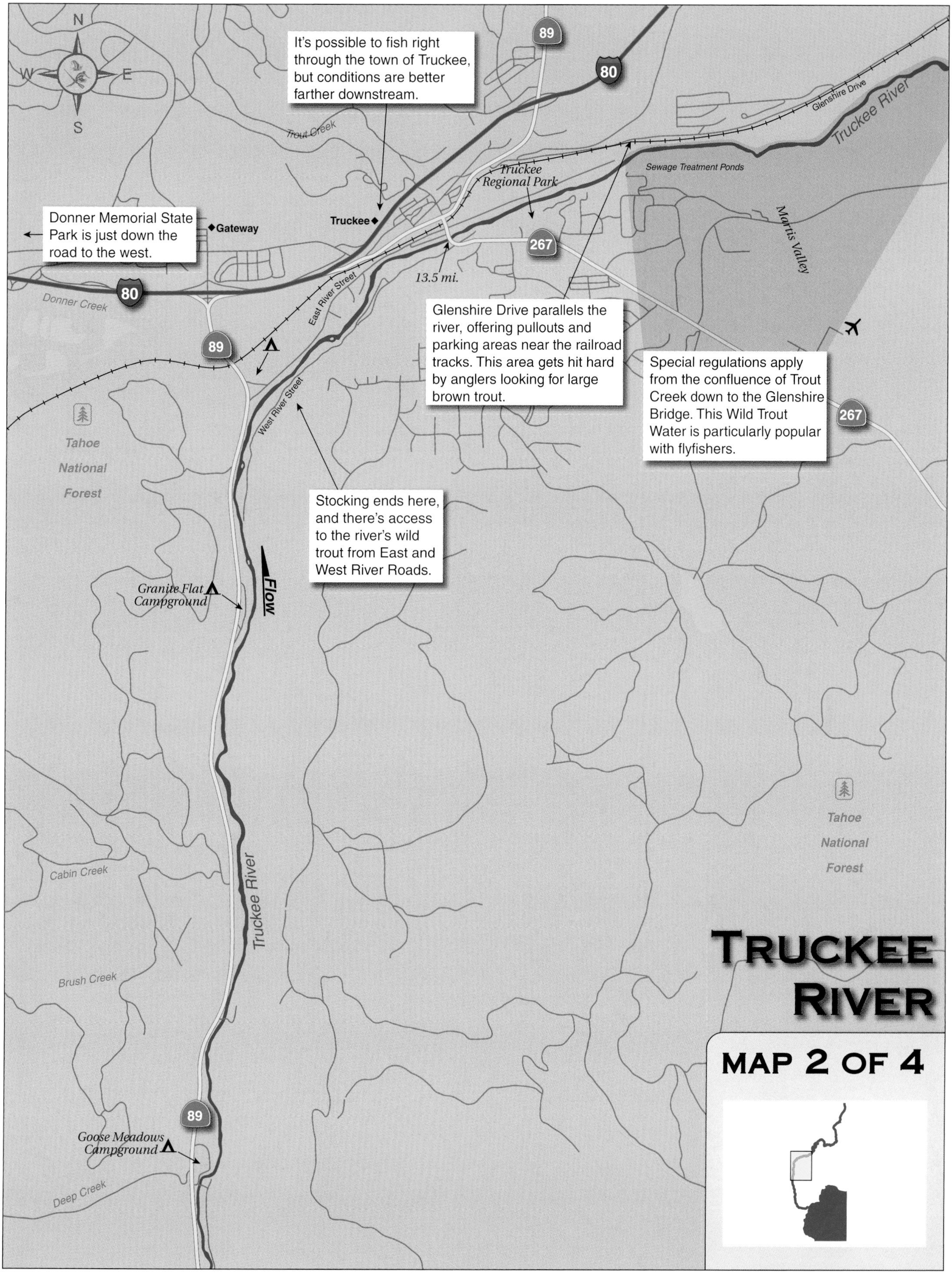
N
W
E
S
It's possible to fish right through the town of Truckee, but conditions are better farther downstream.
89
80
Trout Creek
Glenshire Drive
Truckee River
Sewage Treatment Ponds
Truckee Regional Park
Donner Memorial State Park is just down the road to the west.
Gateway
Truckee
267
Martis Valley
13.5 mi.
East River Street
80
Donner Creek
Glenshire Drive parallels the river, offering pullouts and parking areas near the railroad tracks. This area gets hit hard by anglers looking for large brown trout.
89
West River Street
Special regulations apply from the confluence of Trout Creek down to the Glenshire Bridge. This Wild Trout Water is particularly popular with flyfishers.
267
Tahoe National Forest
Stocking ends here, and there's access to the river's wild trout from East and West River Roads.
Flow
Granite Flat Campground
Tahoe National Forest
Cabin Creek
Truckee River
Brush Creek
TRUCKEE RIVER
MAP 2 OF 4
89
Goose Meadows Campground
Deep Creek

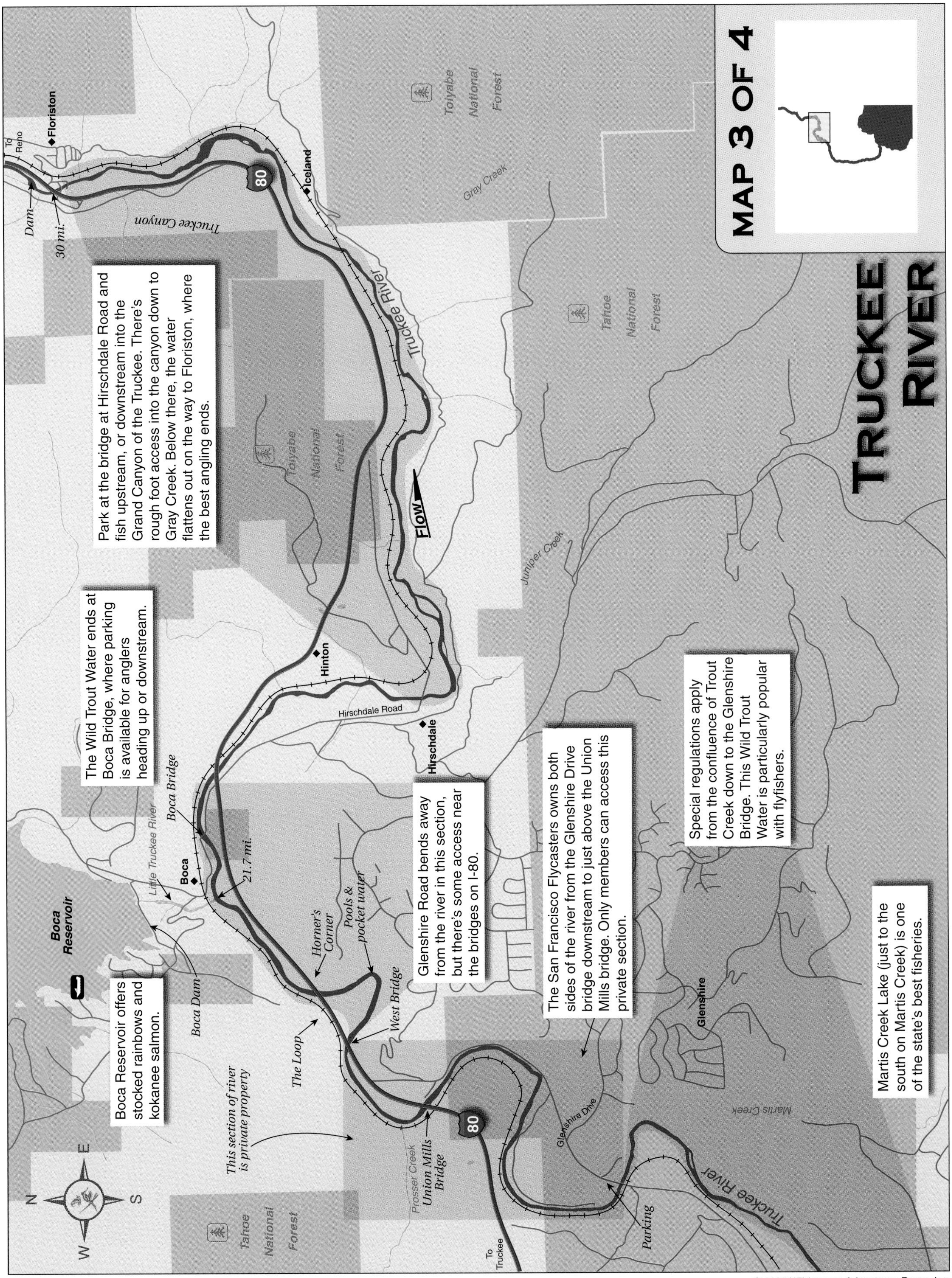

MAP 3 OF 4
TRUCKEE RIVER
Park at the bridge at Hirschdale Road and fish upstream, or downstream into the Grand Canyon of the Truckee. There's rough foot access into the canyon down to Gray Creek. Below there, the water flattens out on the way to Floriston, where the best angling ends.
The Wild Trout Water ends at Boca Bridge, where parking is available for anglers heading up or downstream.
Boca Reservoir offers stocked rainbows and kokanee salmon.
Glenshire Road bends away from the river in this section, but there's some access near the bridges on I-80.
The San Francisco Flycasters owns both sides of the river from the Glenshire Drive bridge downstream to just above the Union Mills bridge. Only members can access this private section.
Special regulations apply from the confluence of Trout Creek down to the Glenshire Bridge. This Wild Trout Water is particularly popular with flyfishers.
Martis Creek Lake (just to the south on Martis Creek) is one of the state's best fisheries.
This section of river is private property
To Reno
Floriston
Dam
30 mi.
Truckee Canyon
80
Iceland
Gray Creek
Toiyabe National Forest
Tahoe National Forest
Truckee River
Flow
Juniper Creek
Hinton
Hirschdale Road
Hirschdale
Boca Bridge
Little Truckee River
Boca
21.7 mi.
Boca Reservoir
Boca Dam
Horner's Corner
Pools & pocket water
West Bridge
The Loop
Prosser Creek
Union Mills Bridge
Glenshire Drive
Glenshire
Martis Creek
Parking
To Truckee
N
E
S
W

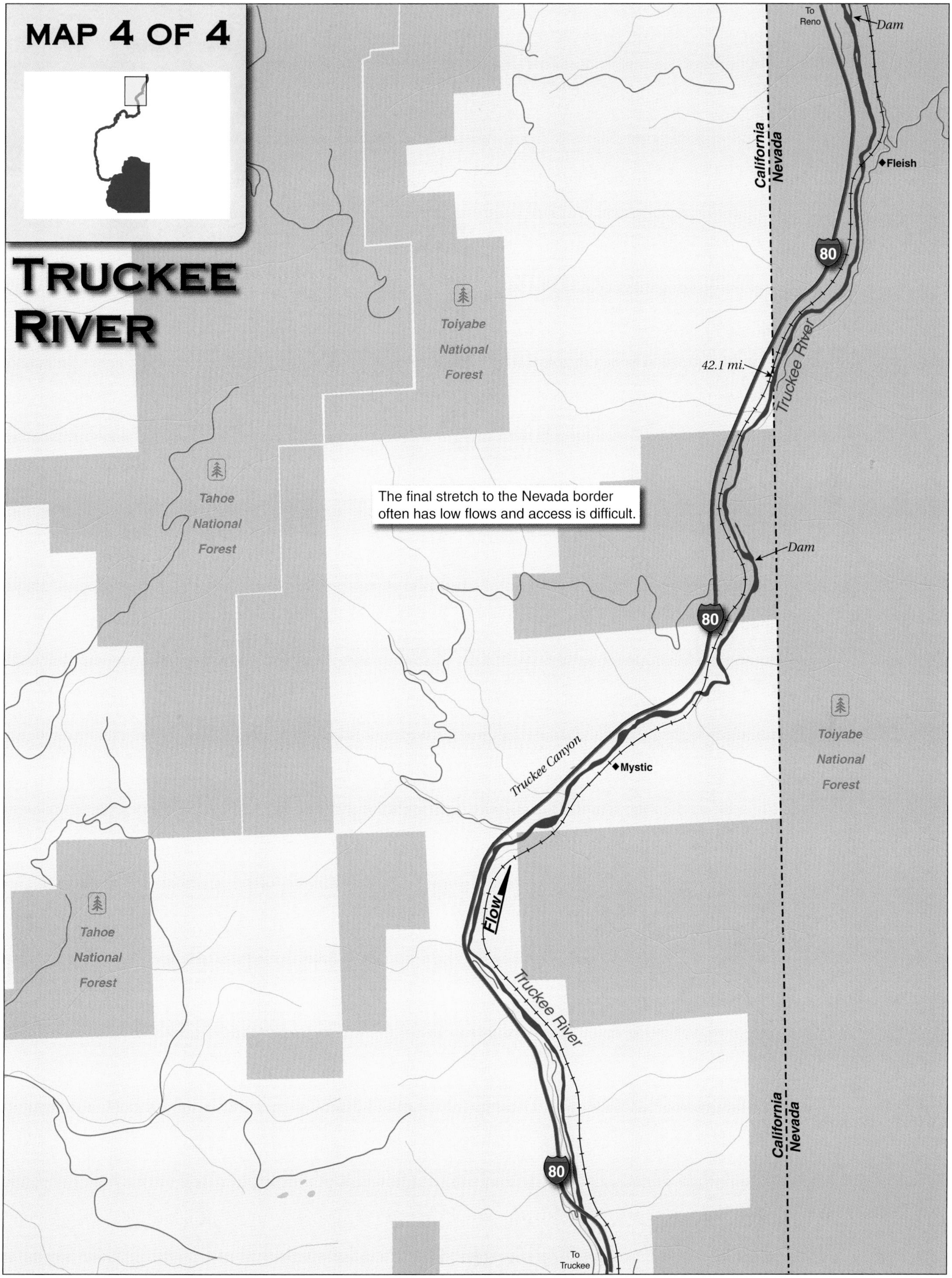
MAP 4 OF 4
TRUCKEE RIVER
To Reno
Dam
California
Nevada
Fleish
80
Toiyabe National Forest
42.1 mi.
Truckee River
Tahoe National Forest
The final stretch to the Nevada border often has low flows and access is difficult.
Dam
80
Truckee Canyon
Mystic
Toiyabe National Forest
Flow
Tahoe National Forest
Truckee River
California
Nevada
80
To Truckee

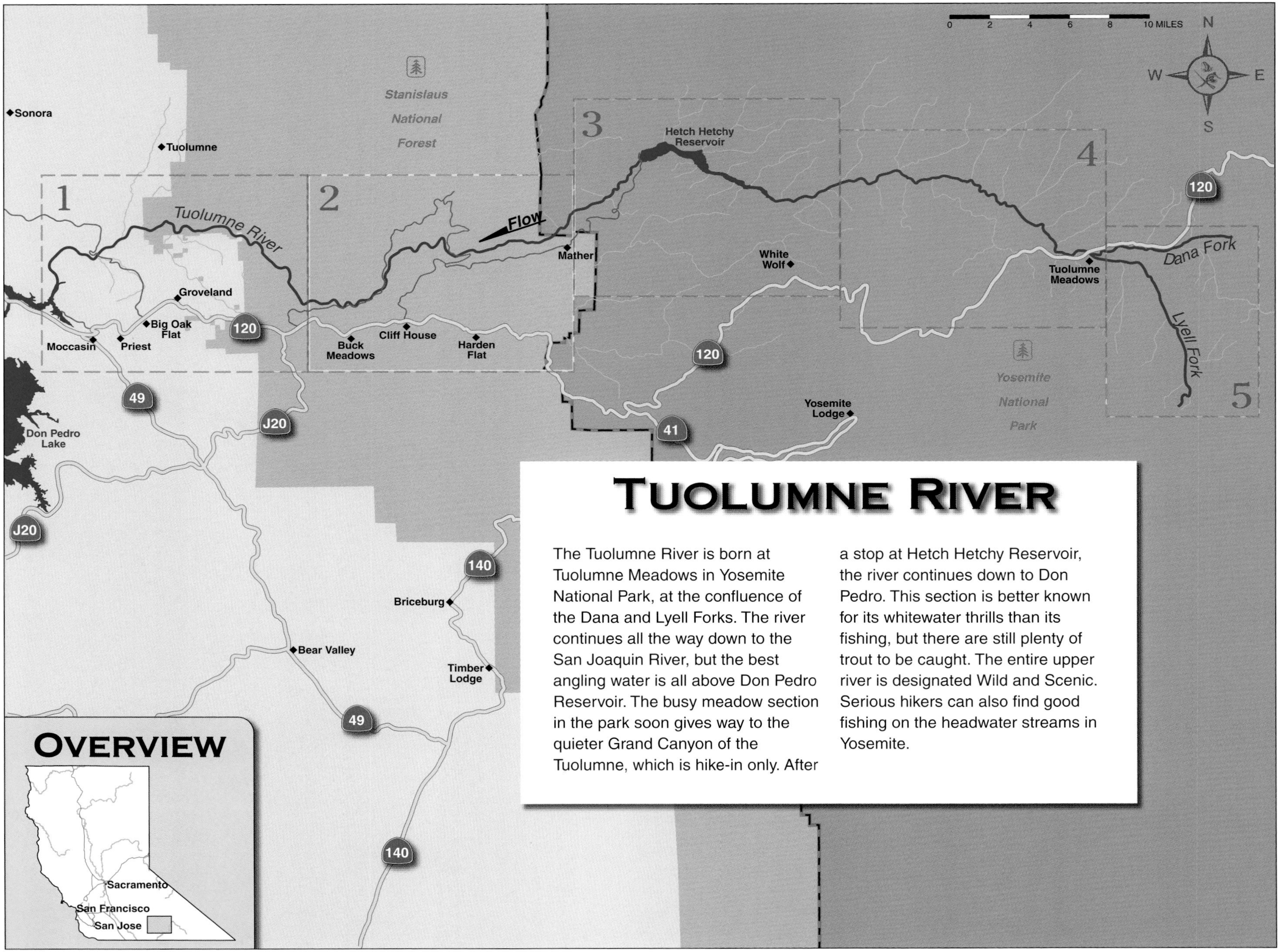

Tuolumne River

The Tuolumne River is born at Tuolumne Meadows in Yosemite National Park, at the confluence of the Dana and Lyell Forks. The river continues all the way down to the San Joaquin River, but the best angling water is all above Don Pedro Reservoir. The busy meadow section in the park soon gives way to the quieter Grand Canyon of the Tuolumne, which is hike-in only. After a stop at Hetch Hetchy Reservoir, the river continues down to Don Pedro. This section is better known for its whitewater thrills than its fishing, but there are still plenty of trout to be caught. The entire upper river is designated Wild and Scenic. Serious hikers can also find good fishing on the headwater streams in Yosemite.

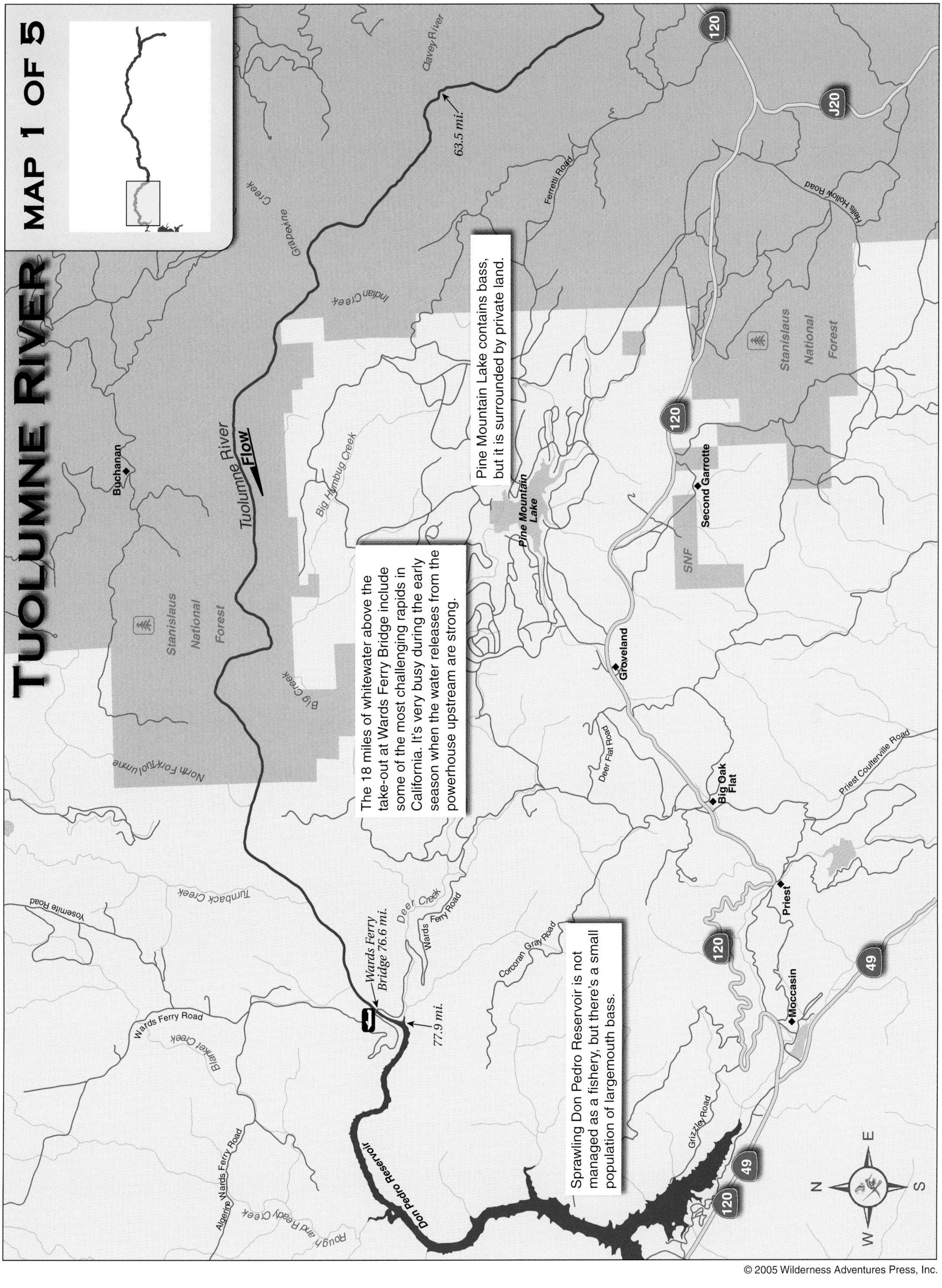
Tuolumne River
Map 1 of 5
The 18 miles of whitewater above the take-out at Wards Ferry Bridge include some of the most challenging rapids in California. It's very busy during the early season when the water releases from the powerhouse upstream are strong.
Pine Mountain Lake contains bass, but it is surrounded by private land.
Sprawling Don Pedro Reservoir is not managed as a fishery, but there's a small population of largemouth bass.
Stanislaus National Forest
Stanislaus National Forest
SNF
Tuolumne River
Flow
Buchanan
Clavey River
63.5 mi.
Grapevine Creek
Indian Creek
Big Humbug Creek
Big Creek
North Fork Tuolumne
Turnback Creek
Yosemite Road
Deer Creek
Wards Ferry Road
Wards Ferry Bridge 76.6 mi.
77.9 mi.
Wards Ferry Road
Blanket Creek
Algerine Wards Ferry Road
Rough and Ready Creek
Don Pedro Reservoir
Corcoran Gray Road
Grizzly Road
Ferretti Road
Hells Hollow Road
Pine Mountain Lake
Second Garrotte
Groveland
Deer Flat Road
Big Oak Flat
Priest Coulterville Road
Priest
Moccasin
120
J20
49
N
E
S
W

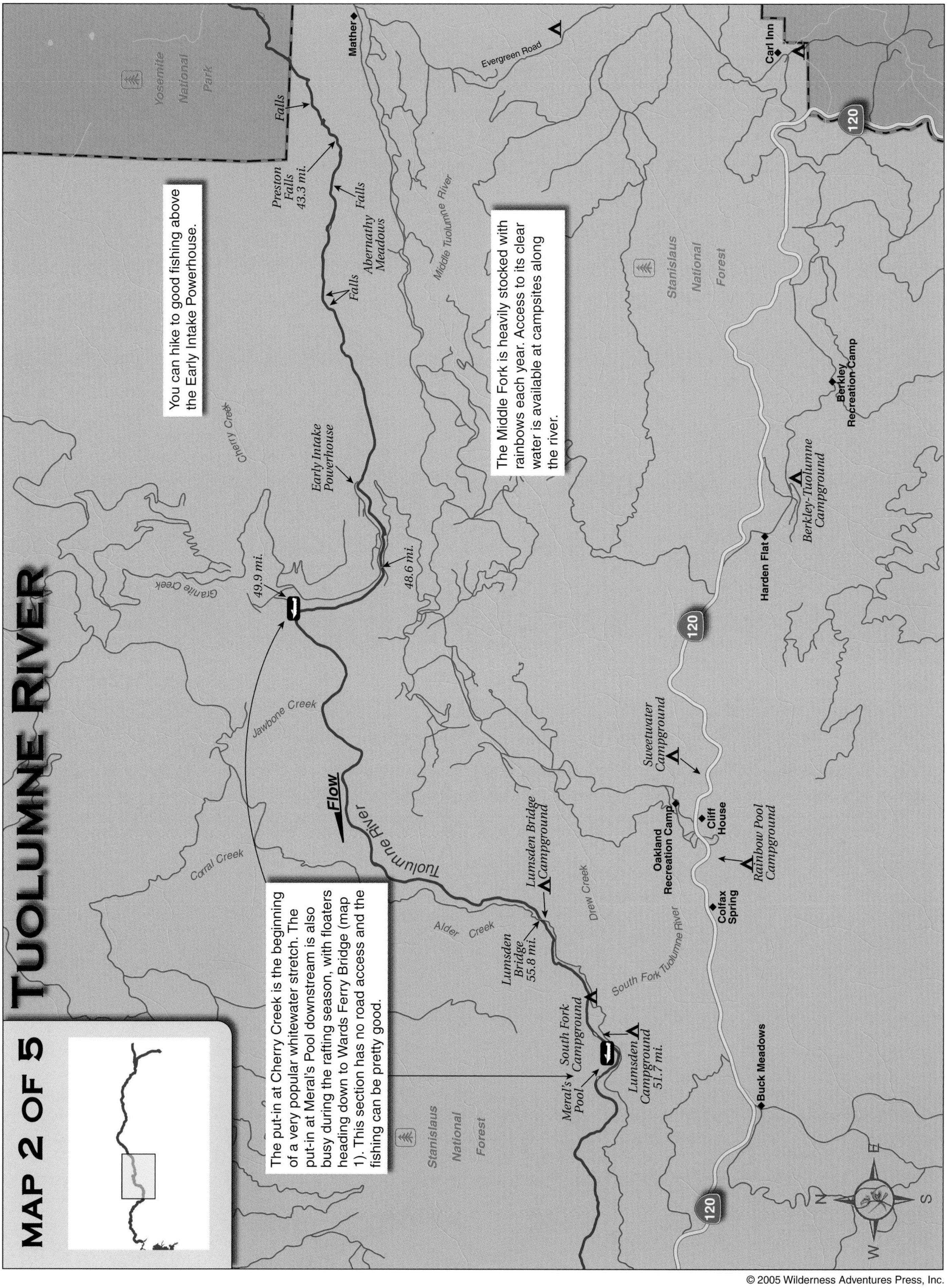
MAP 2 OF 5
TUOLUMNE RIVER
You can hike to good fishing above the Early Intake Powerhouse.
The Middle Fork is heavily stocked with rainbows each year. Access to its clear water is available at campsites along the river.
The put-in at Cherry Creek is the beginning of a very popular whitewater stretch. The put-in at Meral's Pool downstream is also busy during the rafting season, with floaters heading down to Wards Ferry Bridge (map 1). This section has no road access and the fishing can be pretty good.
Yosemite National Park
Stanislaus National Forest
Stanislaus National Forest
Mather
Evergreen Road
Carl Inn
120
Falls
Preston Falls 43.3 mi.
Falls
Abernathy Meadows
Falls
Middle Tuolumne River
Cherry Creek
Early Intake Powerhouse
Granite Creek
49.9 mi.
48.6 mi.
Berkley Recreation Camp
Berkley-Tuolumne Campground
Harden Flat
120
Jawbone Creek
Flow
Tuolumne River
Sweetwater Campground
Cliff House
Oakland Recreation Camp
Rainbow Pool Campground
Corral Creek
Lumsden Bridge Campground
Drew Creek
Colfax Spring
Alder Creek
Lumsden Bridge 55.8 mi.
South Fork Tuolumne River
South Fork Campground
Lumsden Campground 51.7 mi.
Meral's Pool
Buck Meadows
120
N
E
S
W

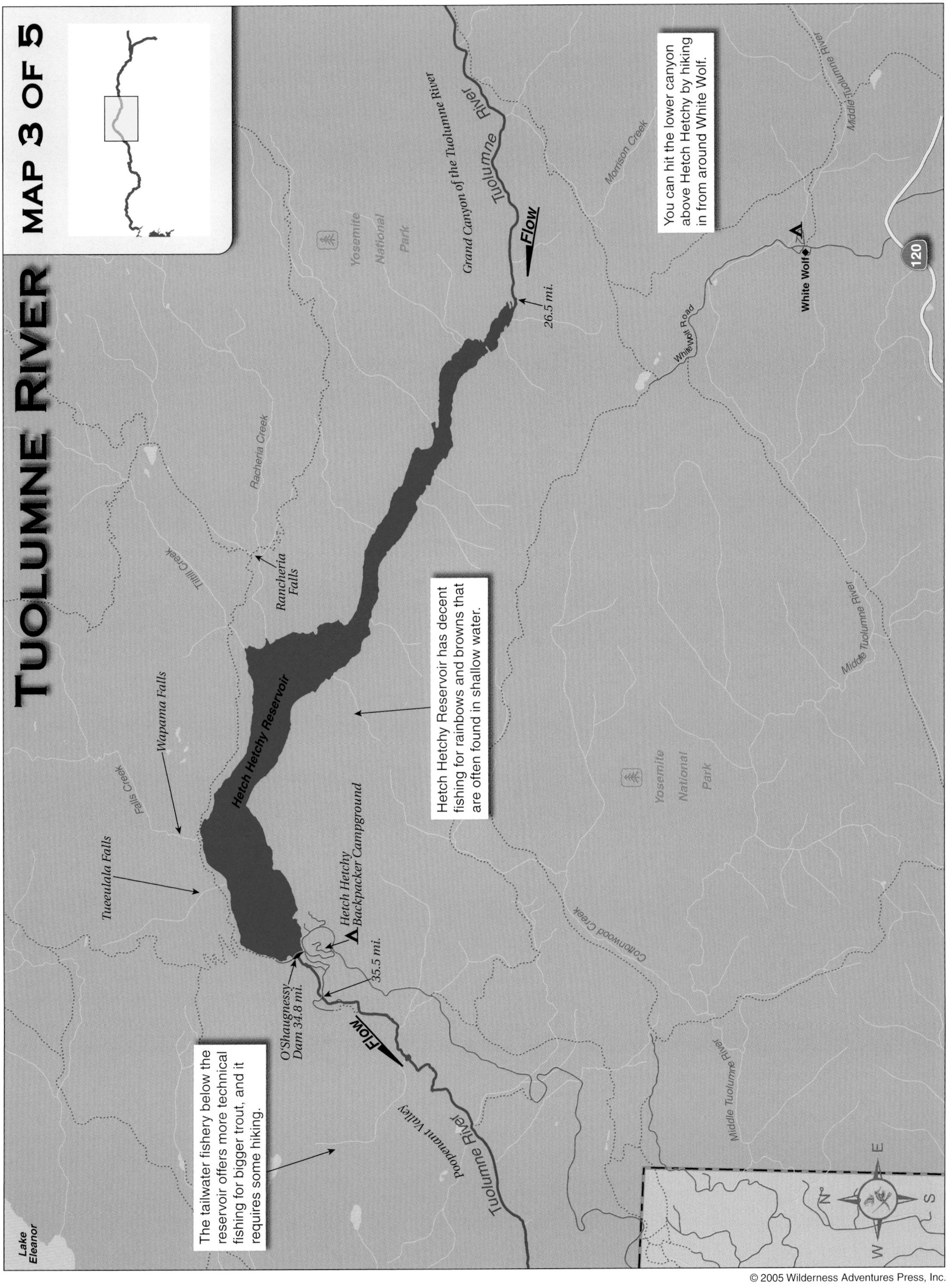
TUOLUMNE RIVER
MAP 3 OF 5
You can hit the lower canyon above Hetch Hetchy by hiking in from around White Wolf.
Hetch Hetchy Reservoir has decent fishing for rainbows and browns that are often found in shallow water.
The tailwater fishery below the reservoir offers more technical fishing for bigger trout, and it requires some hiking.
Grand Canyon of the Tuolumne River
Tuolumne River
Flow
26.5 mi.
Yosemite National Park
Morrison Creek
Middle Tuolumne River
White Wolf
White Wolf Road
120
Racheria Creek
Rancheria Falls
Tiltill Creek
Hetch Hetchy Reservoir
Wapama Falls
Falls Creek
Tueeulala Falls
Hetch Hetchy Backpacker Campground
35.5 mi.
O'Shaughnessy Dam 34.8 mi.
Cottonwood Creek
Poopenaut Valley
Lake Eleanor
N
S
E
W

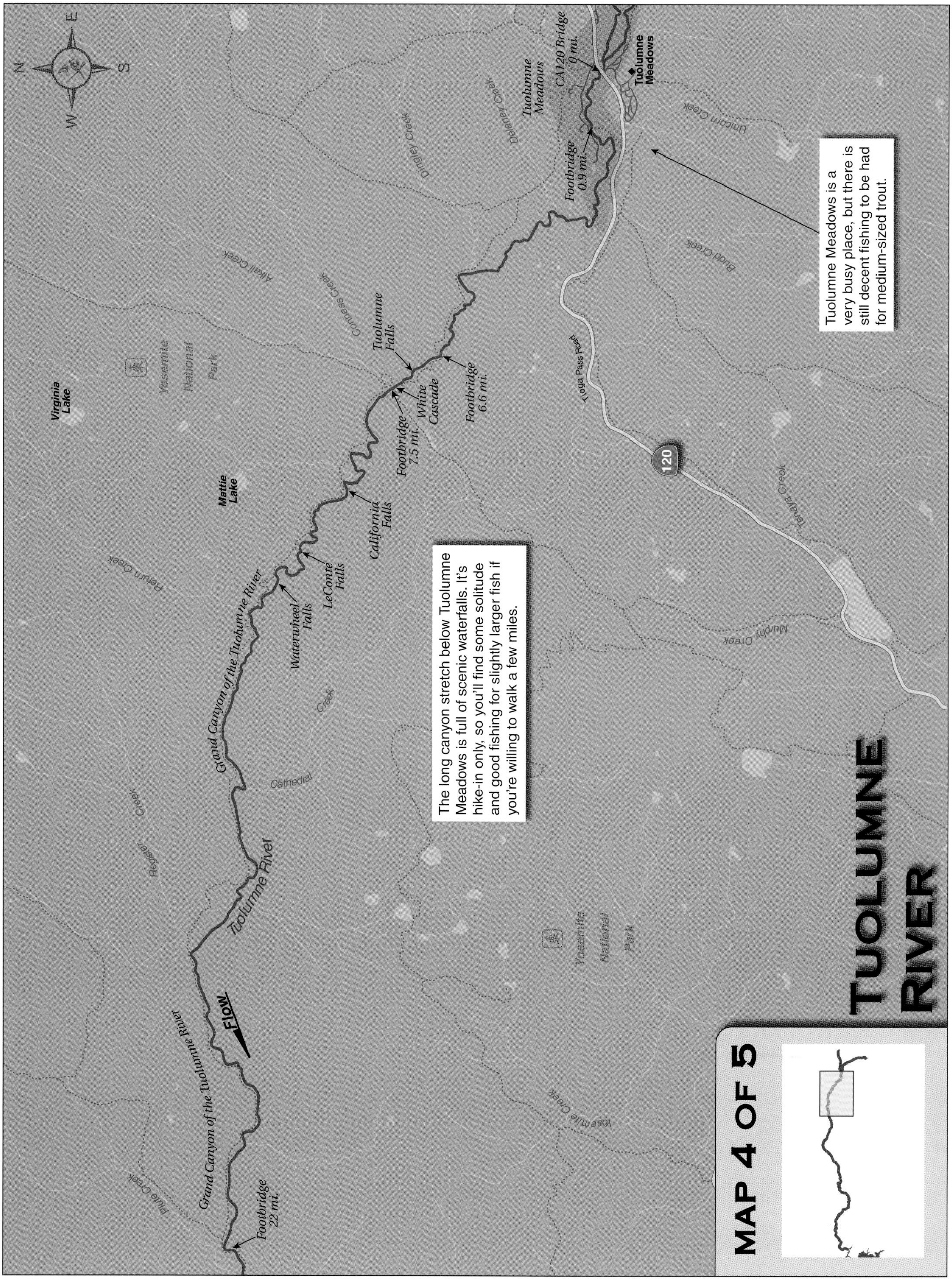

MAP 4 OF 5
TUOLUMNE RIVER
The long canyon stretch below Tuolumne Meadows is full of scenic waterfalls. It's hike-in only, so you'll find some solitude and good fishing for slightly larger fish if you're willing to walk a few miles.
Tuolumne Meadows is a very busy place, but there is still decent fishing to be had for medium-sized trout.
CA120 Bridge 0 mi.
Footbridge 0.9 mi.
Footbridge 6.6 mi.
Footbridge 7.5 mi.
Footbridge 22 mi.
Tuolumne Meadows
Tuolumne Falls
White Cascade
California Falls
LeConte Falls
Waterwheel Falls
Grand Canyon of the Tuolumne River
Tuolumne River
Flow
Yosemite National Park
Virginia Lake
Mattie Lake
Tioga Pass Road
120
Dingley Creek
Delaney Creek
Unicorn Creek
Budd Creek
Alkali Creek
Conness Creek
Return Creek
Register Creek
Cathedral Creek
Tenaya Creek
Murphy Creek
Yosemite Creek
Piute Creek
N
E
S
W

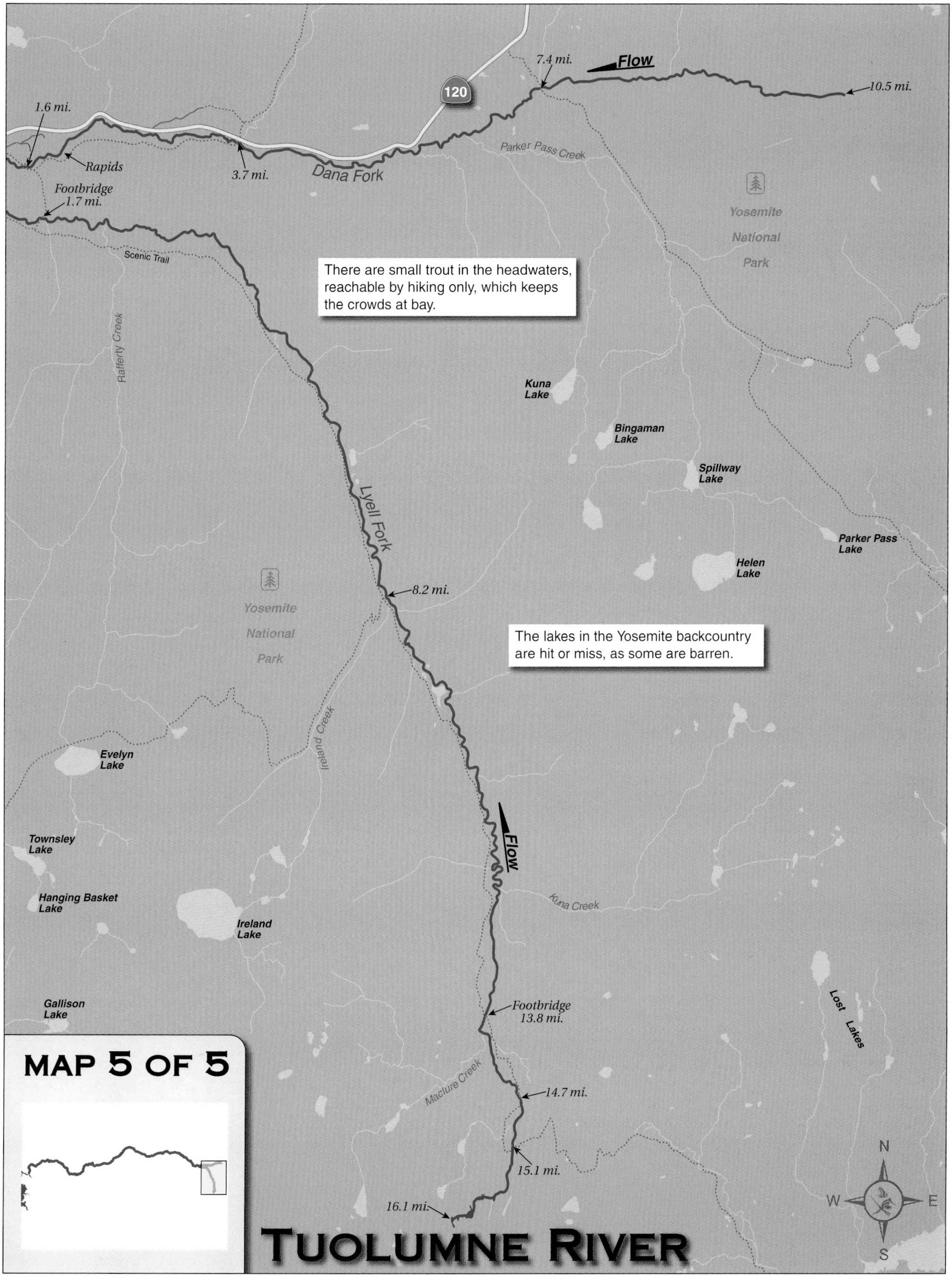

Flow
7.4 mi.
10.5 mi.
120
1.6 mi.
Rapids
3.7 mi.
Dana Fork
Parker Pass Creek
Footbridge
1.7 mi.
Yosemite
National
Park
Scenic Trail
There are small trout in the headwaters, reachable by hiking only, which keeps the crowds at bay.
Rafferty Creek
Kuna
Lake
Bingaman
Lake
Spillway
Lake
Lyell Fork
Parker Pass
Lake
Helen
Lake
8.2 mi.
Yosemite
National
Park
The lakes in the Yosemite backcountry are hit or miss, as some are barren.
Ireland Creek
Evelyn
Lake
Flow
Townsley
Lake
Kuna Creek
Hanging Basket
Lake
Ireland
Lake
Lost
Lakes
Gallison
Lake
Footbridge
13.8 mi.
MAP 5 OF 5
Maclure Creek
14.7 mi.
15.1 mi.
N
W
E
S
16.1 mi.
TUOLUMNE RIVER

East Walker River

The East Walker River rises on the east side of the Sierras in central California, where its headwaters are fed by Green, Dunderberg, and Virginia Creeks. The upper river down to the town of Bridgeport is mostly private, but the area just above Bridgeport Reservoir has good access and fishing. The best fishing occurs below the reservoir in the 8 miles from the dam to the Nevada border, where brown and rainbow trout average 12-17 inches, with some larger browns in the mix. The Bridgeport area is loaded with excellent fisheries, and it's a great location to set up a base from which to try a variety of streams and stillwaters.

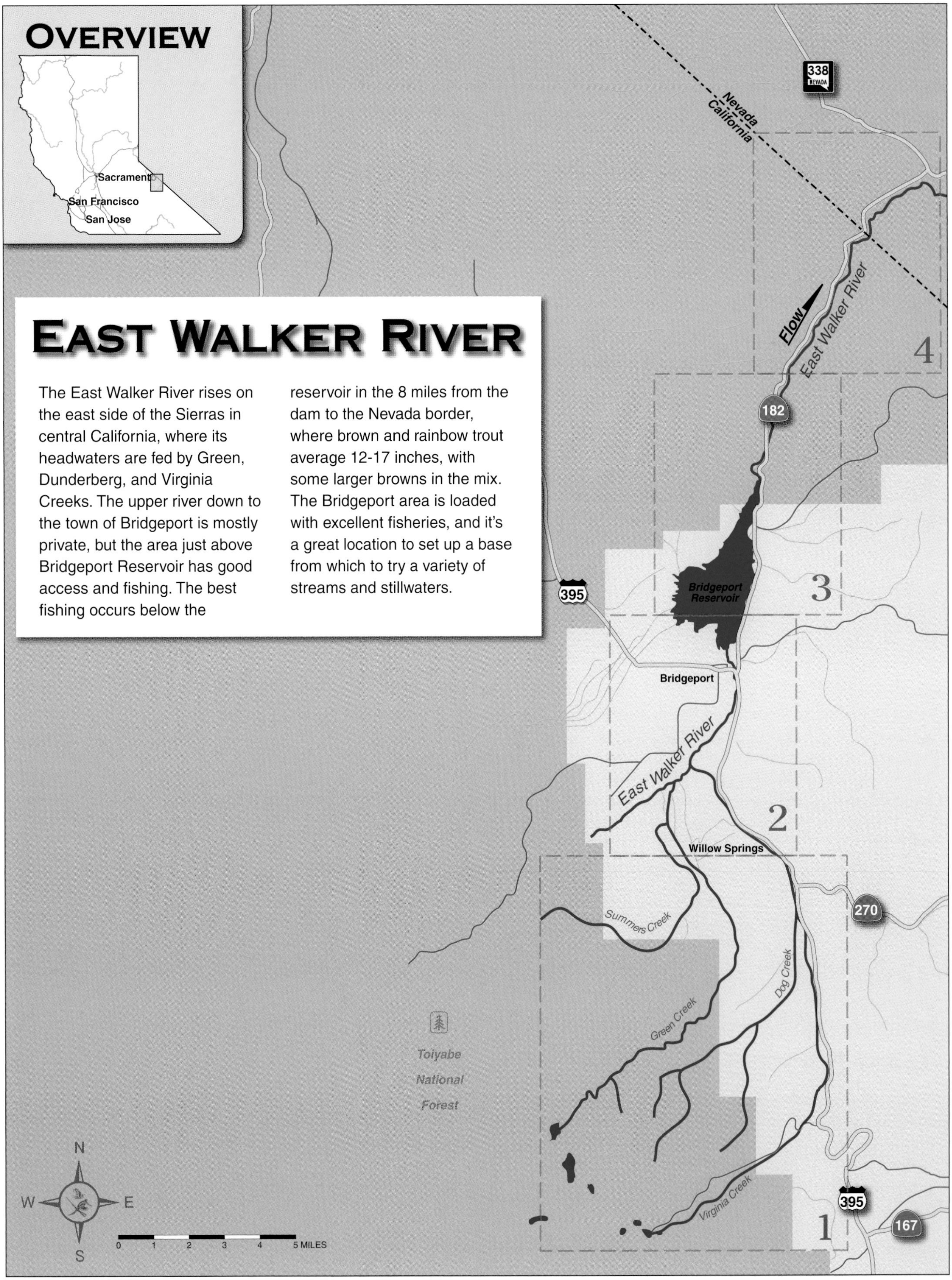

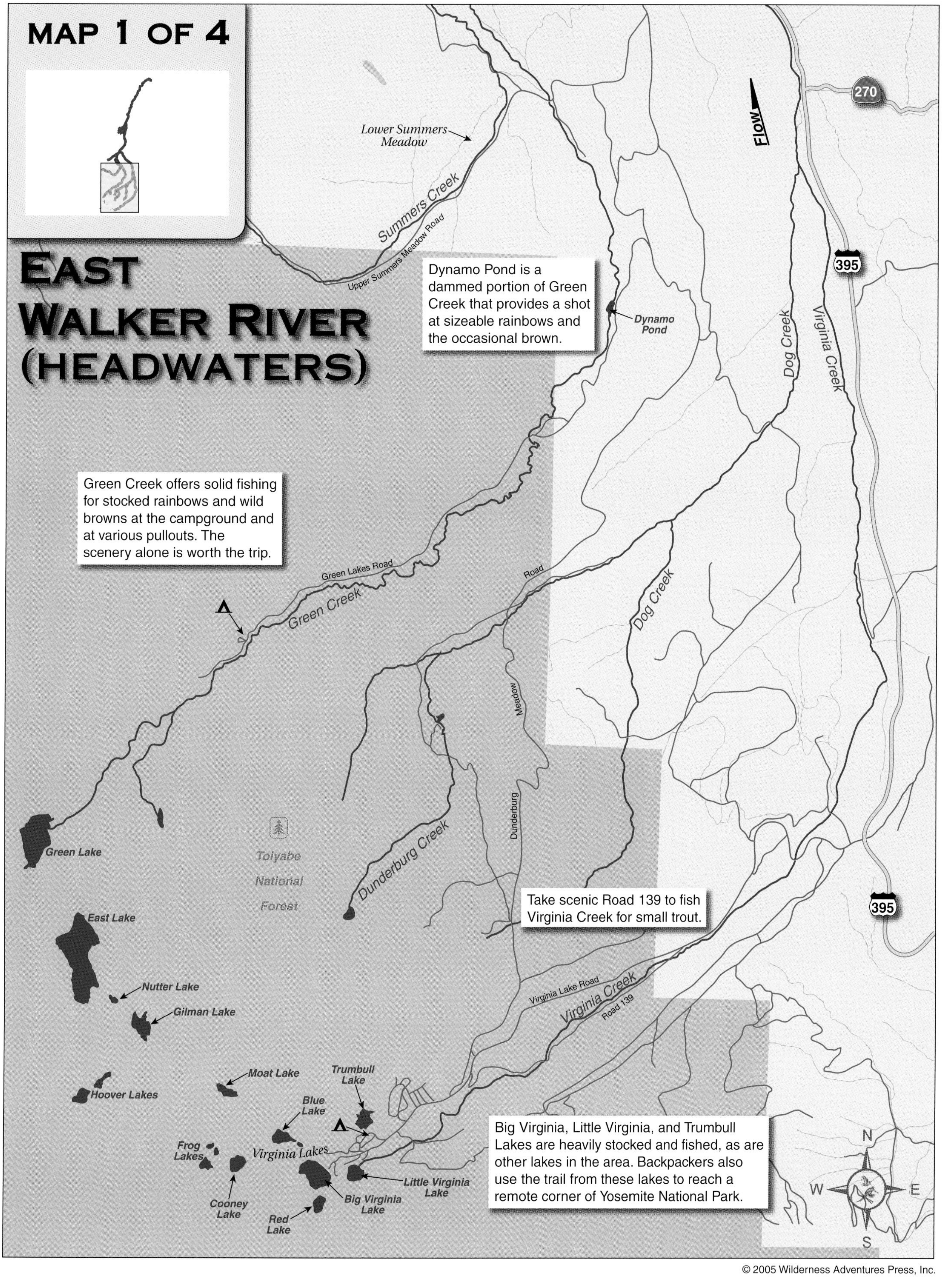
MAP 1 OF 4
EAST WALKER RIVER (HEADWATERS)
Lower Summers Meadow
Summers Creek
Upper Summers Meadow Road
Flow
270
395
Dynamo Pond is a dammed portion of Green Creek that provides a shot at sizeable rainbows and the occasional brown.
Dynamo Pond
Dog Creek
Virginia Creek
Green Creek offers solid fishing for stocked rainbows and wild browns at the campground and at various pullouts. The scenery alone is worth the trip.
Green Lakes Road
Green Creek
Road
Dog Creek
Meadow
Dunderburg
Dunderburg Creek
Green Lake
Toiyabe National Forest
Take scenic Road 139 to fish Virginia Creek for small trout.
East Lake
Virginia Lake Road
Virginia Creek
Road 139
Nutter Lake
Gilman Lake
Moat Lake
Trumbull Lake
Hoover Lakes
Blue Lake
Frog Lakes
Virginia Lakes
Little Virginia Lake
Big Virginia Lake
Cooney Lake
Red Lake
Big Virginia, Little Virginia, and Trumbull Lakes are heavily stocked and fished, as are other lakes in the area. Backpackers also use the trail from these lakes to reach a remote corner of Yosemite National Park.
N
W
E
S

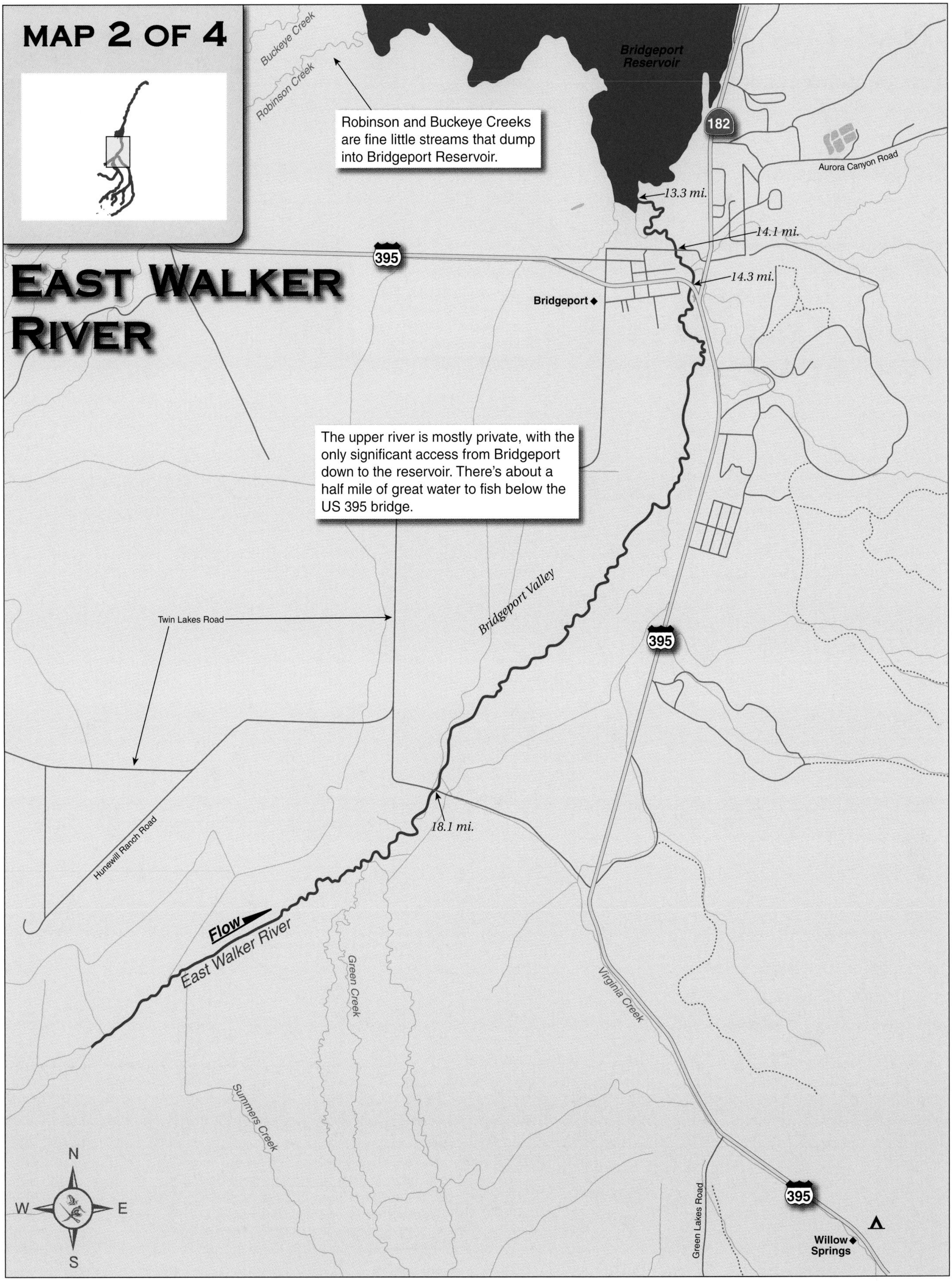
MAP 2 OF 4
EAST WALKER RIVER
Buckeye Creek
Robinson Creek
Bridgeport Reservoir
Robinson and Buckeye Creeks are fine little streams that dump into Bridgeport Reservoir.
182
Aurora Canyon Road
13.3 mi.
14.1 mi.
14.3 mi.
395
Bridgeport
The upper river is mostly private, with the only significant access from Bridgeport down to the reservoir. There's about a half mile of great water to fish below the US 395 bridge.
Bridgeport Valley
Twin Lakes Road
18.1 mi.
Hunewill Ranch Road
Flow
East Walker River
Green Creek
Virginia Creek
Summers Creek
Green Lakes Road
Willow Springs
N
E
S
W

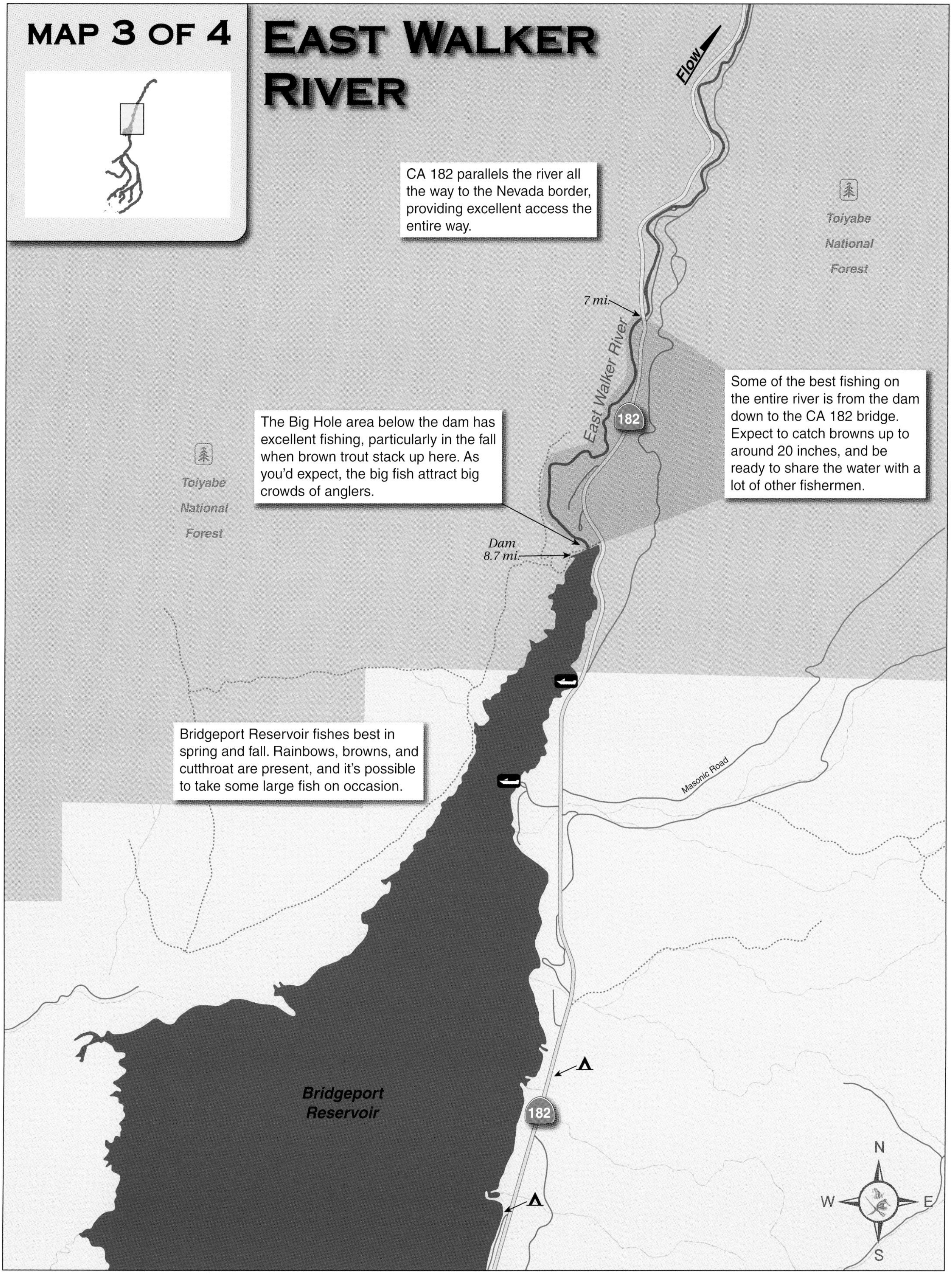
MAP 3 OF 4
EAST WALKER RIVER
Flow
CA 182 parallels the river all the way to the Nevada border, providing excellent access the entire way.
Toiyabe National Forest
7 mi.
East Walker River
182
Some of the best fishing on the entire river is from the dam down to the CA 182 bridge. Expect to catch browns up to around 20 inches, and be ready to share the water with a lot of other fishermen.
The Big Hole area below the dam has excellent fishing, particularly in the fall when brown trout stack up here. As you'd expect, the big fish attract big crowds of anglers.
Toiyabe National Forest
Dam 8.7 mi.
Bridgeport Reservoir fishes best in spring and fall. Rainbows, browns, and cutthroat are present, and it's possible to take some large fish on occasion.
Masonic Road
Bridgeport Reservoir
182
N
W
E
S

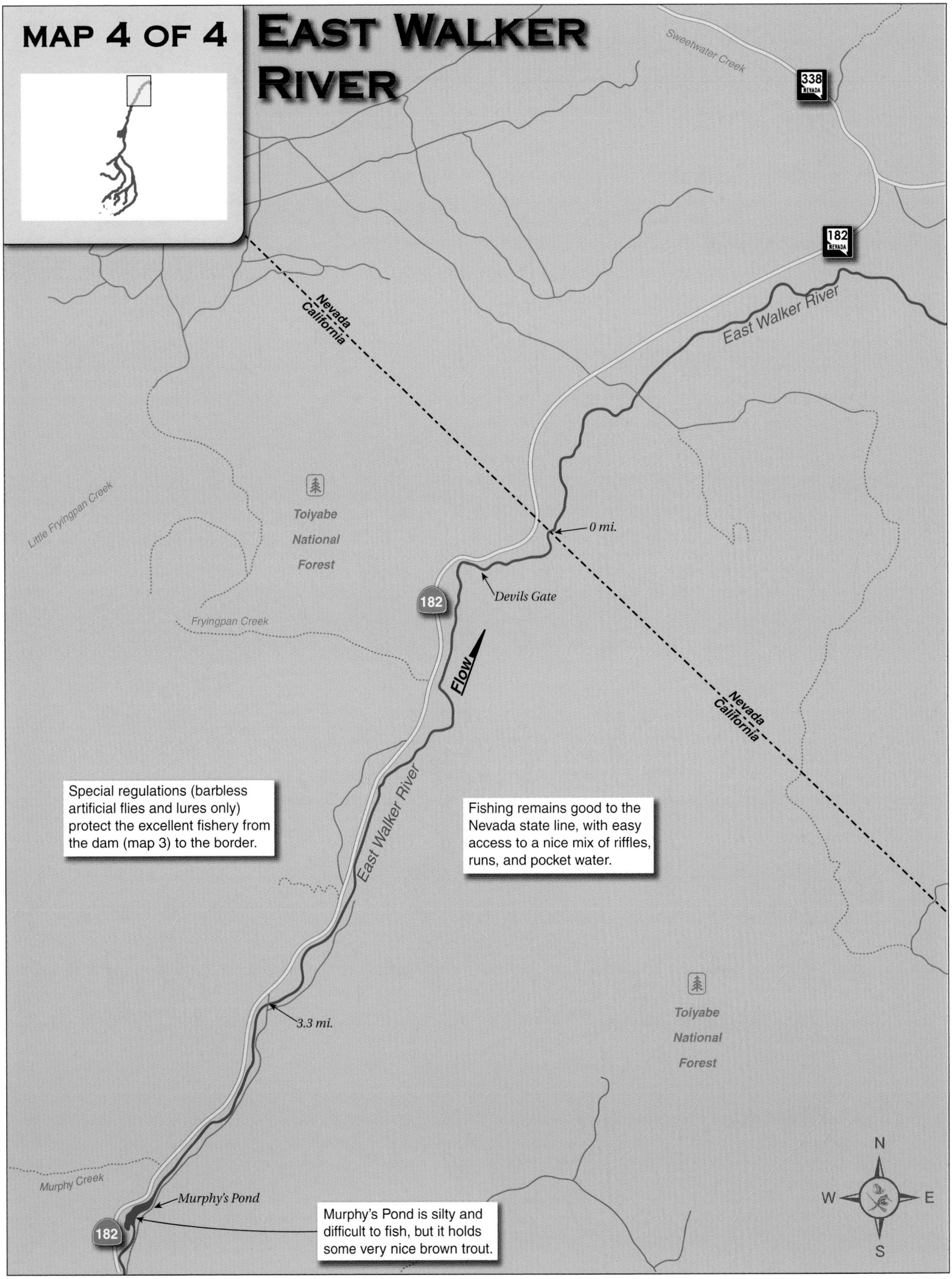
MAP 4 OF 4
EAST WALKER RIVER
Sweetwater Creek
338 NEVADA
182 NEVADA
East Walker River
Nevada
California
Toiyabe National Forest
Little Fryingpan Creek
0 mi.
Devils Gate
182
Fryingpan Creek
Flow
Nevada
California
Special regulations (barbless artificial flies and lures only) protect the excellent fishery from the dam (map 3) to the border.
East Walker River
Fishing remains good to the Nevada state line, with easy access to a nice mix of riffles, runs, and pocket water.
3.3 mi.
Toiyabe National Forest
N
W
E
S
Murphy Creek
Murphy's Pond
182
Murphy's Pond is silty and difficult to fish, but it holds some very nice brown trout.

West and Little Walker Rivers

The West Walker begins high in the Toiyabe National Forest west of Bridgeport, and then flows north to Topaz Lake on the Nevada border and beyond. It doesn't receive the same attention that the prime stretch of the nearby East Walker does, but it's a nice little fishery for medium-sized wild browns and stocked rainbows, along with a few brook and cutthroat trout. The East and West Walkers are entirely separate streams in California, with separate characters and fishing opportunities. The Little Walker River and the many creeks and lakes in the Bridgeport area offer anglers nearly every type of fishing imaginable.

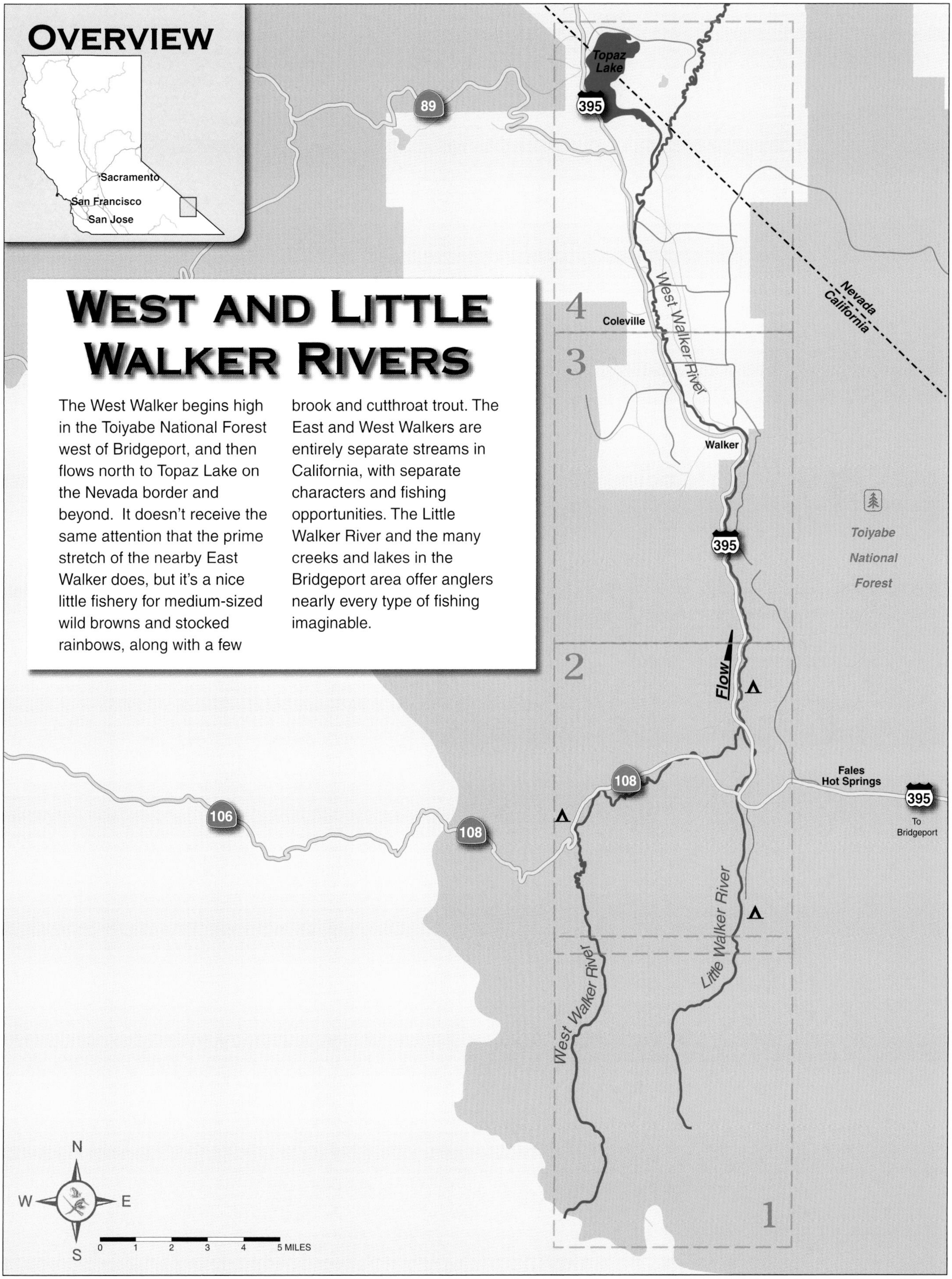

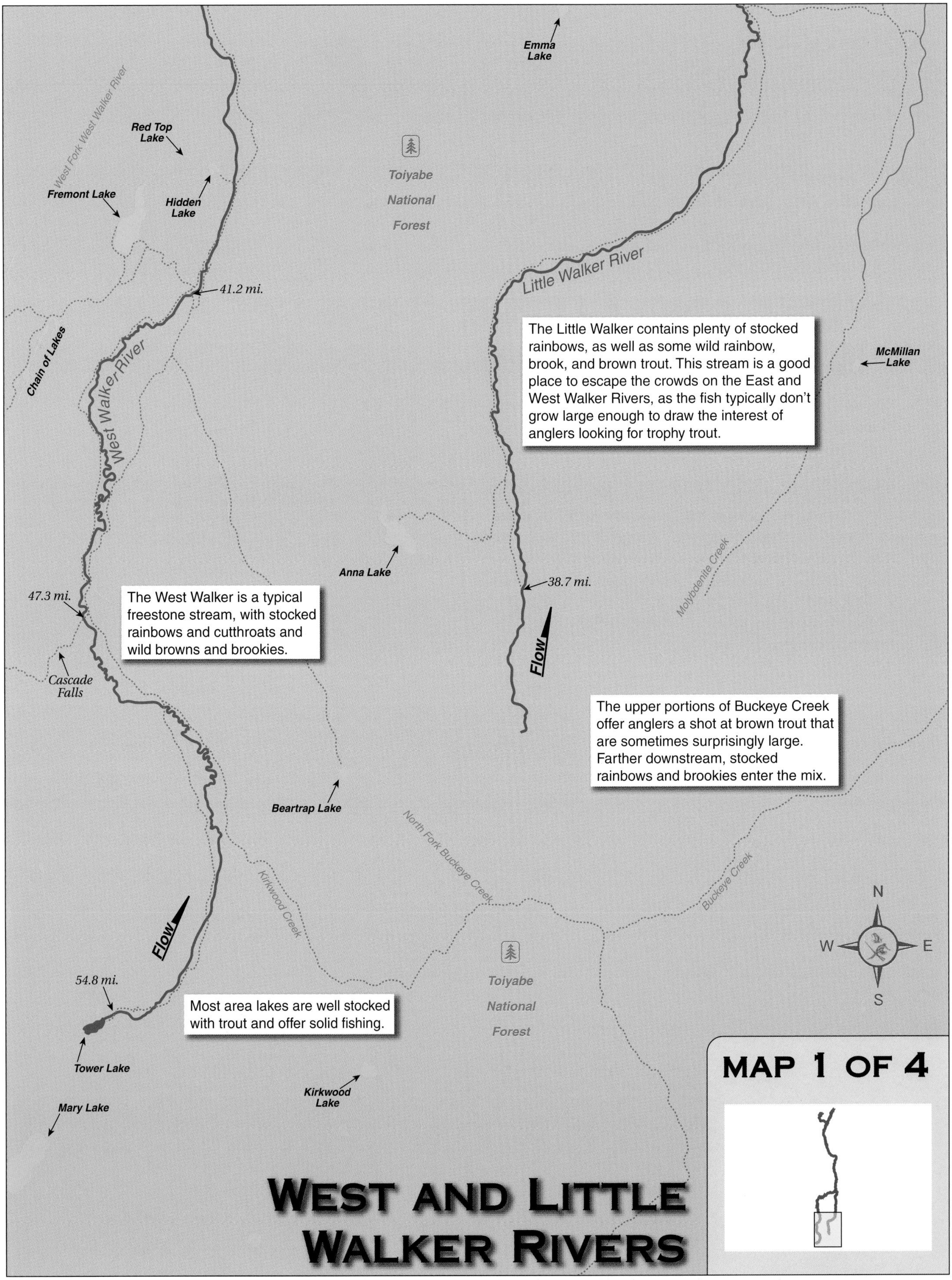
Emma Lake
West Fork West Walker River
Red Top Lake
Fremont Lake
Hidden Lake
Toiyabe National Forest
Little Walker River
41.2 mi.
Chain of Lakes
West Walker River
The Little Walker contains plenty of stocked rainbows, as well as some wild rainbow, brook, and brown trout. This stream is a good place to escape the crowds on the East and West Walker Rivers, as the fish typically don't grow large enough to draw the interest of anglers looking for trophy trout.
McMillan Lake
Molybdenite Creek
Anna Lake
38.7 mi.
47.3 mi.
The West Walker is a typical freestone stream, with stocked rainbows and cutthroats and wild browns and brookies.
Flow
Cascade Falls
The upper portions of Buckeye Creek offer anglers a shot at brown trout that are sometimes surprisingly large. Farther downstream, stocked rainbows and brookies enter the mix.
Beartrap Lake
North Fork Buckeye Creek
Kirkwood Creek
Buckeye Creek
N
W
E
S
Flow
Toiyabe National Forest
54.8 mi.
Most area lakes are well stocked with trout and offer solid fishing.
Tower Lake
MAP 1 OF 4
Kirkwood Lake
Mary Lake
WEST AND LITTLE WALKER RIVERS

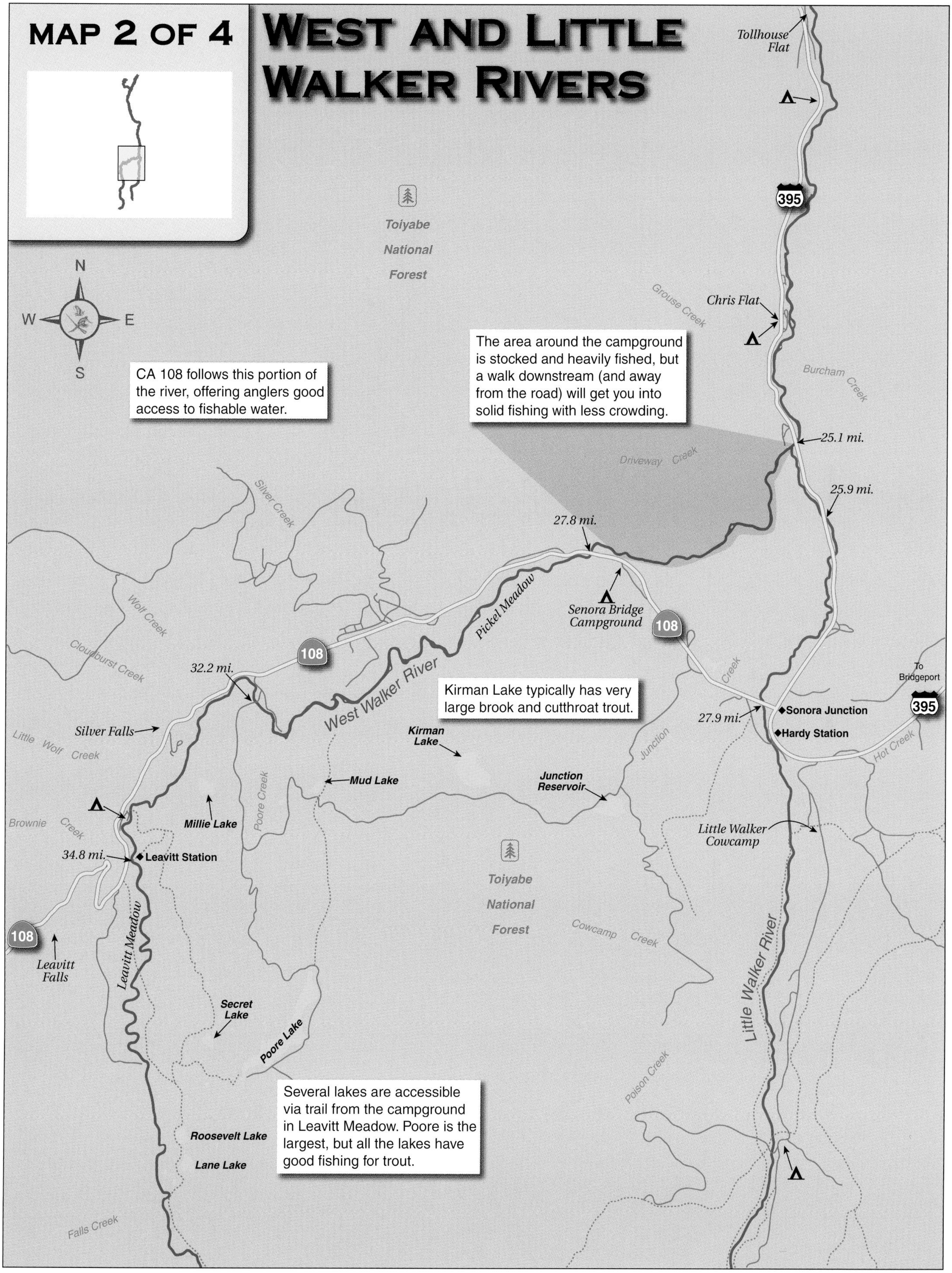
MAP 2 OF 4
WEST AND LITTLE WALKER RIVERS
N
W
E
S
Toiyabe National Forest
CA 108 follows this portion of the river, offering anglers good access to fishable water.
The area around the campground is stocked and heavily fished, but a walk downstream (and away from the road) will get you into solid fishing with less crowding.
Kirman Lake typically has very large brook and cutthroat trout.
Several lakes are accessible via trail from the campground in Leavitt Meadow. Poore is the largest, but all the lakes have good fishing for trout.
Tollhouse Flat
395
Chris Flat
Grouse Creek
Burcham Creek
25.1 mi.
Driveway Creek
25.9 mi.
27.8 mi.
Silver Creek
Wolf Creek
Cloudburst Creek
Pickel Meadow
Senora Bridge Campground
108
32.2 mi.
West Walker River
Creek
To Bridgeport
27.9 mi.
Sonora Junction
Hardy Station
Hot Creek
Silver Falls
Little Wolf Creek
Kirman Lake
Mud Lake
Junction Reservoir
Junction
Poore Creek
Millie Lake
Brownie Creek
Little Walker Cowcamp
34.8 mi.
Leavitt Station
Toiyabe National Forest
Cowcamp Creek
Leavitt Falls
Leavitt Meadow
Little Walker River
Secret Lake
Poore Lake
Poison Creek
Roosevelt Lake
Lane Lake
Falls Creek

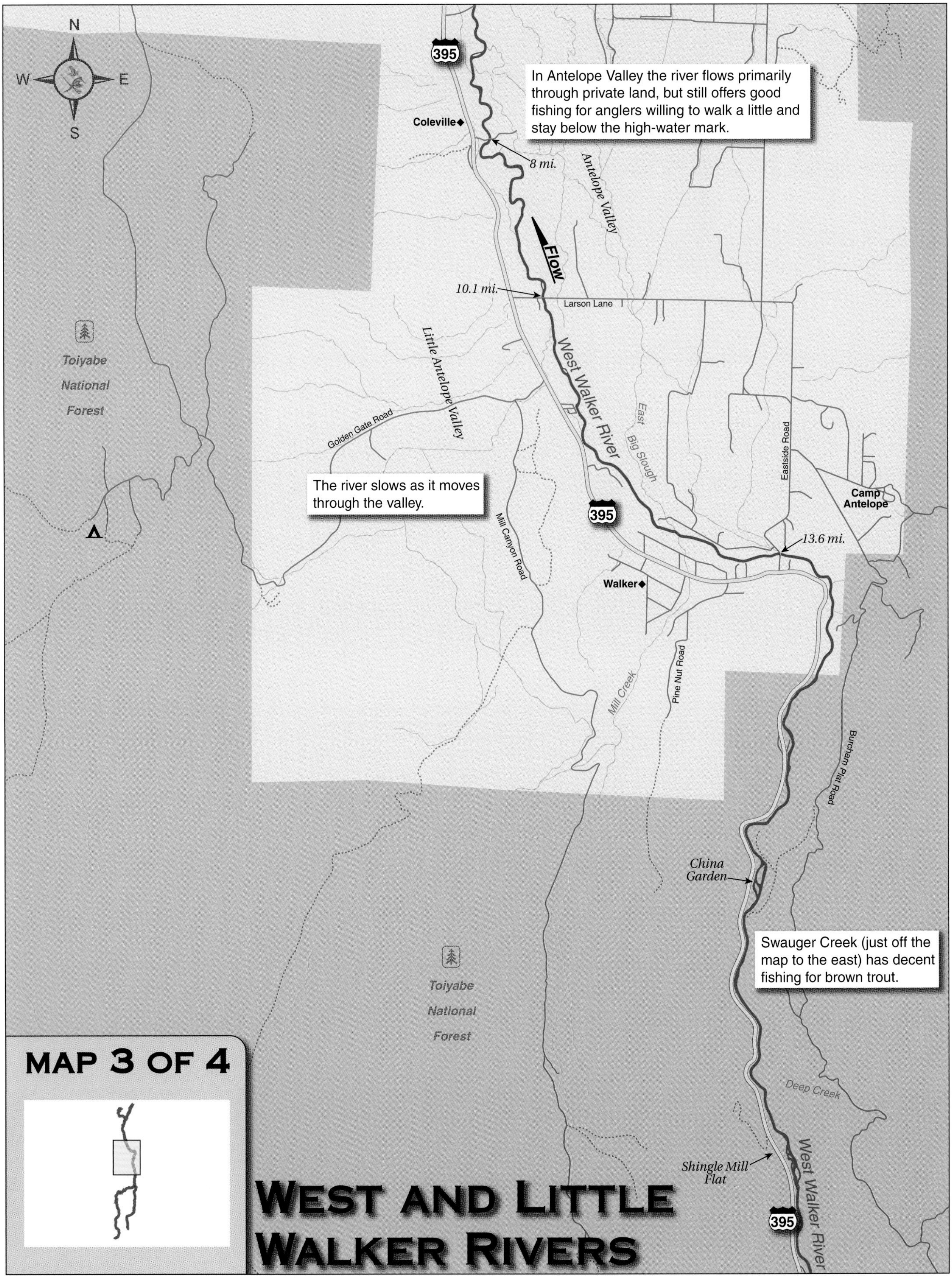
N
W
E
S
395
In Antelope Valley the river flows primarily through private land, but still offers good fishing for anglers willing to walk a little and stay below the high-water mark.
Coleville
8 mi.
Antelope Valley
Flow
10.1 mi.
Larson Lane
Toiyabe National Forest
Little Antelope Valley
West Walker River
East Big Slough
Golden Gate Road
Eastside Road
Camp Antelope
The river slows as it moves through the valley.
Mill Canyon Road
395
13.6 mi.
Walker
Mill Creek
Pine Nut Road
Burcham Flat Road
China Garden
Swauger Creek (just off the map to the east) has decent fishing for brown trout.
Toiyabe National Forest
MAP 3 OF 4
Deep Creek
Shingle Mill Flat
West Walker River
395
WEST AND LITTLE WALKER RIVERS

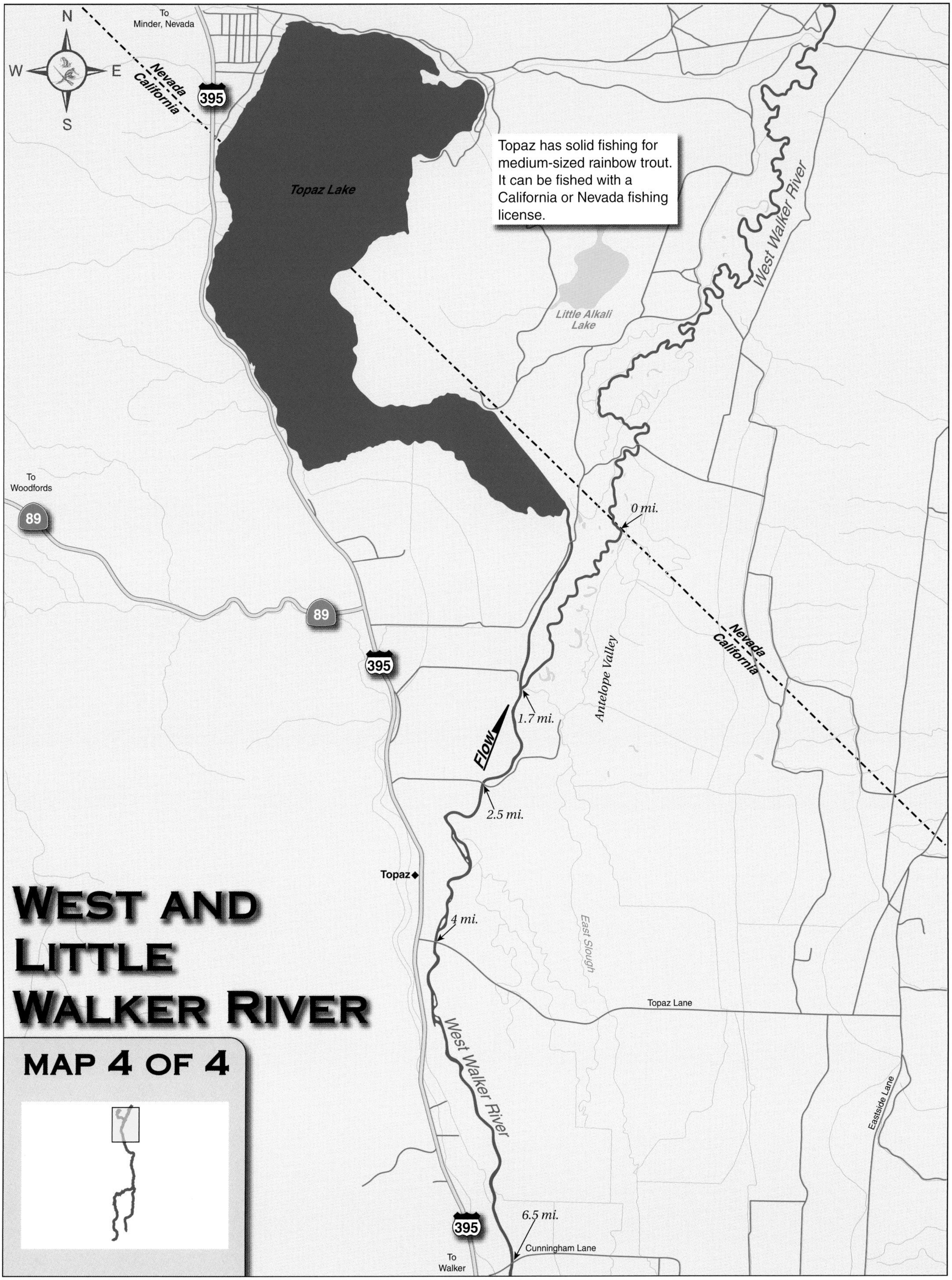
To
Minder, Nevada
N
W
E
S
Nevada
California
395
Topaz Lake
Topaz has solid fishing for medium-sized rainbow trout. It can be fished with a California or Nevada fishing license.
Little Alkali
Lake
West Walker River
To
Woodfords
89
0 mi.
89
395
Nevada
California
Antelope Valley
1.7 mi.
Flow
2.5 mi.
Topaz
WEST AND
LITTLE
WALKER RIVER
4 mi.
East Slough
Topaz Lane
MAP 4 OF 4
West Walker River
Eastside Lane
6.5 mi.
395
Cunningham Lane
To
Walker

Yuba River

The North Fork Yuba River rises in the Tahoe National Forest and runs through New Bullards Bar Reservoir to pick up the Middle and South Forks on the way to Englebright Lake. This 40-mile stretch has great access to rainbows and browns that average just under 12 inches, with some larger fish present. From Englebright to the confluence with the Feather River near Marysville, the 15-mile tailwater stretch of the Lower Yuba hosts rainbows averaging about 12 to 14 inches. Some steelhead enter the river via the Feather, but many of the good-sized rainbows are resident fish. Shad also make a run here around late May. Water flows from Englebright usually dictate how good the fishing will be, so check levels locally before making the trip to fish here. The coldest water is below the dam, and the water warms somewhat as it gets closer to Marysville.

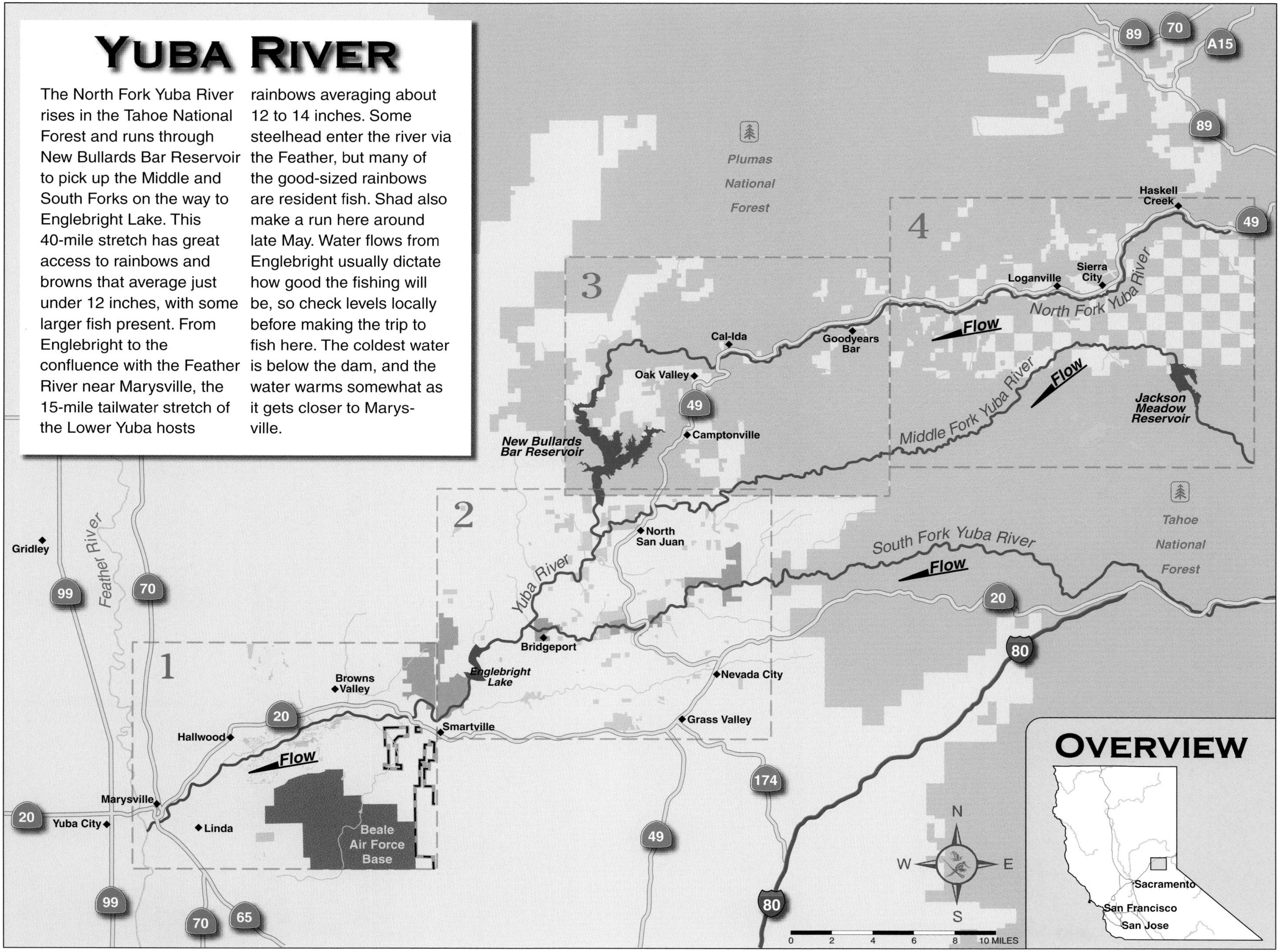

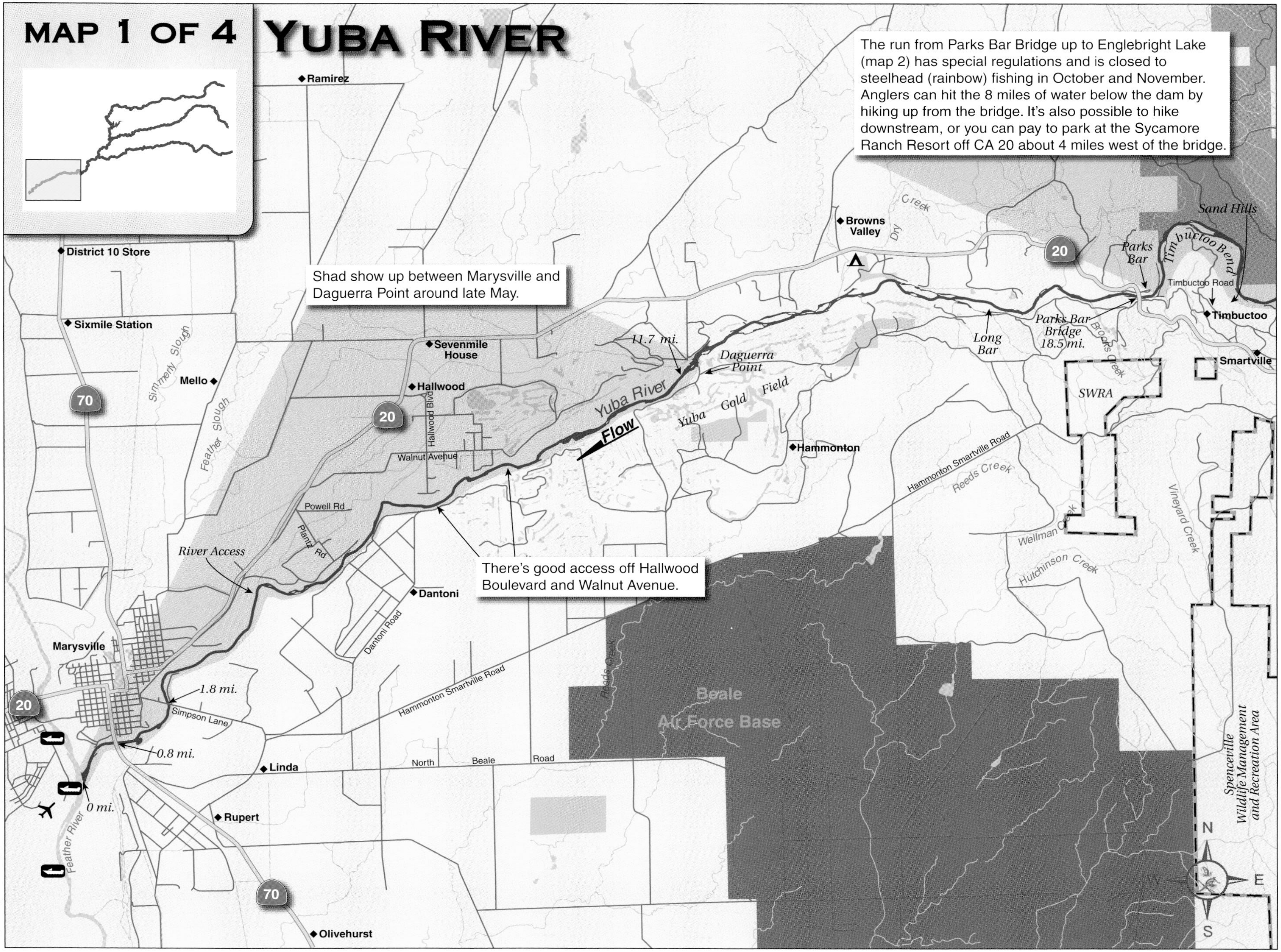
MAP 1 OF 4
YUBA RIVER
The run from Parks Bar Bridge up to Englebright Lake (map 2) has special regulations and is closed to steelhead (rainbow) fishing in October and November. Anglers can hit the 8 miles of water below the dam by hiking up from the bridge. It's also possible to hike downstream, or you can pay to park at the Sycamore Ranch Resort off CA 20 about 4 miles west of the bridge.
Shad show up between Marysville and Daguerra Point around late May.
There's good access off Hallwood Boulevard and Walnut Avenue.
Ramirez
District 10 Store
Sixmile Station
Mello
Simmerly Slough
Feather Slough
Sevenmile House
Hallwood
Hallwood Blvd
Walnut Avenue
Powell Rd
Plantz Rd
River Access
Marysville
Dantoni
Dantoni Road
Simpson Lane
1.8 mi.
0.8 mi.
0 mi.
Feather River
Linda
Rupert
Olivehurst
North Beale Road
Hammonton Smartville Road
Yuba River
Flow
11.7 mi.
Daguerra Point
Yuba Gold Field
Hammonton
Browns Valley
Dry Creek
Long Bar
Parks Bar Bridge 18.5 mi.
Parks Bar
Timbuctoo Bend
Sand Hills
Timbuctoo Road
Timbuctoo
Smartville
Brooks Creek
SWRA
Reeds Creek
Wellman Creek
Hutchinson Creek
Vineyard Creek
Beale Air Force Base
Spenceville Wildlife Management and Recreation Area
N
E
W
S
20
70

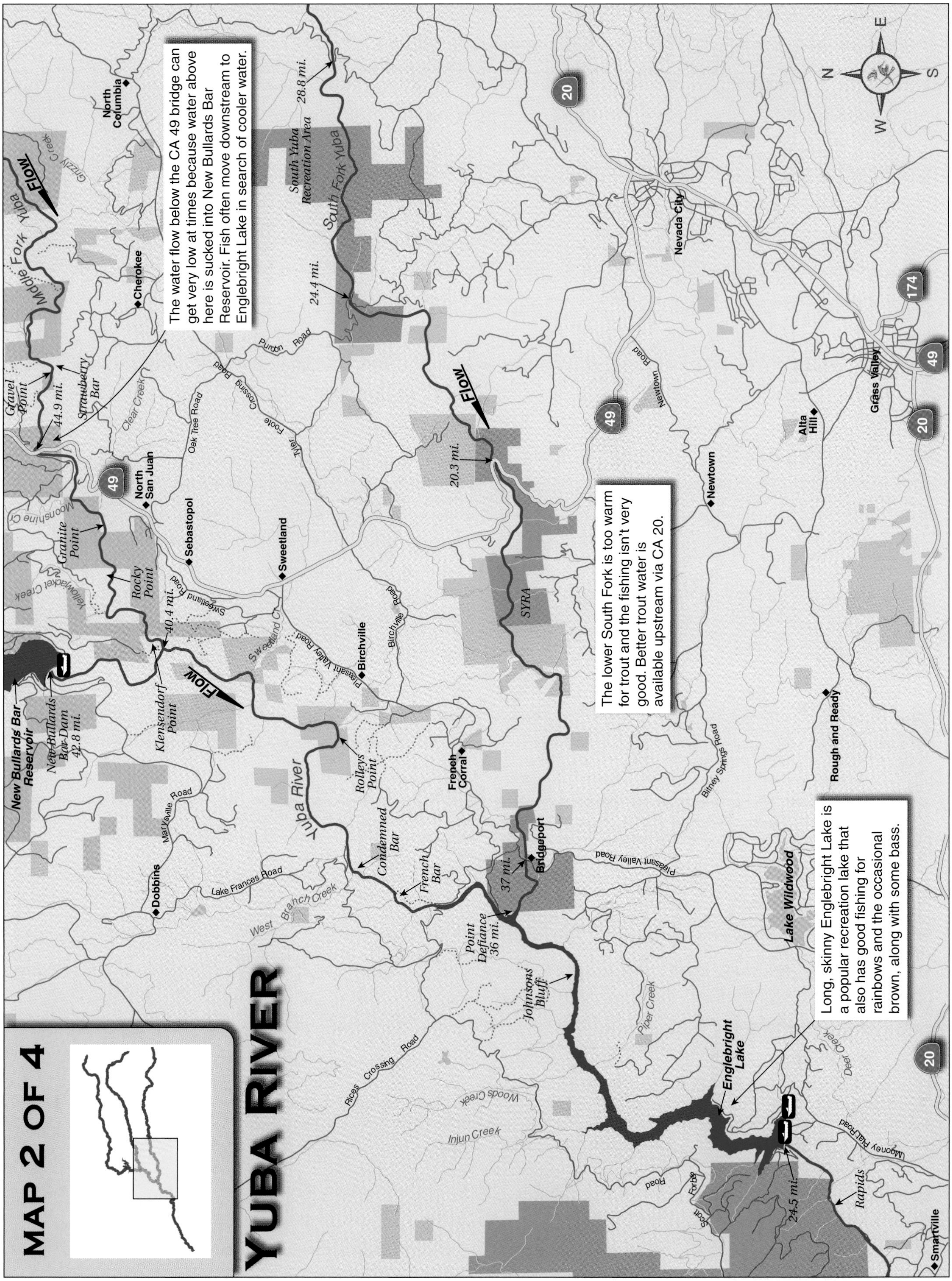
MAP 2 OF 4
YUBA RIVER
The water flow below the CA 49 bridge can get very low at times because water above here is sucked into New Bullards Bar Reservoir. Fish often move downstream to Englebright Lake in search of cooler water.
The lower South Fork is too warm for trout and the fishing isn't very good. Better trout water is available upstream via CA 20.
Long, skinny Englebright Lake is a popular recreation lake that also has good fishing for rainbows and the occasional brown, along with some bass.
New Bullards Bar Reservoir
New Bullards Bar Dam 42.8 mi.
Klensendorf Point
Flow
Rocky Point
40.4 mi.
Granite Point
Gravel Point
Strawberry Bar
44.9 mi.
Middle Fork Yuba
Cherokee
North Columbia
North San Juan
Sebastopol
Sweetland
Birchville
French Corral
Bridgeport
Rolleys Point
Condemned Bar
French Bar
37 mi.
Point Defiance 36 mi.
Johnsons Bluff
Yuba River
South Fork Yuba
South Yuba Recreation Area
28.8 mi.
24.4 mi.
20.3 mi.
SYRA
Nevada City
Grass Valley
Alta Hill
Newtown
Rough and Ready
Lake Wildwood
Englebright Lake
24.5 mi.
Rapids
Smartville
Dobbins
Marysville Road
Lake Frances Road
West Branch Creek
Rices Crossing Road
Woods Creek
Injun Creek
Piper Creek
Deer Creek
Mooney Flat Road
Scott Forbs Road
Pleasant Valley Road
Bitney Springs Road
Newtown Road
Tyler Foote Crossing Road
Purdon Road
Oak Tree Road
Clear Creek
Moonshine Cr
Yellowjacket Creek
Sweetland Road
Sweetland Cr
Birchville Road
Grizzly Creek
20
49
174
N
E
S
W

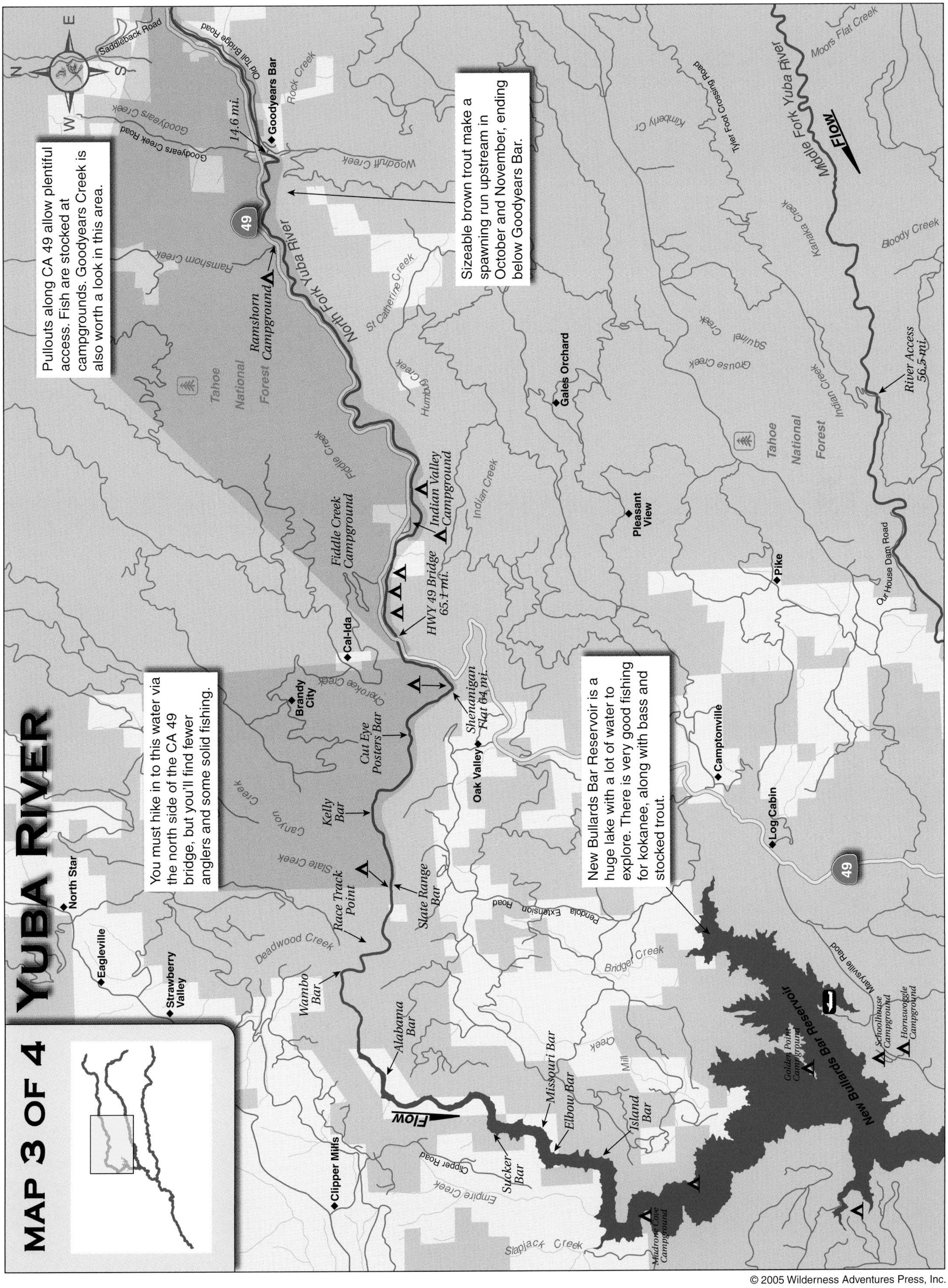
MAP 3 OF 4
YUBA RIVER
Pullouts along CA 49 allow plentiful access. Fish are stocked at campgrounds. Goodyears Creek is also worth a look in this area.
Sizeable brown trout make a spawning run upstream in October and November, ending below Goodyears Bar.
You must hike in to this water via the north side of the CA 49 bridge, but you'll find fewer anglers and some solid fishing.
New Bullards Bar Reservoir is a huge lake with a lot of water to explore. There is very good fishing for kokanee, along with bass and stocked trout.
North Fork Yuba River
Middle Fork Yuba River
Flow
New Bullards Bar Reservoir
Tahoe National Forest
14.6 mi.
Goodyears Bar
Ramshorn Campground
Fiddle Creek Campground
Indian Valley Campground
HWY 49 Bridge 65.1 mi.
Shenanigan Flat 64 mi.
Cut Eye Posters Bar
Kelly Bar
Race Track Point
Slate Range Bar
Wambo Bar
Alabama Bar
Missouri Bar
Elbow Bar
Island Bar
Sucker Bar
River Access 56.5 mi.
Golden Point Campground
Schoolhouse Campground
Hornswoggle Campground
Madrone Cove Campground
North Star
Eagleville
Strawberry Valley
Clipper Mills
Brandy City
Cal-Ida
Oak Valley
Camptonville
Log Cabin
Pike
Pleasant View
Gales Orchard
Saddleback Road
Old Toll Bridge Road
Goodyears Creek Road
Goodyears Creek
Rock Creek
Woodruff Creek
Ramshorn Creek
St Catherine Creek
Humbug Creek
Fiddle Creek
Indian Creek
Cherokee Creek
Canyon Creek
Slate Creek
Deadwood Creek
Pendola Extension Road
Bridger Creek
Marysville Road
Mill Creek
Clipper Road
Empire Creek
Slapjack Creek
Kimberly Cr
Tyler Foot Crossing Road
Moors Flat Creek
Kanaka Creek
Bloody Creek
Squirrel Creek
Grouse Creek
Indian Creek
Our House Dam Road
49
N
E
S
W

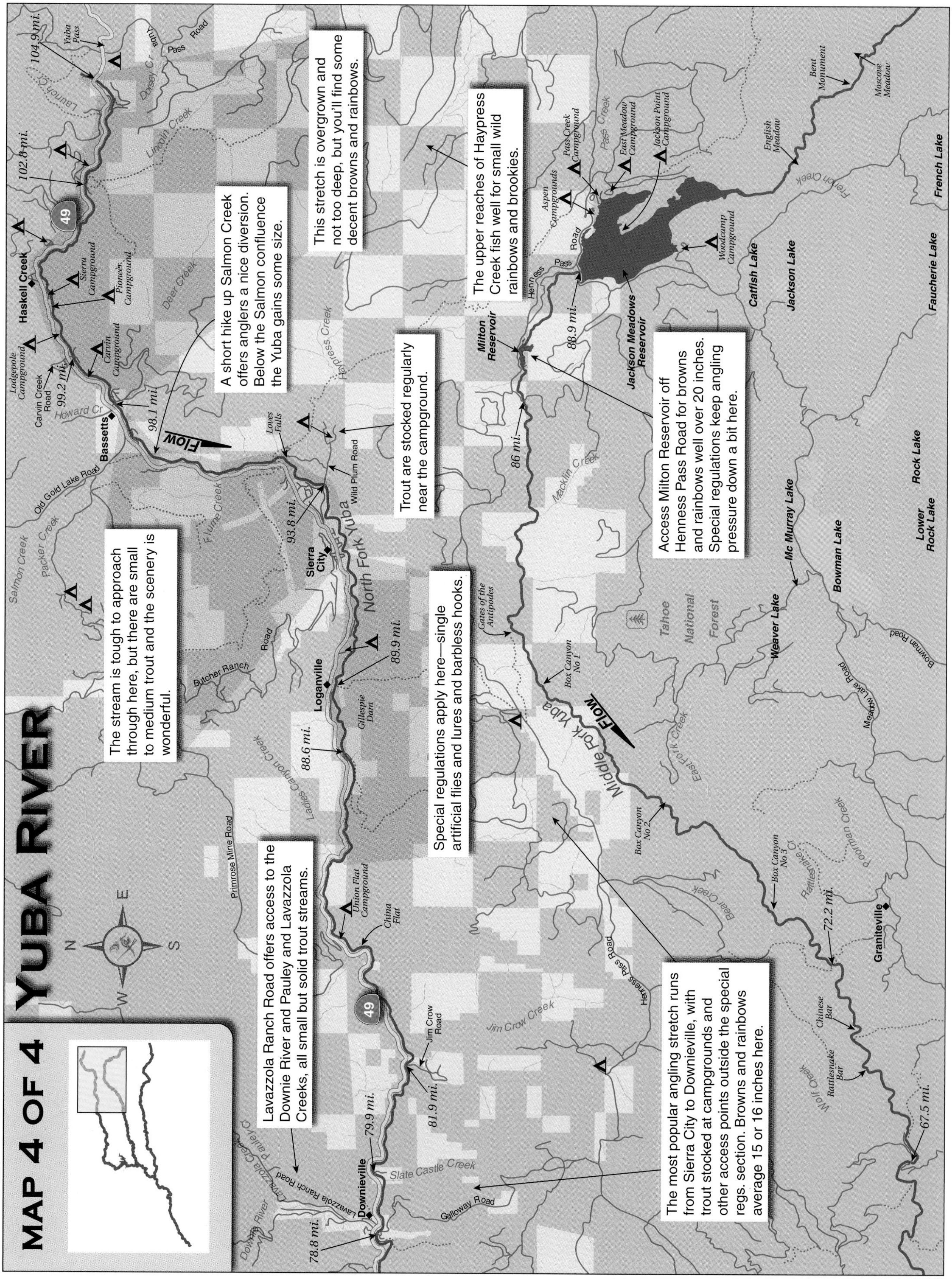
MAP 4 OF 4
YUBA RIVER
The stream is tough to approach through here, but there are small to medium trout and the scenery is wonderful.
A short hike up Salmon Creek offers anglers a nice diversion. Below the Salmon confluence the Yuba gains some size.
This stretch is overgrown and not too deep, but you'll find some decent browns and rainbows.
The upper reaches of Haypress Creek fish well for small wild rainbows and brookies.
Trout are stocked regularly near the campground.
Special regulations apply here—single artificial flies and lures and barbless hooks.
Access Milton Reservoir off Henness Pass Road for browns and rainbows well over 20 inches. Special regulations keep angling pressure down a bit here.
Lavazzola Ranch Road offers access to the Downie River and Pauley and Lavazzola Creeks, all small but solid trout streams.
The most popular angling stretch runs from Sierra City to Downieville, with trout stocked at campgrounds and other access points outside the special regs. section. Browns and rainbows average 15 or 16 inches here.
North Fork Yuba
Middle Fork Yuba
Flow
Yuba Pass
Haskell Creek
Bassetts
Sierra City
Loganville
Downieville
Graniteville
Milton Reservoir
Jackson Meadows Reservoir
Tahoe National Forest
104.9 mi.
102.8 mi.
99.2 mi.
98.1 mi.
93.8 mi.
89.9 mi.
88.9 mi.
88.6 mi.
86 mi.
81.9 mi.
79.9 mi.
78.8 mi.
72.2 mi.
67.5 mi.